POLITE POLITICS

Dedicated to my friend S.K. Lee

Polite Politics
A sociological analysis of an urban protest
in Hong Kong

DENNY HO KWOK-LEUNG

LONDON AND NEW YORK

First published 2000 by Ashgate Publishing

Reissued 2018 by Routledge
2 Park Square, Milton Park, Abingdon, Oxon OX14 4RN
711 Third Avenue, New York, NY 10017, USA

Routledge is an imprint of the Taylor & Francis Group, an informa business

Copyright © Denny Ho Kwok-leung 2000

All rights reserved. No part of this book may be reprinted or reproduced or utilised in any form or by any electronic, mechanical, or other means, now known or hereafter invented, including photocopying and recording, or in any information storage or retrieval system, without permission in writing from the publishers.

Notice:
Product or corporate names may be trademarks or registered trademarks, and are used only for identification and explanation without intent to infringe.

Publisher's Note
The publisher has gone to great lengths to ensure the quality of this reprint but points out that some imperfections in the original copies may be apparent.

Disclaimer
The publisher has made every effort to trace copyright holders and welcomes correspondence from those they have been unable to contact.

A Library of Congress record exists under LC control number: 00134025

ISBN 13: 978-1-138-74023-5 (hbk)
ISBN 13: 978-1-138-74017-4 (pbk)
ISBN 13: 978-1-315-18376-3 (ebk)

Contents

List of Figures and Tables viii
Acknowledgements xi

1 Introduction 1
   Urban Movements: Their Importance in Urban Politics 3
   The Significance of the Study of Urban Protests in Hong Kong 10
   Method and Data 13
   Structure of this Book 17

2 Theories of Social Movements: A Review of the Literature 20
   Introduction 20
   The Classical Perspective on Collective Action 21
   The Resource Mobilization Perspective 26
   The Social Construction of Protest 45
   Toward an Integrated Approach to Collective Action 51

3 The Changing Political Context in Hong Kong 59
   Introduction 59
   The Pre-democracy Stage: 1970-1980 60
   The Stage of Transition to Democracy: 1981-1992 69
   The Grassroots' Response to the Changing Political Structure in the 1980s 75
   Recapitulation 79

4 Public Housing Policy and Urban Minorities 84
   Introduction 84
   The Housing Provision Structure in Hong Kong 84
   Production and Allocation of Public Housing 88
   Public Housing Policy and Urban Minorities 94
   The Nature and Management of the Temporary Housing Areas 100
   Summary 103

vi *Polite Politics*

5	A Brief Account of the Trajectory of the ATHA Protest	106
	Introduction	106
	The Aged Temporary Housing Areas Issue	107
	The Rise of the ATHA Protest	109
	The Actors Involved in the ATHA Protest	118
	The ATHA Residents	122
	Summary	128
6	No Through Road: Limited Political Opportunities for ATHA Residents	134
	Introduction	134
	Two Changing Processes in the Political Structure	135
	Who Cares about the Housing Movement?	145
	The ATHA Issue and the Actors in the Political Structure	159
	Conclusion	164
7	Every Person Counts: The Political Participation of ATHA Residents	171
	Introduction	171
	Forms of Political Participation in the Two ATHAs	173
	The Social Characteristics of Residents in the Two ATHAs	175
	To Participate or Not to Participate: A Case Study in the Kowloon Bay THA	181
	Participation in the Ping Shek THA	193
	Mobilization Potential and Actual Participation	207
	Conclusion	214
8	The Mobilization Process: External Organizers, Local Leaders and the Choice of Strategies	220
	Introduction	220
	The Mobilization Agents	221
	The Creation and Maintenance of the Foundation of ATHA Protest: The Local Concern Groups	233
	Strategy Formation	246
	Success or Failure of the Local Mobilization and Protest	258
	Conclusion	263
9	Conclusion	269
	Summary of the Argument	269
	The Theoretical and Methodological Implications of this Study	289
	Future Development of the ATHA Protest	297

Appendix 1	Methods	300
Appendix 2	A Personal Reflection on Methodology	314
Appendix 3	Survey on the Tenants' Preferences in the Temporary Housing Areas in the Kwun Tong District	322
Appendix 4	Survey on Kowloon Bay THA Residents' Attitudes to "Same District Rehousing" Policy	328
Appendix 5	Survey of the Living Conditions of the Ping Shek THA	335
Bibliography		348

List of Figures and Tables

Figures

2.1	Causal Sequence of Collective Action	22
2.2	Political Opportunity Structure: Summary of the Components Making for Increased Access and Increased Success as Suggested by Tarrow, Kitschelt and Kriesi	42
2.3	Key Variables in Understanding Aspects of Social Movements According to Four Theoretical Perspectives	53
6.1	Summary of the Political Openness, Orientation Towards Taking up Housing Issues, and the Articulation Strategies of the Actors in Different Articulation Channels in Relation to Housing Movements in the Early 1990s	158

Tables

1.1	Frequency of Various Forms of Action Taken in Housing Conflicts, 1980-1991	12
3.1	Distribution of Working Population by Occupation (%)	62
3.2	The Performance of the Economy of Hong Kong in the 1980s	70
3.3	Representation of Five Occupational Categories on the Executive Council, Legislative Council, Urban Council and Regional Council, 1965-1986	72
4.1	Occupied Living Quarters by Type of Living Quarters, 1981, 1986, 1991 (%)	85
4.2	The Production of Public Housing Units by the Housing Authority, 1973-1991	91
4.3	Sources of Fund for Capital Expenditure of the Housing Authority, 1977-1990	93
4.4	Population and Year of Existence of the Temporary Housing Areas as at 1 April, 1991	99

5.1a	A Chronology of the Actions Organized by the Residents of the Kowloon Bay THA in Respect of the ATHA Issue, 1990-1991	115
5.1b	A Chronology of the Actions Organized by the Residents of the Ping Shek THA in Respect of the ATHA Issue, 1990-1993	116
5.2	A Chronology of the Actions Organized by the Joint Committee of the THA Residents Associations for the ATHA Issue, 1990-1993	117
5.3	General Information About Two Local THA Concern Groups	120
5.4	Years of Residency in Hong Kong, Place of Birth, Population, Number of Households, by Residents in the Two ATHAs, as of May 1991 (%)	124
5.5	Years of Residency in THAs by the Residents in Two THAs (%)	125
5.6	Occupation of the THA Residents by THA (%)	126
5.7	Monthly Household Income by THA (%)	127
5.8	Age Group of the THA Residents by THA, 1991 (%)	127
7.1	People to Whom Respondents Turn in Case of Emergency	179
7.2	Respondents' Mobilization Potential in Protest Activities in the Kowloon Bay THA	183
7.3	Characteristics of the Respondents in the Kowloon Bay THA	186
7.4	Odds Ratios for Predicting Four Measures of Participation in Protest Activities Among Kowloon Bay THA Residents, Using Two Logistic Regression Models	189
7.5	Respondents' Mobilization Potential in Protest Activities in the Ping Shek THA	195
7.6	Characteristics of the Respondents in the Ping Shek THA	196
7.7	Odds Ratios for Variables Predicting Four Measures of Participation in Protest Activities Among the Ping Shek THA Residents, Using Two Logistic Regression Models	199
7.8	Reason for Non-participation in Protest Activities by THA	205
7.9	Rate of Actual Participation in the Ping Shek THA	208
7.10	Characteristics of the Actual Participants in the Ping Shek THA	208
7.11	Models Predicting Actual Participation in the Ping Shek THA Protest Activities	210

8.1 Period of Involvement of the Volunteer Organizers in the   224
     Ping Shek ATHA Protest, May 1992-April 1994
8.2 Level of Involvement of the Indigenous Leaders in the   232
     Kowloon Bay THA and the Ping Shek THA, April 1990-
     April 1994
A1.1 Distribution of Interviewees   301

Acknowledgements

I would like to express my thanks and gratitude to my supervisor, Professor Chris Pickvance, for his guidance and supervision on the study. He showed great patience in reading through my drafts, gave valuable suggestions on both the content and the presentation of this study, and provided scholarly advice and personal support.

Special thanks to all the community social workers and volunteer organizers who took part in the Aged Temporary Housing Area protest. Without their gracious assistance, this study could not have been conducted. I wish to extend my thanks to Ms. Samantha Chan who assisted me in finishing the fieldwork; to the postgraduate students in the Urban and Regional Studies Unit, University of Kent at Canterbury, who have helped in many ways; and to Ms. Terry McBride who spent great effort in editing my English.

This study was generously supported by the Staff Development Committee, Hong Kong Polytechnic University.

Finally, I am indebted to the residents of the Kowloon Bay and Ping Shek THAs who patiently answered my questions and let me know how they dealt with the social forces impinging upon their daily lives. I acknowledge with gratitude their willingness to recount their rich experiences and reflection on their protest.

1 Introduction

This study is concerned with an urban movement and its role in urban politics. An urban movement is conceived here as an individual organization 'which make[s] urban demands whatever their levels and effects' (Pickvance, 1985:32). Our focus will be on the origin, the character and the effects of a housing movement in Hong Kong. A housing movement is one of the sub-types of urban movement, in particular arising in relation to issues concerning the management and distribution of housing resources. An issue concerning Aged Temporary Housing Areas (ATHAs) will be taken as a case study in order to throw light on the reasons why, and how, urban minorities in Hong Kong employ collective actions to protect or advance their interests. Furthermore, we shall draw on the findings of this study to shed light on the theoretical discussion about the process of translating a social base to a social force (Pickvance, 1977).

In this chapter, we shall discuss the significance of the study of urban movements in section 1.1. Its significance to the study of urban politics in Hong Kong is presented in section 1.2. Section 1.3 will spell out the method and data used in this study. The final section is about the structure of this book.

Before going into the discussion about the significance of the study of urban movements, it is useful to place the housing movement in Hong Kong in the context of other types of political action. Based on the data collected through a study of the social conflicts in Hong Kong in the period from 1980-91 we found a number of features of the housing movement in Hong Kong.[1] Firstly, in the period from 1980-91 social action related to housing issues was the third most frequent category of conflict issues, following labour and political issues. Secondly, most of the issues were those concerning local and sectoral benefits; 60% of the housing issues were of 'local' scope, 32% of sectoral scope and only 8% of whole-territory scope. Thirdly, as regards the forms of organization involved, 44% and 34% of housing conflicts in Hong Kong in the last decade involved loose groups and community/sectoral groups respectively. However, only 4% of housing conflicts involved federal forms of organization; in other words, organizational alliance was a very insignificant form of organization in the housing movement. Fourthly, as will be shown in detail later, most of the forms of action were confined to petitions, press conferences and sending letters to the media. By contrast, disruptive contests were less likely to be a form of action taken in housing conflicts. This indicates that the most popular form of action taken in housing disputes is 'polite protest actions' which refer to the protest activities that 'eschew or at least avoid the extensive physical damage to property and humans found in violent struggle on the one side and the restraint and decorum of staid politics on the other' (Lofland, 1991:261). These findings support Saunders' description of the nature of urban movements as 'typically fragmented, localized, limited to a narrow range of concerns, and politically isolated from broader radical movements' (1980:551).

Despite being one of the most frequent categories of social action, the housing movement has not developed into a social force with a wide scope for forming an alliance, and its concerns seldom reached issues at territory-wide level. Such features lead us to reconsider the nature of community-based movements. Boyte (1980) explained them by reference to the localism, narrowness of constituency and the dominance of paid staff in community movements. Fisher and Kling (1993) held a positive view on community movements despite the small scale of this kind of collective action. They argued that such grassroots mobilization was the result of the popular strategies of parochial and self-serving kinds.

This study attempts to shed light on these features of the housing movement in Hong Kong and to explore the factors giving rise to these features and the trajectory of working class people's collective action in pursuit of their interests. Also, we are interested in the reasons underpinning the use of 'polite protest actions' as the dominant strategy in housing movements. It will be argued that the concept 'polite protest action' is the key to understanding the nature and character of the housing movement in Hong Kong; and we shall discuss this concept further in the next section.

Urban Movements: Their Importance in Urban Politics

Why should we study urban movements?

An urban movement is an individual organization making urban demands. It is distinguished from 'urban social movements' - a sub-type of urban movement which is reserved for denoting urban movements that can achieve high-level changes (Pickvance, 1985:32). Urban social movements have been regarded as an important agent of social change by a new school of sociological approach known as new urban sociology (Zukin, 1980). The new urban sociology is in fact a critique of the classical tradition of the Chicago School. Urbanization is conceived by the Chicago School to be the result of a natural evolutionary process, and competition and population increase are the impetus for social change. Although acknowledging the hardship and suffering of the underprivileged, the Chicago School 'falls back on oddly mechanical explanations for those facts, such as the purported effects of population density, size and heterogeneity' (Walton, 1993:99). Collective actions by the underprivileged, in the eyes of the scholars of this tradition, are considered to be the result of social disorganization or the psychological imbalance of individuals (Park, 1952).

The new urban sociology approach has a different conception of urban life. It suggests that a city is a fusion of market, political authority and community (Walton, 1993). In a city, there is a regular exchange of goods, by which resources are allocated to meet the demands of people's daily necessities. The market is the location for these kinds of practice. In order to ensure the prosperity of the market in a city, the political and administrative authority develops and regulates the practices of tradesmen and merchants. This entails political control and the creation of rules (Tabb and Sawers, 1978). Community is the third essential component of a city, which refers to 'the urban citizenry united in a corporate unit administrated by authorities who they elect' (Walton, 1993:94). It is also a specific form of association among the urban citizenry who organize collectively to defend, or advance, their interests. These three components entail three kinds of interests. Agents involved in the market are oriented to the pursuit of profit, while the political and administrative institutions regulate the operation of the market and urban life. Community arises in order to protect itself from exploitation by the market and domination by the political system. Because of the involvement of these interest groups, city life is fashioned by social conflicts concerning economic competition and political control (Goering, 1978; Walton, 1979). City life, or urban life, is understood as a process - such as residential segregation, land-use pattern, and the formation of community organizations, etc. - and as the product of the interplay of economic forces, political control and community. Studies of urban conflicts reveal the ways in which private and public agents modify the influence of economic and political forces. The suffering of the underprivileged is hence understood as the consequence of economic exploitation and political domination, and their collective actions are responses to the inherent and fundamental problems of city life.

Marxist urban sociology is one of the strands of the new urban sociology. The proponents of this perspective on urbanization anticipate the development of a new urban politics which is dominated by social conflicts arising from exploitation and domination outside the sphere of work. With the publication of his book *The Urban Question* in 1972, Castells brought the structuralist Marxist tradition into the study of urban politics. In Castells' theoretical framework, urban protests provide the clues to the identification of new social cleavages apart from class conflicts and inequality. Urban politics is seen as an arena in which urban social movements are the agents of social change, and hence the primary task of urban sociology is to examine their origins and effects.

Urban social movements are defined by Castells as 'a system of practices resulting from the articulation of the particular conjuncture, both by the insertion of the support-agents in the urban structure and in the social structure, and such that its development tends objectively towards structural transformation of the urban system or towards a substantial modification of the power relations in the class struggle, that is to say, in the last resort, in the state power' (1977:432). Castells argues that while class conflicts spring from the primary structural contradictions of capitalist relations of production, urban social movements arise as a result of another intrinsic structural contradiction of the capitalist mode of production. However, urban social movements are secondary in the sense that they cannot produce any 'effects' by their own efforts. Class movements are identified as the primary social force generating social and political changes, whilst any other forms of social movement are considered to be unable to give rise to the same effects. The effects of urban social movements are only related to their function of linking secondary structural contradictions in the urban system to the anti-capitalist struggle (Lowe, 1986). Significant as their role in linking different classes may be, the effects of non-class based urban social movements are to be materialized through the mediation of an efficient working class organization. In other words, urban social movements can facilitate class struggle only when they are able to develop linkages with class practices.

This conceptual framework has directed academic attention to the study of whether such a new politics has developed, and about the extent to which urban social movements engender a new and significant challenge to the hegemony of capitalist societies (Saunders, 1980). In particular, the question of the relationship between class struggle and urban social movements has opened up new research directions, including many studies aimed at finding out how these two kinds of struggles are related (Della Seta, 1978; Folin, 1979; Janssen, 1978; Lagana, *et al.*, 1982; Preteceille, 1986). Lagana *et al.* (1982) argued in his study of the urban conflicts in Turin that urban social movements could be an extension of the anti-capitalist struggle from factory to society, and therefore any explanation of urban social movements without such a reference to class contexts would be misleading.

However, there are a number of shortcomings in Castells' framework. Firstly, Castells' analysis is highly functionalist, in the sense that his primary concern is the functions of urban social movements, rather than identifying and examining the actual effects of particular actions. As McKeown argued, 'the consequence of Castells's functionalism...is that he explicitly avoids any analysis which would treat urban processes (such as urban planning and urban social movements) as the outcome of the conscious and calculated decisions and actions of the actors in a capitalist society' (1987:140). Secondly, less emphasis is placed on the study of movement organizations. Castells argues that 'the genesis of an organization does not form part of the analysis of social movements, for only its effects are important' (Castells, 1976:169-70). The reason for this methodological rule is pointed out by Pickvance who says that for Castells 'concrete movement organizations are the locus of *observation*. The point is that they are not the frame of *analysis*. The focus is rather on the 'problems', 'issues' or 'stakes' the organization pursues and their structural determination. It is the structural contradictions which are the crucial level of analysis, and organizations are seen as means for their expression and articulation' (original italics, 1976:199). Castells subsequently fails to explore sociologically an important theme about how the constituency of an urban movement groups together, implements mobilization and makes decisions in pursuit of their interests. Thirdly, since he does not give sufficient attention to the mobilization process, what has not been adequately studied is the nature and political orientations of the constituency which makes up the potential source of an urban movement (Lowe, 1985). Lastly, Castells puts so much emphasis on urban social movements which have a bearing on societal change that little attention is given to those urban movements with a purely local dimension, or to non-protest and quiescence in urban politics. However, the neglect of small-scale territory-based political actions may result in fewer insights into 'the mechanisms of ideological stabilisation which limit the development of broader political movements from organizations around urban issues' (Dunleavy, 1980:158-9). Similarly, as McKeown argued, 'any definition which wishes to exclude these neighbourhood and community-based movements from the general category of urban movement is likely to miss an important part of the politics that take place within urban areas' (1987:190).

In the mid-1980s the structuralist Marxist approach was widely under attack as overly deterministic. Subsequently Castells revised its original formulation. In his later modification, urban movements have been granted their own right to existence as they are held to be a potential link between different social classes, especially the middle class and working class (Lowe, 1985). Along with class movements and other pressure groups, they struggle to impart a particular 'meaning' to a given city against the interests of the institutionalized urban meaning and dominant classes. Castells in his new work redefines urban social movements as 'urban-orientated mobilizations that influence structural social change and transform the urban meanings' (1983:305). Put simply, he attempts to draw out the link between changes in urban meaning and urban social movements. Furthermore, urban social movements are classified by reference to three fronts that each movement works on: collective consumption, community culture and political self-management. Castells argues that only the urban social movements which interconnect these three fronts are capable of effecting social change. However, he has not gone so far as to give up his Marxist political concern about the power of urban social movements to effect social change, and hence did not shift his attention to the study of various forms of urban protest. Above all, as Lowe argued, Castells 'has still not integrated a sociological understanding of the importance of the nature and characteristics of social bases in the mobilization process; and how a social base becomes, or fails to become, a social force' (1985:52).[2]

In view of the problems of Castells' theoretical framework, another strand of urban movement study developed in the late 1980s. This was more oriented to empirical research about local political actions, and focused on the conditions shaping the growth and outcomes of urban movements (Burdick, 1992; Bennett, 1992; Canel, 1992; Eckstein, 1990). This kind of research is based on case studies to illustrate the salience of contextual factors in determining the responses of poor people to grievances and the possibility of being a successful movement. Studies in the Third World illustrated how the urban poor, in the hope of improving their physical environment, united and struggled to secure access to resources, for instance, money, labour, facilities and legitimacy for their movements (Alvarez, 1990; Eckstein, 1977; Schuurman and Naerssen, 1989). Recent attempts have also pinpointed the importance of examining the bearing of state initiatives and forms of response to grassroots movements (Clarke and Mayer, 1986).

In the United States where the structuralist Marxist tradition was less influential, the organizational and mobilization aspects of urban political movements received more attention (Ambrecht, 1976; Bailis, 1974; Brill, 1971; Davis, 1991; Delgado, 1986; Henig, 1982; Jackson and Johnson, 1974; Stoecker, 1994). These studies enrich our understanding of how powerless people forge viable political means of collective action to advance their interests. In particular, the Fainsteins (1974) focused on how people of low income groups became involved in politics. They pointed out the significance of this kind of research. Firstly, urban movements are 'of additional scholarly interest because they represent a type of political phenomenon that usually goes unrecorded' (1974:xiii). Secondly, they represent a new kind of political institution and any inquiry into the experience of these organizations reveals several of the most significant aspects of American politics. Thirdly, they indicate the extent to which citizens with little power, money, or status can use the political system as a lever to increase their relative share of public goods. Lastly, we may obtain the answer as to whether social inequality is destined to perpetuate itself indefinitely, even in a pluralistic, democratic political system.

The merit of this framework lies in its wider field of interest. Unlike Castells who confines his concern to the extent to which urban social movements effect social change, it gives relatively more attention to the character and trajectory of urban movements. Moreover, one of its aims is to illustrate that social and historical contexts are important determinants of the protest pattern of an urban social movement, and therefore the students of urban social movements must be sensitive to a range of factors unique to the social and historical contexts in which an urban movement operates, such as the nature of the class system and the configuration of political power (Friedland, 1982; Katznelson, 1981).

With the lessons learnt from the study of urban politics in the United States and the critique of Castells's analytical framework, the new urban sociology was found to be in need of reformulation and development for the study of urban movements in the mid-1980s. Subsequently two directions have been repeatedly suggested. The first is to incorporate the social movement theories into the domain of urban sociology, such as the resource mobilization theory and the political process model, for the analysis of the mobilization and organizational aspects of urban movements (Hasson, 1993; Lowe, 1985; Pickvance, 1976, 1985). The second is to rectify the overly deterministic tendency of the structuralist Marxist tradition by giving more attention to actors in the study of urban politics. As regards the importance of actors, Smith argued that 'although impersonal conditions constitute the historical context within which people act, people are not merely passive recipients of these structural economic and political conditions. They are creators of meaning, which is also a wellspring of human action and historic change' (1989:355). Flanagan asked us to shift our attention from the structural issues at the most macrological level 'toward the local level where the powerful and the less powerful face choices about how to live today and plan for tomorrow' (1993:141).

This discussion in urban sociology raises the question of how to incorporate the mobilization process, the role of actors, and social and historical contexts into the analysis of urban movements. As we shall argue in Chapter 2, the study of strategies provides us with a starting point for our analysis of the character and trajectory of urban movements. A theoretical formulation of the concept of strategy also gives us the conceptual tools to identify and analyze the interplay of actors' choices, mobilization of resources, and social and historical contexts of an urban movement. In this study, the concept of strategy refers to the types of action by which the originators of strategies expect to materialize certain effects. We shall modify the scheme of ordering types of strategy suggested by Lofland (1985) into a four-category model, in which strategies are classified as 'ordinary politics', 'polite politics', 'protest' and 'violence'. Ordinary politics refers to those actions organized through both formal and informal channels in political institutions, such as lobbying, sending representatives to government institutions, and forming connections with political parties, etc. The strategy of polite politics refers to those acts which make known or evident by visible and tangible means outside the political structure the grievances and demands of the group in question, but this kind of strategy does not lead to any disruption of the prevailing social life and political structure. Protest refers to those actions which are oriented to disrupting current social arrangements, such as rent strikes, non-cooperation, blockades, illegal occupation and system overloading (Lofland, 1985; Piven and Cloward, 1977). Violence refers to those actions which physically damage or destroy property or other humans. With this classification, we shall explore the reasons for the actors choosing the forms of strategy taken throughout the protest.

To sum up, one of the objectives of our analysis of the housing movement in Hong Kong is to develop an integrated approach which takes both actors, and social and political contexts into account in understanding urban movements. In Chapter 2, we shall give a critical evaluation of the theories of social movements and explore the ways of developing such an integrated approach. We shall argue that two social movement theories need close inspection. The first is the resource mobilization theory which stresses the importance of the availability of resources to the protest pattern, and the second is the political process model which emphasises the significance of the political opportunity structure. We shall also evaluate these theories in the light of our study of the urban movement in Hong Kong. Having recognized that neither the resource mobilization theory nor the political process model places emphasis on the active role of actors in collective action, we focus on the strategy adopted by the protest group in order to analyse the mobilization and organizational aspects of an urban movement. We shall also demonstrate how powerless people collectively construct a viable means to counter a dominant political authority and in what ways a locally-based urban movement reveals the nature of a political system.

Our study attempts to break new ground in three respects. First, an integrated approach to urban movements is constructed through a synthesis of the resource mobilization theory, the political process model and the social construction perspective. Second, whereas the forefront of research in the field of urban movements places emphasis on the link between structural conditions and the incidence of urban movements, we aim to advance our understanding of the dynamics of urban movements through the study of actors and their interaction with the social structure. Thirdly, while many studies of urban movements are preoccupied with their social effects, we focus on their character and trajectory, a topic which has been identified as particularly important but has received scant attention, i.e. the process of translating a social base to a social force.

The Significance of the Study of Urban Protests in Hong Kong

In this section, we discuss the significance of this kind of study to the understanding of urban politics in Hong Kong. Our study attempts to fill a gap in empirical research concerning the character and development of small-scale urban movements in Hong Kong. This kind of urban movement has been largely unstudied in the field of urban sociology, and hence we know little about ordinary people's political action in relation to the control of their daily lives. It is our contention that the study of small-scale, or even unsuccessful, protests is very important. As Dunleavy argued, 'a study of urban social movements can provide important cues to the existence of latent grievances and issues, and yield insights into some fundamental but relatively intangible power relationships between state agencies and the mass of the population' (1980:161).

The fact that small-scale urban movements receive little attention is related to the difficulty of access to such kinds of protest. As West and Blumberg pointed out, 'protest politics is an everyday experience in the lives of people around the world... However, many local protest activities are crushed or lose support before they reach the level of mass movements, while others are never recorded as part of political history' (1990:6). Hong Kong differs little in this respect. But two studies are the exception. Lui (1984) studied three urban protests in Hong Kong in the light of Castells' framework and Kung (1984) was concerned with an urban movement pressing for a district hospital. Both employed a similar theoretical framework to explore how an urban movement articulated the structural contradictions of the capitalist mode of production.

These studies provide us with information about the causes and course of urban protests in Hong Kong in the early 1980s. However, there has been little research on such urban protests in the early 1990s when a new era started in Hong Kong. Democracy was introduced into the political system and the 1997 issue had generated more conflicts between the government and the grassroots. The 1990s witnessed the rise of political parties and the dominance of the discussion about the 1997 issue, and there were changes in the configuration of power both inside and outside the political system. It is necessary to see why and how Hong Kong people adopt concerted actions outside the formal political system to fight for their interests. We are interested in the nature of the political system in transition, and how Hong Kong people seek control of their lives in this specific historical context. We will also explore whether territory-based collective action remains one possible type of political action by which Hong Kong people can advance their interests.

A further objective of this study is to contribute to an improved understanding of urban protests in Hong Kong. Although both Lui (1984) and Kung (1984) have provided us with information about how urban protests in Hong Kong developed, their studies remained deeply influenced by Castells' framework, and therefore little attention was paid to the importance of actors. It is true that Lui and Kung recognized the functionalist and overly deterministic tendency in Castells' framework and thereby highlighted the contribution of the external agents to the mobilization process, but they simply assumed that the external agents were important in the supply of resources, without giving sufficient attention to their ideologies, their influence on decisions about the choice of strategies, and the possibility that the external agents could serve as agents of social control. Recent studies in other countries have illustrated the need to examine the nature of external agents. Hasson (1993), in his study of urban social movements in Jerusalem, showed that the ideologies of community social workers influenced the course of protest. Another study, in Brussels, also illustrated how the social work profession was used by the authorities to deal with urban conflicts (Hengchen and Melis, 1980). Moreover the two Hong Kong studies attached little importance to the examination of the nature of actors, and therefore shed little light on the role of the external supportive agents in urban social movements.

The third reason for our study of urban movements in Hong Kong is the dominance of the strategy of 'polite' politics in urban conflicts. As shown in Table 1.1, petitions, press conferences and sending letters to newspapers were the dominant forms of strategy in the last decade. We conceived these activities as polite politics since they take place outside the formal political system and aim at raising public awareness without causing any disruption of the prevailing social and political arrangement.

Form of Action	Frequency	Percentage of actions	Percentage of events*
Petition	178	38	49
Press conference	95	20	34
Sending letters to media	80	17	28
Protest	36	8	13
Action-survey	23	5	8
Meeting	18	4	6
Signing campaign	11	2	4
Civil disobedience	11	2	4
Violence	3	1	1
Total	466	100	

Table 1.1 Frequency of Various Forms of Action Taken in Housing Conflicts, 1980-1991

* The total number of events is 282. The percentage in this column is obtained by dividing 282 by the frequency.

Source: Author's analysis is based on the data provided by Chui and Lai who conducted a survey on the social conflicts in Hong Kong in 1994.

These findings lead us to ask why polite politics remains the most popular form of strategy in urban movements. Lui (1984) explained the choice of strategy by reference to the polity structure and the resources provided by community social workers. Kung (1984) added historical practices of urban struggles in Hong Kong as another factor determining the choice of action forms. The problem in both analyses is their deterministic tendency which prevents them from giving attention to how the protesters made their choice of strategy. It seems that neither study allows any space for the originator of the strategy to choose the direction of their actions. Furthermore, these studies did not explain the lack of disruptive protest and violence. Perhaps the protesters are culturally predisposed to avoid radical action - as Lau (1982) argued that Hong Kong people were pragmatic in attitude, and their concerns about personal material advancement and social stability led to an aversion to aggression. Neither Lui nor Kung was interested in exploring whether the lack of aggressive political behaviour of Hong Kong people was culturally predisposed, or is due to some structural constraints. Therefore, their analysis paid little attention to the constituency of an urban movement. It is our contention that the analysis of the choice of strategies provides us with more clues to answer the 'culture vs. structural constraint' question.

To sum up, we address in this study four questions about the urban movements in Hong Kong. Firstly, why do some Hong Kong people stand outside the formal political system to defend or challenge the provision of urban facilities and social services in an era in which democracy has been introduced into the political system? Secondly, how does a social base in Hong Kong develop into a social force and what strategies are adopted to exert pressure on the political authorities? Thirdly, why does polite politics remain the most popular form of strategy adopted by urban movements? Lastly, what is the nature of the political system in Hong Kong as revealed by urban politics?

Method and Data

Our study focuses on the Aged Temporary Housing Area (ATHA) protest and aims to illustrate how political structure, the organizational specificity of the protest and the actors involved shape the character of a housing movement. The choice of the ATHA protest as a case for the examination of the process translating a social base to a social force is based on the idea that the validity of case study analysis lies not in its ability to verify a theory, but in its ability to shed light on our theoretical claims (Burawoy, 1991; Mitchell, 1983).

The urban movement we shall study was launched by a group of working class people living in ATHAs in Hong Kong in the early 1990s. The function of the Temporary Housing Areas, according to the Housing Authority,[3] is to provide shelter for the 'homeless and people not yet eligible for permanent public housing resulting from clearances, fires, natural disasters and other operations' (The Housing Authority, 1991:80). Although this sort of shelter was understood as 'temporary', ironically by 1990 more than 16 THAs, which had been accommodating more than 24,000 people, had been in existence for more than 10 years. In view of the poor conditions in the ATHAs, a group of organizers, comprising volunteers and community social workers, mobilized the ATHA residents to form grassroots associations and a cross-district coalition to exert pressure on the government and the Housing Authority in order to press for early clearance of the ATHAs.

The protest of the ATHA residents is an indication of their being poorly taken care of by the prevailing public housing policy. The outcry of the ATHA residents through collective actions appears to be a refutation of the story about the success of the public housing policy which the government regards as one of its most outstanding achievements. The protests of the ATHA residents draw attention to the insufficient provision of public housing, and to the fact that some people in Hong Kong have to organize themselves into a social force in order to fight against ignorance, to secure social benefits and to raise their living standards. Nevertheless, we shall argue that the ATHA residents encountered a lot of constraints on their actions. The constraints were of three types: limited political opportunity for expressing their grievances and exerting pressure on the government, difficulties in mobilizing ATHA residents, and ineffective strategies.

We decided to observe closely the activities of two local concern groups in our study, because of limited manpower and resources. Moreover, we considered that these could give us an improved understanding of the dynamics of urban protest.

Our selection of these two areas is based on the following considerations.[4] Firstly, we obtained permission from the coordinator and the chairman of the People's Council on Public Housing Policy to work with them and to be a participant observer of the ATHA protest. Secondly, since there was no mobilization task prior to our fieldwork, we could observe the entire process of mobilization from the very beginning. Thirdly, both ATHAs were in the same district, therefore we could compare two mobilization processes within the same local environment.

In order to support our arguments, our analysis focuses on five aspects of the ATHA protest. The first aspect concerns the social and political contexts of Hong Kong in the 1980s. We aim to draw attention to the changing relationship between the government and the grassroots. The second aspect concerns the rise and role of the THA in the public housing provision system in Hong Kong. Here, we place emphasis on how the formal bureaucratic rules and procedures create and regulate people's access to housing resources. The third, fourth and fifth aspects relate to the three strategies adopted by the ATHA protesters. The third aspect concerns the use of ordinary politics strategy, i.e. lobbying and using persuasion in dealing with government officials and politicians. The fourth aspect concerns the extent to which the internal social structure and the value orientations of the constituency of the ATHA protest influence mobilization. We shall argue that the low level of actual participation renders difficult the use of some forms of polite and disruptive politics, such as large-scale petitions and demonstrations. The final aspect concerns the dominance of polite politics.

As regards the data we employed in this study, the information for the analysis of the social and political contexts in the 1980s is mainly drawn from published articles, official documents and publications, and statistical data provided by the Census and Statistics Department. In respect of the role of the ATHAs in public housing policy, we first draw on the data from unpublished documents of the Hong Kong Housing Authority to delineate both the production and allocation of public housing, and then explore the extent to which the housing policy ignores some urban minorities.

Our analysis of the political opportunity structure relies on three sources of information. The analysis of the institutional structure relies on official government documents and the annual reports of the Housing Authority. This analysis aims to draw out the link between the restructuring of the Housing Authority and the available channels by which the housing movement can access the decision-making domain. The second source is the interviews conducted with politicians, political party members, social workers and trade unionists in relation to THA policy (see Appendix 1). Altogether twenty-four cases are used in the analysis. We also participated in a number of meetings in order to gather information on the politicians' views of the ATHA issue.

Our account of the ATHA protest is based on two sources of information. Our fieldwork was conducted in the period from April 1990 to April 1994, one part of it is an extended participant observation (details of which will be presented later); and the other is questionnaire surveys conducted in three THAs, namely Kowloon Bay, Ping Shek, and Hong Ning Road THAs. The first questionnaire survey began in May 1991 and finished in July 1991. Questions were asked about respondents' socio-economic background, level of satisfaction with living conditions, willingness to move out of the ATHAs, preferred location of rehousing and their willingness to participate in neighbourhood associations (see Appendix 3).

Information for the analysis of the mobilization process of the two local concern groups is drawn from two questionnaire surveys conducted in October 1991 in the Kowloon Bay THA and in May 1992 in the Ping Shek THA (see Appendices 4 and 5). Questions concerned the residents' evaluation of the THA policy, their experience of involvement in the ATHA protest, their willingness to participate in the protest, and their personal evaluation of the political efficacy of ATHA residents. Findings from these surveys provide us with detailed information about the reasons for participation and non-participation. Two sets of ethnographic interviews with both participants and non-participants (16 in the Kowloon Bay THA and 30 in the Ping Shek THA) were used to solicit further information on the value orientations and social structure of the ATHA residents. Interviewees were guided by a list of questions, concerning how to evaluate the social life in Hong Kong, their social networks, evaluation of the THA policy and the performance of the Hong Kong government. All the interviews were tape-recorded and later transcribed for analysis. Through these interviews, we gathered more information on those aspects which were not included in the questionnaire surveys (see Appendix 1).

Given that we are concerned with the dynamics of the ATHA protest relating to the process of strategy formulation, organization formation and the interaction pattern among the members of the local concern groups, we considered it to be necessary to collect information on the organizing and mobilizing processes of the ATHA protest. The analysis of the internal dynamic thus derives from extended participant observation, during the period from April 1990 to April 1994, in the concern group meetings, petitions and protest activities organized by the local concern groups. By undertaking the role of volunteer organizer, it is possible for us to follow the activities of the local concern group closely. This strategy gave rise to some methodological issues which will be discussed in

Appendix 2. During the fieldwork, we conducted more than 50 extensive, open-ended formal and informal interviews with participants, non-participants, community social workers and volunteer organizers involved in the ATHA protest. The interviews focused on these actors' changing perceptions and evaluations of the protest, and on the process of decision-making in relation to the choice of strategy.

We were also able to use the internal organizational documents of a coalition of residents associations known as the Joint Committee of THA Residents Association (JCTRA) in order to examine the relationships between local concern groups. The author also participated in a number of meetings and conducted 8 interviews with the members of this coalition in order to explore the failure of this organization to serve as a viable coalition working for the interests of the ATHA residents. The interviewees were identified as the key persons acting as informal leaders of the coalition in different periods.

Further details about questionnaires and sampling methods are presented in Appendix 1.

Structure of this Book

This thesis has nine chapters. The next chapter is a theoretical review of the literature on social movements. It includes a discussion and evaluation of the classical perspective on collective action, the resource mobilization theory, the political process model, and the social construction model.

Chapter 3 describes the social and political conditions of Hong Kong in the period 1970-90. We stress that the economic boom in this period had two major effects. First, the middle class expanded as a result of the economic growth. Second, the political structure underwent a process of change when the emergence of the 1997 issue became the dominant concern in the polity and led to the opening up of the political structure. As a result, less attention was paid to communal (or urban) issues.

Chapter 4 examines the structure of housing provision in Hong Kong and explores the reasons for the fact that housing problems got worse in the 1980s. This decade witnessed a shortfall of public rental housing, and consequently, the housing demands of various groups were not met. The housing problems of three urban minority groups, the THA residents, the squatters and the single-person households, are identified. Chapter 5 is a brief account of the trajectory of the ATHA protest. It contains a general description of the social demographic background of the ATHA residents, the rise of the ATHA protest, and the actors involved in the protest. In Chapter 6 we detail the relationship between the political context and the ATHA protest. The aim of this chapter is to see whether the ATHA protesters can mobilize support through connections with the actors involved in the formal political system. We shall argue that much political power has been reallocated to non-governmental statutory organizations in which the democratic element is notable for its absence. Consequently, there is little opportunity for the ATHA protesters to have access to the decision-making process. We also examine the interorganizational links between the political rights movement and the housing movement. It will be shown that political rights movement activists established their political parties and paid less attention to community actions, which made it difficult for the housing movement to rally support from the political rights movement.

Having described the political context, we develop our analysis of local mobilization in Chapter 7. The objective of this chapter is to explain the absence of large-scale mobilization at local level, and to see why so few large-scale demonstrations were organized. Three aspects of mobilization will be examined: the extent to which the internal social structure facilitates mobilization; the extent of the mobilization potential of the ATHA residents; and the mobilization efforts initiated by the ATHA local concern groups. We attempt to find out which aspect determines the extent of mobilization.

In Chapter 8, we focus on the internal dynamics of the local concern groups and examine the decision-making process. Our analysis proceeds in three stages. We first identify the social relationships among the actors involved in the local concern groups, and then look at how these actors influenced the choice of strategies and why the strategy of polite politics is so frequently adopted. The third stage is to evaluate the outcomes of the ATHA protest.

Chapter 9 is a summary of our findings. Some recommendations for future research will be made. We also discuss the role and the likely development of such small-scale social movements in the post-1997 era.

Notes

1. The features of housing movements is identified by the author on the basis of the analysis of the raw data collected by Chui and Lai (1994) in a study of social conflicts in Hong Kong.
2. The typology of urban social movements has been regarded by Pickvance (1985) as problematic in the analysis of the changing incidence and militancy of urban movements. For details about the exchange between Castells and Pickvance, see Castells (1985), Lowe (1985) and Pickvance (1985, 1986).
3. Details about the Housing Authority will be given in Chapter 4. A brief introduction is given here. The Housing Authority is a statutory body, established under the Housing Ordinance, being responsible for coordinating all aspects of public housing. The terms of reference of the authority are stated as follows: 'The authority advises the Governor on all housing policy matters and, through its executive arm (the Housing Department), plans and builds public housing estates, Home Ownership Scheme courts and temporary housing areas for various categories of people as determined by the authority with the approval of the Governor. It also manages public housing estates, Home Ownership Scheme courts, temporary housing areas, cottage areas, transit centres, flatted factories and the ancillary commercial facilities throughout the territory, and administers the Private Sector Participation Scheme and the Home Purchase Loan Scheme. On behalf of the government, the authority clears land, prevents and controls squatting, and plans and co-ordinates improvements to squatter areas' (The Hong Kong Government, Annual Report, 1990: 177).
4. Initially, we planned to study Hong Ning Road THA as well. However, the ATHA protest there ended after one year of action and we had no time to prepare our involvement in this ATHA.

2 Theories of Social Movements: A Review of the Literature

Introduction

The study of social movements became popular in the 1960s, an era in which protests and direct actions outside the formal political system played an important role in social change. This led to a growth in the general sociology literature of work informed by resource mobilization theories which considered protests and social movements to be the products of the political participation of rational people. This view is contrary to that offered by the dominant classical perspective which deemed collective action to be initiated by irrational people. Resource mobilization theorists emphasize the study of the process of collective actions and their impacts on social change. In urban sociology, Pickvance (1977) suggested that it might be fruitful to adopt this perspective to study the process of translating a social base to a social force. The study of this aspect in urban sociology seems necessary since the development and dynamics of urban movements have received little attention (Hannigan, 1985). Later Pahl (1989) in his evaluation of class analysis pointed out that the analysis of urban movements often invoked a structure-consciousness-action chain to theorize its origin, but had in practice given little attention to the mechanisms by which the social group in question acquired the 'consciousness' that guided and informed its actions. Despite such awareness of the need to study the relationship between action and structure, little effort has been put into this question (Giddens, 1984).

This chapter reviews the existing literature on social movements, and in doing so brings out the main theoretical issues concerning the analysis of urban movements. Our aim is to develop a more useful and coherent theoretical framework to understand urban movements in a specific social and political context. Another objective of this chapter is to bring out the theoretical issues pertinent to the analysis of locally based urban movements. We shall argue that the strategy of an urban movement is an adequate dependent variable, and that the analysis of the process of its formulation and implementation is the key to unravelling the complexity and dynamics of urban movements. We shall start with a brief review of the classical perspective on collective action in section 2.1. Section 2.2 discusses the resource mobilization perspective. Although there are problems in this perspective, we shall draw on the analytical classification of resource acquisition for the study in this thesis. In sections 2.3 and 2.4, we explore and examine two recent theoretical models, that is, the political process model and the social construction of protests, and try to show that these two models are complementary to the resource mobilization perspective. At the end of each section, we point out the major shortcomings of the perspectives. In section 2.5, we link up the resource mobilization perspective with the political process and social construction models, and illustrate a possible way of using their conceptual and analytical elements in our analysis of social movements.

The Classical Perspective on Collective Action

To start with, we briefly elucidate the main tenets shared by different models within the classical perspective, and then go on to argue that this perspective develops on the basis of a problematic distinction between unconventional collective behaviour and institutionalized politics.

Five models can be classified under the 'classical perspective': mass society, collective behaviour, status inconsistency, rising expectation and relative-deprivation models. Their object of study is non-institutionalized collective action and covers social unrest, riots, religious cults, crowd action, revolution, etc. Despite variations among these models, they start from the conception that collective actions can be linked to the psychological state of individuals. As McAdam *et al.* pointed out, in this perspective 'the origin of social movements tended to be explained by reference to the same dynamics that accounted for individual participation in movement activities' (1988:696). This perspective suggests that rapid social change disturbs and frustrates those who are not able to cope with tensions, breakdowns and drastic changes, and as a consequence, disturbed individuals set in motion a series of transient and unorganized non-institutionalized activities in order to restore their psychological equilibrium.

In all these models, individual strain is the proximate cause of collective behaviour, and some macro-social factors are identified as structural causes of the strain. Participation in collective action is seen as the means of managing the psychological tensions of a stressful social situation. The logic of the collective behaviour perspective can be represented in a causal sequence, as shown in Figure 2.1. The sequence can be understood as moving 'from the specification of some underlying structural weakness in society to a discussion of the disruptive psychological effect that this structural "strain" has on society. The sequence is held to be complete when the attendant psychological disturbance reaches the aggregate threshold required to produce a social movement' (McAdam, 1982:7).

Structural Strain ▶ Disruptive Psychological State ▶ Social Movements

Figure 2.1 Causal Sequence of Collective Action

Source : McAdam, D. (1982:7)

The models which share the classical perspective, despite variations in concepts and methodology, adopt the above causal sequence to explain the emergence of collective actions. The mass society model suggests that social movements are the result of the experience of personal psychological anxiety and alienation which are engendered by social atomization (Kornhauser, 1959). The collective behaviour model stresses the feeling of anxiety, fantasy and hostility springing from 'normative ambiguity' (Smelser, 1962). The status inconsistency model emphasizes psychological strains generated by a loss of community and drastic social change (Arendt, 1951; Broom, 1959; Geschwender, 1967; 1971; Lenski, 1954; Selznick, 1970). The relative deprivation model suggests that discontent arising from the perception of relative deprivation during adverse socio-economic change is the basic instigating condition for participation in collective violence

(Davies, 1969; Grofman and Muller, 1973; Gurney and Tierney, 1982; Gurr, 1970).

The classical perspective makes a distinction between conventional political action and collective actions. Conventional political activities are taken as the normal, long lasting and proper institutional structure, and as able to influence social change in the long run. Collective action on the other hand does not channel discontents and political demands through the formal political structure. Since participants are psychologically disturbed and hence detached from normal social life, they tend to avoid the formal political structure which is part and parcel of the social normative integration mechanism. This perspective regards collective actions as guided by irrationality and as essentially temporary, transitory and spontaneous outbursts, and therefore are not accorded the capacity to influence political change and societal development. Based on this distinction, the collective behaviour perspective suggests that it is necessary to employ two different theoretical models for the analysis of these two kinds of activity.

This distinction is based on a pluralist assumption about political power (Mayer, 1990; McAdam, 1982). Pluralists believe that a democratic political system is effective in expressing individuals' grievances and political preferences, and involvement in such a system is the logical and reasonable response for any rational individual. Conversely, launching a social movement, i.e. non-institutionalized action, reflects the participants' rejection of rational, self-interested political action. Pluralists treat the refusal of movement participants to use the proper channels of politics as proof that the motives behind their actions are somehow distinct from those leading others to engage in ordinary politics. In this sense, participation motivation in collective behaviour must be arational, if not outright irrational, and irrational motivation is not capable of sustaining long term and persistent political activities like those of political groups in the formal political structure. Hence, social movements are seen as social problems posing a threat to the established socio-political order.

In short, all these models conceptualize collective action as emergent collections of psychologically disturbed individuals who are seeking to alleviate personal disturbance generated by social change. This conception then leads the proponents to focus on the social psychology of individuals in order to explain the origin of a social movement.

This perspective has been criticized for being oversimplistic. First, this perspective assumes that collective action is motivated by psychological strains arising from drastic social change. Participation in collective action is seen as a means for curing participants' personal psychological strain arising from feelings of isolation and anxiety. Hence movement participation is interpreted as therapeutic in nature rather than political. However, this argument is rejected on empirical grounds.[1] Empirical research has found a low statistical association between social psychological variables and participation in collective actions (Aberle, 1965; Barnes and Kaase, 1979; Bolton, 1972; Marx and Wood, 1975; Muller, 1980; Petras and Zeitlin, 1967; Portes, 1971; Snow and Phillips, 1980; Useem, 1980, 1975). In other words, the classical perspective lacks empirical support for a link between psychological strain and political participation. In contrast, recent research has found the use of rational skills in recruitment, the formulation of tactics, and negotiation with the authority (Bowen et al., 1968; Muller, 1972; Synder and Tilly, 1972). As shown in these studies, the assumption of irrationality underlying collective behaviour is an ideological one.

Secondly, this perspective makes a problematic distinction between collective action and conventional political activities. McAdam (1982) has argued that this distinction was based on a questionable pluralist image of the political power structure (Mayer, 1990). The pluralists assume that democracy ensures a relatively even distribution of political power because no political force can afford the use of force and violence against their opponents. Also, a democratic political system creates equal opportunities for participation for social groups of whatever size because groups 'simply lack the power to achieve their political goals without the help of other contenders...Any attempt to exercise coercive power over other groups is seen as a tactical mistake' (McAdam, 1982:6). However, the assumption about the openness of a pluralistic political system which ensures equal access to power is not borne out. Even the major proponent of pluralism, Robert Dahl, admitted that equality in terms of participation opportunity, as often existed in the United States, did not entail equality of power, and in fact giant economic corporations could secure more power by the possession of large amounts of economic resources than could the dispossessed and deprived (Dahl, 1982). Parenti (1970) also pointed out that the democratic structure of the United States excluded and exploited working class people. In view of the limited channels in the formal political structure for the exploited class to advance its interests, collective action appears to be the only rational reaction to express grievances and demands.

Thirdly, the classical perspective underestimates the significance of macro-political and organizational dynamics in social movements (Lipset and Wolin, 1965). It is true that this perspective gives some attention to these aspects but it is limited to analyzing the features of the macro-structure in the pre-movement period in order to find out the causes of individual psychological strain (McAdam *et al.*, 1988). Since attention is largely devoted to exploring participants' motivations, this perspective is preoccupied with the emergence stage of social movements, and little emphasis is placed on the dynamics of movements, their growth, change and demise (Zald and Ash, 1966).

Lastly, scant attention is given to the goals and effects of collective behaviour on the political structure and social change. There is a lot of historical and contemporary evidence about the impacts of social movements, for example, the civil rights movement, the feminist movements, the environmentalist movements, etc. They were found to be able to effect policy change and the restructuring of political power. It is clear that we cannot afford to neglect this aspect of collective movements (Carden, 1974; Frankland and Schoonmaker,1992; Ferree and Hess,1985; Gelb and Palley, 1982; Morris, 1984; Piven and Cloward, 1977).

The political struggle and social conflicts that dominated the political scene of the United States in the 1960s stimulated the revision of the classical perspective. With more academic social scientists' involvement in and sympathies with social movements such as the civil rights movement, feminist movements, and the anti-Vietnam war and ecology movements, increasing criticism was directed to the classical perspective. A new framework, known as the 'resource mobilization perspective', emerged (Freeman, 1973, 1983). With its denial of the view that movement participants are irrationally motivated, this perspective suggests that non-institutionalized collective actions are largely taken by rational actors who are marginalized to the fringe of society. In the last two decades, this perspective was regarded as more promising, and considered to be useful in the study of urban social movements (Pickvance, 1976, 1985).

The Resource Mobilization Perspective

We first present the basic assumptions and prepositions of the resource mobilization perspective, and then discuss its strengths and weaknesses.

Starting as a critique of the classical perspective, a number of proponents of the resource mobilization perspective draw on microeconomic and sociological theories so as to develop analytical tools for the study of collective actions. We know that there is no firm agreement on the main assumptions, propositions and family of concepts in this perspective. At the risk of overgeneralization, we identify two basic assumptions of the resource mobilization perspective.

Firstly, resource mobilization theorists are critical of the classical perspective which regards collective action as an irrational response to structural strains. Instead, they regard social movement participation as a behaviourial reflection of rational political intentions, and members of social movements as rational actors who are able to instrumentally formulate their political goals and are committed to the idea of reforming the existing social structure (Gamson, 1975; Gerlach and Hine, 1970; Jenkins, 1983; McCarthy and Zald, 1977, 1987; Olson, 1965). Their objectives embrace improving the social positions of disadvantageous social groups, obtaining entry to the polity through political insurgency, and seeking a better distribution of resources. To the theorists of this perspective, a social movement is 'a ubiquitous form of political action and [...] constitutes a set of rational collective actions by excluded groups to advance their interests in the context of a restrictive polity' (Jenkins, 1985:1).

Secondly, resource mobilization theorists consider unconventional political actions to be an extension of institutionalized political action. Rebellious activities are the means and resources employed to achieve political aims by those who are excluded from the formal political structure (Lipsky, 1968). Therefore, there is no real difference between the nature and objectives of unconventional political actions and of political actions originated by political parties, interest groups and lobbyists inside the conventional political structure (Eisinger, 1973; Gamson, 1975; Lipsky, 1968; Lipsky and Levi, 1972; Piven and Cloward, 1977). This perspective suggests that despite the different forms of action adopted in social movements and conventional politics, it is appropriate to use the same conceptual framework and methodological tools to study both kinds of political action.

On the basis of these assumptions, the resource mobilization theorists pose two questions. First, what are the underlying factors generating social movements, i.e. why do they emerge? Second, what are the factors which shape the formation, trajectories, development, success or failure, and the growth and demise of a social movement? These two questions lead to three thematic concerns: the origin of a social movement, its forms of resource acquisition, and its success or failure.

The Origin of Social Movements

Central to this model is an analytical distinction between a social movement (SM) and social movement organizations (SMOs).[2] Social movement refers to a set of preference structures, ideas and beliefs directed to some sort of social and political change, whereas a social movement organization is a complex and formalized structure that assumes the role of centralized direction and of translating individual efforts into collective activities in conformity with the advocated beliefs and preferences of a social movement (McCarthy and Zald, 1977; Zald & Ash, 1966; Zald and McCarthy, 1980).[3] It is possible and indeed usual for a social movement to be represented by more than one social movement organization (Garner and Zald, 1985).

Resource mobilization theorists argue that the roles of moral and movement entrepreneurs are important in the interpretation of discontents and grievances, the supply of resources, and the formulation of strategies and tactics. They argue that grievances are structurally given, ever present, and are possibly 'manufactured' and transformed into political demands and purposive political actions by the mobilizing efforts of movement activists and leaders (Jenkins, 1983, 1985; Jenkins and Perrow, 1977; Klandermans, 1991; Mayer, 1990; McAdam *et al.*, 1988; Oberschall, 1973).[4] To quote Jenkins: 'grievances were seen as collective and derived from structural antagonisms built into social institutions. Grievances were real and significant, but the central factors explaining the emergence of the social movements were increases in organizational capacities and political opportunities, not the intensity of individual discontents' (1985:xiii). Hence emphasis should be placed on how political actors mobilize and organize resources in order to translate grievances and deprivation into social movement activities.

In the resource mobilization perspective, the reason for participation is not taken as the reason for the emergence and development of social movements. The proponents of this perspective criticize the collective behaviour perspective for failing to acknowledge that knowing peoples' reasons for participation does not provide any explanation about how a social protest emerges and develops. As McAdam *et al.* point out,

> the two processes - movement emergence and individual recruitment - are expected to go hand in hand. It is important to keep in mind, though, that they are two separate processes. Explaining why an individual comes to participate in collective action does not suffice as an account of why a particular movement emerged when it did. By the same token, knowing what processes produced a movement tells us little about the factors that encouraged particular individuals to affiliate with that movement (1988:704-5).

Accordingly, the resource mobilization theorists suggest that the question of 'why social movements emerge?' should be replaced by the question 'how do they emerge?' (Klandermans, 1986; Melucci, 1984). If the classical perspective is overconcerned with the 'why' problem and pays no attention to the 'how' problem, the solution put forward by the resource mobilization theorists is to collapse the two questions into one. The origin of social movements is considered to be dependent on how social movement originators mobilize resources, organize action and maintain the movement. Attention is directed to the study of the availability of the resources. It has been hypothesized that the greater the amount of resources available, the greater the likelihood that a social movement organization emerges and operates (McCarthy and Zald, 1987). As Jenkins and Perrow argued, 'what changes, giving rise to insurgency, is the amount of social resources available to unorganized but aggrieved groups' (1977:266). This argument draws our attention to the interjection of external resources which is seen as the essential factor in the emergence of social movements.

Since resources are critical to the emergence and development of social movements as well as the maintenance of social movement organizations, the focal concern is on the resource acquisition methods, including the recruitment of human resources, like members and leaders (Fernandez and McAdam, 1989; Gerlach and Hine, 1970; Jenkins, 1983; Klandermans, 1988, 1989; McAdam, 1990; Molotch, 1970; Oberschall, 1973; Rich, 1980; Snow *et al.*, 1980); and resources acquired through interorganizational links (Aveni, 1978; Curtis and Zurcher, Jr., 1973; Jenkins and Perrow, 1977; McCarthy and Zald, 1977).

Resource Acquisition

For the purpose of studying the means and extent of resource mobilization, we identify in the literature of the resource mobilization perspective three different modes of resource acquisition, namely market-managerial, interorganizational linkage and communal modes.

The market-managerial mode of resource acquisition is identified by some proponents of the resource mobilization perspective, who, drawing insights from micro-economics, conceive social movement organizations as economic entities competing for resources with other sectors of society (Zald and McCarthy, 1987). Based on the economic metaphor, politics is seen as a free market, in which political groups compete with each other for various kinds of resource, such as funding, mass support, participants, knowledge, legitimacy, etc. As Mayer points out, in the resource mobilization perspective, 'social movement behaviour is viewed as the consequence of competition between various SMOs [social movement organizations] as they calculate and execute actions that give themselves notoriety and expand their membership in the same way a corporation would engage in advertising campaigns to increase sales and profits' (1991:65). Social movement activists are seen as 'managers', soliciting resources by means of campaigns, advertising and professional fund-raising strategies, etc. The mobilization target is the 'potential consumers' - the isolated constituents who are portrayed as atomized individuals rather than being tied into certain local social ties and relationships. Individuals are also assumed to be rational actors whose decisions about participation are based on a cost-benefit calculation (Muller and Opp, 1986). This conception leads to an interest in marketing problems, for instance, organizational effectiveness in fund-raising (Godwin and Mitchell, 1984; Johnston, 1980; Oliver and Marwell, 1992; Sabato, 1981).

One of the major tasks in the study of mobilization is to deal with Olson's 'free-rider problem'. Olson (1965) assumed that rational people calculate the cost and benefits of participation. In the case of pressing for collective goods, he argued that a rational person will understand that they stand to gain what other participants get even if they are not involved. Therefore, non-participation appears more rational than participation. In other words, provided that people are rational, collective action will have difficulty motivating people to join and hence no collective benefits will be realized. The solution to overcome the free-rider problem, according to Olson, is the provision of 'selective incentives' - which refers to the inducement or reward offered exclusively to those who have contributed to the social movement organization in question - to participants by the organizers of social movements.[5] Following Olson's assumption of rational calculation and the necessity of incentives, some proponents of the resource mobilization perspective stress the use of selective incentives and non-collective material benefits as rewards to motivate people to participate. Empirical studies have also examined the effectiveness of an incentive structure for membership recruitment (Barkan *et al.*, 1993; Gamson, 1975; Knoke, 1988; Knoke and Adams, 1987; Knoke and Wright-Isak, 1982; O'Brien, 1974, 1975; Oliver, 1984; Opp, 1986; Sharpe, 1978).

Another strand deviates from the assumption of rational calculation and explains political activism by resorting to variables such as group interests and solidarity, ideology, local insurgency culture and moral commitments to the broad collectivities in whose name a movement claims to be representative and to act (Ash, 1972; Carden, 1978; Fireman and Gamson, 1979; Klandermans and Oegema, 1987; McAdam, 1986; McAdam and Paulsen, 1993; Mitchell, 1979; Scott, 1990; Wilson, 1973). The proponents of this strand argued that the rational choice model failed to consider the significance of group norms to an individual's decision about participation, and they therefore downplayed both the importance of selective incentives and the individual's rational calculation of cost and benefit in participation. Instead, more emphasis was placed on indigenous communal resources, for example existing social relationships, ethnic communities and localized moral traditions, etc. (Fireman and Gamson, 1979; Katznelson, 1981; Castells, 1983; Oberschall, 1978). This leads to the study of the communal mode of mobilization, a topic which will be discussed later.

The second mode of resource acquisition is the organizational-entrepreneurial mode which focuses on the organizational formats and performance of social movements (Morris and Herring, 1987).

In the resource mobilization perspective, the social movement organization is the essential component of a social movement. It serves as the centre for recruiting movement participants and as a formal organization 'that attempts to interject the interests of excluded groups into centres of power. Its major task is extending and deepening indigenous organization while harnessing it to the goals of insurgency' (Jenkins, 1985:8). Advocates of this view suggest using the tools of organizational analysis to examine the organizational effectiveness of a social movement in acquiring resources.

Some proponents have attempted to link internal organizational structure with the success or failure of a social movement (Gamson and Schmeidler, 1984; Hobsbawm, 1984; Jenkins, 1979; Piven and Cloward, 1977). Organizational structures are analytically divided into 'centralized' vs. 'decentralized' (Breines, 1980, 1989; Gamson, 1975; Lawson, 1983; McCarthy and Zald, 1977), 'isolated' vs. 'federated' (McCarthy and Zald, 1977), and 'bureaucratic' vs. 'non-bureaucratic' (Knoke, 1989). There has been a debate surrounding the type of organizational structure that best facilitates the growth and effectiveness of a social movement (Gamson, 1975; Gerlach and Hine, 1970; McCarthy and Zald, 1977). Recent discussion appears to have reached the conclusion that the search for the most effective organizational type is chimerical. This implies that there is no ideal organizational form independent of the complexities of social movement organizations and different historical contexts (Gamson and Schmeidler, 1984; Goldstone, 1980). With the knowledge that no organizational form is perfect, research focus has been shifted to examine how movement leaders tackle management dilemmas, such as direct democracy vs. effectiveness, arising in organizational structures (Barkan, 1979; Walsh and Cable, 1989).

Resources mobilized through organizational links are another concern. Resource mobilization theorists stress that interorganizational competition and cooperation within and between social movement industries affect the acquisition of resources (MaCarthy and Zald, 1977; Duffhues and Felling, 1989; Marger, 1984; Zald and McCarthy, 1980). Inter-organizational networks can be cooperative and supportive, or in some situations contain conflicts and competition (Aveni, 1978; Barkan, 1986; Curtis and Zurcher, 1973; Garner and Zald, 1985; Haines, 1984; McCarthy and Zald, 1977; Morris, 1984; Oberschall, 1973; Zald & Ash, 1966; Zald and McCarthy, 1980). In the light of this view, the focus of study is placed on the examination of patterns of interorganizational linkage. Klandermans recently attempted to theorize this pattern by the concept 'multiorganizational field' which is defined as 'the total possible number of organizations with which the movement organization might establish specific links' (1992:95). He went further to divide the multiorganizational field into two sectors, namely, *alliance system* and *conflict system*.

The alliance system refers to the totality of groups and organizations which support a social movement. A social movement organization is likely to obtain more resources by establishing some sorts of connection with an alliance system. It has been found that involvement in an alliance system affected objective formulation, selection of tactics and resource mobilization (Aveni, 1978; Carden, 1989; Gerlach and Hine, 1970; Levine and White, 1961; McAdam *et al.*, 1988; McCarthy and Zald, 1987; Zald, 1969).

The conflict system on the other hand refers to the representatives and allies of the opponents of a social movement, as well as to countermovement which is defined as the 'mobilization of sentiments initiated to some degree in opposition to a movement' (Lo, 1982; Maguire, 1995; Mottl, 1980; Zald and Useem, 1987). The conflict system emerges in the context of a high degree of competition for scarce resources among social movement industries. This competition may lead to changes of mobilization techniques and the rise of innovative tactics for resource acquisition. As was found through empirical research, social movement organizations were compelled to try out new ideas and strategies in order to capture the support of the constituency and to distinguish their vision and efficacy from that of their competitors (Barkan, 1986; Conover and Gray, 1983; Oberschall, 1980; Staggenborg, 1986). This reveals that competition within or between social movement industries for resources, as well as struggle with countermovements, is associated with the extent of resource acquisition.

In short, the resource mobilization perspective posits that the performance of an SMO in competition and alliance determines the flow of resources which in turn affects the survival, failure or success of a social movement. Empirical evidence lends support to this idea (Burstein *et al.*, 1995; Kriesi, 1989; della Porta and Rucht, 1995).

The third mode of resource acquisition is the communal mode. In contrast to the two other modes of resource acquisition which seek support from a greater number of geographically dispersed individuals and organizations, the communal mode confines its mobilization efforts to a particular locale, aiming at obtaining resources such as funding, personal commitment and the direct involvement of people living within a community. Lo (1992) argued that communal resources were important to social movement organizations which were small in size and excluded from the polity, because this sort of organization had little money to employ the market-managerial type, and had few relationships with the organizations involved in the polity.

The communal type of resource acquisition involves face-to-face interaction between movement activists and supporters. This raises the question of how the activists and supporters create the necessary commitment and consensus for collective action (Bailis, 1974; Jenkins, 1983a; Judkins, 1983; Morris, 1981). To explain how a social movement organization can sustain participation over time, the resource mobilization theorists turned to examine the conversion and persuasion process (Snow et al., 1980; Snow et al., 1986; Snow and Benford, 1988). Morris (1984) however, argued that a social movement can only effectively mobilize resources within the indigenous base rather than those provided by external assistance. Preexisting institutions, organizations and social networks could contribute to the rise and continuity of social insurgency (Breines, 1989; Morris, 1984). Piven and Cloward (1977) also pointed to the importance of the communal mode of mobilization. They argued that the organizational mode led only to organization building and resulted in suffocating the initiatives of grassroots movements.

Early resource mobilization theorists in fact ignored locally based movement organizations which were based on the communal mode of resource acquisition. This type of organization is characterized by being less formal and bureaucratized, by informal interaction and by its reliance on membership participation (Henig, 1982a; Roberts, 1973). Without any formal rules governing its activities, the organization is fluid and transitory, and depends on personal commitment and involvement (Hertz, 1981; Rosenthal and Schwartz, 1989).

Success or Failure of a Social Movement

The resource mobilization perspective addresses the question of the effects of a social movement. A number of factors have been highlighted, such as leadership, external support, effective tactics and its capacity for mobilizing resources. However, there is no firm agreement on the most appropriate measure of success or failure of a social movement. In general, resource mobilization theorists maintain that success is more likely to be achieved when an interjection of resources takes place and when opponents are disunited and/or tolerant of the social movement (Jenkins and Perrow, 1977).

Gamson (1975) appears to be one of the few to put forward precise criteria for measuring the success of a social movement. He focuses on two dimensions: a) the provision of tangible benefits that meet the demands of a social movement organization; and b) the formal acceptance of the social movement in question by its opponents as a legitimate representative of a set of interests. From these two factors, four possible movement outcomes are thus derived: full success (i.e. having gained both acceptance and benefits); cooptation (gained acceptance but not benefits); preemption (gained benefits but no acceptance) and failure (gained neither acceptance nor benefits). Several factors are found to be associated with movement success, namely reliance on centralized and bureaucratic organization, use of selective incentives, pursuit of narrowly defined goals and use of 'unruly' tactics (Morris and Herring, 1987). Piven and Cloward (1977) on the other hand stressed the use of mass insurgency, in contrast to those who had empirical evidence proving the importance of organization (Morris, 1984; Gamson and Schmeidler, 1984). However, as Morris and Herring pointed out, 'it is clear that organization, resources, strategies, and the nature of repression/facilitation affect movement outcomes depending on the nature of the goals pursued. What is not clear, however, is *how* these factors affect outcomes and what their relative importance is in determining outcomes' (1987:175). This clearly indicates a direction for future research in relation to movement outcomes.

Besides, Gamson's criteria for measuring success and failure raises a number of issues. One critic points out that apart from gaining full acceptance, a social movement can be seen as successful when it achieves other forms of intangible gain. A social movement may lead to electoral shifts and changes in coalition within the state, and these two possible gains must be taken into consideration (Jenkins, 1983; Tarrow, 1982). Another criticism comes from students of new social movements whose objectives are more associated with consensus and identity building among members of a social movement. As Mueller argues, apart from winning concessions from opponents, a social movement can be regarded as successful if the experience and the sense of solidarity formed in the process of a social movement can be 'recycled as a resource for a second movement phase' (1989:91). Basically, both critiques charged that Gamson employed a very narrow concept of success which only dealt with tangible forms of benefits but failed to offer a measure of change in social power.

In summary, we have briefly elucidated three thematic concerns in the resource mobilization perspective. We see that resource mobilization theorists dismiss the individual-oriented and social-psychological method of the classical perspective and argue that personal strain and grievances are not fundamental to the emergence of social movements. They link mobilization efforts with the origin of social movements, and their foci of study include social movement organizations, and the extent and effectiveness of resource acquisition methods. Above all, this perspective sensitizes us to acknowledge the role of social movement organizations.

There are however some shortcomings in this perspective. As regards the origin of a social movement, the resource mobilization perspective cuts itself off from any macro-structural analysis since it assumes that the 'grievances' and 'deprivation' arising from structural problems are not enough to generate a social movement (Zald, 1991). However, this perspective ignores the fact that different historical epochs and different stages of social development will generate different types of social movement. Macro-sociological studies have shown that advanced capitalist democracies promote social movements which put more emphasis on identity formation, but less on formal organization and involvement in formal political institutions (Donati, 1984; Eyerman, 1992; Habermas, 1985; Melucci, 1980, 1984; Offe, 1985; Scott, 1990). In urban studies, it has been argued that the crisis in the provision of collective consumption in urban areas was more likely to generate urban movements (Castells, 1983; Fainstein and Fainstein, 1985). Pickvance (1985) also identified rapid urbanization, the increasing provision of collective consumption by the state, the ability of political parties to articulate urban issues, and specific social and historical conditions as the important factors determining the ebb and flow of urban movements. Kitschelt (1985), in his study of new social movements, emphasises the significance of the crisis in the welfare state to the growth of new 'life chance' movements. These empirical findings and theoretical discussions point out that, apart from the efforts of social movement organizations, political and societal contexts are critical for the formation of social movements.

Resource mobilization proponents have not identified the extent to which resources could make a difference to the development, success, or failure of a social movement. Silence in this respect renders it difficult for this approach to yield any falsifiable propositions. As Kitschelt argues: 'whenever a movement occurs, one is able to identify some kind of resource [...] that will be held responsible for a collective mobilization. The theories would lose their arbitrariness only if one could tell when [and] which resources should make a difference for the career of a specific movement' (1991:336). The extent of the significance of resources remains ambiguous in this perspective. The rational choice variant is concerned with the extent to which incentive systems can mobilize human resources, while the variant concerning interorganizational linkages merely concentrates on the internal organizational structure. Neither look closely at the significance of resources.

On the other hand, the proponents of the resource mobilization theory place too much emphasis on the market-managerial and organizational modes of resource acquisition to the neglect of the communal mode. Most empirical studies have been concerned with nationally based, federated organizational structures which were more likely to adopt a market-managerial mode of resource acquisition. The increasing interest in nationally based social movement organizations is the result of McCarthy and Zald's analysis which proclaimed that modern social movements were led by professional movement organizations which 'control larger resource pools' (McCarthy and Zald, 1977:1221). As a result, locally based groups remain undocumented in research. Without acknowledging the significance of the communal relationship to mobilization, the internal social structure of communities receives scant attention. However, as Pickvance (1977) pointed out in his review of the study of urban social movements, the social relationships within a social base should be examined because the social integration mechanism embedded in a community might be able to absorb social grievances and political demands, and thereby urban protest would be less likely to emerge in this context (Frohlich and Oppenheimer, 1970; Granvotter, 1973; Liu and Duff, 1972).

Resource mobilization theorists have also failed to relate the choice of mode of resource acquisition to the strategic position of social movement organizations. We can identify three types of structural restriction that would shape the behaviour of social movement organizations. The first restriction is created by the political structure which delimits the access channels for a social movement. Recent research has shown a high degree of association between the openness and flexibility of the political structure to political demands on the one hand, and the forms of strategy, the development process and the nature of social movement organizations on the other (Eisinger, 1973; Kitschelt, 1986; Kriesi, 1991; Tarrow, 1989). Active state intervention constitutes the second constraint on social movements. In some cases, the state leaves a social movement little room for manoeuvre, and in extreme cases, state repression totally eradicates a social movement. The resource mobilization perspective is weak in theorizing the active role of the state (Jenkins, 1995; Mayer, 1991; Pickvance, 1995). The third restriction is related to the social location of a social movement organization which affects the disposable resources of a social movement organization (Mueller, 1992). In Weberian terms, the macro-social structure determines the distribution of life chances, which in turn affects the distribution of political power. Piven (1975) has pointed out that the strategic position of workers provided them with more political leverage to obtain concessions than the poor and the unemployed. Since the workers were essential to the industrial system, enterprise owners were more likely to concede when the workers brought the factory system to a halt by strike. By contrast, protests by the unemployed and welfare recipients had little significance other than temporarily disturbing the tranquillity of a few marginal governmental agencies.

The mode of resource acquisition is not necessarily determined by structural factors; however, the rationality of actors is crucial in this respect. There has been increasing criticism of the simplistic model of rationality in the resource mobilization perspective (Ferree, 1992; Ferree and Miller, 1985; Hirsch, 1986; Kitschelt, 1991; Mayer, 1991; Taylor and Whittier, 1992). Kitschelt has criticized the assumption that the goals and objectives of a social movement are taken as given, and as a result, the aims of a social movement are not regarded as 'being subject to internal and external communication and learning in which the actors (and their adversaries) bring facts, values, reasons, and experiences to bear on strategic choices and purposes. Objectives are a fixed "second nature" of social movements' (1991:331).

This criticism clearly points to one of the drawbacks of the resource mobilization perspective. As this perspective is obsessed with the analysis of organizational effectiveness, the extent to which actors determine the selection of strategies and organizational forms are under-researched. The life experiences, consciousness and worldviews of the participants have not been identified and integrated into its framework of social movements (Oliver, 1989). As Gamson pointed out 'there is little here of loyalty, commitment, solidarity, consciousness, or the role of face-to-face interaction. The meanings that participants give to their involvement in collective action are made to seem largely irrelevant' (1987:6). Ferree and Miller (1985) argued that the ideology of social movement activists played a critical part in the selection of strategies and the interpretation of goals. This argument is substantiated by Downey's (1986) case study of the Clamshell Alliance where it was found that rather than the availability of resources, ideology was a more important factor in the development of the protest group. To say that ideology is an important factor in decision-making is not to reject the rational choice variant of the resource mobilization perspective. We suggest that it is necessary to examine the interplay of ideology and rational choice in the process of strategy selection. This echoes Ferree's argument that we need a theory which would recognize that 'there are different types of rationality associated with different forms of social organization' (1992:47).

The neglect of movement activists' ideology leads to a further weakness in the resource mobilization theory that this perspective is unaware of the need to link internal conflicts with the pattern of social protests. We notice that the formation of the meaning of grievances must undergo a process of interpretation, in which both participants and non-participants play active parts (Klandermans, 1984; Oliver, 1983). Conflicts between leaders and followers may emerge when there is disagreement or a conflicting interpretation of grievances and strategies. We argue that the articulation of the objectives and goals of social movements, and the choices of strategies, are the result of the interaction between leaders and participants.

Furthermore, because the resource mobilization perspective gives prominence to the role and effects of external supporters, it fails to meticulously examine the effects of elite involvement and to consider the impact of elites opposed to social protest. We agree with McAdam (1982) that the power relations within society are more complicated and the involvement of elites is not as positive and helpful to an insurgency as the resource mobilization perspective implies. Elite involvement may turn out to be a cooptative mechanism when the elites hold different political preferences and orientations from the mass. For example in one study, external assistance provided by professional social movement organizations was found to be playing the role of social control and resulted in the suppression of a social movement (Troyer, 1984). Also, there are numerous examples of professionals who work independently of their potential constituency (McCarthy and Zald, 1987; Pinard and Hamilton, 1989). In many community development projects, welfare professionals were engaged in collective action as 'organizers' (Collier, 1976; Dore and Mars, 1981; Eckstein, 1977; Gilbert and Ward, 1984, 1985; Nelson, 1979). It was found that they did not act in line with the views of the people whom the professionals claimed to represent since they carried a particular set of objectives, ideology and beliefs and preferred to deal with problems in ways different from the mass whom they claimed to work for (Freeman, 1979; Troyer, 1984).

In summary, the resource mobilization perspective is grounded in an analysis of social movement organizations. Focusing on the resource acquisition methods and their effectiveness also broadens our vision to include an understanding of the complicated dynamics of social protests. However, this perspective raises a number of issues. It places too much emphasis on the link between organizational structure and outcomes, and does not clearly theorize the reasons for the selection of mobilization acquisition modes. The proponents of the resource mobilization perspective overlook the possibility of conflicts between providers of external assistance and the mass base, and fail to notice the negative impacts of external assistance. It is clear that there is a need for the study of the power relationship between sources of external assistance and the indigenous leadership as well as the mass base. Moreover, political context and the ideology of a social movement are not taken into consideration. In response to these drawbacks in the resource mobilization perspective, two different perspectives have developed, namely, the political process and social construction of protest models. In the following sections we examine these models.

Political Process Model

Perrow (1979) classified the political process model as one variant of the resource mobilization perspective and called it 'resource mobilization theory I'. Advocates of this model, however, feel uneasy with this term because the resource mobilization perspective only 'identifies the amassing or spending of resources as the absolutely central phenomenon, and to the extent, distracts away from power struggles and from group organization' (Tilly, 1983, quoted in Morris and Herring, 1987:165). They also argue that the study of resource acquisition is not an exclusive concern of social movement theorists. Focusing on resource mobilization constitutes a critical theoretical domain which does not demarcate social movement theories from those in other sub-fields of sociology. For example, the study of political parties and interest groups also examines resource acquisition. The resource mobilization perspective is unclear about whether the organization under study should be conceptualized as a movement organization or interest group (Morris and Herring, 1987). Hence, as political process proponents argue, the resource mobilization perspective may leave unnoticed many important characteristics of a social movement.

Central to the political process model is the idea that social movements are 'challengers', who receive neither recognition nor advantages from the authorities. They usually operate outside the formal political structure. The focus of study is the process by which groups adopt collective action and become involved in conflict with the political authority. This model raises a number of questions, including (1) why some groups are engaged in collective action; (2) what kinds of condition facilitate or hinder their operations; and (3) what factors determine the choice of strategy, with a specific concern with 'unruly' practices (Gamson, 1975; Tilly, 1978). Advocates of this model seek the answers by reference to three levels of analysis. The origin of a social movement is largely explained by the limited political channels available to powerless social groups. Thus, they argue that it is necessary to examine how the political structure excludes social groups from the formal structure. With respect to the conditions facilitating the growth of collective action, emphasis is placed on the resource base and pre-existing organizational structure. It is clear that the political process model does not deny the insights provided by the resource mobilization perspective about the importance of organization and mobilization. The third level is to study the varied strategic choices that confront movement leaders and participants. It indicates that this model 'attributes an active role to participants and leaders, for the strategic choices will affect the growth and spread of collective action' (Morris and Herring, 1987:169).

Recent work however shifts attention from the strategic choice of movement leaders to study of the formal political structure. The concept of 'political opportunity structure' has been suggested by different theorists for the conceptualization of the link between social movement and political context. It refers to the formal political structure, and the political alliance and opposition system which a social movement encounters. There is no firm agreement about the essential features of political opportunity structure, but a few attempts have been made to break it down into components. In Figure 2.2, we present the components of the political opportunity structure suggested by Tarrow, Kitschelt and Kriesi.

Figure 2.2 illustrates the difference between the three versions of the concept 'political opportunity structure'. The components belong to three categories, namely the nature and characteristics of formal access to the political structure; the configuration of the political groupings including political parties, interest groups, alliance and opponents; and the capacity of the state to deal with external social forces. These views suggest the hypothesis that the greater the number of favourable components a political structure has, the more favourable political conditions are to the emergence of social movements.

	Input Process		Output Process
	The wider social and political context (outside the formal political structure)	Access	The capacity of the state
Tarrow (1988)	- the stability of political alignment; - the presence of allies and support groups;	- a high degree of openness of the polity; - the presence of divisions within elites; - the elites' tolerance of protest	- the presence of divisions within elites, increasing the possibility of social movements winning concessions;
Kitschelt (1986)	- the simultaneous appearance of several movements contesting the institutions of social control; - the availability of normative, remunerative and informational resources in the political context;	- strong patterns of interaction between government and interest groups, and favourable electoral laws; - a high degree of openness of political regimes;[a]	- the output phase of the policy cycle offers social movements points of access and inclusion in policy making;[b]

	Input Process		Output Process
	The wider social and political context (outside the formal political structure)	Access	The capacity of the state
Kriesi (1992) (N.B. Kriesi's focus is mainly on the political context of New Social Movements)	- the formation of an alliance with the political party on the left;[c] - fragmented union systems leading to considerable competition among unions: some unions appeal to the constituency of social movements;	- a low degree of centralization and concentration of the power of the formal institutional structure, i.e. a weak state; - a low degree of coherence, internal coordination and professionalization of the public administration; - the presence of institutionalized direct democratic procedures, such as popular initiatives and referendums, which allow social movements to put an issue on the political agenda;	- a weak state which is coherent, federal, and fragmented, providing a favourable mobilization context for collective action; - the use of inclusive informal procedures and strategies at the implementation stage;

Figure 2.2 Political Opportunity Structure: Summary of the Components Making for Increased Access and Increased Success as Suggested by Tarrow, Kitschelt and Kriesi

Notes:
[a] The degree of openness is higher when (i) there is a large number of political parties, which makes it difficult for the political system to confine electoral interest articulation to the 'cartel' of parties in power; (ii) the legislature is electorally accountable and more sensitive to public demands, and capable of developing and controlling policies independently of the executive; (iii) there are 'fluid' and pluralist links providing more access for new interests to the decision-making centres; and (iv) there are viable procedures to build effective policy coalitions.
[b] This is more likely (i) when a centralized state apparatus provides social movements with a clear policy implementation process to target their demands on; (ii) when there is strong control by the state over economic resources available for social movements to challenge policies; and (iii) when the judiciary is little involved in resolving conflicts over policy implementation.
[c] This is more likely (i) when a proportional electoral system leads to more competition between parties; (ii) when there is a unified left; (iii) when the left is in opposition; (iv) when the presence of the New Left both puts competitive pressure on the state and pursues the same goal, uses the same strategies as the new social movements; and (v) in the presence of the Green Party.

The concept 'political opportunity structure' is employed in two ways. First, it is used as an analytical tool to delineate the 'environment' in which a social movement operates and to abstract its stable properties. The analytical strategy assumes that the political environment is stable and goes on to examine how the actors formulate their strategy and actions within this context (Kriesi, 1991). Second, it is treated as one of the important factors determining the growth and decline of social movements (McAdam, 1982; Piven and Cloward, 1977), or is conceived as one of the factors determining the choice of mobilization strategy (Eisinger, 1973; Kitschelt, 1986; Kriesi, 1991; Tarrow, 1988). Simply put, this concept implies that the choice of strategies of social movements is strongly associated with the specific properties of the political opportunity structure (Eisinger, 1973; Kitschelt, 1986; Kriesi, 1991). For example, in Kitschelt's framework (1986), a political opportunity structure with a higher degree of openness is said to be more likely to induce or invite confrontational movement strategies while a higher degree of closure leads to compromising strategies.

Nevertheless, as has been shown, we should note that this concept refers to three component categories. In our view, these three categories are different in nature. Formal access refers to the structural elements of a political structure, while interorganizational linkage refers to the configuration of power among allies or opponents. The capacity of the state is related to the possible means for the state to resolve or intervene in social conflicts, including repression, assimilation, cooptation and facilitation. Also, whereas formal access refers to a somewhat static aspect of the polity, the capacity of the state refers to the readiness of the state to act. These two aspects of the polity differ in nature and implications, and should not be mixed up. It is clear that these three components in a polity refer to different dimensions of the political structure, and therefore lumping them into one concept seems to add to the confusion. We suggest that different dimensions of the polity should be analytically separated in order to develop a fruitful analytical tool. We shall come back to this issue in section 2.5.

In evaluating the concept 'political opportunity structure', Rootes (1992) argued that this concept mixed up structural aspects and the contingent products of the political system, for example the shifting balance of political competition. Furthermore, as he pointed out, it is right to identify the formal institutional structure as constituting the structural aspect of a political system, however it is problematic to regard the character of a social movement as a direct result of the structural aspects of a political system. Besides, it is necessary but not sufficient to explain the character of a social movement by merely making reference to the structural aspects of a political system. Drawing on his comparative analysis of the environmental movement in Britain and in Germany, Rootes found that the character of this social movement was 'shaped both directly by the formal structures of the political system and by the contingent effects of those structures as they are mediated by political competition' (1992:10). He suggested that it was necessary to place greater emphasis on the contingent factors, in addition to the structural factors, in order to find out the factors which influence the opportunities presented to a social movement.

Furthermore, the concept 'political opportunity structure' only seeks to abstract the features and characteristics of a political structure and there are few theoretical statements concerning the mediating process through which the conditions shape the actor's choice of strategy (Dalton, 1995; della Porta and Rucht, 1995). We argue that the interplay between actors and context should be spelled out in order to analyze the extent to which the political opportunity structure determines the political action of movement actors. In addition, this concept seems to define political context in structural terms, as something given and as having a relatively stable environment (Kriesi, 1991; Kriesi and van Praag, Jr., 1987). This leads to the neglect of the state as an active agent of social control whose strategies could influence the growth and development of a social movement (Clarke and Mayer, 1986). We suggest that more effort should be invested in finding out how state action affects the balance of power of a polity, or on investigating how the state manipulates formal access to reduce the ability of social movement organizations to influence the decision-making process. The state should be seen as an actor, and the impact of its tactics upon a social movement should be taken into account (Gale, 1986; Jenkins and Klandermans, 1995; McCarthy *et al.*, 1991).

Another problem with the political process model is related to the analysis of the composition of state elites. Except for Tarrow who has warned against statism, other proponents of this strand treat the state simply as an entity and overlooked its internal divisions. However, it has been shown that sub-groups inside the state differed in their responses to social insurgency (Jenkins and Perrow, 1977). We should treat the different orientations of the state elites toward social movements as an important factor that could shape responses to social movements (Dearlove, 1973; Pickvance, 1976). Rootes also pointed out that a political system 'may be relatively open or closed to different kinds of issues and/or groups, and this makes the global characterization of political systems hazardous if not entirely arbitrary' (1992:17).

To sum up, the concept 'political opportunity structure' introduces three components of a political structure and provides us with an analytical tool to conceptualize the political context in terms of formal access of the state, the balance and configurations of power of the interorganizational networks among political parties and interest groups, and the capacity of the state. However, we argue that the role of the state is inadequately conceptualized and more attention should be given to the possible internal divisions of the state. Moreover, advocates of the 'political opportunity structure' concept merely draw our attention to the political structure, but we should bear in mind that the political process models advocated by Tilly (1978) and McAdam (1982) not only stress the analysis of political contexts, but also emphasize analysis of the organizational and resource base, and the strategic choices of movement leaders and participants. However, we notice that the political process models are weak in theorizing the links between political context, organizations and actions. Morris and Herring (1987) suggested that the study of the role of ideology may provide insight into the links. Therefore we now turn to examine the social construction of protest model to see how far this can solve the theoretical issue of the role of ideology.

The Social Construction of Protest

Recent discussion in the field of social movements raises the issue of the role of ideology in collective action. In fact, this is the result of a revival of academic interest in the social psychological aspects of social movements. The resurgent social psychology is not to repudiate the idea that movement participants are rational actors, but essential to this new trend is the argument that rationality and emotions are not irreconcilable (Killian, 1984). One of the suggestions posits that consciousness, ideology, solidarity and collective identity play a critical role in defining and interpreting the individual's situation (Cohen, 1985; Gamson, 1992). The analysis of ideology seems to give us the means to explain 'what makes people define their situation in such a way that participation in a social movement seems appropriate' (Klandermans, 1992:77). Klandermans (1992) uses the term 'social construction of protest' to refer to the constructionist approaches that share a common interest in understanding the transformation in subjective consciousness of the actors involved. The theoretical issue about 'meaning' draws attention to the definition of the actor, the social context within which meanings are developed and transformed, and the cultural content of social movements (Mueller, 1992). Advocates of the social construction model are increasingly aware of the importance of meaning attribution and subjective interpretation in the process of defining grievances, interests, strategies and the formation of identity.

We identify three main strands within the social constructionist approach to the meaning attribution process. The first focuses on the social psychological level of individuals and looks at how an individual is motivated to participate in collective action. The second is concerned with the persuasion process through which movement organizers are able to establish among a target population a collectively agreed definition of a situation and a belief in the necessity of adopting collective action to push for common interests. The third strand has a strong assumption that actors are not atomistic individuals, but are group embedded. Hence, the analysis of movement participation is not to focus on an individual's choices and decisions, but on the group context for constructing grievances, opportunities, and resources. This new development is interesting and needs more discussion.

The first variant of this perspective attempts to deal with reasons for participation. Its focus is on the process by which individuals become active participants. It is argued that an individual's motivation to participate depends on two kinds of acceptance. First, an individual has to accept the cause of a collective effort and second, to accept the view that collective action is an appropriate and necessary form of action to solve one's problem. Klandermans suggests the concept 'consensus mobilization' to examine the first acceptance and 'action mobilization' for the second acceptance. Consensus mobilization refers to the readiness of a group of people to participate in collective action, while action mobilization refers to their acceptance of the goals and means of action adopted. As regards the analysis of consensus mobilization, Klandermans suggests three dimensions in terms of people's expectations: a. expectations about the number of participants; b. expectations about one's own contribution to the probability of success; and c. expectations about the probability of success if many people participate (Klandermans, 1984).

Klandermans reiterates the critical role of the subjective decision-making of potential participants in relation to participation in collective action. He assumes that movement participation is the consequence of a reasoning process rather than simply the outcome of some psychological factors such as grievances and alienation. The unit of analysis in the framework suggested by Klandermans is the social psychological factor at the individual level. In conceptualizing individual support for social movements in general, Klandermans and Oegema (1987) introduced the concept 'mobilization potential' which refers to the aggregate of individuals' readiness to participate in a future social movement campaign. This concept is a measure of the extent to which a social movement organization at 'a given moment of time can count upon active support, should they decide to mobilize overtly for action campaigns' (Kriesi, 1992:24). Clearly, this is an attitudinal concept referring to individual predispositions. But whether this potential is translated into actual participation in a social movement is not entirely dependent on individual predispositions. An intervening variable is introduced for the study of the mediating process, which refers to the mobilization strategy of organizers who are supposed to be the actors able to create participation opportunities and/or overcome barriers. With respect to this aspect of mobilization, advocates of this strand suggest the study of the participation opportunity structure, the interaction contexts in which mobilization strategy is carried out, and the interplay between mobilization potential and mobilization strategy.

By contrast, another strand of the social construction approach takes the standpoint which approximates that of a movement organizer. It is concerned with mobilization strategy which attempts to establish a match between individual identity and a collective identity advocated by a social movement (Gamson, 1992; Melucci, 1989; Snow and Benford, 1988; Snow et al., 1986). Analysis starts with an assumption that 'some sets of individual interests, values, and beliefs and social movement activities, goals, and ideology are congruent and complementary' (Snow et al., 1986:464). The concept 'frame' was employed to study the signifying work of social movements. In this framework, actors are signifying a social condition when they 'frame, or assign meaning to and interpret, relevant events and conditions in ways that are intended to mobilize potential adherents and constituents, to garner bystander support and to demobilize antagonists' (Snow and Benford, 1988:198). The mobilization and activation of participants are rendered possible when social movement organizers can achieve frame alignment, which refers to a correspondence in terms of interpretive orientations between individuals and social movement organizers. Hence, the aim of analysis is to examine the alignment processes by which collective action is made possible.

The frameworks suggested by Klandermans and Snow *et al.* seem to suggest that the formation of mobilization and action consensus, or frame alignment is a prelude to collective action. The key point is that the dominant cultural code does not always define situations as problematic or encourage collective action. For the formation of a social movement, it is necessary to anchor in the target population an interpretation of the situation which is different from the dominant code, and persuade them that collective effort is plausible and feasible. This is similar to the idea suggested by Piven and Cloward (1977) that participation is more likely when an individual loses his/her attachment to dominant meaning systems. The constructionists' concerns are about the conditions in which people think differently, accept collective action, and form a collective identity which sustains social movements. This theoretical issue leads to a growth of interest in the study of the conditions giving rise to collective identity, and another strand of social construction perspective develops.

The third strand has a different unit of analysis from that of the previous two strands. Rather than examining the individual's reasoning process or the movement organizers' efforts in frame alignment, this strand places emphasis on face-to-face interaction. It assumes that actors are group embedded or socially located. Groups constitute a social network in which actors are engaged in specific social locations. Such social locations, as Mueller pointed out, 'intersect and overlap in providing cultural materials that are drawn upon by a meaning-constructing actor who participates with others in interpreting a sense of grievances, resources, and opportunities' (1992:7). We notice that this strand places importance on the contextual analysis of interaction. Its focus is on the informal primary interactions through which protest meanings are constructed, the social inequality dominant in daily life is discerned, a sense of shared fate is constituted, and the forms of resistance are worked out. Moreover, analysis must take into account the context in which the negotiation process takes place. For this purpose, McAdam suggests the concept 'micromobilization context' to study the condition referring to 'any small group setting in which processes of collective attributes are combined with rudimentary forms of organization to produce mobilization for collective action' (McAdam *et al.*, 1988:709). The micro-mobilization context provides primary sources of resources and renders possible social insurgency. One of its essential components is the preexisting social organizations which constitute social networks. Inherent in a social network are bonds of friendship and love which constitute strong social ties among people. Informal social networks then facilitate communication and the dispersal of a common identity and shared fate which are decisive for solidarity (Marwell and Oliver, 1984). McAdam has pointed out that 'the failure of a new movement to take hold and the rapid spread of insurgent action have been credited to the presence or absence of such an infrastructure' (1982:46). Tilly (1978) coined the term *catnet*, which refers to the amalgam of category and network, to indicate the importance of preexisting social relationships to the formation of collective identity.

Advocates of this strand of the social construction approach point out that resource mobilization and political process models fail to identify and conceptualize the oppositional component in a social movement. Where do political ideas and claims which oppose the dominant values come from? The advocates then argue that we should throw light on informal and face-to-face interaction. As they argue, in advanced industrial societies where there is a hegemonic process which continuously justifies the prevailing social inequality and domination, 'face-to-face interactions not only form the building blocks of larger aggregations and organizations but also serve as the social context in which hegemonic belief systems are broken down' (Mueller, 1992:13). Hence, it is necessary to focus on interaction within the group in order to see how oppositional belief flourishes.

The advantage of this perspective is that it provides an analytical tool for studying the communal mode of resource acquisition. The social constructionists stress the role of ordinary people and conceive them as active actors who are able to think, interpret, and interact with political activists and leaders. This perspective also draws our attention to the possibility that the social networks, worldviews, and the modes of daily life of potential participants are the principal factors influencing the occurrence of a social movement. In other words, we avoid seeing people as being simply passive, only waiting for external mobilization and assistance. On the contrary, we should focus on how people interact in a group context, how they construct their meanings, and how they define grievances, opportunities and the choice of actions. Regarding the choice of strategies, whereas the resource mobilization perspective and political process model look for answers in the availability of resources and the political opportunity structure, social construction proponents focus on informal and face-to-face interaction where the construction of meaning, and the defining of grievances, opportunities, and strategies takes place.

Nevertheless, this perspective has two shortcomings. The first criticism is applied to the first strand of this perspective which merely focuses on the reasoning process in relation to movement participation, and therefore in our view is not able to provide theoretical insights for the study of the development of a social movement. As for the shortcomings of the social construction model as a whole, we would note its lack of concern about the possibility of conflicts in interest articulation and the choice of tactics and strategies, and about how conflicts affect the behavioural pattern of a social movement. In our opinion, the decision-making process in relation to political participation is not straightforward, beginning with people who are unaware of their own interest, who are then transformed through becoming aware of their collective interests and who finally act. On the contrary, the process may involve a series of conflicts of interpretations of the situation. Internal conflicts over the goals and means of a social movement would affect the selection of tactics and strategies, and increase the degree of internal fragmentation. This would entail a reduction in the organizational capacity of a social movement organization. Indeed, empirical evidence lends support to this idea. Heisler and Hoffman (1989) point out in their study of unemployed blue-collar workers that the identification of grievances leads to factionalism and organizational splits. This indicates a connection between the selection of grievances and organizational problems. Barkan (1979) found that conflicting values and attitudes among anti-nuclear protesters resulted in a particular set of dilemmas, and subsequently the movement encountered difficulties in the choice of issues, tactics and modes of organization. In another study of civil rights movements, Barkan (1986) showed that interorganizational conflicts arose because of different ideological and tactical considerations within movements. Walsh and Cable (1989) also found that the creation of a new social movement organization was in fact a form of solution to the ideological disputes over goals and tactics. Walsh and Warland (1983) showed that social movement organizations became unstable and short-lived, given conflict existing between actors and organizers. Clearly, through understanding internal conflict over the definition of interests and objectives, and over the ideological principles of protests, we can obtain more information to account for the development path and direction of a social movement.

In short, the social constructionist perspective has not given us any clear theoretical statements about such the link between the character of a social movement on the one hand, and subjective perceptions of grievances, the formation of identity and internal conflicts on the other.

Toward an Integrated Approach to Collective Action

This section briefly summarizes the previous discussion about the perspectives on social movements, and then suggests an integrated approach to the study of an urban movement in Hong Kong.

At the outset we note that the perspectives we have discussed in the previous sections have different concerns. Figure 2.3 summarizes the major concerns, the dependent variables and the key independent variables suggested by the four perspectives. It is clear to us that the dependent variables in these perspectives differ. In the classical and resource mobilization perspectives, the rise and fall of a social movement is taken as the dependent variable. Advocates of the classical perspective and the rational choice variant of the resource mobilization perspective assume that the survival of a social movement depends on the expansion of membership, and hence the study of the reasons for movement participation is said to be the key to understanding the origins of collective action. They attempt to explain participation by reference to the decision-making process of individuals. In these models, the rise and fall of a social movement is in turn associated with the expansion and contraction of membership. The organizational variant of the resource mobilization perspective is also interested in the maintenance of a social movement, but its advocates emphasize the organization's capacity to mobilize resources. Hence, they examine both the link between organizational type and movement outcome, and that between organizational structure and the extent of resource mobilization. Accumulation and expenditure of resources are regarded as an indication of the operation of a social movement. By the same token, the rise and fall of a social movement is explained by the extent of mobilizable resources.

Advocates of the political process model also aim to explain the rise and fall of social movements. Tarrow (1988) attempted to identify the factors shaping the cycles of protest in Italy during the 1965-75 period. McAdam's book on the civil rights movement (1982) takes the life cycle of this movement as a dependent variable. The interest of both students remains the rise and fall of a social movement. A new attempt informed by the political process model is that suggested by della Porta and Rucht (1995) who coined the concept 'social movement family' to describe a group of social movement organizations that have similar basic values and organizational overlaps. The focus of their study is the factors which shape the characteristics of a social movement family. This study resembles those studies which are more interested in the behaviourial pattern of a social movement than in its growth and decay, or rise and decline. The political process model as suggested by Tilly is a case in point. The dependent variables in this framework include the rise and fall of a social movement, and its behaviourial pattern. The third strand of the social construction perspective has the same focus of study. It attempts to understand the link between the construction of meaning and the cause and course of social protest.

Aspect of social movements of interest	Key variable(s)
a) the origin of social movements	CPC - structural breakdown engenders grievances and irrational actors RMT - a) resources provided by external agency b) preexisting social networks PPM - unequal distribution of power and resources and the closure of political system SCT - a) preexisting social networks b) formation of collective identity
b) the rise and fall of social movements	CPC - formation of emergent norms and generalized beliefs RMT - a) the expansion and contraction of membership b) the social movement organization's capacity to mobilize resources PPM - a) the political opportunity structure b) mobilization of members and the strategic use of resources SCT - formation of collective identity

Aspect of social movements of interest	Key variable(s)
c) the character of social movements	CPC - (uninterested) RMT - availability of resources, the rules and limitations of rational action, strategic problems, organizational dilemma PPM - the character of the political opportunity structure SCT - ideology, preference formation, frame alignment
d) the nature of the participants	CPC - the character and action of actors are determined by the crises and problems in social structure RMT - actors are assumed to be rational and their actions are bound by the rules and limitations of rational action PPM - the room for manoeuvre for social actors, who are rational people, is constricted by the political organizational imperative and structure SCT - a) actors' collective identity provides the foundation from which social movement emerges b) their actions are associated with their interpretation of the situation and decisions regarding their mode of activity
e) success or failure of a social movement	CPC - (uninterested) RMT - realization of movement objectives PPM - realization of movement objectives SCT - consciousness raising

Figure 2.3 **Key Variables in Understanding Aspects of Social Movements According to Four Theoretical Perspectives**

Key: CPC - Classical perspective on Collective action
RMT - Resource Mobilization Theory
PPM - Political Process Model
SCT - Social Construction Perspective

Another major concern of these perspectives is with the character of social movements and the nature of participants. With the assumption that actors are rational, resource mobilization theorists suggest that the character of social movements is shaped by the external constraints and opportunities, and that social movement activities largely depend on the capacity of a social movement to mobilize resources in order to overcome the constraints. Advocates of the political process model also share this view and emphasise the capacity of social movement organizations to accumulate and strategically use resources. By contrast, advocates of the social construction model criticize the assumption in these perspectives that social movement participants are rational. They argue that social movement participants are so embedded in social groups that collective social life produces specific ideologies, preferences and interpretations of situations which together assume central importance in social movements. Hence, as suggested by the social construction theorists, a key step in the study of social movements is to analyse the process of activating collective identity and to see how this process gives rise to a continual engagement in the production of meaning which in turn serves as a cognitive foundation for concerted action (Gamson, 1992; Melucci, 1988). Furthermore, the forms of action adopted by social movement participants are also related to their capacity to perceive and evaluate the limits and opportunities offered by the social context.

The essential point of our discussion is to point out the simple fact that these perspectives are asking different questions and use different dependent as well as independent variables. Therefore, in relation to our choice of perspectives we should be clear whether we are asking the same kinds of question as the ones posed by these perspectives. So it is necessary for us to set out clearly the questions we address in this thesis. As has been pointed out in Chapter 1, we pose four questions about urban movements in Hong Kong.

1. Why do some groups of Hong Kong people stand outside the formal political system to advocate or defend their interests in an era in which democracy has been introduced into the political system?
2. How does a social base develop into a social force and what strategies has the social force adopted to exert pressure on the political authority?
3. What effects can such an urban movement bring about?
4. What is the nature of the political system in Hong Kong as revealed by urban politics?

Our concerns in this study thus include the origin of the urban protest, its behaviourial pattern and its effects. Our study adopts an integrated approach which combines the key variables suggested by the resource mobilization, political process and social construction perspectives. Less emphasis will be placed on the classical perspective since we reject the view that social movement actors are irrational, and that the complexities of social movements can be understood by an analysis of the breakdown of the social structure. As regards the other three perspectives, we consider that they are not mutually exclusive, and that the importance of the variables suggested by these perspectives varies in different social and political contexts. With this assumption, our study will seek to find out to what extent (if any) the key variables suggested by these perspectives are significant to the origin, the character and the outcomes of an urban movement - the Aged Temporary Housing Areas (ATHA) protest in Hong Kong studied here.

We should point out that the choice of the ATHA protest is theoretically based. It was made for three reasons. First, the ATHA protest mainly involves disadvantaged people who lack resources. This kind of social protest gives us a chance to see how a collective action is possible even if resources are difficult to mobilize. Secondly, since the ATHA protest is a community-based collective action, our study may illustrate how the communal mode of mobilization, one aspect of social movements which goes unnoticed by the resource mobilization theorists, is implemented. Thirdly, it is easier for us to become involved in a relatively small-scale social protest to examine how the actor's preferences and identity are formed.

Turning to the research strategy of this study, we will be mainly focusing on the four questions we posed. In the analysis of the origin of the ATHA protest, we shall focus on the availability of resources, the functions of the external agencies, preexisting social networks in the ATHA and the unequal distribution of power and resources, and the degree of closure of the political opportunity structure. We attempt to examine why a social movement must employ non-institutionalized means to advance its interests.

In relation to the second question, we first examine how a social base developed into a social force. We recognize that urban movements may not have a stable organizational structure. In fact, as the Fainsteins pointed out, 'social movements are emergent social groups ... [and] social movements never assume a permanent form - hence the description "emergent" [is important]' (1985:189). Our major concern is how the protesters can maintain continuous engagement among the participants. Therefore, we examine the availability of resources to mobilize the participation, the willingness of the potential participants to become involved in protest activities, and the preexisting social networks which may facilitate the formation of collective identity. The second aspect we shall study is the character of the ATHA protest. We argue that the forms of strategies adopted provide an appropriate way of focusing on the activities of urban movements. What is original in our study is its synthesis of the resource mobilization and social construction perspectives which enable the formation of identity to be linked to the choice of strategies. [6] As shown in the general literature on social movements, the social construction theorists only attempt to link identity formation to participation in social movements, without giving consideration to the importance of identity in the choice of strategies. By contrast, in the resource mobilization perspective, actors are presumed to be bound by the constraints of rational action. The choice of strategies is not seen as negotiable and influenced by actors' ideological and cultural predispositions, so the complexities of the process of choice of strategies is inadequately grasped. It is our contention that in the study of the strategic aims of social movement actors, it is necessary to examine the actors' strategic preferences and interpretations of situations. We agree with Gamson who pointed out that social movement actors do not make strategic judgements based on their expectations about costs and benefits, but that 'any strategic paradigm necessarily supposes a theory of identity' (1992:57). Our position also echoes the argument suggested by Rootes that 'any attempt to explain the choice of tactics must reckon with the political values of the actors and the way in which tactical and strategic preferences were dictated by those values' (1992:19). Moreover, we should point out that the actors' preferences and the strategic intent of a social movement remain indeterminate until they are analysed in the light of the social background of the actors themselves and the political environment. In the following analysis, we shall explain the character of the ATHA protest by reference to the availability of resources, the strategic preferences of the actors involved, and the political environment in which the ATHA protest operates.

As regards the question of the success or failure of the ATHA protest, we pay attention to the two aspects suggested in Figure 2.3, namely, the realization of the objectives of the protest and consciousness raising. By analyzing the origin, character and outcome of the ATHA protest, we shall be in a position to reflect on the nature of the political structure in Hong Kong on the basis of the findings of this study.

To sum up, our analysis focuses on three areas. The first is the political opportunity structure. Our aim here is to find out the reasons why a social movement must employ non-institutionalized means to press for its interests, rather than using institutionalized means or entering ordinary politics. The second area concerns the social characteristics of the potential participants, including their preexisting social infrastructure, their social relationships, and their mobilization potential. All these constitute the social context which may determine the choice of strategy. The third area concerns the way in which the actors involved in a social movement group define grievances, identify resources and opportunities, and choose strategies. We explore how the socially located actors interact and react to the social and political contexts which they face. Our study of the ATHA protest will use this framework to analyze the causes and course of this urban movement, and the strategies put into action. Chapters 3 to 5 provide a brief account of the social and political background of the protest and the ATHA residents. Chapter 6 investigates the political opportunity structure and illustrates the extent to which the channel of ordinary politics is blocked. Chapter 7 examines the social infrastructure, the social relationships and mobilization potential of the ATHA residents, and explores the impacts of the mobilization efforts on the residents. Chapter 8 focuses on the nature and political orientations of the actors involved in the local concern groups. The tendency to choose polite politics strategy will be explained by reference to internal conflicts, political orientations and the resources available to the protesters.

Notes

1   It is true that some social movement organizations have a 'therapeutic' orientation. Smith and Pillemer argued that 'self-help groups' are characterized by the 'therapeutic' use of personal interaction as a means of altering or ameliorating certain kinds of personal problems of the participants (1983:214). Thus it does not imply that all types of social movement are therapeutic in nature.

2   The concept 'social movement industry' has been regarded as a more useful concept than 'social movement'. Rucht wrote that 'as a rule, social movements do not act as isolated units but exist within the context of other overlapping, complementary or oppositional movements' (quoted from Tarrow, 1988:431). Oberschall used the concept 'loosely-structured' collective action to characterize the complicated relationships among units of a social movement. Melucci (1985) suggested that it is

3. more appropriate to use movement networks or movement areas to refer to the network of groups and individuals sharing a conflicting culture and a collective identity.

3. McCarthy and Zald distinguish social movements from the organizational aspect of collective action. They define a social movement as 'a set of opinions and beliefs in a population representing preferences for changing some elements of the social structure or reward distribution, or both, of a society'. Social movement organizations are defined as 'complex, or formal, organizations that identify their goals with the preferences of a social movement and attempt to implement those goals' (1977:1217-18).

4. The debate around the significance of grievances to movement participation did not reach any conclusion. Some research revealed that individual attitudes were at best weak predictors of riot participation (Bowen et al., 1968; Grofman and Muller, 1973; McPhail, 1971; Muller, 1979; Tilly et al., 1978). However, Walsh and Warland (1983) argued, provided participation opportunities existed, grievances were positively associated with social movement participation (see also Walsh (1981)). Similarly, Useem (1981) found that grievances were salient in the Boston Antibusing Movement when sudden threats to a group increased. Both grievances and resource mobilization are factors which can explain participation in social movements. Heisler and Hoffman (1989) argued that grievances could directly affect ongoing process of mobilization, organization and outcome.

5. Olson's logic was subjected to empirical tests but the results ran against it. Kaplowitz and Fisher (1985) found that telling people they have the option of free-riding, surprisingly, reduces their tendency to do so. Tillock and Morrison (1979) studied one environmental movement organization and came to the conclusion that Olson's theory 'is of limited application in explaining collective action for noneconomic, large-scale, expensive, nonexcludable public goods.' See also Bonacich et al., 1976; Chamberlin, 1978; Frohlich et al., 1975; Frohlich and Oppenheimer, 1970; Oliver, 1980).

6. There are some case studies of social movement strategy, but the identity, ideology and political value are not highlighted. See Barkan (1979), Lawson (1984), Lofland (1985), Morris (1984), Shapiro (1985), Turner (1970) and Wilson (1961).

3 The Changing Political Context in Hong Kong

Introduction

More than a decade has passed since the first surge of political rights movements in Hong Kong. Today such groups are no longer excluded from politics, as was the case before the 1980s. Since then, politically active social forces appear to have carved out larger sites of conflict between the state and the grassroots. This chapter attempts to depict the changing relationship between the state and social and popular movements in the late 1980s.

It is our contention that economic development and the changing political structure have transformed the fabric of social and political forces. In order to delineate such a transformation, we have periodized the changing process into two stages, namely the *pre-democracy stage* in the 1970s and the stage of *transition to democracy* since 1980. In the pre-democracy stage, the transformation of the economic structure led to the expansion of the tertiary sector and a growth of the middle class. The political system remained a closed system, dominated by government and business interests. As two riots in the late 1960s appeared to indicate an increase in social grievances, a new local administrative system was formed to build up a new link between the government and the people, and as a responsive measure, more social services, public housing and economic infrastructure were provided. In the 1980s, the opening up of the formal political structure led to a phase which we describe as the stage of transition to democracy. This stage is characterized by the unprecedented process of introducing elections into the political structure. A District Board system was set up in 1981 and in 1986 the government opened up the Legislative Council by replacing some nominated members with elected members.[1] Subsequently, representatives of local communities appeared to have access to the highest echelons of the administrative structure and to have secured their positions in the polity. In retrospect, the introduction of electoral politics into the polity attracted more political activists, most of whom were of middle class background and were committed to playing a significant role in articulating grassroots interests. In 1991 the Hong Kong United Democrats, a political party mainly comprised of middle class political activists, achieved a landslide victory in the direct election to the Legislative Council, signalling a new political configuration in the formal political structure (Lau and Louie, 1993). In short, electoral politics in the 1980s changed the political configuration of Hong Kong.

This chapter delineates the changing political context in two stages. In section 3.1 we examine the economic and political situation of Hong Kong in the pre-democratic stage, and highlight the changing economic structure, the increasing intervention of the government into the social life of Hong Kong people, and a new political integration mechanism between the government and the grassroots. Section 3.2 describes the new political situation in the 1980s and section 3.3 examines the response of the grassroots to the changing political structure. Here the importance of pressure groups and community groups in grassroots politics is highlighted. The final section is a summary of the arguments of this chapter.

The Pre-democracy Stage: 1970-1980

The pre-democracy stage during the 1970s was characterized by rapid economic growth, an expansion of the middle class, and the dominance of the colonial government in the polity. Although these changes did not give rise to any social unrest or drastic change, as we shall illustrate, there was a subtle change in the political climate of Hong Kong in the 1970s; in particular the government became less paternalistic and authoritarian, and more committed to greater expenditure on social policy. On the other hand, it created a new local administration system, putting more emphasis on rule by consent and consultation so as to secure its colonial rule in the 1970s. This section will describe such changes and examine their impacts on citizen participation in Hong Kong.

The post-war industrialization of Hong Kong started in the 1950s and reaped its rewards in the 1970s. The economy is undoubtedly successful in terms of growth. The average annual growth of real Gross Domestic Product (GDP) is impressive: in the period 1973-1979 the average real growth rate in GDP was about 9%, higher than Singapore and Taiwan which were 8.7% and 8.6% respectively in the same period (Krause, 1988).

The rapid growth of the economy in the 1970s was partly the result of a thriving manufacturing sector and partly due to the opening up of the China market. Domestically produced exports grew in the period 1960-1980 at an average compound rate of 10.8% in real terms, roughly twice the growth rate of world trade (Lin and Ho, 1982). Having revitalized its re-export sector, Hong Kong's re-exports to China grew at the rate of 514% and 253% in 1979 and 1980 respectively.

Meanwhile, Hong Kong was developing into a fast-growing financial centre in the Asian-Pacific region in the mid-1970s and became one of the major international financial centres. The financial sector gained its momentum in the mid-1970s and continued to perform well, even though the world oil crisis affected its ascendancy in the mid-1970s. Whilst in 1961 it only accounted for 11% of the GDP, in 1981 its share reached 24% of the total GDP.[2]

The structural transformation of the economy had a spillover effect on the employment structure. With the growing importance of Hong Kong as an entrepot and as a financial centre, more of the labour force became involved in the tertiary sector. By 1971 about 43% of the total working population were employed in the tertiary sector, while by 1981 this figure had increased to 48.2%. If we only consider the growth rate of the labour force in the financial sector, we can see that it increased dramatically: in 1971 it was 2.7% of the total labour force but by 1981 it had increased to 4.7% (Ho, Y., 1986).

It seems that the growth of the tertiary sector was partly due to the expansion of the public sector. It is reported that in the period 1949-1985 the real GDP increased only 17 times, whereas the real government expenditure on Consolidated Account increased 36 times (Ho, H., 1989). Government expenditure per capita at 1980 prices increased from HK$1,857 in 1971-1972 to HK$4,377 in 1980-1981. The growth rate in this decade was 136%, a very impressive expansion. Expansion was found in virtually every field of human and social services (child care, school social work, youth services, family planning services, marriage counselling, elderly services, community social work, public housing provision, social security, etc.) Out of the total government expenditure in the period from 1974 to 1980 the share of social services increased from 40% to 44%.[3] The category 'social services' obtained the largest share in the 1970s, accounting for 40% of total government expenditure. The expansion of the public sector entailed a growing public sector work force. In the period from 1977-1980, the civil service achieved an average growth rate of 7% per annum.

Above all, the 1970s witnessed an expansion of the middle class, precipitated by the growth of workers engaged in the tertiary sector and the public service. In spite of the difficulty in defining class, we can rely on the official data of the occupational structure in order to get a rough idea of the class structure of Hong Kong in this period. In Table 3.1, we can see that the two categories 'professional, technical and related workers' and 'administrative and managerial workers' have both recorded an increase since 1971. The middle class, which refers to all non-manual workers (i.e. the first five categories in Table 3.1), made up 41.3% of the total labour force in 1971, increasing to 46.8% by 1981.

Occupation	1971	1981	1986	1991
Professional, technical and related workers	5.2	6.0	8.3	8.7
Administrative and managerial workers	2.4	2.7	3.6	5.1
Clerical and related workers	8.3	12.2	14.6	18.6
Sales workers	10.6	10.3	11.7	11.5
Service workers	14.8	15.6	16.2	18.7
Agricultural workers and fishermen	3.8	2.1	1.9	0.9
Production and related workers, transport equipment operators and labourers	52.3	50.4	43.3	36.2
Armed forces and unclassifiable	2.6	0.7	0.4	0.3
Total	100.0	100.0	100.0	100.0

Table 3.1 Distribution of Working Population by Occupation (%)

Source: Chau, L.C. 1989; Hong Kong Government, 1993. Hong Kong 1991 Population Census: Main Report

Despite its growing size, few political challenges originated from the middle class. It has been argued that although there was a growing union membership among non-manual occupational groups in community and social services in this period, the middle class contributed little to the overall effectiveness of the trade unionist movement (Levin and Jao, 1988). As will be discussed later, the political implications of the rise of the middle class were revealed in the 1980s, but not in the 1970s.

Nevertheless, even if the middle class did not exert any great pressure on the political structure, the political system was undergoing a process of restructuring during this stage. In the 1970s there was an expansion of the public sector in terms of infrastructure and social welfare provision. It is our contention that this expansion of the government was partly attributable to the two riots in the late 1960s, and partly to the economic recovery in the mid-1970s.

Before the two riots, the political domain was characterized by the domination of the colonial government and a small number of businessmen (Davies, 1977; Rear, 1971). A secluded bureaucracy was secured by controlling access to the Legislative Council and the Executive Council.[4] Not surprisingly, there was no direct election for membership of the two councils. The members of the councils were either unofficial members nominated and appointed by the government, or official members who were civil servants at the highest echelons of the bureaucratic structure (Leung, 1990; Rear, 1971). In order to further exclude external social and political forces for the purpose of curbing any anti-government, non-conformist or deviant social forces, the government was keen to 'stamp out all nascent sources of independent political power' (Lau, 1982:37). Also, the government refrained from providing too much in the way of social services and welfare to the grassroots in order to deter any politicization of social issues.

The two mass social disturbances in the late 1960s however, served as a warning signal to the government that its links with the grassroots had weakened. Several reforms were consequently initiated by the government as remedial measures to deal with the discontents revealed in the disturbances, including more provision of social services and welfare, the formation of a new local administrative structure, and the combat of corruption in and reform of the civil service (Scott, 1989). Of these changes, the first two had greater implications for the political context in the 1970s.

In order to secure its centralized political power and its right to rule, the government started to provide more public goods and social services to deal with the possible detrimental effects of the riots on its ruling. As Scott argued:

> after the 1966 and 1967 disturbances, it was particularly vulnerable to the charge that it was an unresponsive colonial regime. To survive, it needed positive public support. More representative institutions and the introduction of direct elections were thought to be out of the question. The only course of action seemed to be to meet the rising level of expectations by setting social policy targets and letting people judge the government on its record (1988:152).

Promising more public goods and social services appeared to be a means by which the government could mobilize greater political support and reduce further friction between itself and the grassroots. In 1972, the Governor MacLehose pledged the government to a new plan for the provision of more public goods and social services in housing, education, social welfare and recreation (Ho, D., 1989). The government appeared to be aware of the potential social unrest arising from problems in social life, as was reflected in the Governor's announcement in 1972 of the ten-year public housing programme:

> the inadequacy and scarcity of housing and all that this implies, and the harsh situations that result from it, is one of the major and most constant sources of friction and unhappiness between Government and the population. It offends alike our humanity, our civic pride and our political good sense (Hong Kong Hansard Session 1972/73:4-5).

On the other hand, the increasing government intervention into the social life of Hong Kong is related to the economic development of the 1970s. When economic growth engendered more demand for land, the government planned to put greater emphasis on creating more industrial land in new towns. Public housing policy is important to the formation of new towns because it moves people from urban areas to the new towns in order to build up a pool of labour. As Lui pointed out, 'the rapid growth of these new towns and the expansion of the provision of public housing not only mean a greater capacity to accommodate the increasing population but also an increase in the supply of land for industrial development, in communities where the industrial capitalists can find an abundant supply of labour' (1984:64).

The ten-year public housing programme had a great impact on the spatial development of Hong Kong (Wang and Yeh, 1987). Under the aegis of a new town programme, by 1983 slightly more than a million people were accommodated on public rental housing estates. Most of these people moved to the new towns which are located in the New Territories - areas which are quite distant from the urban areas (Bristow, 1989; Wong, 1982; Yeh, 1986).[5] The rate of internal geographical mobility is shown in the 1981 Census which states that 'in 1971, 81.1 percent of the total population of Hong Kong lived in the main urban areas, but by 1981 [this percentage] had decreased to 72.9 percent. On the other hand, the proportion of the total population living in the new towns increased from 9.8 percent in 1971 to 17.1 percent in 1981' (Yeh, 1985:64). Besides this, in 1981 about 70% of the population increase in the new towns was effected through public housing.

Although this massive scheme of land formation and geographical mobility is considered to be successful, the government's involvement in the urbanization process has generated social conflicts throughout the implementation process. There was increasing dissatisfaction with rehousing locations, compensation methods and the rate of redevelopment, etc. According to a study of social conflicts, about 18% of the total number of social conflicts in the late 1970s were related to housing problems and 33% to urban development (Cheung and Louie, 1991). Another study reported that in the period 1966-81, there was a steady increase in the number of conflicts involving consumption problems, from 5 events in 1966 to 30 in 1981. As far as urban protest is concerned, the average number of events per year in the 1960s was 3.1 which increased to 18.8 in the 1970s (Lui, 1984). According to Lui (1984), the frequency of urban protest at that time was about half that of industrial action, hence this kind of urban issue was not negligible in the 1970s.

A new local administrative system was established in the 1970s, signalling the government's strategy of strengthening its relationship with the grassroots, and perhaps can contain the mounting political challenges from the grassroots. Before the two riots in 1966 and 1967, the old local administrative system relied on a network in which the colonial government worked closely with local elites and indigenous charitable organizations. This network was the product of the 'indirect rule' policy of the British authority. The government relied upon a select group of Chinese leaders and organizations to mediate between the government itself and the governed. The main component in this network was the traditional kaifong (or neighbourhood) association, whose activities include relief work, running evening schools, provision of free or cheap clinics, free libraries, educational exhibitions, etc. This network served as an intermediary between the people and the government, and through it the government could solicit local opinion and the support of the grassroots (Leung, 1982; Wong, 1972).

After the two riots in the late 1960s, the government decided that the kaifong association network was no longer adequate to serve as a link between the government and the grassroots, and it decided to establish a new administrative structure in local districts in place of the kaifong associations. Reform of the local administrative structure began in the early 1970s. One component of this structure is the district-based City District Office Scheme (CDO), where the office in each district is composed of 20 appointed local leaders and representatives from relevant government departments, and chaired by an appointed local leader.

Another component is the Mutual Aid Committee Scheme (MAC) which was launched in 1973. The basic unit of organization of a MAC is an individual building block and its scope of activity is confined to environmental improvement, prevention of fire and crime, and management of the building block. A MAC is designated as a voluntary association of residents, working under the scrutiny and supervision of a CDO liaison officer who would frequently visit MACs to ensure they did not work beyond a pre-determined scope of activity (Lui, 1984; Leung, 1982). Since 1973, the CDOs had operated at district level while the MACs have worked at block level in their role of informing the public about government policies and articulating public opinion. However, the performance of this local administrative structure was not satisfactory in representing grassroots' interests. As Leung pointed out:

> Although the government had created a district consultative framework in the 1970's, the representatives of the members was narrow and participation highly regulated. The traditional organization were undemanding groups heavily dependent on the government for support and recognition, who frequently became passive recipients of information from the government (1990:46).

Nevertheless, this new local administration system had its impact on local politics. First, the kaifong association network became less significant to community politics as an intermediary after many of its functions were taken over by the new structure. Second, the declining significance of the kaifong associations discouraged the local Chinese elites from participating in such associations. Local leaders turned to the new local administrative system and hence the kaifong associations were short of local leadership. As Lau succinctly pointed out, 'the gradual extension of official recognition to the Chinese elite based on individual achievements and expertise drives members away from those intermediate organizations which in the past had played a significant role as an intermediary between the government and the ordinary people, [and] which increasingly suffer from a shortage of leadership talent' (1982:127). Thirdly, as the CDOs and MACs constituted a government sponsored advisory structure, the government tended to appoint those with a pro-government attitude, and hence membership was mainly confined to the representatives of traditional kaifong associations, MAC officials, businessmen and professionals. Consensus turned out to be the norm inside this structure. The local administrative system can be conceived as a cooptation mechanism that could select a group of Chinese elites to participate in the bureaucratic structure through appointed membership. This enlargement of the administrative process was interpreted as 'an administrative absorption of politics' which in essence involved further administrative penetration into the grassroots and channelling political participation into administratively endorsed paths (King, 1981).

We notice that two features of the social and political context were conducive to the growth of grassroots movements. Firstly, the increasing provision of social services and public housing in the 1970s attracted the attention of community activists. In the late 1970s, many religious groups, voluntary agencies and students groups worked actively at a grassroots level to identify common concerns and problems, organizing social protests, as well as the formation and mobilization of grassroots organizations. Adequate housing provision, environmental improvements and the provision of communal amenities were their foci. Secondly, dissatisfaction with the pro-government attitude of the members of the new local administrative structure was the main reason for the decision of some community groups and student groups to act outside the formal political system. The lack of trust between the insiders and the outsiders generated more protests in the late 1970s. As Leung noted, 'a decade of protest movements and community activism has not produced any strong grassroots organizations and networks, but a handful of indigenous leaders and community organizers have emerged' (Leung, 1986:364).

There are three notable features of the community actions at that time. The first feature is that most social conflicts around urban problems tended to be issue-based and did not develop into a coherent force capable of challenging the political structure. Another feature is the lack of involvement of indigenous organizations. Due to the limited trust between the MAC and local leaders, student groups and community social workers became the two main sources of input (Lui, 1984). Community protest actions were initiated by a handful of student leaders and voluntary agencies in order to draw residents together to solve their immediate environmental problems. The third feature is pertinent to the strategy and tactics employed. Among the leaders of these groups, most were social workers who employed an Alinsky-style approach to community development in order to force the government to make concessions to their demands. In the 1970s, we had Caritas, the Neighbourhood Action Advice Council, Tsuen Wan Ecumenical Social Service Centre, the Society for Community Organizations and the Hong Kong People's Council on Public Housing Policy, etc. Rapid formation of community groups was deemed by the community activists to be an effective way of mobilizing the deprived to obtain power to improve their plight (Leung, 1986; Wong, 1972). Non-conventional methods (for example, mass gatherings, petitions, demonstrations, sleep-ins, sit-ins, strikes, etc.) and confrontational stances were commonly employed. In the late 1970s, local politics were characterized by a trend towards an expanding repertoire of urban protest (Lui, 1984; Leung, 1990).

All in all, we can identify the following characteristics of the social and political context of the 1970s. First, the 1970s witnessed a phenomenal economic growth and an expansion of the middle class. Second, although the polity continued to be dominated by the colonial government, there were subtle changes in the relationship between the government and the grassroots, such as more social services provision and the establishment of a new local administrative system. Precisely because of the two riots in the late 1960s, the government began to provide more public goods and social services for the purpose of redressing social discontent which might otherwise have translated into social unrest. Third, the establishment of a tightly controlled local administrative structure in place of the traditional intermediate associations did not lead to a higher degree of citizen participation. Instead it coopted and drained local elites and indigenous leaders, and rendered the formation of local collective actions more difficult. Lastly, community groups and student groups entered the domain of community politics and played a significant role in acting for the grassroots interests and against the conservative local administrative structure.

Having examined the social and political context of the 1970s, in the next section we turn to the 1980s to study the extent to which this context changed.

The Stage of Transition to Democracy: 1981-1992

In this stage, the economy was basically characterized by continual growth, though with some fluctuations. There was a downturn at the beginning of the 1980s, but the economy revived in the mid-1980s. In 1982, the growth rate in real terms declined to 3% but recovered slightly to 6.5% in 1983. It reached its peak in 1987, recording a 13.6% growth rate in GDP per capita in real terms, but dropped drastically all the way down to 1% in 1989 (see Table 3.2). Although not as prosperous as in the 1970s, the economy was proficient enough to maintain a certain degree of growth. This can be attributed to two factors. The first is the continuous opening up of the market in China. In this period, China became the largest re-export market and the second largest export market of Hong Kong (Lau, 1986). Re-exports grew at an annual compound rate of 35.5% and domestic exports at 18.3% per annum in the period 1978-1988 (Ho, H., 1989:65). The second factor is the continuous expansion of the financial sector and the public sector. In the fiscal year 1982-1983, the relative size of the public sector reached a historical record of 19% of GDP, and in 1990 it still accounted for 17% of GDP.

As in the 1970s, the size of the middle class continued to grow. Table 3.1 shows that the middle class, which refers to the first five rows in the table, accounted for about 47% of the total working population in 1981, while in 1991 it had expanded to about 63%. By contrast, the proportion of manual workers decreased from 50.4% to 36.2% in the same period.

Unlike the situation in the 1970s, the dominance of the colonial government and business interests within the political structure was no longer maintained. The polity was opened up, allowing more channels for representatives of different interest groups to penetrate the decision-making process. The opening up of the formal political structure began in the early 1980s. The District Boards scheme was established in 1982 which took the unprecedented step of electing a number of its board members on the basis of universal adult franchise. In the mid-1980s, direct election was introduced into the Legislative Council. In addition to 10 official members and 12 appointed members, the new Legislative Council included 26 elected members returned by 9 functional constituencies and 12 by electoral college who were members of the Urban Council,[6] the Regional Council[7] and the District Boards. Even if there was no full direct election to the council, the previously 'closed' political system became comparatively open and the Hong Kong people have subsequently gained access to the political domain.[8]

Year	GDP per capita (HK$)	Rate of growth of GDP per capita in real terms (%)	Rate of growth in Exports in real terms (%)
1981	31,827	9.4	8.1
1982	35,393	3.0	-2.7
1983	38,832	6.5	14.6
1984	46,097	9.5	21.9
1985	47,871	0.1	5.7
1986	54,193	11.2	15.2
1987	65,602	13.6	33.0
1988	74,917	6.1	n/a
1989	85,325	1.0	n/a

Table 3.2 The Performance of the Economy of Hong Kong in the 1980s

Note :   n/a - not available

Source: Scott, 1989. Table 6.5; Data for 1987-89: Hong Kong Annual Report, 1987-90

Since then, the membership of the councils has changed, reflecting a new reality in Hong Kong politics. Davies pointed out that one feature of this change was an 'increasing presence of an articulate and influential body of educated, professional, middle class people who were themselves the major beneficiaries, in job terms, of the expansion of government' (Davies, 1989:53). Simply put, the opening up of the political system led to a decline of the predominance of business and expatriate interests on high-level councils. Table 3.3 shows the dominance of business interests and bureaucrats on the councils, including the Executive Council, the Legislative Council and the Urban Council, in the 1960s. In 1965 77.5% of the places were occupied by these two categories of interest. By contrast, representatives of the local voice, which Davies refers to as the representatives of caring professionals and labour associations, were totally excluded.[9] This situation changed auspiciously in 1986: the caring professionals and the labour representatives obtained 38 places which accounted for 27.4% of the total number of places on the councils. Clearly, the predominance of businessmen and bureaucrats in the polity was in decline.

Nevertheless, the monolithic and authoritarian political structure of Hong Kong had not been totally replaced by a pluralist one in which different interests are potentially represented. We notice that only the local level of the political domain, i.e. the District Board System, was opened up to grassroots participation. The core of the political structure, which comprises the Legislative Council and the Executive Council, was still dominated by conservative groups. There were 'ten official members and a phalanx of twenty-two appointed members, vastly over-representing conservative economic interests, who could be relied upon in most circumstances to vote with the government' (Scott, 1989:277). Members returned by functional constituencies were caring professionals and the labour representatives who had a greater share of the total number of seats on all the councils, but the majority of their places were merely those held at a local level. Only a few grassroots representatives successfully entered the District Boards system and the Urban and Regional Councils, while none entered the Legislative or the Executive Council.[10] In other words, the representatives of grassroots interests had not penetrated the 'core' of the decision making domain in the 1980s and, not surprisingly, the core of the political system in the mid-1980s remained conservative and biased in favour of the economic elites.

72 Polite Politics

Category	1965		1970		1975		1982		1986	
Business@										
Total	25	(36.6)*	23.5	(36.2)	30	(44.1)	32	(36.0)	51	(37.0)
Exco	6	(36.7)	6.5	(43.3)	6	(40.0)	6	(37.5)	7	(43.0)
Legco	10	(38.5)	8.5	(32.7)	9	(30.0)	11	(22.0)	23	(40.0)
Urbco	9	(34.6)	8.5	(43.7)	15	(62.5)	15	(65.2)	11	(37.0)
Regco	n/a		n/a		n/a		n/a		10	(28.0)
Civil Service										
Total	26	(39.9)	26	(39.9)	22	(32.2)	30	(33.7)	18	(13.0)
Exco	7	(46.7)	7	(46.7)	7	(46.7)	7	(43.75)	7	(47.0)
Legco	13	(50.0)	13	(50.0)	15	(50.0)	23	(46.0)	11	(19.0)
Urbco	6	(23.1)	6	(23.1)	0	(0)	0	(0)	0	(0)
Regco	n/a		n/a		n/a		n/a		0	(0)
Professionals										
Total	12	(17.1)	12.5	(17.4)	13	(18.4)	16	(18.0)	17	(12.3)
Exco	3	(16.7)	1.5	(10.0)	2	(13.0)	3	(18.7)	1	(10.0)
Legco	2	(7.7)	2.5	(9.6)	4	(13.3)	7	(14.0)	10	(18.0)
Urbco	7	(26.9)	8.5	(32.7)	7	(29.0)	6	(26.1)	4	(13.0)
Regco	n/a		n/a		n/a		n/a		2	(5.5)
Caring Professionals										
Total	3	(3.8)	4	(5.1)	4	(5.0)	8	(9.0)	33	(23.9)
Exco	0	(0)	0	(0)	0	(0)	0	(0)	0	(0)
Legco	0	(0)	1	(3.8)	2	(6.7)	6	(12.0)	11	(19.0)
Urbco	3	(11.5)	3	(11.5)	2	(8.3)	2	(8.7)	12	(40.0)
Regco	n/a		n/a		n/a		n/a		10	(28.0)
Labour										
Total	0	(0)	0	(0)	0	(0)	3	(3.4)	5	(3.5)
Exco	0	(0)	0	(0)	0	(0)	0	(0)	0	(0)
Legco	0	(0)	0	(0)	0	(0)	3	(6)	2	(4.0)
Urbco	0	(0)	0	(0)	0	(0)	0	(0)	2	(7.0)
Regco	n/a		n/a		n/a		n/a		1	(3.0)
Sub-total**	67	(100.0)	67	(100.0)	69	(100.0)	89	(100.0)	138	(100.0)
Elected#	10	(12.8)	10	(12.8)	12	(17.0)	11	(12.3)	60	(43.5)
Non-elected	57	(87.2)	57	(87.2)	57	(83.0)	78	(87.7)	78	(56.5)
Sub-total	67	(100.0)	67	(100.0)	69	(100.0)	89	(100.0)	138	(100.0)

Table 3.3 Representation of Five Occupational Categories on the Executive Council, Legislative Council, Urban Council and Regional Council, 1965-1986

Note: n/a not available
  *   percentage of the total number of members in the councils
  #   Elected refers to those members gaining seats through direct election in the Urban Council.
  @   The percentage in this row refers to the percentage of this category of all the Councils.
  ** The figures in this row include the 'other/unknown' category which is not shown in this table.

Source: Davies, 1989. Tables 1-5

The reasons underlying this transformation of the political structure are yet to be confirmed. There are two explanations of the change in the formal political structure. Davies (1989) argued that with population growth and the expansion of the middle class, more political demands and challenges arose and the government found it difficult to maintain its 'ascriptive' representation in the 1980s. Therefore the lower tier of the political structure had to be opened up to allow for a more balanced power structure. Another explanation suggested by Scott (1989) points to the government's awareness of a possible legitimacy crisis in the transition period to 1997. According to Scott, decentralization of power is a tactic enabling the British and Hong Kong government to establish a new basis for legitimacy in the transitional period.

In our view, these two explanations are not mutually exclusive and can be integrated into a coherent framework to make sense of the conservative tendency in the democratization process of Hong Kong. We agree with Scott that the government appeared to be worried about the emergence of political turbulence arising from uncertainty about the future of Hong Kong under a communist regime. Moreover, the Hong Kong government could avoid being tarnished with an image of a 'lame duck' government when the influence of the Chinese government became stronger. Accordingly, with the aim of building up an image of an efficient government and maintaining a stable business and political climate, the government resorted to constructing its legitimacy on the basis of popular support. This intention was reflected in the green paper on representative government issued in July 1984 in which the government admitted that Hong Kong needs 'a system of government, the authority for which is firmly rooted in Hong Kong, and which is more directly accountable to the people of Hong Kong...'(Hong Kong Government, 1984:3).

Nevertheless, the government clearly knew that the western idea of democracy by direct election would be undesirable in Hong Kong since direct election entailed a real share of power for different external social forces. Without any measure to ensure desirable outcomes, direct election might invite social and political forces which would be beyond the government's control.

Facing the choice between an authoritarian structure and direct election, the government seemingly found that a corporatist strategy, which in terms of functional representation was a middle-of-the-road tactic, would be the most suitable measure to realize its aims. The government could thus be said to be accountable and at the same time real power need not to be shared with any threatening social forces. There arose a question as to the selection of appropriate groups with whom the government shared political power. Under such circumstances, the government selected those sectors which are functionally important to the economy and which would be likely to have representatives with a pro-government attitude. With hindsight, the government's logic of choice seems to have been based on two considerations. First, as Davies (1989) argued, the middle class occupied critical positions in various sectors and were developing into an important social and economic force. Thus it would not be advisable to exclude them from the political arena. Second, there was no sign indicating that the middle class might become threatening to the political regime. The low profile of the new middle class in politics appears to be one of the reasons why the government chose to coopt them into the decision-making process. This idea was reflected in the green paper which stated that in the development process of the political system 'full weight should be given to representation of the economic and professional sectors of Hong Kong society which are essential to future confidence and prosperity. Direct elections would run the risk of a swift introduction of adversarial politics, and would introduce an element of instability at a critical time' (Hong Kong Government, 1984:9).

All in all, we argue that the government only opened up the lower level of the political system to the grassroots, while representatives of business and professional interests were more likely to obtain seats on the councils at the higher level. In other words, the government's corporatist tactics favoured the business and professional elites, while the decision-making process at the higher level of the formal political structure remained closed to the majority of Hong Kong people. In the next section, we shall argue that this change in the formal political structure led to changes in the nature of Hong Kong politics during the 1980s which were reflected in the grassroots' response to the political reform originated by the Hong Kong government.

The Grassroots' Response to the Changing Political Structure in the 1980s

This section focuses on the grassroots' response to the opening up of the formal political structure. As has been discussed, the establishment of the District Board system offered a new channel for the grassroots to enter into the lower level of the political domain.

In support of candidates on the District Boards, a number of local concern groups sprung up, working in areas relating to urban issues such as housing, transportation, the environment, etc., in order to strengthen local support. A survey found that there were 26 district concern groups in 1986 (Leung, 1990).[11] The impact of these local concern groups has not been negligible. In some districts, for instance Tsing Yi and Shamshuipo, the local concern groups built up close connections with the grassroots, and through the process of election penetrated the District Board system.[12] It was estimated that about 41% of the elected district board members in 1985 were associated with pressure groups, electoral alliances and quasi-political groups (Lau and Kuan, 1985).

On the other hand, it is necessary to point out that the political situation became more complicated when negotiation over the 1997 issue and the signing of the Sino-British Joint Declaration attracted considerable attention. Increasing numbers of pressure groups emerged, placing more emphasis on the struggle over the introduction of direct election into all levels of the political system. This political demand was related to the 1997 issue as it would seem to be a way of ensuring a better future for Hong Kong people under the communist regime. In order to attract more popular support, most pressure groups, apart from the struggle for democracy, also laid emphasis on the improvement of the standard of living of the low-stratum people. One of the strategies for rallying support was involvement in community politics (Kung, 1987).

District Board members, pressure groups and neighbourhood associations filled the void between the government and the Chinese society in the 1980s, following the decline of the traditional link, i.e. the kaifong associations (Leung, 1982; Wong, 1972).[13] Lau and Kuan have succinctly described their characteristics, indicating that 'what distinguishes the newly emergent pressure groups from the decadent traditional organizations are their confrontational posture, their adoption of unconventional influence tactics, their appeal to mass sentiments, and their mobilizational fervour'

(1986:28). It has been difficult for the government to coopt pressure group leaders into the formal institutions of the political structure as most had learnt western ideas on democracy and aspired to build up a society based on freedom and equality (Cheung, 1979; Chan, 1979). As a result, the intermediary between the government and the people was no longer predominately filled by leaders with a pro-government attitude, on the contrary, there were increasing numbers of political activists placing more emphasis on the protection and advocacy of the rights and interests of the grassroots.

There are common features between the local concern groups and pressure groups. Most members of these groups were veterans of the student movement in the 1970s. They were young, well-educated and of middle class background. According to a study of the 1982 and 1985 District Board elections, educationists, social workers, professionals and office workers accounted for 34.7% and 53.2% of the total elected District Board members respectively (Lau and Kuan, 1985). Also, most had experience in social and political movements; especially the social workers whose activism in community development brought them into close contact with the government and the real situation of the poor in Hong Kong. Such a learning process provided them with relevant knowledge about social problems and the administrative style and orientation of the government. Owing to the nature of their work, mainly concerning the protection of the rights of deprived people, social workers were more likely to become involved in community issues. We see that not only did they contribute to the formation of neighbourhood organizations or concern groups on specific issues, but also actively participated on the District Board. There is scant information about the exact number of social workers involved in community politics, but the number of candidates for the District Board election provides us with an indirect indication of the extent of the social worker's involvement in community politics. In the 1985 election, 22 out of 470 candidates, 4.7%, were social workers while in the 1988 election, 39 out of 490 candidates (8.3%) were social workers (Fung, 1994). Nevertheless, they were small in size and had narrow memberships, and as a result were unable to command sufficient resources to mobilize the grassroots.[14]

However, we found that the relationships between pressure groups and local concern groups became unstable and their connections weakened in the late 1980s. From our examination of the relevant literature and interviews with experienced local leaders, we can identify the following reasons for the weakened relationships.

First, immediately after the opening up of the political system, pressure group politics were thriving and many political leaders were ready to assume a significant role in the government-sponsored political structure. Although most pressure groups failed to enter the highest level of the political structure, their successful election to the District Board signalled that they had a chance to become involved in the formal political structure. This was encouraging for the local activists. A subsequent expansion of pressure group politics drew in leaders from local levels. Many leaders of local concern groups then shifted their attention from local issues to those at territory-wide level. Some of the local concern groups moved into areas of politics which conventional residents' organizations had not participated in, such as building links with political groups, forming alliances, and becoming involved in extra-district issues such as the drafting of the Basic Law (Leung, 1986). As a result, local issues received less attention from local political leaders.

Secondly, we noticed that some local leaders, after entering the district boards, put more emphasis on their role as politicians. They considered that working through the government-sponsored participatory system was a better strategy than using non-institutional activities. The leaders of neighbourhood associations believed that they would be able to assist the grassroots to get what they wanted through their presence on the District Boards. Therefore, they staked a great deal on using institutional access to express their views and grassroots' demands. Ma (1986) compared the institutional and non-institutional means of action in the housing struggle and found a dramatic increase in the utilization of institutional means to influence housing policy. This change in the choice of strategies led to more cooptation onto the district boards system. According to Leung:

> Most pressure groups have chosen to co-operate with government-sponsored institutions instead of being completely dependent on outside mass protest actions. Overt and public protests have been replaced by informal contacts and formal committee work between community spokesmen and public officials. The opening of political channels has resulted in a reduction in the militancy of pressure group activities. To stay within the system, they are more prone to compromise than to seek clear-cut victories (1986:366-7).

Thirdly, many local leaders, who were also representatives inside the system, became more conscious of the possibilities of getting the greatest benefits from politics and therefore minorities were considered to be insignificant to re-election. Hence they were less likely to be interested in representing the minorities inside the formal political system. To obtain the greatest benefits, the leaders acted in a calculated way and were more likely to employ compromising rather than confrontational tactics in electoral politics. It is probable therefore that the interests of the grassroots were sacrificed when the leaders on district boards were expected to compromise with other interest groups. As a consequence, the problems of some grassroots minorities did not receive sufficient attention and their situations as well as their problems were marginalized. An experienced and elected district board member said that:

> it was reasonable for the elected district boards members to give more attention to the interests of the majority of the residents. I know that the growing distance between some minorities of grassroots, say, the Temporary Housing Areas tenants and the local activists, is owing to the fact that the former were just a small group of people. Moreover, most of them are newcomers, have not been here for seven years in Hong Kong, and are not allowed to vote, so quite reasonably, the district boards members ignored their interests in the past few years.[15]

Lastly, the pressure groups changed their strategies for influencing decision-making. Once inside the political system, the leaders of local concern groups and pressure groups shifted away 'from the use of single-issue protests and mobilization tactics to the use of more sophisticated and diversified tactics based on rational arguments, researches and surveys, lobbying and elite coalition' (Leung, 1990:56). One social worker explained that, besides the shortage of leadership in community politics, a further problem was related to the leaders' views that community issues could be solved through district board politics. Accordingly, direct action and non-conventional means were temporarily put aside in local politics.[16] In addition, with improved accessibility to policy-makers and decision-making processes, and more communication channels with the government, the pressure groups looked towards a more intellectually-oriented, rationalized base of support, and became less militant (Chui, 1987). This new form of pressure group strategy has prevailed since the mid-1980s. Since most leaders were well-educated, they were competent at using surveys and research findings, at lobbying, and at employing rational arguments in pursuit of their goals. This meant that mobilization at neighbourhood level was no longer perceived by the leaders to be an essential means of obtaining support. Instead of focusing on the creation of a stable and consistent institutional structure with the grassroots, most pressure groups preferred to mobilize residents occasionally through wide publicity on specific issues. Leung defined this strategy as one of 'organizations of organizers', for which mass support was just the target of ad hoc mobilization. As a result, there emerged a trend in the late 1980s wherein 'elite mobilization and alliance as a strategy of change and building up the power-base have been revived and are becoming popular' (Leung, 1986:367).

In this section we have argued that the opening up of the formal political system triggered community activists' interest in the mobilization and formation of local concern groups and pressure groups. However, there were four factors which checked their growth, namely the institutionalization of social conflicts, the fact that more resources and efforts shifted to territory-wide concerns from local concerns, the increasing use of compromising strategies by politician and local leaders, and the diminishing importance of grassroots mobilization.

Recapitulation

In this chapter, we have highlighted the different features of the economic and political context in the 1970s and 1980s. We periodized these decades into two stages, namely the pre-democracy and the transition to democracy stages. The first stage was characterized by continual economic growth, the expansion of the middle class and the increasing intervention of the government into the social life of Hong Kong people. Most importantly, the government's increasing involvement in the provision of social welfare and in the urbanization process, and the establishment of a conservative local administrative structure politicized the relationship between the government and the grassroots, leading to a proliferation of local concern groups in the 1970s. Increasing community actions were organized to advocate the grassroots' rights and interests at local level and more non-institutional and unconventional methods of direct action were adopted in order to express their grievances and demands. However, community action was not powerful enough to effect any change in the formal political system, which remained dominated by the colonial government and business interests.

The political situation changed in the second stage when the government gradually opened up the formal political structure. Throughout this stage, the government allowed mainly middle class representatives, especially the professionals, to enter the core of the formal political structure. In effect, those dissatisfied with this reform organized a number of pressure groups to fight for a genuine democratic system. With the establishment of the District Board, pressure groups put their candidates forward for election and were keen to be involved in electoral politics. However, this change weakened the connection between the pressure groups and the local concern groups in community politics. Firstly, more resources were allocated to issues concerning political development. Secondly, granting politicians the right to access the formal political channels led to an institutionalization of social conflicts, because local leaders believed that working through the formal political system was feasible. Thirdly the leaders inside the formal political system became calculating in their ambition for political gain, and thereby the interests of urban minorities were largely left unattended. Fourthly, leaders in the formal structure tended to rely more on lobbying and compromise, while confrontation and an antagonistic stance were unlikely to be employed. For the politicians, it became less necessary to mobilize the grassroots, and hence their connection with the grassroots was weakened.

All in all, we argue that there were urban minorities in the late 1980s whose interests and needs were largely neglected. To further substantiate this argument, we shall identify the urban minorities by showing how the public housing policy overlooked their housing needs.

Notes

1. The Legislative Council is mainly for the passing of laws, the granting of supply of finance to the executive branch of the government and the scrutiny and control of the acts of the executive. For details, see Miners (1991).
2. This change is exemplified by the presence of a large number of international financial intermediaries. In the period 1969-78, the financial sector was characterized by the rapid growth of foreign-owned financial institutions. The representative offices of foreign banks increased from 352 in 1969 to 851 by 1978. Moreover, out of the 80 licensed banks registered in 1979, 46 were foreign banks incorporated outside Hong Kong. In addition, among 'the 234 registered DTC's (registered deposit-taking companies), about half are subsidiaries or joint ventures set up by foreign commercial banks, merchant banks, and investment houses' (Jao, 1979:676). Jao's study further revealed that of the top 100 commercial banks of the world, some 64 were operating in Hong Kong in one form or another. See also Ho (1986).
3. The category 'social services' includes five sub-categories, namely, Education, Medical and Health, Housing, Social Welfare and Labour. The actual amount spent on social services in 1971-2 was HK$ 1,057 million, increasing to HK$ 5,187 million by the fiscal year 1978-9. If we break down the category to see the trend of growth in the subcategory 'social welfare', we find that the actual expenditure on social welfare increased from HK$ 154 million in 1973-4 to HK$ 2,027 million in 1983-4. It further increased from HK$ 2,355 million in 1985-86 to HK$ 4,074 million in 1989-90; a 73% growth over a period of five years. The expenditure on subsidies to voluntary agencies also increased from HK$ 448 million to HK$ 933 million in the same period; a 125% growth.
4. The Executive Council serves like a cabinet in a Westminster-style system. It consists of four *ex-officio* members - the Chief Secretary, the Commander British Forces, the Financial Secretary and the Attorney General - together with members appointed by the Governor and approved by the Secretary of State of the British government. In 1991, there were ten appointed members in the Council. The Governor is required by the Royal Instructions to consult the council on all important matters, but the proceedings are confidential and only some of its decisions are made public. In short, the Governor in Council, that is the Governor acting in consultation with the Executive Council, is 'Hong Kong's central and most important executive authority' (Hong Kong Annual Report, 1992:19). For details, see Miners (1991).
5. The New Town Programme in Hong Kong was intended in its early stage to provide land for postwar rapid industrial expansion and population growth. Since 1973, it has been providing more land to support the massive public housing programme. The plans for the formation of new towns in the 1970s were based on districts which located in the New Territories. The planning of new towns adopted the concepts of 'self-containment' and 'balanced development' of British new town planning. The impact of this programme has been phenomenal: the population in urban areas has been significantly decentralized into the once rural areas of the New Territories. For details, see Yeh (1986).

6   The Urban Council is a statutory council with responsibilities for the provision of municipal services in the urban areas. It is granted with executive authority and is charged with full responsibility for a wide range of municipal functions, including street cleaning, refuse collection and control of environmental hygiene. Control of hawkers and street-traders, and provision and management of public recreational facilities are also the responsibilities of the council. The council consists of 40 members of which 15 are elected from district constituents, another 15 are appointed by the Governor, and the rest are representative members from the urban district boards. The council is financially autonomous.

7   The status of the Regional Council is similar to its counterpart in urban areas - the Urban Council. Their responsibilities and terms of reference are similar. It consists of 36 members, of which 12 are elected directly, 9 are representatives of the nine district boards within the Regional Council, and 12 are appointed by the Governor.

8   From 1995, all members of the Legislative Council are elected on the basis of direct election.

9   The caring professionals are identified as 'social workers, teachers, church leaders, charitable organization leaders, etc', categorically different from professionals in general which refers to doctors, accountants, architects, engineers, lawyers and those 'employed using professional skills' (Davies, 1989:68).

10 In order to look into the degree of openness of the political structure, Davies arranged the representative structure of the Hong Kong government into a four-tier structure, of which the top tier is the tip of the hierarchy of the power structure where important territory-wide issues are discussed and policies decided. In his view, the councils form a hierarchy in which the Executive Council is the most powerful, representing the core of decision making. The Legislative Council belongs to the second tier, the third is the Urban and Regional Council and at the bottom is the District Board. Davies noticed that 'throughout this long 23 year sequence and while the voice of business has been steadily eroded, first in the third tier councils, and then in the second tier council, that voice in the highest, wholly appointed council has remained comparatively untouched' (1989:55). In 1986, according to Davies' findings, representatives of business held as many seats as the bureaucrats. Seven seats out of 15, about 47% of the total on the Executive Council, were occupied by businessmen. These two groups together held 94% of the seats on that council. In the Legislative Council, they had 59% of the seats. Obviously, the local voice remained underrepresented. Only 2 labour representatives elected by functional constituency and 11 personnel from the caring professions had entered the Legislative Council.

11 The district groups have different names, for instance, 'concerned groups for people's livelihood', 'district research centres', 'district development centres', 'social service centres', and 'service groups', etc. See Hong Kong Council of Social Service (1986).

12 In the 1991 District Boards Election, the Tsing Yi Concerns Groups supported seven candidates and all of them won in the election. In Shamshuipo district, the Democracy and Livelihood Corporate Associations supported eight candidates who also defeated their competitors. This is a good indicator to show the strengths of the pressure groups at local level.

13 The kaifong associations in Hong Kong had a long history of providing a link between the government and the Hong Kong Chinese. The first formal kaifong associations were founded in 1949. This kind of local organization was intended for relief work, the promotion of public health, and the provision of social welfare, medical and educational services. Though serving like social welfare agencies, the leading figures in the kaifong associations acted as local representatives.

14 Lo's findings (1988) reflected the fact that the pressure groups in the 1980s only had small memberships. The total number of members in any one pressure groups did not exceed 500.

15 A personal interview with Lee wing-tak, who is now a member of the political party - the United Democrats of Hong Kong - and actively involved in discussions over housing policy in Hong Kong.

16 A personal interview with the full-time workers of two community work organizations, who are Ip Chiu-ping, the chief coordinator of the Hong Kong People's Council on Public Housing Policy and Yeung Sik-Chung, a community worker of Tsuen Wan Ecumenical Social Service Centre.

4 Public Housing Policy and Urban Minorities

Introduction

This chapter is devoted to a brief overview of public housing policy which provides an essential context for understanding the issue surrounding Aged Temporary Housing Areas (ATHAs) discussed in the following chapters, and also identifies the urban minorities whose housing needs are ignored. Section 4.1 depicts the structure of housing provision in the early 1990s, and in particular the range of public housing provision. The production and allocation policies of public housing flats are outlined in section 4.2 where a shortfall of public rental housing flats is highlighted. In section 4.3 we point out that the housing needs of some urban minorities have received insufficient attention in public housing policy. We examine further the nature and management of Temporary Housing Areas (THAs), and their role in the public housing policy in section 4.4. Our main argument is that squatter area clearance is one of the means by which the government regulates the pattern of land use in urbanization. The main function of the THAs is to rehouse squatters who are affected by the government's clearance policy but are not eligible for public rental housing. In this way, possible political tensions arising from clearance will be reduced. The final section summarizes our arguments in this chapter.

The Housing Provision Structure in Hong Kong

This section briefly delineates the types of living quarters in the early 1990s. The living quarters in Hong Kong are classified in the 1991 Census into two sectors, permanent and temporary. There are six sub-types in the permanent sector (see Table 4.1). The 1991 Census revealed that just over 50% of the total occupied living quarters consisted of permanent private living quarters and 45.5% permanent public housing flats (including rental and owned). Only 4.2% were temporary living quarters. As shown in Table 4.1, among the public permanent living quarters, 38.2% were rental flats and 7.7% homeownership scheme flats.

Type of Living Quarters	1981	1986	1991
Housing Authority Rental Blocks	38.0	37.9	38.2
Housing Authority home ownership estates	0.7	4.2	7.7
Private housing blocks			
self-contained	39.4	38.4	41.5
non self-contained	0.4	0.1	0.0
Villas/Bungalows/Modern village houses	2.1	3.0	3.3
Other permanent housing*	9.4	8.7	5.1
Roof-top structures	0.7	0.5	0.2
Temporary housing	10.0	7.7	4.2
Total	100.0	100.0	100.0

Table 4.1 Occupied Living Quarters by Type of Living Quarters, 1981, 1986, 1991 (%)

Note: * This type includes simple stone structures, institution type, and other permanent types.

Source: Hong Kong Government, 1993, Census Report

Among the various permanent private living quarters, the self-contained flat was predominant throughout the 1980s, constituting about 42% of the total occupied living quarters. Other types of permanent housing in the private sector, including simple stone structures, accommodation provided by institutions and non-domestic accommodation units comprised a mere 5.1% of the total occupied living quarters. Less than 4% were villas/bungalows/modern village houses. In addition, the 1991 Census reported that a very large proportion of domestic households occupied the whole flat, and only 7.6% of the total domestic households were living in rooms and bedspace. Together, temporary housing and roof-top housing shared a negligible proportion.

The price of private housing increased at a fast rate in the late 1980s. It is estimated that between 1986 and 1990 the price index for small flats of less than 40 square metres saleable area rose from 54 to 115, an increase of 106% (Lau, 1991:357). Between the fourth quarter of 1990 and that of 1991 alone, the general prices of domestic property soared by almost 52% (Wong and Staley, 1992:322). It is a well known fact that in Hong Kong the escalating property prices outpaced the rate of salary increases. As regards the private flats, rent indices also increased in the same period by about 90% (Lau, 1991:357). Hence, faced with increases in property prices and rents, the provision of public housing means a lot to the low and middle income households.

The range of public housing flats is as varied as the types of private housing. Before discussing this range, it is necessary to give a brief account of the institutions responsible for the provision of public housing.

Public housing policy is formulated by two implementing agents, namely, the Housing Authority and the Housing Department. The Housing Authority is a statutory organization, established in 1973 under the Housing Ordinance. All of its members are appointed by the government. Until 1988, the role of the Chairperson was assumed by the Secretary of State for Housing, establishing a link between the Housing Authority and the government. In 1988 financial independence and administrative autonomy was granted to the Housing Authority, giving it sufficient flexibility to 'deal with the priorities under the government's Long Term Housing Strategy' (Hong Kong Government, Annual Report, 1992:180). Its terms of reference are stated by the government as follows:

> It advises the Governor on all housing policy matters and through its executive arm, the Housing Department, plans and builds housing estates, either for rent or ownership, and temporary housing areas. The authority also manages public housing estates, ownership courts, temporary housing areas, transit centres, flatted factories and the ancillary commercial facilities throughout the territory, and administers the Private Sector Participation Scheme and the Home Purchase Loan Scheme. It acts as the government's agent to clear land, prevent and control squatting, and maintain improvements to squatter areas (Annual Report, Hong Kong Government, 1992:180).

The Housing Department is a government department, responsible for the execution of policy passed by the Housing Authority. It can be seen as the executive branch of the Housing Authority. The Housing Department provides shelter to eligible Hong Kong citizens in temporary accommodation units and permanent blocks. There is only one type of temporary shelter, that of the THAs.

Permanent blocks are divided into four types, namely Group A rental blocks, Group B rental blocks, Housing Society rental blocks and Housing Authority homeownership estates. Group A rental blocks refers to those previously known as Government Low Cost Housing and those built by the former Hong Kong Housing Authority. Group B rental blocks are converted from the Mark I and Mark II blocks built in the 1950s and 1960s, generally known as the 'old' type of public rental housing. Housing Society rental blocks are built and managed by the Hong Kong Housing Society whose terms of reference are similar to those of the Housing Authority, except that it enjoys a higher degree of administrative and financial autonomy than that of the Housing Authority. Housing Authority homeownership estates are built for sale at prices below market value to lower-middle income families and public housing tenants. In order to promote home ownership, public flats for sale have been constructed since 1980 under the Home Ownership Scheme (HOS) and the Private Sector Participation Scheme (PSPS).[1] These two schemes have two objectives. Firstly, to satisfy people's desire to own their flats. Secondly, as more tenants of rental public housing estates become homeowners through the two schemes, more public rental housing flats can be re-allocated to those in need of public rental housing.[2] Though many critics have commented that this policy is obviously a form of privatization, the Home Ownership Scheme has been hailed by the government as a feasible alternative for people to satisfy their housing needs (Chan, 1992; Ho, 1992; Lee, 1992; Wong, 1992).

The Housing Authority homeownership estates can be seen to be at the top of the hierarchy of the public housing provision structure since they serve those households which can afford to purchase their own flats. In 1991 there were 144,000 self-owned flats on 95 Housing Authority homeownership estates (Hong Kong Government, Annual Report, 1992:179). Most households living on these estates belong to relatively higher income groups. In 1991 the median monthly income of these households was HK$12,000 (Hong Kong Government, 1993).[3] The

Housing Society rental blocks, together with the Group A and Group B rental blocks, can be conceived as standing in the middle of the hierarchy since they mainly serve lower-middle income households. Of these, there were 645,000 flats on 146 rental estates and the median monthly household income of the sitting tenants was HK$9,985 in the Housing Society rental blocks, HK$8,393 in Group A rental blocks and HK$6,843 in Group B. At the bottom are the THAs which provide mainly for people cleared from the squatter areas, or victims of disasters, until they are eligible for permanent rental flats. Most of these households are lower income groups. In 1991 the overall median monthly household income of Hong Kong as a whole was HK$9,967 while that of the temporary housing areas was HK$6,000. By the end of 1991, there were 72,000 people living in 65 THAs.

The public housing hierarchy can also be described in terms of rent level. The 1991 Census shows that the median monthly household rent of private housing blocks was HK$1,600 in 1991. The median monthly household rent in the public housing sector was comparatively lower than that of the private sector: HK$1,350, and HK$669 for the Housing Authority homeownership estates and public rental blocks respectively (Hong Kong Government, 1993:67). There is no data in the Census Report about the median monthly rent level of the public temporary housing units. But we know that the rent of a four-person unit in 1991 was less than HK$100. In short, within the public housing sector, the monthly rent of the homeownership estates is the highest, then the public rental blocks, and at the bottom the THAs. Having outlined the hierarchy of housing in Hong Kong, we move on to delineate the production and allocation policy of public housing flats in the next section.

Production and Allocation of Public Housing

Public housing policy in Hong Kong is considered to be successful by the government. Both the quality and quantity of public housing improved in the 1980s. New types of public rental housing estates were built, such as the Trident Blocks and Harmony Blocks, based on improved standards of space and a dedication to improving quality. Nevertheless, in 1985 about 12.3% of the total population of public housing households were living in areas of less than the minimum 35 square feet per person. In order to alleviate the problem of overcrowding, the minimum living area was increased from 35 square feet to 50 square feet per person.

Different criteria are employed to control access to public housing flats. Flats for sale under the HOS and PSPS schemes are targeted at two groups of people. The first group consists of sitting tenants on Housing Authority and Housing Society rental estates, as well as the Housing Authority's prospective tenants which include households on the waiting list, junior civil servants, and people displaced by clearance and the Authority's redevelopment programme. The other group comprises families from the private sector. Applicants in this second group must not own any domestic property and are subject to a limit on household income, which was set for the year 1990 at HK$11,500 per month.[4]

Access to rental housing is either through the waiting list or categorization as a household with definite housing needs. Waiting list applicants are subject to the following eligibility criteria:

1. the applicant must be at least 18 years of age;
2. at least 2 related persons must be living together, although single person applicants can also register on a separate Waiting List;
3. monthly household income must not exceed the income limits;
4. the applicant or family members must not be for two years prior to their application, an owner of any domestic property nor enter into any agreement to purchase such property; and
5. on allocation the applicant and the majority of family members must have been resident in Hong Kong at least 7 years; in the case of two-person families both members must have lived in Hong Kong for at least 7 years (Hong Kong Housing Authority, 1994).

As is reported by the Housing Authority, the average waiting time 'for applicants on the Waiting List ranged from two to eight years for estates in new towns and extended urban areas, to about nine years for those on popular urban estates' (Hong Kong Housing Authority, Annual Report, 1994:44).

The second category of applicants includes: (1) families affected by redevelopment programmes; (2) sitting residents of the THAs affected by redevelopment or clearance programmes; (3) junior civil servants; (4) emergency cases, such as victims of natural disaster; and (5) compassionate cases referred by the Director of the Social Welfare Department. With the exception of (4), the majority of (3), and the THA residents with less than 10 years' residence in THAs,[5] the applicants of this category are not subject to a means test. Throughout the 1980s about one-third of the public rental flats were allocated to this category while the rest were assigned to waiting list applicants.

For those who are not eligible for public rental housing, the government provides interim accommodation known as the Temporary Housing Areas, which are 'for people not yet eligible for permanent public housing but who have been rendered homeless by development clearance and fires or natural disaster' (ibid.:56). There is no strict eligibility criterion for THAs, except that applicants must be legal residents of Hong Kong. As regards rehousing in permanent public housing flats, before July 1993 THA residents had to have had seven years' residence in Hong Kong, and one year's stay in a THA. The current policy, however, has relaxed this requirement. We shall examine the nature and characteristics of this kind of accommodation in detail in section 4.3.

By 1991 the public rental housing estates in Hong Kong accommodated nearly 2.5 million, nearly half the total population. The rate of production of public housing flats, including rental units and units for sale, was maintained at a stable flow, around 45,600 units per year in the late 1980s (see Table 4.2). As shown in Table 4.2, the annual production levels of the various types of public housing increased in all but five years during the period 1974-1989, though it declined in 1989-1991.

Between 1979-1989 the tenant population increased by 23%. During this decade 354,326 public housing flats were allocated to 1,467,521 people, with an average of 133,400 people moving onto public housing estates per annum.

However, these figures conceal a shortfall in public rental housing. It is estimated that at least 219,000 households, or roughly 13% of the territory's total population, were still inadequately housed by the end of 1992 (Leung, 1993). The shortfall in the provision of public rental housing was also substantiated by a Housing Authority review, issued in 1993, concerning the problems and difficulties in meeting the outstanding demand of those who were inadequately housed under the current public housing policies. The review pointed out that there would be 610,000 families still in need of housing from 1993 up to the end of the century (Hong Kong Housing Authority, 1993).

Year	Rental Flats	HOS	PSPS	Housing Society	Total	Growth Rate#
1990-1991	32,684	5,250	4,880	3,158	45,972	-13.1
1989-1990	35,863	6,492	7,064	3,470	52,889	-4.8
1988-1989	40,885	5,810	5,020	3,840	55,555	29.2
1987-1988	31,887	7,610	2,716	780	42,993	-0.8
1986-1987	30,237	6,838	4,866	1,391	43,332	-10.1
1985-1986	29,386	6,688	11,902	213	48,189	25.7
1984-1985	26,354	10,168	1,408	419	38,349	-0.9
1983-1984	28,564	7,877	2,240	10	38,691	5.7
1982-1983	27,879	7,508	760	442	36,589	-7.3
1981-1982	31,346	4,399	-	3,725	39,470	5.1
1980-1981	26,769	8,674	1,500	618	37,561	13.8
1979-1980	29,759	2,439	-	800	32,998	115.0
1978-1979	14,130	-	-	1,220	15,350	13.5
1977-1978	13,020	-	-	504	13,524	33.8
1976-1977	9,620	-	-	486	10,106	-40.9
1975-1976	14,900	-	-	2,190	17,090	74.6
1974-1975	9,200	-	-	586	9,786	15.4
1973-1974	-	-	-	325	8,495*	-

Table 4.2 The Production of Public Housing Units by the Housing Authority, 1973-1991

Note: # This figure is calculated by using the production in year t+1 (e.g 1987-1988) minus the production in year t (e.g. 1986-1987) and then divided by the production in year t, and times 100.

* This figure includes the number of public housing units transferred from the former Resettlement Department and the Government-Low-Cost-Housing scheme in 1973. The department and the scheme were incorporated into the Housing Authority which has been responsible for all the construction, maintenance and management of public housing estates in Hong Kong since 1973.

Source: Lau, 1989

This shortfall in public rental housing provision was explained by the government as a consequence of the shortfall in land supply, which was in turn due partly to delays in land development projects and partly to the slowness of public rental housing tenants to become homeowners (Hong Kong Housing Authority, 1993:12).

Nevertheless, it is our contention that the shortfall in the production of public rental housing flats is a result of the government's attempts to withdraw its involvement in the provision of public housing since the early 1980s. This tendency has been reflected in two ways, the financial arrangement of the Housing Authority, and the expansion of the Home Ownership Scheme - a form of privatization of public housing.

In 1973 the Housing Authority was established as a statutory institution and granted its financial independence. Subsequently a large portion of its income came from rents, with the remainder deriving from sales of HOS flats and the letting of commercial facilities to private business undertakings. During the 1970s, the Housing Authority was able to secure financial support from the government through the Development Loan Fund, but this support drastically declined in the early 1980s. As shown in Table 4.3, in 1977-1978 government loans accounted for 34% of the Authority's total capital expenditure, increasing to as much as 80% in 1981-1982. In 1989-1990, however, this figure dropped to 31% of the total.

In 1988 the government decided to sever its formal institutional tie with the Housing Authority, and granted it complete administrative autonomy. A new financial arrangement was set up. The government offered a 'one-off' grant of about HK$27 billion, regarding it as the government's capital injection to the Housing Authority. In 1990 another HK$10 billion government cash injection was loaned to the Housing Authority.[6] This loan was repayable with interest. According to the calculation of some social activists, by 1992 the Housing Authority had repaid HK$4 billion to the government. Rather than offering more financial support, the government actually draws considerable financial resources from the Housing Authority, and as a result the latter's capacity to provide public rental housing is reduced. Many studies have pointed out that the high rents for public housing are a direct result of the new stress on public housing as a self-financing programme and the outflow of financial resources. Also, high rents result in a high level of political mobilization in protest against rent increases (Ho, D. 1989; Lau, 1991; Lui, 1984; Scott, 1989).[7]

Year	Housing Authority	Development Loan Fund	Total
1977-1978	319 (66%)	164 (34%)	483 (100%)
1878-1979	313 (36%)	573 (64%)	885 (100%)
1979-1980	375 (28%)	964 (72%)	1,344 (100%)
1980-1981	418 (21%)	1,390 (79%)	1,946 (100%)
1981-1982	462 (20%)	1,690 (80%)	2,302 (100%)
1982-1983	755 (27%)	1,900 (73%)	2,794 (100%)
1983-1984	1,107 (39%)	1,600 (61%)	2,825 (100%)
1984-1985	n/a	n/a	n/a
1985-1986	n/a	n/a	n/a
1986-1987	1,248 (42%)	1,700 (58%)	2948 (100%)
1987-1988	1,459 (49%)	1,550 (51%)	3,009 (100%)
1988-1989	1,811 (60%)	1,200 (40%)	3,011 (100%)
1989-1990	2,140 (69%)	950 (31%)	3,090 (100%)

Table 4.3 Sources of Fund for Capital Expenditure of the Housing Authority, 1977-1990

Note: n/a - not available

Source: *Figures for the years 1977-84 are from Ho (1986:343) and the rest from Lau (1989:266)*

Similarly, the government's tendency to withdraw its commitment to the provision of public rental housing is manifest in its promotion of the Home Ownership Scheme (HOS). In 1987 the government promulgated its Long Term Housing Strategy, with one of the objectives as the promotion of home ownership. This aim was later translated into a public commitment to achieving an overall homeownership rate close to 60% by 1997. In the hope of achieving a reduction in housing demand, the government expected to see on the one hand a high out-mobility by public rental housing tenants, which would lead to a subsequent increase of vacant flats for those on the waiting list, and on the other hand a high take-up rate of HOS flats among those affected by clearance in squatter areas, THAs and public housing estates under the redevelopment scheme. Given an unchanged total production of public housing, and considerable resources being reallocated from the public rental housing sector to that of the HOS, the provision of public rental housing was inevitably reduced. Additionally, the HOS failed to attract as many clearees as expected, with only 3% to 9% of the clearees taking up HOS flats in the period 1990-92 (Hong Kong Housing Authority, 1993:7). Such failure further exacerbated the shortfall in public rental housing.

The shortfall means a prolonged waiting time for those in need of public rental housing, especially for three categories of urban minorities who were hitherto accorded a lower priority in the housing allocation policy, namely small families,[8] including one and two person households, squatters and THA residents. We argue that insufficient attention to the housing needs of urban minorities generates disputes and conflict with the government. In the next section we examine the extent to which the allocation policy of public rental housing meets the needs of urban minorities.

Public Housing Policy and Urban Minorities

The shortfall in public rental housing affected three types of urban minorities in the late 1980s, namely, one person and two person families, the squatters and the THA residents.

One Person and Two Person Families Living in THAs

In the early 1980s, small families were only allowed to opt either to live in THAs or to receive the 'rehousing allowance' in lieu of rehousing. In addition, one person and two person families in THAs were not eligible for public rental housing. Although this restriction was abandoned in 1985, the housing allocation policy has long accorded a very low priority to this category and as a result these kinds of families spend a long time on the waiting list. Since 1984 they have been supplied with 'old' units, such as those converted from Group B or former Government Low Cost Housing flats, most of which were built before 1973. Besides these, a small number of new flats started to be offered to small families in 1984. In December 1990 the Housing Authority proclaimed that 9,000 flats per annum were to be constructed for one person families.

Although new public rental housing flat, and 'old' flats obtained from the conversion of casual vacancies on old public housing estates have been allocated for one person and two person families, the demand for small units has yet to be met. The government calculated that about 15% of the total Hong Kong population, estimated to be 0.98 million, were small families, and surely there was a great housing demand. Moreover, it was reported that at the end of 1989 about 25,000 applications out of a total of 160,000 on the waiting list (15.6%), were one person household applicants (Hong Kong Government, 1990). According to a Housing Authority estimate in 1991, the shortfall of small family flats within the period 1991-1997 would be 10,038 for single person households and 5,176 for two person households (Hong Kong Housing Authority, 1991).

The Housing Authority attributed the shortfall to limited resources. We argue, however, that because only 7% of the total production of public rental housing was designated for small family flats, the fact that supply fell short of demand should have been a foreseeable outcome. In fact, the government has long discriminated against one and two person households. Only when a fire broke out in December 1990, resulting in the death of more than ten aged single persons, did the housing problem of one person households come to the attention of social commentators and the general public, forcing the government to look for a solution to the housing needs of one person households.[9]

We noticed that the Housing Authority's response to the shortfall in public rental flats for the small family has been a strategy of cutting short the waiting list instead of exploring extra resources for small families. For example, when the Housing Authority revised the income limit on applications for public rental housing in April 1991, the income limit for households of more than one person was increased by 10.9% to 20.2% whereas for single persons, the income limit was increased by only 3.2%. It appears that the Housing Authority regulated the demand for housing by one person households by avoiding registering too many of them on the waiting list, rather than increasing the production of one person flats.

In view of the increasing housing needs of one person and two person families, disputes about public housing provision have inevitably grown. Given that the total annual production did not increase, allocating more resources for small families means less for the needs arising from other categories, like those affected by squatter and THA clearance, by redevelopment and those on the waiting list. This is a zero-sum game. The shortfall in the annual production of public rental housing has become a seedbed of social conflict.

Squatters

Since the 1960s, squatter clearance has been undertaken by the Housing Authority in order to create more land for development. In the late 1980s, a large scale clearance project was drawn up in order to clear the squatter areas in urban districts. This project is estimated to resettle about 17,000 squatters per year. The government reported that about 48,000 people moved to squatter areas after the 1984-1985 registration (People's Council on Squatter Policy, 1991a). Despite a reduction in the urban squatter population from 183,000 in 1985 to 66,000 in 1990, the squatter problem continued (Hong Kong Housing Authority Annual Report, 1991). We notice that the clearance project focused more on squatter areas in urban districts while most in the New Territories were not adequately dealt with. An official estimate points out that there were 264,100 people living in non-urban squatter areas in 1990. In 1990 the government reported that there were 330,100 people living in squatter areas across the territory (Hong Kong Government, 1990). In 1992 the squatter population was 58,000 in urban areas and 230,000 in the New Territories. The squatter problem still baffled the government (Hong Kong Government, Annual Report, 1992:189). Undeniably, the obstacle to the success of squatter clearance was the shortage of public rental housing flats.

Small families in the squatter areas found themselves in an even worse position. The resettlement policy for squatters accorded different treatment to different sizes of families, and small families in squatter areas were placed at a lower position on the priority list. Except for those who were able to fulfil a number of criteria relating to age and special circumstances, they were admitted only to THAs, and not to public rental housing.[10] It is estimated that in the early 1990s, only three-tenths (about 30%) of the small family squatters had the right to rehousing (People's Council on Squatter Policy, 1991). Upon clearance, they are entitled to opt for rehousing in THAs or a lump sum as compensation in lieu of rehousing. Obviously, granting rehousing rights to larger families to the virtual exclusion of small families is unfair, but the authority shows no intention of changing its policy or providing any justification for it to the public.

The position of larger families is comparatively better. They are entitled to rehousing on public rental housing estates upon clearance. The basic requirements are: the households must have been registered in the 1984-1985 squatter registration, and more than half of the household members must have lived in Hong Kong for at least ten years (Hong Kong Housing Authority, Annual Report, 1987).

In short, the public housing policy did little to accelerate the resettlement process of the squatters. Although most squatters would be rehoused upon clearance, the small families in squatter areas and those living in non-urban squatter areas were largely neglected and discriminated against by the public housing policy.

The Temporary Housing Areas (THAs)

The living conditions of the THAs are easily overlooked by the public. Unlike the squatter areas which are located on hillsides or unpopular locations and lack sufficient basic facilities, the temporary housing areas appear to be well maintained, with the provision of basic facilities and, most importantly, at low rent. To the public, the THA residents at least have a place to stay. Moreover, as the THA residents were believed to be staying there temporarily and would eventually be rehoused on public housing estates, the public would not consider their living conditions to be worse than those of the homeless and squatters.

There are two types of THAs, namely semi-finished and fully-built. Before 1974 the government allowed eligible households to erect their own huts in permitted areas so as to 'solve' the housing problems of those ineligible for public rental housing. Since 1974, the government has provided semi-built temporary housing blocks for those in need of housing, designating them as 'Temporary Housing Areas'. The government flattened some areas and put up poles supporting the roof of the blocks. Eligible families had to erect four walls of wooden material for the partition. In this first generation of THAs, basic facilities such as electricity, water, and public toilets were provided. Since 1984, the second generation THAs have been completed with a fully-built structure, i.e. with walls and partitions. A block of temporary housing would be sectioned into twenty cubicles, about 100 square feet each for a four person household. Compared with the second generation THAs, the first generation was much worse in terms of facilities and environment.

As shown in Table 4.4, the total population of the THAs until 1st April 1991 was 82,243 people, one half of whom were living in first generation THAs, i.e. the semi-finished THAs. According to a survey conducted in 1992, 92% of THA residents were immigrants (Lui, Wong and Ho, 1994). Most had spent more than a decade in Hong Kong; the survey indicated that the mean length of residence in Hong Kong of these immigrants was 16.7 years. The THA residents were mostly low-income people; their median income was found to be HK$7,000 in 1992, which was less than half the Hong Kong average in 1992 ($14,527). More than a quarter (27.5%) of the households were one person households and about one fifth (21.5%) were two person households. Three to five person households accounted for nearly half (46.8%), and households with six persons or more were very uncommon (4.3%). More than half of the households (56.5%) were nuclear families, and about one tenth (10.9%) were extended families. Seven-tenths (70.5%) of the households were eligible for public rental housing.

Furthermore, we notice that although the areas were called 'temporary', in 1990 there were more than 16 areas which had existed for more than 10 years. These were referred to by the residents as 'Aged Temporary Housing Areas' (ATHAs). The ATHAs were characterized by deteriorated, badly-painted, rat-infested buildings, lack of fire safety facilities and poor hygiene. In 1989 an unpublished Housing Authority report on the building structure of 2,306 temporary housing blocks admitted that 575 blocks, about 25% of the total, were regarded as 'needing engineering work to strengthen the structures of the buildings'.[11] It was estimated that there were 24,248 residents living in poor living conditions with below standard facilities in the ATHAs.

Another problem in the THAs was related to the policy of adding new family members to the tenancy. Strict rules apply to one person families in this respect. Firstly, the applicants have to move, together with the new members, to the THAs in the New Territories or to the casual vacant units in urban THAs. Secondly, they are rehoused in a unit comprising less than 80 square feet even though their family size has increased. Thirdly, the proposed new member must prove that they are unable to find their own place of residence. Fourthly, they have no right to resettlement in public rental housing flats. Lastly, they are not allowed to enjoy the same privileges in the purchase of HOS flats as the sitting tenants of public rental housing. These strict conditions were only applied to one person families.

This measure which discriminates against one person families led to the reduction of the number of people eligible for rehousing upon clearance.

Years of Existence since Created as at 1.4.1991	No. of THAs	Total Population	Percentage of Subtotal	Percentage of Total
Semi-Finished Units 1975-1984				
16	2	4,842	11.6	5.9
14	2	2,160	5.2	2.6
13	6	7,491	18.0	9.1
12	4	3,744	9.13	4.6
11	2	6,011	14.7	7.3
9	6	10,934	26.3	13.3
8	3	6,418	15.4	7.8
Sub-total	25	41,600	100.0	50.6
Fully-Finished Units 1984-1991				
6	2	1,722	4.2	2.1
5	7	8,728	21.5	10.6
4	9	7,501	18.5	9.1
3	16	13,615	33.5	16.6
2	7	6,321	15.6	7.7
1	6	2,756	6.8	3.4
Sub-total	47	40,643	100.0	49.4
Total	72	82,243	-	100.0

Table 4.4 Population and Year of Existence of the Temporary Housing Areas as at 1 April, 1991

Note: S : Semi-finished units
        F : Fully-constructed units

Source: This figure is computed from the official data provided to the members of the Housing Authority in Housing Authority document number: MOC 56/91

To conclude, although the production rate of public rental housing appeared promising, most of the people in these three categories were still in need of, and waiting for, public rental housing flats. As has been argued, the existence of these housing needs was actually a consequence of the government's lowered commitment to public housing. In the following section, we further explore the extent to which the neglect of urban minorities by the public housing policy conditioned the rise of the ATHA protests.

The Nature and Management of the Temporary Housing Areas

As our study is concerned with the ATHA issue, this section focuses on the policy concerning THAs.[12] The THAs are designated as transitory housing areas and are provided for 'the homeless and people not yet eligible for permanent public housing who have been displaced by clearances, fires, natural disasters and other operations' (Hong Kong Government, Annual Report, 1992:189). To the government, the THAs are a suitable method of housing people in need and of rehousing the squatter affected by clearance. As described in the previous section, the THAs are constructed with a simple wooden framework and only basic facilities, such as electricity and a water pipe, are supplied. Surely they are considered to be 'temporary' in nature.

To understand the role of THAs in public housing policy, it is necessary to spell out the relationship between the squatter and the THA.

The government has long expected to freeze the population of squatters in order to achieve its long-term plan of eradicating the problem of squatters by 1995. In 1985 the government registered all occupants of squatter dwellings and adopted the policy that only registered occupants would be eligible for resettlement in clearances, and any other occupants would have no rights of resettlement. However, lack of resettlement rights did not impede the appearance of new squatter areas. In order to deal with the unregistered squatters upon clearance of the areas, the current squatter policy allows the unregistered to move to THAs. It appears that the THA carries a political mission: to rehouse unregistered squatters upon clearance in order to minimize the chance of massive opposition to clearance. When the land occupied by squatters is needed and clearance is inevitable, the provision of THAs is a method of dealing with possible resistance and controversy. Hence the government utilized land that was not due to be developed in the near future to temporarily accommodate those people affected by clearance who were not yet eligible for public housing.

There are three ways in which the THA residents can apply for rehousing. The first of these is clearance. Residents who have been living in a THA for more than one year and have at least seven years of residency in Hong Kong are eligible for permanent public rental housing.[13] Secondly, trawling is an occasional method of providing 'old' public housing flats in urban areas or new public housing flats in the New Territories. The trawling exercise is a special measure for THA residents. Occasionally a number of public rental housing flats in the New Territories are set aside for those THA residents who fulfil the admission requirement for public rental housing. Allocation is not according to the applicant's position on the waiting list. Not all eligible THA residents can enjoy this opportunity because the Housing Department only offers it to certain designated THAs.[14] The third way is through the waiting list which is open to all Hong Kong citizens.

Two further schemes are available to THA residents to facilitate their move out of the THAs. In order to encourage the THA residents to purchase their own houses, the Housing Authority grants them priority in the purchase of HOS flats or makes them eligible for interest-free loans under the Home Purchase Loan Scheme. Most THA residents are not attracted to these two schemes as the majority are low-income families who cannot afford to buy their own flats. Most THA residents expect to be rehoused in permanent public housing through one of the three aforementioned ways.

We now examine the management of the THAs. There are two agents responsible for the management of the THAs, namely the Housing Authority and the Housing Department of the Hong Kong Government.

With regard to the management of the THAs, responsibility for policy has been delegated to the Management and Operations Committee of the Housing Authority, which oversees planning, construction, maintenance and clearance policy. This committee is basically policy-oriented, and policy execution is delegated to the Temporary Housing Affairs Section of the Housing Department. Routine management tasks of the THAs, including allocation, management and clearance, are to a large extent carried out by this section of the Housing Department.

Nevertheless, the Housing Authority does not include THAs among its properties and assets, and posits that its management of the THAs is carried out on behalf of the government. The THA residents are thus not regarded as public housing tenants, and there is no landlord-tenant relationship between the Housing Authority and the THA residents. Although the THA residents are not recognized as the tenants of the Hong Kong Authority, the burden of constructing and managing the THAs still falls on the Housing Authority. Yet the Housing Authority is subject to two constraints in respect of the management of the THAs.

Firstly, the construction of THAs is constrained by limited land supply. In view of their transitory nature, the government's urban planning policy does not take into consideration the demand for land arising from the construction of THAs. Basically, all land for THAs is provided by the government on a lease basis. A piece of land is leased to the Housing Authority provided that the area is crown land and will not be utilized in five years by any government department. If these two conditions are satisfied, the Housing Department liaises with the Land Development Department and applies for the right to use the area on a lease basis. Generally, a lease is given for five years and is renewable for a shorter period if the area is not earmarked for development by another government department. Hence, the construction of temporary housing depends on the availability of land and the cooperation of other departments. If a department is reluctant to lease the land under its control or to extend the lease, there is no other option for the Housing Authority to acquire land for THAs.

Secondly, the Housing Authority is not free to determine the clearance schedule since this largely relies on the supply of public rental housing flats and on whether another government department claims the land back. As a corollary, as an official of the Housing Department explained, there was no long-term planning as to how many public rental housing flats should be set aside for THA residents affected by clearance, because of the lack of information provided by other departments about when land would be claimed back. Faced with this constraint, the Housing Authority merely works out a tentative schedule, which, to ensure flexibility in response to unexpected demands from other departments, is not announced to the public. The Housing Authority normally announces a clearance schedule one year in advance of clearance. Clearly, this practice reflects the fact that the demand for the land of other departments is put before any other considerations such as the life span of the THAs, or the length of stay and the living conditions of the THA residents. As long as the THAs are not dangerous, the government is still willing to take advantage of them for the purpose of rehousing squatters evicted by clearance.

Summary

This chapter has provided a brief overview of the housing provision structure in Hong Kong. We have considered the range of public housing types, as well as the production and allocation policy of public rental housing. Despite a remarkable growth in the rate of production, the supply of public housing in the 1980s was inadequate, and subsequently the housing needs of the urban minorities, namely one and two person families, squatters and ATHA residents, received insufficient attention. With decreasing financial support from the government, the Housing Authority appeared unable to efficiently rehouse these categories of people in permanent public housing. We argue that it was the shortfall in public rental housing production that generated the issues of the ATHAs. In the next chapter, we examine in detail the characteristics of the ATHAs and how the ATHA issue became politicized.

Notes

1 The Home Ownership Scheme (HOS) was established in the late 1970s for the purpose of providing flats for sale at below market prices to lower-middle income families and public housing tenants. As an incentive to encourage purchase, public housing tenants are accorded higher priority than private sector applicants in selecting HOS flats, but they are required to forgo their rights to rental accommodation. Both categories of HOS applicants are able to enjoy favourable mortgage terms provided by 50 financial institutions. There are two sets of eligibility criteria for these schemes. The first enables public housing tenants, residents of Temporary Housing Areas, those on the waiting list for public housing, junior civil servants, and people affected by the government's redevelopment policy, to apply for purchase on the 'green form' which means that they have the privilege of selecting their units in advance. Residents of public housing estates have to move out of their units and give up their public housing tenancy. The second group includes those living in private sector housing who need to apply on a 'white form'. Applicants are subjected to a means test and no member of

the household may own any domestic property. Before April 1991, the income ceiling for the applicants was HK$11,500, which has now been increased to HK$14,000. The purpose of the Home Purchase Loan Scheme (HPLC) is to assist the lower-middle-income families and public housing tenants to buy flats of their own in the private sector. In 1992, eligible applicants had two options: either to accept an interest-free loan of $130,000 over 20 years or to make a monthly mortgage contribution of $2,000 for 36 months which is not repayable. This scheme has been offered to public rental housing tenants, prospective tenants and tenants in the private sector who are eligible to apply for HOS flats. It had already benefitted 6,550 households up to 1991.

2   The PSPS scheme aims to create an opportunity for the private sector to become involved in the production of housing when the demand for private housing is affected by the increasing supply of public housing. See *The Long Term Housing Strategy* and the Chairperson of the Housing Authority speech at the First Open Meeting on 11th April, 1991.

3   The exchange rate of Hong Kong Dollar to Pound in 1991 was 14 to 1.

4   Eligible applicants are ranked by ballot to determine the priorities of selecting their flats. Sitting tenants of public rental estates and Temporary Housing Areas affected by redevelopment and clearance are given first priority, followed by prospective rental housing tenants. Applicants from the private sector are given a lower priority in selecting flats.

5   The residential requirement was abandoned in May, 1991.

6   The Housing Authority has encountered deficits since it became a statutory body. In 1973 its liabilities were HK$135 million, growing to HK$1,836 million in 1989. There are two reasons to account for such a deficit in its balance sheet. First, the deficit is created on account of the large amount of maintenance cost for the B-type public housing estate. In the period 1983-1987 the A-Type rental public housing generated HK$121 million surplus while the deficit in rental public housing was about HK$682 million. On balance, it had an overall deficit of HK$561 million. Second, the land provided by the government has been counted in monetary terms and put into the liabilities side of the balance sheet as 'Hong Kong Government Contribution to Domestic Housing'. The land cost increased from HK$5,377 million in 1976 to HK$41,432 million. The Housing Authority receives no grants but only loans from the government. The large-scale construction projects are supported by money borrowed from the government. In 1986-1988, more than half of the authority's expenditure came from government loans. The Housing Authority borrows money from the government at an interest rate of 5 % and repays it over 40 years. But the government does not take the interest back. Instead, it returns it to the authority in loan form. In this way, the loan is accumulating insofar as the interest becomes another loan and thereby interest to be paid also progressively increases.

7   For the relationship between the financial arrangement of the Housing Authority and the rise of social conflicts, see Castells, (1988); Lau, (1989); Lui, (1984); Ho, D. (1989).

8   The term 'small families' is persistently and insistently used by social activists committed to minorities' housing movements. They argue that housing policy does not

treat single and two-member families as 'families' which are totally excluded from consideration in public housing policy. Hence, calling them 'family' has critical ideological implications in the confrontation with the Housing Authority.

9   Public attention and criticism of the government's ignorance led to a review of accommodation for small households. For details, see the Hong Kong Housing Authority, 1991.

10 According to the squatter clearance policy, 'those aged below 50 are eligible for accommodation in Temporary Housing Areas (THA) or a cash allowance in lieu of housing. The elderly and those rehoused on compassionate grounds can be allocated individual public housing units or can opt voluntarily to share larger flats. Individual units will only be allocated in the extended urban areas and the New Territories. Rehousing is also subject to a seven year residence qualification' (Hong Kong Housing Authority, 1991:4).

11 See the Housing Authority document no. 56/91, p.2.

12 We do not deny the significance of conflicts arising from squatters and small families to urban politics. But at the time of our study only the ATHA issue was articulated and protest groups concerning this issue formed.

13 The seven year residency requirement was abolished in June 1993 to encourage more THA residents to move to permanent public housing in order to provide vacant units to accommodate squatters.

14 Before May 1991, residents of temporary housing areas could apply for transfer to public housing estates in the New Territories, providing more than half of their family members had been living in temporary housing areas for more than one year and in Hong Kong for more than seven years. If more than half of their family members had been in Hong Kong for more than ten years, they would be exempt from the means test whose criteria are the same as when applying for public housing units through the master waiting list. In May 1991 the Management and Operations Committee of the Housing Authority decided to expunge the requirement of a means test.

5 A Brief Account of the Trajectory of the ATHA Protest

Introduction

The aim of this chapter is to describe the development of the protest over the Aged Temporary Housing Areas (ATHAs). The first section provides an account of the background context essential to understanding the emergence of this issue. We contend that the government intended to retain the ATHAs for the purpose of rehousing squatters affected by its clearance programme. Not until the sites of the ATHAs were reclaimed by other government departments did the Housing Department demolish the physically deteriorated ATHAs. Dissatisfaction with this clearance policy was one of the reasons for the rise of the ATHA issue. Section 5.1 presents a brief account of the development of such protests. As our study is primarily concerned with protest at local level, we have selected two ATHAs as the focal point of our study, namely Kowloon Bay II & III THAs and Ping Shek THA. In order to provide more detailed information about such protests, in section 5.2 we examine the trajectory of the local protests in these two ATHAs. Section 5.3 describes the key actors involved in the mobilization process, including the concern group members of the two ATHAs, paid community social workers, and volunteer organizers. We consider the background of these actors, with particular reference to the organization they represent, for our study of the mobilization process in the following chapters. Section 5.4 examines the demographic characteristics of the two ATHAs. The final section is a summary.

The Aged Temporary Housing Areas Issue

The ATHA issue arose when the residents started pressing for early clearance of the ATHAs. To understand the emergence of this issue, we need to know the reasons for the government's reluctance to demolish the physically 'unfit' THAs, on the one hand, and why the ATHA residents were unwilling to move out through the formal rehousing procedure on the other. The aim of this section is to find the answers to these two questions.

It is our contention that the preservation of the physically 'unfit' THAs is related to the political function and the management of the THAs.

As has been discussed in Chapter 4, the main function of the THAs is to rehouse the squatters who are affected by the government's clearance policy but are ineligible for public housing flats. When clearance of urban squatters was carried out in the early 1980s, in order to create more urban land for the construction of subways and infrastructure, for the provision of recreational facilities and for land sales, it was necessary to rehouse the affected squatters who were not eligible for public housing flats so as to avoid provoking any political disputes. We argue that as long as there are ineligible households in squatter areas affected by the squatter clearance programme, the THAs remain politically necessary.

Due to their important political function, the government managed to retain enough THAs to support its policy of squatter clearance. As a corollary, despite the continued existence of many aged and deteriorated THAs, the government showed no intention of demolishing the problematic blocks, and just strengthened the structure and did simple refurbishment to the ATHAs. According to the Housing Department's official explanation, the clearance of a THA is dependent on three factors: whether the land is needed, the availability of public rental housing units, and financial support.[1] We see that a THA will be cleared if the land it is located on is urgently needed for development and resources are available. Apparently, neither the age of the THA, nor the fact that many residents are compelled to tolerate unpleasant living conditions, are considered to be priorities in THA clearance policy.

In the late 1980s, the government was reluctant to clear the THAs because two problems had exacerbated the existing shortage of public housing flats. First, the physical deterioration of public rental housing estates became an issue in the 1980s, and in response the government initiated a redevelopment programme in the mid-1980s.[2] At the same time, a comprehensive redevelopment project had already been implemented, aimed at demolishing or converting the Mark III-VI estates that were suffering from structural defects. Both redevelopment programmes were considered a drain on housing resources. As the government had committed itself to these programmes and had promised to rehouse all the affected tenants, more public rental housing flats were earmarked. The number of people rehoused in public rental housing flats through the redevelopment or conversion programmes increased from 9.9% in 1981-1982 to 27.4% of the total population who are allocated public housing flats in 1988-1989. These programmes subsequently absorbed a substantial proportion of public housing resources.

Second, as has been discussed in Chapter 4, insufficient housing production was related to the government's reluctance to commit more resources to public rental housing.

Faced with these two problems, the government was unwilling to demolish problematic THAs in order to avoid generating more demand for public housing flats. We contend that the THA clearance policy is basically development-led, in the sense that a THA is cleared only when the piece of land on which it is located is needed for development. When the Housing Authority has no clear idea when the other government departments will claim the land back, it is difficult for the Housing Authority to figure out a long-term THA clearance schedule. As was admitted by the Housing Authority, 'it was not possible for the Department to draw up, unilaterally, a longer-term THA clearance programme because there might be changes to the plans of client departments, thus affecting the clearance programme'.[3] Without any long-term planning for the clearance of THAs, there was no long-term plan for the provision of public housing for THA residents affected by clearance. This is one of the reasons for the existence of ATHAs.

We now turn to the question of why most of the ATHA residents did not apply for rehousing through formal channels, which include the Home Ownership Scheme (HOS), trawling, and the waiting list. However HOS flats are not attractive to many THA residents as they are simply unable to afford them.[4] Applying for rehousing through trawling and the waiting list do not appear to be attractive either.[5] Public rental housing flats available to the applicants through these two means were largely located in the New Territories.[6] By virtue of the distance between the new towns and the urban areas, most THA residents were reluctant to move into the New Territories.

In our survey of three ATHAs in 1991, 78% of the respondents had not applied for rehousing through the trawling exercise. In addition, the survey asked the respondents to show their preferred location, assuming that they had freedom of choice. Only 2.3% would have chosen to move to Tseung Kwan O - a public rental housing estate in a peripheral urban area, whilst 92% preferred to be rehoused in urban districts, and 5.7% gave no answer.[7] This situation was admitted by the Chairperson of the Housing Authority in his opening speech at the First Public Meeting of the Housing Authority on 11th April, 1991. As he pointed out, there were insufficient job vacancies for newcomers in the new towns and, coupled with a poor transportation system, this situation encouraged the belief that living in the new towns would entail a lot of additional hardship. The possible hardship arising from moving into the new towns discouraged the THA residents from applying for rehousing through trawling and the waiting list.

It appears that waiting for clearance is the most attractive strategy for the THA residents, because they are entitled to rehousing in public rental flats in the same district upon clearance. Hence, pressing for early clearance means pressing for early rehousing to public rental housing in the same district.

This section has explained the reluctance of the government to clear the ATHAs, and the reasons underpinning the ATHA residents' preference for waiting for clearance. In the next section, we focus on how the ATHA protest arose and developed.

The Rise of the ATHA Protest

First we state the objectives of the ATHA protest and then move on to delineate the development process.

The ATHA protest has three major objectives:

a. pressing for early clearance of all the ATHAs which are defined as having existed for at least seven years;
b. pressing for the stipulation of a long-term clearance schedule (i.e. at least a five-year plan);
c. during the protest the ATHA issue made a new political demand for the rehousing of eligible THA residents in the same district upon clearance.[8]

The Housing Department gave three explanations for its reluctance to accept the THA residents' demands.[9] First, urban public rental housing flats were mainly intended to cater for the housing demands arising from redevelopment of the aged public housing estates, as a result of the government's promise that all public housing residents evicted through the redevelopment programme would be rehoused in the same district. Hence, housing resources would not be sufficient to deal with the demand for public housing created by speeding up the clearance of ATHAs.

Second, it would be impossible for Housing Department officials to draw up a five- year clearance schedule as clearance was subject to the need for land originated by other government departments.

Third, the Housing Department official explained that the public rental housing estates where eligible THA residents were to be rehoused were located in 'extended urban areas' such as Tseung Kwai O, Shatin, and Tsuen Wan. Thus, the rehousing measure offered to the ATHA residents already conformed to the current rehousing policy.[10]

The conflict between the ATHA residents and the government over the timing of clearance was the main issue in the ATHA protest.

To describe the development of the ATHA protest, we have traced this issue back to 1989. The ATHA protest effectively began with a newspaper article in 1989.[11] The article derived from a government press release about the findings of a technical report on the structural condition of THA blocks.[12] The press release did not disclose details of the report but indicated that a number of THAs needed some sort of structural repair.[13] This article attracted the attention of a group of community social workers who were involved in an organization called 'The Concern Group of Temporary Housing Area Policy' (CGTP).[14] The CGTP subsequently contacted the Housing Department and requested more details about the safety of the THAs. The Housing Department neither admitted the existence of any survey or research on the allegedly 'problematic' THAs nor accepted that there was any deterioration in the building structure of some of the blocks. After a number of unsuccessful attempts to obtain more information, the CGTP decided to conduct a survey of 18 THAs.[15] The survey was done in collaboration with a pressure group - the People's Council on Public Housing Policy (PCPHP).[16] A number of teams were formed and assigned to those THAs where no social work team was already working.[17] Basically, the teams aimed at conducting the survey, while at the same time mobilizing, consolidating and assisting the residents to establish their own local concern group in some of the ATHAs. Four ATHAs, namely Lai Chi Kok Road, Ping Shek, Kowloon Bay II & III, and Hong Ning Road were selected to be their focal areas. The chairman of the CGTP was responsible for managing the survey and mobilization tasks in the Lai Chi Kok Road THA and the PCPHP undertook the same tasks in the other three THAs. In November 1990, the survey was finished and 2,668 questionnaires had been completed. The findings were released on 12th December 1990 at a press conference. They indicated a lot of problems in the physical structure, hygiene and environment of the 18 ATHAs.[18]

In fact, during the period from April to December 1990, the CGTP started mobilizing the residents in the selected ATHAs. A meeting was held involving various THA representatives, including those from Cheung Pei Shan, Pak Kok, Cheung Wan, Fat Kwong Street and Tai Wo Ping THAs. Later, they defined those THAs which were more than seven years old as 'ATHAs', and decided to establish a coalition composed of ATHA representatives.[19]

The coalition worked for one year from mid-1990 to mid-1991, involving the residents of Cheung Wan, Cheung Pei Shan, Lai Chi Kok, Tai Wo Ping, Pak Kok, Fat Kwong Street, Ping Shek and Kowloon Bay THAs. However, the residents of Pak Kok THA did not show up after a couple of meetings, and both the Cheung Wan THA and Cheung Pei Shan representatives withdrew in late 1990 because the government had announced the clearance date of their THAs.

During the early period of the ATHA protest, the CGTP made two decisions about the direction of the activities of the whole movement. The first was to acquire more technical information about the building structure of the ATHA blocks. The second was to consolidate the coalition by inviting more ATHA residents to participate. However, neither objective was achieved. No technical survey report pertaining to the building structure of the ATHAs was located. Besides this, the coalition formed by the CGTP dissolved in mid-1991 due to the departure of the leading organizers. The leadership of the ATHA protest was handed over to the Joint Committee of the THA Residents Association (JCTRA) which re-formed a coalition concerning the ATHA protest in late 1991, and served as the spokesperson for all the ATHA residential associations. After that, a number of press conferences, demonstrations and petitions were launched.

The JCTRA also attempted to organize protest activities at local level, and carried out the task of liaising with all the local concern groups.

Since 1992, the JCTRA has put less effort into the ATHA issue. Although there were local concern groups which remained active in pressing for early clearance, the leadership of the JCTRA considered the ATHA issue to be a settled case. From the leadership's point of view, the 1992-93 clearance schedule had been announced by the Housing Authority in 1992; and even if some of the ATHAs were not yet included in the schedule, few local representatives participated in the JCTRA. Accordingly, it was decided that there was no point in continuing to lead the protest. The JCTRA promised to keep an eye on the development of the ATHA issue and to be ready to assist the residents to launch action upon request.

In 1992 only the Ping Shek THA residents insisted on struggling for early clearance. Later, the concern group of the Shun Lee THA began pressing for early clearance of their THA. But the concern groups worked independently and no local coalition was formed.

In late 1992, a new coalition was established again by the JCTRA, involving mainly the Mui Lee THA and Ping Shek THA representatives. The revival of the JCTRA's interest in the ATHA issue was engendered by a series of protests by the residents of the Ping Shek THA, whose concern group organized petitions and whose 18th anniversary ceremony succeeded in generating publicity. Subsequently, the JCTRA was reminded of the ATHA issue and managed to put it back on the agenda. Nevertheless, the coalition was hardly successful in playing its role of leading the ATHA protest.

Throughout the protest, the local THA concern groups played a very significant role, and were relatively successful in arousing public interest. Demonstrations to the Housing Authority, the Housing Department and the District Board were organized, and the concern groups made efforts to seek the support of political activists and members of District Boards. A Small Joint-Districts Committee was also set up by three ATHA concern groups in the Kwun Tong district in late 1990. This committee dissolved after the Kowloon Bay and the Hong Ning Road THAs were included in the clearance scheme in April 1991.

The Ping Shek THA concern group was very active in the period 1992-1994. In June 1993, the Housing Authority announced a clearance schedule indicating that half of the Ping Shek and Shun Lee THA blocks were due to be cleared in 1994. Dissatisfied with this schedule which still left half of the two ATHAs intact, the two THA concern groups continued their mobilization and protests, pressing for clearance in one go. In June 1994, another clearance schedule was announced in which the remaining parts of the two THAs were also planned for clearance at the end of 1994. The concern groups of the two ATHAs then turned to fight for the right to be rehoused in the same district.

To sum up, throughout the protest we can discern two kinds of organization involved in the ATHA issue. First, there were local THA concern groups who organized protest activities. The second type is the coalition - the JCTRA which consists of representatives from local THAs.

Below is a chronology (Table 5.1a) of the ATHA protests organized by the two local ATHAs we studied, followed by a chronology (Table 5.1b) of the protest activities organized by the JCTRA.

Date	Event
9.4.90	Survey
14.4.90	Residents' Meeting (clearance issue)
19.4.90	Demonstration at Kwun Tong District Board (clearance issue)
28.4.90	Residents' Meeting (clearance issue)
29.4.90	Press Conference
7.5.90	Reformation of Residents' Concern Group
11.5.90	Visit by District Board members & letter to Editorial Board
4.6.90	Letter to Housing Department (environmental issue)
14.6.90	Demonstration at Housing Department & District Board Office (clearance issue)
1.6.90	Concern Group registered as a legal organization
22.7.90	Press Conference with the Joint Meeting of THA Social Workers
26.7.90	Demonstration at Housing Authority with Joint Committee of THAs Residents Association
17.12.90	Demonstration at Housing Authority with Fat Kwong Street THA residents
1.1.91	Letter to Housing Department (requesting place for meeting)
18.1.91	Meeting with DB members
22.1.91	Meeting with the Joint Meeting of THA Residents Association
28.1.91	Meeting with OMELCO members with Joint Meeting of THA Social Workers
3.3.91	Visit by the candidates of the District Board Election
5.4.91	Meeting with Housing Department & letter to Editorial Board
7.4.91	Meeting with Mr. Lee Wing-tak, Member of the Hong Kong Democratic United

11.4.91	Meeting with Housing Authority (HA's Public Meeting) with Joint Committee of THA Residents' Association
17.4.91	Announcement of the date of clearance
20.4.91	Letter to Housing Department (clearance issue)
	Letter to Housing Department (environmental issue)
17.5.91	Meeting with Housing Department (local rehousing issue)
3.6.91	Letter to Housing Department (environmental issue)
8.6.91	Visit of King Lam Estate
10.6.91	Signatures collected from the campaign sent to the Housing Department
13.6.91	Letter to Housing Department (local rehousing issue)
15.6.91	Signature petition (requesting local rehousing)
28.6.91	Mass meeting
1.7.91	Meeting with Housing Department (local rehousing issue)
20.7.91	Mass meeting (election for the committee of the concern group - failed to return new members)
7.8.91	Mass meeting
9.8.91	Mass meeting
14.8.91	Visit by District Board members (local rehousing issue)
22.8.91	Meeting with the chairman of the Housing Section of the District Board
27.8.91	Mass meeting
1.8.91 - 30.9.91	Survey on the preference of the residents
10.8.91	Meeting with District Board members (local rehousing issue)
3.9.91	Mass meeting (election for the committee of the concern group)
6.9.91	Mass meeting
10.9.91	Mass meeting
13.9.91	Mass meeting and donation campaign
18.9.91	Letter to Editorial Board (local rehousing issue)
	Meeting with the Clearance Section of the Housing Department
20.9.91	Mass meeting and the Chairperson of the concern group resigned
24.9.91	Mass meeting
25.9.91	Mass meeting
	Letter to Chairperson of Housing Authority
26.9.91	Demonstration at Housing Authority (requesting meeting with MOC members), resulting in a confrontation with the staff members of the Housing Department
28.9.91	Meeting with Legco member - Mr. FUNG Kim-Ki
5.10.91	Visit of DB members - Mr. LEE Wah-ming & Mr. Szeto Wah
17.10.91	Meeting with MOC members and a demonstration took place
10.10.91	Nine mass meetings

Date	Event
25.10.91	Received letter from Mr. Poa Ping-wing - the Chairperson of the MOC (announcement of the delay of clearance)
31.10.91	Letter to MOC members
1.11.91 - 15.11.91	Four mass meetings
3.12.91	Meeting with OMELCO members

Table 5.1a   A Chronology of the Actions Organized by the Residents of the Kowloon Bay THA in Respect of the ATHA Issue, 1990-1991

Note: OMELCO - Office of Members of Executive and Legislative Councils
DB - District Board
MOC - Management and Operation Committee of the Housing Authority

Source: Author's fieldnotes and minutes of meetings of the two local concern groups, 1990-1993

Date	Event
10.11.90	Visited by other THAs
17.12.90	Demonstration with other THAs (Housing Authority Opening Ceremony)
28.1.91	Letter with Residents' signatures to Boys & Girls Association (objection to the closure of children centre)
29.1.91	Meeting with District Board member - Ms. AU Yuk-kar (expressing concern about ATHA problems)
13.2.91	Letter to editorial board (objection to the closure of children centre)
22.2.91	Visit by Chief Coordinator of Boys & Girls Association
24.2.91	Report & press visit (children centre issue)
11.4.91	Report & press visit (clearance issue)
6.5.92	Demonstration (Housing Department, requesting clearance by 93-94)
15.6.92	Visit by District Board members - Mr. LEE Wing-tat & Mr. Szeto Wah
16.6.92	Residents meeting
20.6.92	Letter to Kwun Tong District Board Matters on Housing & Editorial Board
28.6.92	Meeting with Housing Department (along with Ms. AU Yuk-har)
13.8.92	Kwun Tong District Board rejected proposal to establish the concern group of aged THAs
16.8.92	Demonstration (Housing Authority)
24.8.92 - 10.9.92	Survey I
5.9.92	Meeting with MOC members & demonstration (clearance issue)

10.10.92	Visit by SCMP
31.10.92	Invitation to Governor (requesting him to visit Ping Shek THA)
1.11.92 - 30.12.92	Survey II
21.11.92	Letter to Editorial Board & District Board members (18th Anniversary Opening Ceremony)
22.11.92	Demonstration at Governor's House (giving invitation card to Governor)
9.12.92	Demonstration at the Choi Chuk THA (requesting Governor to participate in 18th Anniversary Opening Ceremony)
13.12.92	18th Anniversary Opening Ceremony
19.12.92	Letter to Housing Department (requesting meeting with HD)
2.1.93	Shun Lee NLCDP Team begin to work in the Ping Shek THA
6.2.93	Residents meeting (concern group's work report) & letter to Editorial Board (clearance issue)
10.2.93	Meeting with Housing Department & demonstration (clearance issue)
23.2.93	Meeting with MOC members
2.6.93	Report & visit by SCMP
3.6.93	Letter to Urban Council (asking for the planned land use of Ping Shek THAs)
12.6.93	Letter to Governor (clearance issue)
19.6.93	Residents neeting
23.6.93	Visit by Governor & announcement of the 1st clearance in 93-94
10.7.93	Report & visit by SCMP
15.7.93 - 30.9.93	Survey III
7.11.93	Residents meeting
16.11.93	Letter to Chairperson of Housing Authority & Housing Department (requesting a place for meeting within the THA)
12.12.93	Meeting with Housing Department in Ping Shek THAs/ Report & visit by TVB & Cable TV (announcing the 2nd clearance in 94-95)
13.12.93	Visit by Chairperson of Housing Authority - Ms. Wong Yik-ming

Table 5.1b   A Chronology of the Actions Organized by the Residents of the Ping Shek THA in Respect of the ATHA Issue, 1990-1993

Source: Author's fieldnotes and minutes of meetings of the two local concern groups, 1990-1993

Date	Event
1.8.90	Signature campaign of all ATHAs
8.8.90	Letter to media about the ATHA issue
19.8.90	Meeting with Housing Authority (* ATHA issue)
12.12.90	Demonstration at Housing Authority opening ceremony (*all THA issues)
4.3.91	Letters to OMELCO, media, and politicians about THA issues
8.3.91	Meeting with Housing Department (* all THA issues)
22.3.91	Joint THAs demonstration at Housing Authority MOC meeting
2.2.92	Meeting with Housing Authority
8.2.92	Letter to Housing Department, media
19.3.92	Meeting with Mr. LEE Wing-tat (Legco member)
23.3.92	Letter to Legco member
25.3.92	Meeting with Mr. FUNG Tung (Director of Housing Department) (* asking about the clearance schedule)
8.4.92	Letter to Mr. LEE Wing-tat
8.4.92	Meeting with Housing Department
5.7.92	Letter to Mr. LEE Wing-tat (* discussion on 'same district rehousing' policy)
8.7.92	Letter to Housing Department (* clarification of THA policy)
9.9.92	Meeting with Housing authority
1.10.92	Establishment of the ATHA concern group
1.11.92	Invitation letter to Governor to participate in the 18th anniversary ceremony of the Ping Shek THA
2.2.93	Collection of THA information from political parties
8.3.93	Signature campaign at ATHAs (* ATHA issue)
- 10.3.93	
15.3.93	Collection of information about 'same district rehousing' issue
1.3.93	Survey of all THAs
- 30.6.93	
21.5.93	Sit-in & demonstration at Legco meeting (* ATHA issue)
23.5.93	Petition of Housing Department (* ATHA issue)
28.5.93	Meeting with OMELCO (* ATHA issue)
30.5.93	Meeting with Housing Department (* ATHA issue)
1.7.93	Dissolution of ATHA issue group
16.7.93	Meeting with Housing Department
18.7.93	Letter to Housing Authority (* one-person household issue)
1.9.93	Letter to Housing Department (* one-person household issue)
5.9.93	Letter to Mr. Szeto Wah - a member of Legislative Council
18.9.93	Establishment of Action Planning Group

Table 5.2 A Chronology of the Actions Organized by the Joint Committee of the THA Residents Associations for the ATHA Issue, 1990-1993

Source: From minutes of JCTRA monthly meeting, 1990-1993[20]

The main points emerging from these chronologies of actions by the residents in the two areas and the JCTRA are as follows. Firstly, the major form of protest activities were meetings, including mass meetings, meetings with politicians, and meetings with members of the Housing Authority and the Housing Department. Demonstrations were very infrequent. It appeared that 'orderly politics' and 'polite politics' were the major strategies adopted by the local concern groups. Radical actions, for example sit-ins, sleep-ins, rent strikes, etc., were seldom taken in the course of the protest while more polite and diplomatic actions were consistently employed. Secondly, most activities were planned and implemented by the local concern groups themselves, rather than working through a coalition with other ATHAs. In particular we found a weak relationship between the JCTRA and the local concern groups. Thirdly, only a few internal mobilization campaigns were organized, such as signature and donation campaigns, and mass meetings. Clearly, the Kowloon Bay THA concern group organized more mass meetings, especially in the later stage of the protest, than the Ping Shek THA concern group. Fourthly, mass activities were seldom organized, except for the mass meetings held within the ATHAs. This indicates that the local concern groups did not exercise their political power on the basis of their 'numeric' strength. Lastly, both the JCTRA and the local concern groups adopted the strategies of orderly and polite politics, and there was little division of labour between the two types of protest organization.

We will return to discuss these features of the protest activities of the two THAs in the following chapters. But first, we provide more detailed information on the groups involved in the protest and the social characteristics of the residents.

The Actors Involved in the ATHA Protest

The ATHA protest involved various protest groups which can be broadly regarded as a loosely structured coalition. This reflects the effective absence of a centre which could have served as a directing and decision-making agent. There were three kinds of actor involved in the protest. The first were the residents associations (or local concern groups) in each of the ATHAs. The name of the residents associations varied but most shared the same basic objectives, that is, pressing for early clearance of the ATHAs. The second kind of actors were the community social workers who were the paid staff of voluntary social work agencies.[21] Although regarded as voluntary, they were partly funded by the government. The third kind were the social activist groups, composed of volunteer organizers. Most of the volunteer organizers have a full-time job as community social workers, though a few were recruited from previous protests. We now focus on the nature and characteristics of the three kinds of organization involved in the ATHA issue.

The Local Concern Groups

These groups were made up of indigenous THA residents. The leadership was formed by a small group of active residents, but there were no strict rules and regulations governing the administration of the concern groups. Meetings were called and relevant documents were prepared by the organizers, who were either community social workers or volunteer organizers. Use of standing orders in meetings and acting in conformity with the constitution, if any existed, happened rarely and seemed to be unimportant. For example, although the Kowloon Bay THA residents association had drawn up a constitution, few members referred to it or mentioned it throughout the protest. The members appeared to have no idea about the importance of a constitution. Furthermore, there were no formal rules about eligibility for membership. All the residents of a THA were supposed to be members and simple majority voting was the usual method of election.

Local concern groups were the only social organization in the areas serving as the voice and representatives of the THA residents. In 1990 there were five local concern groups pressing for the early clearance of the ATHAs. Table 5.3 presents some information about the two in the areas we focused on.

120 *Polite Politics*

Name of Local Concern Group	Date of Establishment	No. of Core Members	Organization Involved	Nature of the External Organizers
Kowloon Bay THA residents association	April 1990	9 - 12 (1st committee) 12 (2nd committee)	PCPHP* & Cooperative NLCDP team (since Feb. 1991)	3 volunteers from PCPHP & 3 social workers from Cooperative
The Caring Groups of the Ping Shek THA	May 1990	4 - 10	PCPHP & Christine Service Centre	2 volunteers of PCPHP (from Jun. 1990 to Dec. 1991) 7 volunteers of CPHP (from May 1992 to April 1994) and 3 social workers from Christine Service (from Jan. 1993 to Apr. 1994)
	May 1992 (the second committee)	4 - 11	NLCDP team (from Jan. 1993 to April 1994)	

Table 5.3   General Information About Two Local THA Concern Groups

Key: PCPHP : the People's Council on Public Housing Policy
       NLCDP : Neighbourhood Level Community Development Projects
       CGTP : Caring Group of Temporary Housing Policy
Note: the name of the two organizations are changed

Source: Author's survey

Social Workers

A second category of actor is social workers. These can be divided into two types.

The Community Social Workers In Hong Kong social workers have played a critical role in community development. Under the auspices of the Division Office of Community Development of the Federation of Social Services, a programme known as the 'Neighbourhood Level Community Development Projects' (NLCDP) was launched in the early 1980s.

Although there were different interpretations and understandings of the nature and objectives of the project, the project workers were expected to oversee all the demands for social services and assistance by the residents of squatter areas, public housing estates and THAs. One NLCDP team, which normally consists of three full-time social workers and one clerical worker, would be allocated to an area with more than 3,000 residents and given the responsibility for organizing all social services provision.[22] In some situations community social workers have had to take on the role of organizer to help residents to push for their rights.

The Volunteer Organizers It is quite difficult to distinguish this group from the community social workers. The majority of the volunteer organizers involved in the ATHA issues were trained social workers, and most had their own paid jobs in the social work profession (the author was the only volunteer organizer who had no social work training).[23] In the two ATHAs we studied, the volunteer organizers worked in the name of the PCPHP but relationships were loosely structured and the PCPHP exerted little influence on their actions.

In 1990 the PCPHP established a small Joint-Districts Committee among three ATHAs in the Kwun Tong District, namely the Ping Shek, the Kowloon Bay, and the Hong Ning Road THAs. There was little residents' involvement in this committee, so the local coalition became a forum for the volunteer organizers to figure out strategies and tactics. However, nothing substantial was achieved in this small committee. Information exchange seemed to be its sole purpose.

The Coalition - JCTRA

Lastly, an across-district committee called 'The Joint Committee of the THA Residents Association' was founded by the community social workers for the purpose of overseeing all the issues pertaining to the welfare of the THA residents. It consisted of community social workers and the indigenous leaders of local THA concern groups. The THA residents were supposed to be the core, formal members, while social workers were expected to serve the committees as facilitators, providing skills, resources and information. The committee was established in 1985, with the objectives of building up solidarity and fighting for the rights of the THA residents. It was incorporated into the formal structure of the People's Council of Public Housing Policy but has a very high degree of autonomy.[24]

The coalition organized actions ranging from meetings to petitions. The ATHA issue seized the JCTRA's attention in mid-1990, but was largely ignored between June 1991 and November 1992 when it came back as a major issue, and a specific sub-group was formed to address it. Since the summer of 1993, the JCTRA has become less interested in this issue (see Table 5.2b).

We have briefly presented the nature and organizational structure of the actors involved in the ATHA protest. Since the target of mobilization by community social workers was the ATHA residents, it is necessary to understand the demographic characteristics of the ATHA residents and this is the subject to which we now turn.

The ATHA Residents

There is limited data on the demographic features of the residents living in the ATHAs. The data used here is mainly drawn from the survey we conducted in May 1991.[25] This survey covered three ATHAs in the Kwun Tong District, namely, Kowloon Bay, Ping Shek and Hong Ning Road THAs. Since our case studies of local mobilization in the following chapters will not include the Hong Ning Road THA, information about the residents of this THA will not be included here.

The three ATHAs we surveyed in 1991 were located within the Kwun Tong district which has developed into an industrial-residential area since the 1950s (see Figure 5.1). In the 1950s, a large area of reclaimed land was used for building industrial premises and the government rehoused a large number of working class people on public housing estates there, and subsequently it became a district of predominantly public housing. The population of this district was estimated to be 617,300 in 1991.[26] By 1991 the public housing estates accommodated 473,050 people, about 77% of the total population of the Kwun Tong District. In 1989 there were 18 THAs in Kowloon East, most of them situated in the Kwun Tong District. Kowloon East had the highest figure in terms of population of THA residents. In that year, there were 30,397 THA residents, comprising about 28% of the total population of the THAs. By contrast, in Tsuen Wan, also one of the first generation new towns in the New Territories, there were 16 THAs which accommodated 13,193 people, about 12% of the total. By the end of 1990, the population in the THAs of Kwun Tong District was 22,166, comprising about 25% of the total THA residents in Hong Kong. The Kwun Tong District was also prominent for having the largest number of ATHAs and the largest population of ATHA residents. By the end of 1990, 8,227 people were living in these ATHAs. This figure represents nearly half the total population of Hong Kong residents still being accommodated in THAs that were built in the 1970s. The first THA was the Ping Shek THA which opened in March 1975 and the other two oldest THAs are the Kowloon Bay and the Hong Ning Road THAs.

One of the THAs we studied - the Kowloon Bay THA - was very near another industrial area, the Kowloon Bay area, which was being developed in the early 1980s (see Figure 5.2). The Ping Shek THA was on the fringe of the Kwun Tong District. The land occupied by the Ping Shek THA was originally planned to be used as a playground.[27] But by 1991 the government had given no indication of the future usage of the land. The Kowloon Bay THA was scheduled to be demolished at the end of 1991. This clearance plan was announced in April 1991. Prior to that, there had been no information about its future use. Its clearance then can be interpreted as a result of the residents' protest which began in April 1990.

As shown in Table 5.4, in 1991 the populations of the Kowloon Bay and the Ping Shek THAs were 2,406 and 2,084 respectively, and the numbers of households were 738 and 757 respectively. Three quarters of the ATHA residents (76%) were immigrants, mostly from mainland China. About half of them lived in Hong Kong for less than 10 years: 52% and 48% of the Kowloon Bay THA and the Ping Shek THA respectively. Table 5.5 shows that about four-fifths (81%) of the Kowloon Bay THA residents and seven-tenths (73%) of the Ping Shek THA residents had lived in THAs for less than seven years, and the vast majority of them had been resident from three to seven years. Although the two THAs have existed for more than 15 years, only a small proportion of the residents had been living there for more than 10 years. About 9% of the Kowloon Bay THA residents and 13.6% of the Ping Shek THA residents had been living there for such a long period. Newcomers, i.e. those residents who had been living in the THAs less than two years, accounted for 14% of the total population in these ATHAs.

	Kowloon Bay THA	Ping Shek THA
Year of residency in Hong Kong		
Less than 6	16.6	17.5
6 – 10	35.0	30.0
11 – 15	35.0	32.0
16 – 20	5.1	6.5
21 or over	8.3	14.0
Total	100.0	100.0
Sample size (n)@	1,196.0	638.0
Place of Birth		
Hong Kong	392.0	228.0
Others	1,195.0	638.0
Unknown	63.0	42.0
Immigrants (%)	76.2	74.9
Sample Size (n)	1,650.0	908.0
Population#	2,406.0	2,084.0
Number of households#	738.0*	757.0**

Table 5.4 Years of Residency in Hong Kong, Place of Birth, Population, Number of Households, by Residents in the Two ATHAs, as of May 1991 (%)

Note: @ Non-response and no information categories are excluded.
\# The figures in this row are drawn from official document of the Hong Kong Housing Department
* This figure is as at October 1991.
** This figure is as at December 1991.

Source: Author's Survey

Year of Residency in THA	Kowloon Bay THA	Ping Shek THA
1 – 2	12.1	16.6
3 – 7	69.0	56.7
8 – 10	9.2	13.2
11 – 18	9.4	13.6
Total@	99.7	100.0

Table 5.5 Years of Residency in THAs by the Residents in Two THAs (%)

Note: n 1 650 and 2 084 respondents in the Kowloon Bay and the Ping Shek THAs respectively
@ The total is not 100 since the percentages of giving no response are not included.
Source: Author's survey

According to our findings, 79% of the THA respondents had moved from squatter areas.[28] 66% of the residents had moved to the three ATHAs because of squatter clearance. 12.5% had been rehoused in the THAs as a result of natural disaster. The rest had moved for other reasons, for example, the splitting up of a household (0.8%) or the demolition of private housing (3.1%). The majority of households had previously resided for a long time in the Kwun Tong district and geographical mobility within the district appeared low. As many as 78% of the respondents had lived in Kwun Tong before moving to the current THAs.[29]

We notice that the workplace of 71% of the working population was located in either Hong Kong Island or Kowloon.[30] As most of the respondents were immigrants, it is not surprising to find that none of the residents were professionals, managers, administrators, or associate professionals. As shown in Table 5.6, 55% of the residents in the two ATHAs were either manual or unskilled workers. A negligible portion were self-employed (1.3%) or hawkers (1%). Clerical workers (3%), skilled workers (6%), and service workers (12%) accounted for a small proportion. 12% were retired. A small unemployed population existed, accounting for 4.4% of the working population in these two THAs. The ratio of non-working members to working members in the two THAs was higher than that of the Hong Kong population as a whole. In 1991 the overall ratio of Hong Kong was 1 while that of the two ATHAs was 1.2.

This implies that the working THA residents have to take care of more family dependents.

The income levels of most of the THA residents were not high, as shown in Table 5.7. More than 90% of the THA households reported that their household incomes were lower than the median household income in 1991 of Hong Kong as a whole, which was HK$9,964.[31] The income bracket HK$6,000-9,000 stands out as a significant modal group in the case of the Kowloon Bay THA with about two-fifths (39.3%) of its residents falling into it. But we notice significant variations between the two THAs. One-third (32%) of the Ping Shek THA residents fall into the income bracket of less than HK$ 3,000 while about one-fifth (22%) of the residents of the Kowloon Bay THA fall in the same bracket. The residents of this ATHA may encounter more hardship than the Kowloon Bay THA residents.

Occupation	Kowloon Bay THA	Ping Shek THA
Manual*	24.5	26.4
Unskilled*	32.4	26.0
Skilled	6.0	5.8
Clerical	3.4	2.4
Self-employed	0.9	1.6
Services	9.1	14.7
Hawkers	0.9	1.2
Unemployed	4.8	4.0
Retired	11.3	11.9
No Answer	6.7	6.0
Total	100.0	100.0
Sample size (n)	879.0	497.0
Working population**	738.0	418.0
Non-working population	912.0	490.0
Ratio of working members to non-working members	1.24	1.17

Table 5.6 Occupation of the THA Residents by THA (%)

Note: * Manual workers include drivers, workers in the construction sector, and workers in decoration and renovation. Unskilled workers refer to deliverymen, watchmen and factory workers.
  ** The figures exclude the retired and unemployed.

Source: *Author's survey*

Monthly Household Income (HK$)*	Kowloon Bay THA	Ping Shek THA
less than 3 000	21.6	32.0
3 000 - 6 000	34.5	33.6
6 000 - 9 000	39.3	26.0
over 9 000	4.6	8.5
Total	100	100

Table 5.7   Monthly Household Income by THA (%)

Note: * 1 Pound = $HK14 in 1991
      ** The median of household income in 1991 was HK$ 9 964 (Hong Kong Census and Statistics Department, 1993:139)
Source: Author's survey

Table 5.8 also shows a higher percentage of children under 15 than the overall percentage of Hong Kong. By contrast, the percentage of elderly residents is close to the overall percentage of Hong Kong. The lower percentage of the age group 15 - 34 indicates a smaller population of young people in the ATHAs.

Age Group	Kowloon Bay THA	Ping Shek THA	Overall percentage of Hong Kong*
Under 15	30.2	28.2	20.9
15 - 34	28.8	28.5	36.5
35 - 64	32.1	33.9	33.9
65 or over	8.9	9.4	8.7
Total	100	100	100
n	1,645	905	5,522,281

Table 5.8   Age Group of the THA Residents by THA, 1991 (%)

Note: * Figures in this column are drawn from Hong Kong Census Report, 1991.
Source: Author's Survey

The sex ratio in these ATHAs is similar to that of Hong Kong. Our findings indicate a slightly higher percentage of males in these ATHAs, accounting for 56% of the population in 1991. In Hong Kong the percentage of males was 50% in the same year. Perhaps the larger male population in the THAs is due to the one person households which are predominately male.

In brief, most of the ATHA residents were immigrants, the majority of whom were engaged in manual and unskilled work, had more young dependents to feed, and had resided in Kwun Tong for almost a decade. Their household income was much lower than that of most Hong Kong people. We can understand why they chose to stay in the poor living conditions of the ATHAs. Waiting to be rehoused by the Housing Department in permanent accommodation seemed be their only option, since most of them could not afford to purchase flats in either the public or private sector. The ATHA residents were not only suffering from their relatively deprived social positions, but also from the inequality engendered by the inaction of the Housing Department in respect of clearance of ATHAs.

Summary

This chapter has attempted to identify the reasons why the ATHAs became a political issue. The first factor is related to the Housing Department's reluctance to clear the ATHAs because ATHAs continue to fulfil an important political function as long as clearance of squatter areas is needed. We also see that the ATHA residents were compelled to take the issue to the street because there was no alternative for them to be rehoused. HOS flats were too expensive and the public rental housing flats obtained from trawling were too far away from the urban districts. Consequently they were obliged to wait until appropriate flats could be allocated, or clearance carried out.

We also delineated the chronology of the ATHA protest and described the characteristics of the people involved in this issue. As we shall be discussing the specific forms of action and the organizational structure of these activists in the following chapters, we did not discuss these in detail here.

To sum up, the following features of this protest have been highlighted. Firstly, the issue was articulated by local concern groups in various ATHAs with the support of volunteer organizers and community social workers. Their involvement gave rise to the formation of a coalition among various ATHAs, an acronym which refers to THAs which have existed for more than seven years. Secondly, the protest lasted for almost four years. It is interesting to note that this kind of urban minority can succeed in conducting a protest campaign with this degree of continuity. Thirdly, the form of action taken by both the coalition and individual THA residents groups tends to be 'polite'. Compared with the protests of the 1980s, the degree of militancy appears to have lessened. As shown by Lui (1984), throughout the protest against rent increases in the early 1980s the THA residents used sleep-ins to pressurize the Hong Kong Housing Department - the organization responsible for THA policy. In the early 1980s the urban movements were more radical in their forms of action and violent protest actions were occasionally taken. This comparison raises the question of why radical action was not employed in this case. Lastly, another prominent feature of the ATHA protest was the lack of politicians' involvement. It is surprising to see that when Hong Kong is undergoing a process of democratization, politicians seem uninterested in urban politics.

In the following chapters we shall make use of the theoretical model presented in Chapter 2 to analyze the ATHA protest in order to understand why local protest has the features described. The ATHA protest also raises several questions concerning the origin of the protest activities, the development process, the strategies as well as tactics employed by protesters, and the effect of the protest activities, which will be analyzed and discussed in the following chapters. In the next chapter we examine the relationship between the ATHA protest and the political opportunity structure, and seek to comprehend why the ATHA issue could not be handled within the formal political structure.

Notes

1. See the memorandum of the Committee of Management and Operation of the Housing Authority, *The Clearance Plan of Temporary Housing Areas - A Five Year Forecast*. Document Number MOC 100/90 p. 5.
2. Redevelopment is a remedial policy enabling the government to solve the problems caused by corruption in the 1960s. In the early 1980s the government admitted that there were 26 blocks on public housing estates which were below safety standards. Although they had only been built within the past 20 years, their building structure showed deficiencies and they were regarded as not strong enough. All these problems were owing to corruption between the officials and the constructors involved in the public housing construction projects. In the mid-1980s the court sent some of the construction company bosses to jail and the government proposed a redevelopment project to demolish all the twenty-six problematic estates. Later, the government announced that about 100 blocks on public housing estates built in the 1960s and 1970s were not up to construction standards. Therefore, the sub-standard blocks were to be demolished according to the schedule of the redevelopment policy. On the other hand, the Mark I and II (or B-Type) estates built in the 1950s were old and undoubtedly fell below contemporary living standards, both in terms of facilities and space. Consequently, the redevelopment policy also covered the demolition and redevelopment of such aged public housing estates. It was reported by the Chairperson of the Housing Authority that in 1991 it would need 78,000 units to cater for those affected by redevelopment in the coming 6 years, which is about 34% of total production in the same period.
3. See Hong Kong Housing Authority. 1993. *Memorandum for the Management and Operations Committee: Clearance Programme for Temporary Housing Areas*. 6 December 1993. File Ref. : L/M (1) in HD(H) THCHQ 2/25/1.
4. A survey shows that only 2.1% of the respondents indicated their preference for HOS flats. See Lui, Wong and Ho, 1994. In our survey on three ATHAs, only about 10% of the respondents reported that they planned to purchase HOS flats.
5. Since the 1970s, the lack of urban land has forced the government to create usable land in the New Territories in order to meet the demand arising from growth in the industrial and commercial sectors (Ho, D., 1989; Keung, 1985; Sit, 1982). Public rental housing estates in the New Territories facilitated internal geographical mobility, allowed people to move to the new towns and created more space in urban areas (Leung, 1980; 1983; Sit, 1982). Moreover, the population in Kowloon and New Kowloon dropped from 2.5 to 2.0 millions in the 1980s. The share of these areas in the total population decreased from 49.2% to 35.8%. By contrast, the population of the New Territories recorded a significant growth in the 1980s. The population increased from 1.4 to 2.4 millions, and its share of the total population increased from 26% to 42%. In the last decade the population of public housing tenants in Hong Kong Island and Kowloon dropped slightly, whilst Shatin and Tsuen Wan increased by 240,000 and Tuen Mun plus the rest of the New Territories increased from 40,534 to 384,744. The fourth generation new town Tseung Kwan O in Junk Bay was built in the

mid-1980s and within two years from 1987 to 1989, 24,398 people moved into the three public housing estates in this new town. See Hong Kong Government, 1993: 46-47.

6   The 1991 Census Report substantiated this view, finding that 'the importance of Housing Authority housing in the new towns compared with other sectors is clearly shown. Of the 203,900 households having moved into the new towns, 76,500 were residing in Housing Authority rental blocks (Group A) and a further 37,700 in Housing Authority home ownership estates' (Hong Kong Government, 1993:113).

7   A territory-wide survey of THA residents found that 'a general tendency was that households preferred locations of rehousing which were within or close to the district they were now living in. It was particularly evident among districts in urban areas such as Hong Kong (95%) and Kowloon/Tsuen Wan/Kwai Chung/Tsing Yi (94.7%) where the majority of households held such preference' (Lui, Wong and Ho, 1994:19). This supports the argument about the reluctance of the THA residents in urban districts to move to the New Territories.

8   The eligibility of THA residents for public housing estates was stated in Chapter 4. Before November 1991, all eligible THA residents were entitled to be rehoused in the same district. However, the Housing Department usually neglected this right.

9   These explanations were given by the Housing Department official on different occasions at which the author was present.

10 These three locations had been categorized as new towns, situated on the fringe of the urban areas before the late 1980s. Since then they were redefined by the government as extended urban areas.

11 In 1988 the Pak Tin THA launched a protest against the THA clearance policy which ignored the long existing THAs. At that time, the Pak Tin ATHA protest was merely a single localised instance, having not elevated the issue to a territory-wide protest.

12 See The Oriental News, 25th September 1990. According to the article, the report admitted that among the 23 THAs which have been in existence for more than seven years about 10% had leakage problems and deterioration; 2,000 units had water leakage and 372 units were affected by white ants.

13 See *Newsletter of the Caring Group for the Temporary Housing Policy*. April 1990, Issue No. 1.

14 CGTP is a sub-committee of a neighbourhood association called the Joint Committee of the Temporary Residents Association (JCTRA). This sub-committee is basically composed of social workers whose aim is to obtain and analyze information relevant to current housing policy in order to facilitate the actions taken by the JCTRA. In the early 1990s, one THA resident was so interested in policy analysis that he was involved in the sub-committee. The JCTRA is a coalition, formed by THA representatives and aided by community social workers. The objectives of this neighbourhood association are to scrutinize, examine and evaluate current THA policy. If necessary, social actions are organized to influence the development of THA policy.

15 The eighteen THAs are Tai Wo Ping, Hong Ning Road, Kowloon Bay II & III villages, Ping Shek, Shun Kee, Shatin Tau, Tai Chung Kiu, Lai King phase I-V, Welfare Road, Wong Chuk Hang, Fat Kwong Street, Lai Chi Kok Road, Pak Tin, Shuen Wan, Yue

Wan, Lai King, Pak Kok and Cheung Wan. Some information about the relatively older THAs is given in Table 4.4.

16. The Hong Kong People's Council on Public Housing Policy (PCPHP) has long been a pressure group on public housing policy, and it serves as an 'umbrella' organization linking up different local neighbourhood associations in Hong Kong. The CGTP is one of its affiliates, although the PCPHP never exercises its authority to influence the operation of the CGTP. The two groups function with total autonomy.

17. It was found that a convention prevails in the community social work field. When an NLCDP team is already working in an area, other social work organizations will avoid being involved in the same area. We contend that this kind of territoralization pervades the community social work field, and the volunteer organizers of the CGTP are bound to observe this tacit convention.

18. The findings of this survey supported the social workers' concern about the deterioration of the THAs. As for the problem of water leakage, 65% of the respondents' answers were affirmative. About 45% of the respondents said that they had encountered the white-ants infestation problem. When asked what solution they preferred, 54% indicated clearance, 15% wanted serious repair, 6% preferred clearance once the lease of the land expired and 9.4% gave no answer.

19. A leader explained that this definition was adopted after an official document of the government mentioned that the THA blocks were planned to exist for seven years.

20. It is necessary to point out that some of the actions may not be mentioned in this chronology. The author has obtained as much information as possible. However, some activities may not have been recorded in the minutes, and some minutes are missing. The files on which this chronology is based were provided by a community social worker who had been deeply involved in the leadership of the JCTRA.

21. The voluntary agencies are in part supported by the community chest which is funded by public donation. The government supports these voluntary agencies with a small amount of money. All the voluntary agencies enjoy full administrative autonomy; the checks and balances mechanism among them comes under the jurisdiction of the Hong Kong Federation of the Social Services, which serves as the link between the government and individual voluntary agencies.

22. In February 1990 the NLCDP team known as the Hong Kong Cooperative Kowloon Bay Community Development Programme was sent to Kowloon Bay, with responsibility for the provision of social services to about 3,800 residents in Kaki Yat, Kaki Tai and Kowloon Bay THAs.

23. This has some implications for the methodological formulation of this study. For discussion see Appendix 2.

24. Another group called the 'Joint Meeting of Temporary Housing Area Social Workers' is a forum for the exchange of information and experience across the NLCDP teams of different THAs. Its members normally meet once a month and by nature are not action-oriented. This joint meeting is insignificant to the ATHA protest except that it serves as a forum for the paid community social workers to exchange information.

25. See Appendix I for full details of the methods of this survey.

26 These are the estimated figures for urban planning. See *Urban Planning Report - 1988, Kwun Tong District*. Hong Kong: Hong Kong Government.
27 This plan was stated in a document distributed to the District Board in 1990, entitled *The Report on the Progress of the Engineering Plan in Kwun Tong District*, the Urban Council, 1990. As stated in an official document entitled *Kwun Tong District Programme, 1988 Edition*, the proposal for the land currently located in the Ping Shek THA was to build a playground. We did not find any plans for the use of the land occupied by the Kowloon Bay THA. This indicated that in 1989-90 the government had no plan for the future usage of this piece of land.
28 Less than one-tenth (7.6%) of the ATHA residents had moved from public and private housing. About one-tenth of respondents either gave no answer, or had moved from mainland China. Only 3.5% moved from other THAs.
29 The percentage of residents living in Kwun Tong before moving to the Kowloon Bay and the Ping Shek THAs were 79% and 71% respectively.
30 There is no variation across the THAs. But the figures may not reflect the real situation of the residents. About one-third of the interviewees were not able to indicate the work location of some of their household members. The no response rate to this question in the Kowloon Bay, the Ping Shek, and the Hong Ning Road THAs were 35.9%, 22.1% and 23.3% respectively. The figures in the text excluded the cases giving no answer.
31 The data about income may be incorrect. There are three factors which may have affected the quality of the data obtained from our survey. Firstly, the respondents might be sensitive to this sort of question as there was no trust between the interviewer and the respondents. If the respondents thought that the data might be obtained by the Housing Department, they might lie. On the other hand, most respondents or the breadwinners were wage earners, and their wages might not be fixed. Hence, it would be quite difficult for them to figure out their exact monthly household income. Thirdly, some respondents did not know the income of other family members.

6 No Through Road: Limited Political Opportunities for ATHA Residents

Introduction

In this chapter we shall discuss the role that the political opportunity structure played in the mobilization process of the Aged Temporary Housing Areas protest. Drawing on the theoretical frameworks elaborated in Chapter 2, we highlight three aspects of the political context: the formal political structure, the competition and the shifting balance of political power among the actors who are involved in the channels of articulation, and the social composition of these actors. We argue that together these three aspects determine the potential for a social movement to become involved in the political system and to have an effect on policies.

Our discussion starts with a brief summary of the changing political context of the late 1980s, pointing in particular to two processes of change involving the formal political structure and the channels of articulation. We shall argue that these changes to a very large extent determined the possibility of the two THA local concern groups securing third party support. We shall be looking at how the government responded to the change in the political system, and the impact of this response on the social movement sector. We will be arguing that the government established more statutory organizations in order to reduce its involvement in many areas of public and social services, thereby rendering itself less likely to be the target of political demands from the grassroots.

As has been illustrated in Chapter 3, the 1997 issue and the introduction of direct election into the formal political system attracted much attention among politicians and social activists. Thereafter the focus of political discourse fell mainly into the areas of Sino-British relations and the democratization of the political structure. Since democracy was considered to be the best means of ensuring the autonomy of Hong Kong vis-à-vis the Chinese Government, the political parties and pressure groups focused their attention on consolidating the democratic elements in politics through electoral politics, rather than participating in direct action. As most elected politicians were eager to strengthen their positions inside the formal political structure, which was regarded as the only 'legitimate' channel for influencing political decisions, lobbying and working through the formal political structure were encouraged while confrontation strategies were to a large extent regarded as inappropriate in an era of democratization. Many political parties and pressure groups dissociated themselves from the housing movement, and consequently, the ATHA issue was unable to attract much third party interest and support.[1] We contend that this change had an impact on the housing movement in general and on the ATHA protest in particular. We contend that the ATHA issue emerged and developed in a context where minorities' housing issues were likely to be edged off the political agenda of pressure groups and political parties.

Having outlined the changes in the political structure in Chapter 3, we place more emphasis here on examining the relations between the actors and the political system. In section 6.1 we look at the restructuring of the state and its impacts on the housing movement. Section 6.2 considers the actors involved in the articulation channels and looks at how competition and the shifting balance of political power in the formal political structure led to the marginalization of housing issues. Section 6.3 examines the relationships between the ATHA protesters and the actors involved in the polity. In the final section, we draw on our analysis to put forward some remarks about the relationship between the working class protests and the structure of political opportunities.

Two Changing Processes in the Political Structure

In Chapter 3, we periodized the 1970s and the 1980s into two respective stages, namely the pre-democratization stage and the stage of transition to democracy. During the first period, Hong Kong experienced an unprecedented explosion of urban movements in a political context dominated by a closed colonial administration. In the hope of undermining the legitimacy of the colonial, undemocratic and anachronistic regime, grassroots political organizations focused on the attendant problems in transport, social welfare, housing, education, and on grassroots discontents in order to expose the poor administration of the government. Among them, coalitions and alliances were formed as a result of their advocacy of anti-colonialism and pro-democratization. In the context of a colonial adminstration characterized by few channels of political participation, pressing for welfare rights is equivalent to implicitly pressing for political rights. Hence, urban movements were considered to be a viable and necessary social force for protesting against the colonial government, for the advocacy of populism, and for promoting the welfare of Hong Kong people. In short, this period was quite favourable to the growth of urban movements.

In the period of transition to democracy, the political system remained to a large extent closed and controlled by the government. The two Councils, namely the Legislative and the Executive Councils, were still dominated by the interests of capitalists and ex-British trading companies (Davies, 1989; Lau, 1982; Scott, 1989). Nevertheless, there were increasing political challenges to the political dominance of the government. In response, the state initiated a process of restructuring and established a group of policy-making bodies which were largely unaccountable to the Legislative Council. Also, direct election was introduced into the Councils. We contend that the political conditions in this period were not as favourable for the urban movements as they had been in the previous period, because the political rights movement gradually detached itself from the urban movement. In the following pages, we outline and discuss the impacts of these changes in order to substantiate this argument.

The Structural Change of the Political System: The Effect of the Creation of the Housing Authority on External Challenges

In the early stage of transition to democracy when the District Boards system was established and the Legislative Council was opened up, the political dominance of the colonial regime and pro-government politicians was being challenged. As has been discussed in chapter 3, the introduction of direct election on the basis of universal franchise and the establishment of functional constituencies allowed elected grassroots representatives to participate in the decision-making process on territory-wide policies through the Legislative Council. In the late 1980s, with a majority of elected members (39 out of 60) returned from geographical and functional constituencies, the proportional representation of the electoral system was significantly increased. This victory seems to indicate the strong political power of grassroots representatives and an expansion of political opportunity. Pressure groups and interest groups subsequently took the formal political system to be their major platform for the advancement of the grassroots' interests.

Nevertheless, we should not lose sight of a noteworthy restructuring of the formal political system which diminished the Legislative Council's scope of authority. This restructuring involved the growth of 'non-departmental appointed public agencies' (hereafter, NDAPAs) - a term suggested by Johnson that denotes 'the appointed public agency established by statute or ministerial decision to perform executive tasks in place of a central government Department or elected local authorities' (1982:207). The situation in Hong Kong is slightly different from the nature of the NDAPAs defined by Johnson. While the NDAPAs in Britain have been designated to perform executive tasks, their counterparts in Hong Kong are policy-making or recommendation-making bodies. The NDAPAs in Hong Kong are responsible for areas which have a direct effect on the livelihoods of the grassroots, including transport, medical services and public housing.[2]

Some distinct features of this kind of NDAPA can be identified: 1) all the members are appointed by the government; 2) they are responsible for assisting the government to plan and work out policies in the areas concerned; 3) they differ in their degree of autonomy to make policies and/or recommendations; and 4) they are accountable to the government, not to the public.

As far as the provision of public housing is concerned, the Housing Authority is the statutory body responsible for the construction, maintenance and management of all public housing estates. We argue that in the early 1970s, the Housing Authority had both an economic and a political function: it was a strategic means by which the government could minimise its spending on public housing, and counter public protest.

In our view, the primary reason for establishing the Housing Authority is associated with the changing economic and political context in the early 1970s. Prior to this, the provision of public rental housing had been crucial to the government's role in land administration. As shown in Chapter 4, squatter clearance and urban renewal moved people out of the valuable urban areas, creating more land for sales and for meeting the demands arising from industrialization and urbanization. Forced removal of the squatters and tenants from urban renewal areas without rehousing them, however, would engender grievances and ignite political tension. It was necessary for the government to provide public housing in order to minimize the risk of an eruption of political challenges (Keung, 1985).

In the 1970s, housing demands arising from squatter clearance in urban areas decreased, but after the riots in the late 1960s, the government was forced to recognize the raised political consciousness of the Hong Kong people and their increasing demands for government involvement in the provision of basic needs. Moreover, the two riots had shown that dissatisfaction with social hardship could translate into a political threat. To counteract any such threat, the government was compelled to tackle the housing problems. In 1973, a Ten Year Housing Programme was announced, aiming at rehousing 1.8 million people. Since this new public housing policy involved a massive amount of resources and funding, the government was forced to find a means of reducing its financial commitment to public housing provision (Ho, 1989; Pryor, 1983; Smart, 1992).

The restructuring of the Housing Authority to a statutory body in 1973 provided the government with a mechanism to minimize the financial burden of public housing provision. The government imposed the principle of self-financing onto the Housing Authority and thereby found its justification for reducing its direct cash injection. Since then, excepting that land is provided free and a special interest rate is granted, all the Housing Authority's loans, whether through the Government's Development Loan Fund or direct cash injection, must be repaid. As has been pointed out, with this measure there is no provision of 'direct outlays of public funds that are not recoverable' (The Hong Kong Justice of Peace Commission, 1979:64). On the other hand, rent became the major source of funding for the provision of public housing, and was set at a level which made it possible to cover the recurrent estate expenses, the cost of construction work and the repayments to the government. It has been pointed out by Lui that the financial constraints imposed by the self-financing policy subjected all forms of public housing to the need for a constant review of rents, and hence created 'conditions for making the rent issue a tension between the government and the public housing tenants' (1984:75).

Apart from its economic aim, the Housing Authority was expected to perform the political function of countering public protest. This was reflected in the composition of its membership. The Housing Authority coopted prominent members of the community onto its committees. These appointments comprised professionals, businessmen, and most importantly, the grassroots representatives put forward by residents associations. As grassroots representatives were coopted, the government proclaimed that the Housing Authority was representative of the public interest and that policies were largely formulated in accordance with the grassroots' preferences. However, in our view, the claim that public housing policies were being passed with consensus is an illusion. The membership of the Housing Authority was dominated by business interests, and pro-government appointed members always outnumbered those connected with grassroots associations.[3] This arrangement offered the government a means of ensuring the involvement of business interests in the decision-making process. The appointed members in turn could implicitly function as gatekeepers, whose efforts would ensure that public housing policies were kept largely in line with the general guidelines laid down by the government.

Moreover, the grassroots representatives in the Housing Authority found it difficult to develop a strong opposing political force inside the authority vis-a-vis the pro-government and business interests because they were assigned to different sub-committees responsible for different policy areas. This aptly illustrates how the government took advantage of the Housing Authority to deal with the mounting tensions of public housing issues.

Since 1988, the economic and political functions of the Housing Authority have been reinforced. As discussed in Chapter 4, since that time the Housing Authority has been both administratively and financially independent. After granting the Housing Authority its autonomy, the government was no longer responsible for the provision of public housing, except that it provides land for this purpose. The administrative link between the government and the Housing Authority was severed in 1988 when the government cancelled the post of Secretary for Housing. The parameters for public housing policies were laid down by the government in the Long Term Public Housing Strategies which sets the target for total production before 2001 and the proportion of each type of building to be constructed. Working under these basic guidelines, the Housing Authority is only accountable to the Governor of Hong Kong.

This restructuring of the Housing Authority resulted in a relocation of decision making in respect of public housing policies from the formal political system to a statutory body, effectively constructing a barrier against external political challenges.

The first thing to note, is that with the establishment of the Housing Authority, the Legislative Council appears to have nothing more to do with public housing policy. The only available channel for the Legislative Councillors to influence public housing policy is through the Housing Committee of the Council. This committee can summon the Head of the Housing Department to explain any problems which concern the councillors. However, as the Housing Authority is not accountable to the Legislative Council, the councillors have no authority over it.[4] This clearly shows the lack of accountability of the Housing Authority to the public, and this is still the major criticism levelled by social activists and politicians. The removal of the Housing Authority from the formal political structure renders fruitless any external challengers' efforts to work through the Legislative Council to influence decision-making pertaining to public housing issues.

Second, the small number of grassroots representatives, scattered among different sub-committees of the Housing Authority, are not strong enough to secure grassroots interests. This point is supported by a member of the Hong Kong United Democrats Party (HKUD), Mr. Lee Wing Tat, who claimed that despite being a member of the Housing Authority, he was of little help to the housing movement because he was not a member of the Management and Operations Sub-Committee which is responsible for all policies relating to the production and allocation of public housing.[5] Additional problems arise when the grassroots representatives appointed by the government have different backgrounds and political orientations, which makes it difficult for them to form a strong coalition within the Housing Authority.[6]

Thirdly, the division of responsibility between the Housing Department and the Housing Authority leads to confusion about which agency is responsible for public housing policy. It is not easy for the public to distinguish between policy and administration matters. Confusion about the responsible agents for public housing policy creates a bureaucratic hurdle that the housing movement activists must surmount in order to influence public housing policy. This is also one of the difficulties the ATHA protesters encountered. As far as THA policy is concerned, social activists and social workers find it difficult to locate the person responsible for clearance policy.

In short, in the 1980s the degree of openness in the formal political structure was relatively higher in the Legislative Council than before. However, the government has reduced the scope of influence of electoral politics on public housing policies by the establishment of an undemocratic body, namely the Housing Authority. Moreover, the small number of grassroots representatives on the committees of the Housing Authority are not powerful enough to develop an opposing political force to the pro-government Housing Authority members. Therefore, confronted with the dominance of pro-government members and the lack of any democratic procedures in the Housing Authority, external challengers are unable to gain access to the decision-making process in respect of housing policies.

Changes in the Social Movement Sector

Having examined the characteristics of the formal political system, we now move on to explore the shifting balance of power and political competition in the polity of Hong Kong. We will be focusing on two aspects of the political context, the changing relationship between political rights movements and urban movements, and the growing dominance of political parties.

In the early 1990s, competition within the social movement sector emerged because of two changes, namely, the separation of the political rights movement from urban movements, and the formation of political parties. We argue that the restructuring of the formal political system precipitated these two changes with the result that housing movement organizations, such as residents associations, community action groups, local concern groups, neighbourhood associations etc., began competing with the political parties.

We have examined the restructuring of the formal political system in Chapter 3, therefore only a summary of its salient features is presented here.

As has been discussed, the period of pre-democracy was characterized by a political system which was effectively closed off to the grassroots, and few grassroots political activists were involved in the formal political system as polity members. Although the government established the City District Offices (CDO) and the Mutual Aid Committee Scheme (MACS) in order to form a link with the grassroots, political activists distrusted these two schemes because they were government-sponsored and dominated by pro-government members. Activists of the political rights movement and urban movements therefore consolidated their strength by working with the grassroots. These 'outsiders' or 'challengers', defined as excluded groups 'whose interests are routinely 'organized out' of institutionalized political deliberations because of their lack of bargaining leverage' (McAdam, 1982:24), spent many years rooting out social inequalities and injustices, highlighting the poor living conditions of some Hong Kong people and, through their use of unconventional tactics, pressuring the government to deal with social problems. By articulating social problems and housing problems, not only were the protests drawing attention to the poor living conditions of working class people but also to the undemocratic nature of the formal political system. At this stage, the urban movements and political rights movement went hand-in-hand and enjoyed a period of 'honeymoon' (Lui, 1984; 1993).

In addition to their strong links, the urban and political rights movements shared three common characteristics. First, in contrast to the established political groups, or polity members, who 'regularly consult with governmental authorities and routinely provide input into decision-making bodies and [who] have some effect on the policies adopted' (Lo, 1992:230), neither type of movement was recognized by the authority or received any political advantage. Secondly, neither type of movement adopted the *market mode of resource mobilization* which relies on paid staff to obtain resources through enlisting widespread support. Instead, they employed a *communal mode of mobilization* relying on substantial personal commitments and limited community resources. Their objective was to mobilize people of a common category to participate in protest and disruptive activities to fight for their interests, and they needed highly committed activists whose availability could match the ebb and flow of specific local confrontations. Thirdly, most of their intervention strategies took the form of direct action, known as a 'tenant movement' or 'community action'. When an issue or a problem was identified, the activists organized meetings, set up representative groups, worked out the objectives of the protest and then set in train a series of social protests. Their legitimacy came from the community's participation and their power was acquired by the solidarity of people.

In the period of transition to democracy, the opening up of the formal political system led to changes in the social movement sectors. As has been pointed out in Chapter 3, there were a number of changes in the political context. Firstly, through election more political and social activists gained seats on the District Boards, and most believed that this access to the formal political structure would enhance the capacity of the grassroots to influence policy change. Secondly, the intensity of the political debates on the 1997 issue diverted the attention of political and social activists towards the struggle for greater democracy in the formal political system and the question of Hong Kong's future relations with mainland China. Full democratization of the formal political system was perceived to be one of the most important means of ensuring the political autonomy and economic prosperity of Hong Kong after 1997.[7] Accordingly, political activists invested most of their efforts in pressing for full direct election. As a result, urban movements received less attention from political groups. The political rights movement gradually detached itself from the urban movement as a result of their different political concerns and demands.

In the late 1980s, the relationship between the two movements was further undermined when political parties were formed and came to play the leading role in Hong Kong politics. The growing significance of the political parties had the effect of widening the gap between the political rights movement and the urban movements. There were differences between them in terms of objectives and strategies. The political parties were primarily concerned with political issues related to direct elections and the future relationship of Hong Kong with mainland China. Therefore urban problems and housing issues were relegated to a lower position on the political agenda.

As far as strategy is concerned, political party members, having become polity members, were more inclined to adopt the market mode of mobilization, wielding their influence by lobbying public officials, preparing reports, and shaping public opinion.[8] Lui argued that electoral politics entails a different logic from that of community politics. Community politics are essentially issue-specific, with emphasis on sectional interests, spontaneity and confrontation, whereas political parties 'are election-oriented, with an eye on the development of their influence over various constituencies. Their emphasis is on the form of organization and political negotiations. Although they must be responsive to the interests of their constituencies, they have to accommodate wider concerns and be ready to make compromises' (Lui, 1993:340). With less involvement in communal modes of mobilization, most political party members had little experience or knowledge of urban movements in general or of housing policy in particular. In our fieldwork, we found only a few political party members with past experience and a personal interest in urban issues. Confining our attention to the housing movement, we found a small number of political party members who were well informed about controversial issues in public housing policy. For example, the Hong Kong Association for Democracy and People's Livelihoods, one of the three pro-democracy political parties, basically consists of social workers and District Board members who are experienced in urban movements. Its chief coordinator, Mr. Fung Kin Kee, an elected Legislative Councillor and an appointed member of the Housing Authority, was the former chief coordinator of a pressure group - the People's Council on Public Housing Policy (PCPHP). Another example is Mr. Lee Wing Tat, a committee member of the largest political party, the United Democrats of Hong Kong, and a member of a sub-committee of the Housing Authority. He was active in the Kwai Chun and Kwai Ching Districts, and remained active in articulating housing issues. Both seemed to be more knowledgeable about housing issues than their parties. In brief, because there were only a few leading political party members who were interested in public housing issues, the lobbying activities of the housing movement activists were directed towards them. However, the sympathy of a few leading political party members was not enough to secure a link with the urban movement.

On the other hand, the leadership of the housing movement are wary of trusting the politicians. During the period of coalition, political groups developed with the support of local concern groups and made use of their resources for election campaigning. However, from the point of view of the grassroots leadership, there was no guarantee that the activists would follow the wishes of local concern groups 'when there were differences between the "party lines" of political groups and the demands of residents' associations' (Lui, 1993:338).[9] In addition, they worried that the politicians were promising much in their election campaigns and doing little for the grassroots afterwards. The response of the leadership was to retain the organizational autonomy of the local concern groups in order to protect the interests of the grassroots. They resisted any intrusion by politicians into the leadership of local concern groups. As a result, the division between political parties and the urban movement sectors widened. As shown in the 1991 election, the leading grassroots organization in the housing movement, the PCPHP 'made a U-turn, ended its "honeymoon" with electoral politics and moved back to its original position of a pressure group on public housing issues' (Lui, 1993:334).

This lack of trust was apparent on a number of occasions. First, we observed that some of the concern groups involved in the housing movement discouraged political party members from making appearances at protests. For example, in one protest, the staff members of the PCPHP did not allow the politicians to have access to the public address system in order to prevent them from giving a speech in front of the protesters. Second, we heard in our field observation that many leaders of the housing movement doubted the politicians' loyalty to the local concern groups. The leaders complained that the politicians were overconcerned with votes, rather than the genuine needs and problems of the grassroots. Third, some community social workers who played a crucial role in local mobilization promoted the concept of a 'civil society', putting more emphasis on the autonomy of grassroots organizations and less on working with politicians. The implicit aim of this move was to protect the interests of the local concern groups from any encroachment by political groups and parties. All these instances reflect the lack of trust and friendly relations between the two movement sectors.

In a nutshell, the growth of electoral politics has changed the relationship between the political rights movement and the housing movement. Alliances between them, though not impossible, are difficult to establish when they differ so fundamentally in terms of their mobilization strategy and political concerns, and trust and friendly relations between them are difficult to sustain.

Who Cares about the Housing Movement?

Having described the changes in the formal political structure and in the social movement sector, we now move on to examine the extent to which these changes have restricted the effectiveness of the articulation channels and of the actors involved in putting housing issues on the political agenda. We will do this by identifying the potential channels of articulation, examining the political orientation and practice of the actors involved in these channels, and evaluating their effectiveness in the articulation of housing issues. We identified six possible articulation channels that housing movement activists can use for lobbying and mobilizing support, namely, the Legislative Councillors, the District Board members, the political parties, interest and pressure groups, the trade unionists and social workers. The first three are in fact polity members whereas the other three basically act outside the formal political structure despite some connections with polity members.

The Legislative Councillors

We have argued that the Legislative Council is very weak in dealing with housing policy issues. As has been pointed out, the Council remained dominated by businessmen and professionals whose pro-government orientations reduced their commitment to working class people's interests. For the elected members, there is little formal political leverage available to influence housing policies. On account of the formal structure between the Council and the Housing Authority, the Council has no formal right to intervene in the policies passed by the Housing Authority.[10] The Housing Section of the Council, which is composed mainly of elected councillors, has the right to 'invite' Housing Department officials to attend its meetings and explain any relevant public housing policies. However, few changes can be achieved through this kind of involvement because the section is only entitled to clarification and explanation from the Housing Department and there is no formal authority for it to demand any alteration of policy. In a meeting between a pressure group and the Housing section, one of the members clearly expressed this sense of limited capacity:

> I think you know our situation. We can't do anything. Our section has no power to change the policies decided by the Housing Authority. Unless we change the Housing Ordinance which grants independence to the authority, it is useless for us to talk about the public housing policy (Mr. Pang, Legislative Councillor).[11]

Nevertheless, the councillors seemed to take this structural restriction as given, and had no intention of changing it. Recognizing the Legislative Council's lack of formal power to influence the decisions of the Housing Authority, the housing movement activists are aware that protest action directed toward the Council is of little help. Although protest activities, for example petitions, demonstrations and meetings, have been targeted at the

Legislative Council, most protestors thought of these actions as wasted effort.[12]

The District Boards

Like the Legislative Council, the District Boards have no formal connection with the Housing Authority. They are advisory institutions for local matters, such as public hygiene, administration of the hawkers, and organizing recreational activities. Executive tasks are passed to two implementing departments, namely the District Office and the District Management which are responsible for taking appropriate enforcement measures.[13]

Under each District Board is a Committee on Housing Matters through which members of the boards can channel their advice, criticism and suggestions about housing issues to the Housing Department. Members are entitled to seeking clarification and explanation of public housing issues. In addition, the committee can establish a special committee on a specific issue. In doing so, the Board members can exert pressure on the officials of the Housing Department. However, the possibility of establishing a special committee depends on the internal dynamics and the configuration of power among the political groups on different District Boards. The feasibility of putting a housing issue on the agenda of the District Boards varies across districts. We shall come back to discuss the role of District Boards in relation to the ATHA issue in the next section.

Generally speaking, by virtue of its lack of formal power, the District Boards system as a whole possesses very limited power to influence either the Housing Department or the Housing Authority. But the members of the District Board are helpful in obtaining relevant information on public housing policy.

To sum up, due to the arrangement of the formal political structure, neither the Legislative Council nor the District Boards are effective in articulating public housing issues.

The Political Parties

As suggested by the literature on political opportunity structures, for the purpose of understanding the relationship between political parties and housing movements, we should take into account a) the configuration of power in the political system which is said to be associated with the extent to which the issues of a social movement will be put on the political agenda (Kriesi, 1991) and b) the extent to which the formal electoral system shapes the articulation methods of the political parties.

We first examine the configuration of power in the political system. In the early 1990s, the configuration of power in the political system was largely constituted in terms of the major political issue concerning the future development of the electoral system, and the protagonists of this struggle were the pro-government/anti-direct election parties and the pro-democracy parties.[14] The Cooperation Resources Centre (CRC) represents the former type, and is mainly composed of the appointed members of the Legislative and Executive Councils. The three pro-democracy parties comprise the HKUD, the Meeting Points (MP) and the Hong Kong Association for Democracy and People's Livelihoods (HKADPL).

The pro-democracy wing was developed on the basis of community politics in the 1970s and the political rights movement in the 1980s, whereas the pro-government wing was basically composed of businessmen and professionals. For this historical reason, the pro-democracy wing insisted on pressing for more social services and advocating the interests of working class people. In contrast, the pro-government wing was very inexperienced in this respect. The CRC was averse to any growth in social welfare provision.

Nevertheless, the housing movement found it increasingly difficult to rally support from the pro-democracy political parties. There are several reasons for this.

First, competition in the political party system shapes the extent to which political parties are interested in housing issues. In 1992 the government announced that full direct election would be introduced into the Legislative Council in 1995. In other words, none of the members would be appointed members. This anticipated change led to competition between the pro-democracy and the conservative wings for future electoral support. One of their main targets was the middle class. The reason why the votes of the middle class became critical is clear. Public housing tenants, who account for almost half of the total population in Hong Kong, are surely the most important source of electoral potential. To the HKUD however, its members' long-term efforts in community betterment, localized mobilization and social movements had built up a very good reputation among most public housing tenants, hence they were confident of their ability to mobilize the support of the working class people (Tsang, 1993). In contrast, it was difficult for the CRC to form any allegiance with the public housing tenants because it had few connections with local concern groups and grassroots organizations. It would have been hard for them to compete with the HKUD for the support of the working class, especially since there is a general assumption that the votes of working class people are the 'cast iron' votes of the pro-democracy wing. But both the HKUD and the CRC conceived of the middle class vote as the major battleground because, whereas most working class people tend to vote for the pro-democracy parties, the majority of the middle class are neither entirely pro- or anti-democracy. Their political preferences were uncertain. Hence, articulating their interests is a means of gaining their electoral support. In 1992, the HKUD and HKADPL pressed for public housing specifically for middle class people. Despite being opposed to state intervention, the CRC supported this cause. Their action can be interpreted as an appeal to the middle class for the 1995 direct election. Simply put, the political parties have been compelled, by the changing formal political structure and political competition, to take a more active stance in rallying the support of the middle class.

Secondly, given the political context of keen competition in electoral politics, whether or not a housing issue is articulated by the political parties depends on the degree of electoral significance the people in question have. Because political parties are election-oriented, housing issues involving large populations are more likely to be taken up by them. The disputes over the Double Rent Policy affecting a large proportion of sitting public housing tenants and the provision of public housing to middle class people are typical cases. In contrast, the housing needs of minorities, such as single-person families, THA residents and squatters, only occupied a marginal position on the agendas of the political parties.

Apart from the political configuration of power, the formal electoral system has also to some extent determined who the responsible actors are for the articulation of local issues and shaped the extent to which the political parties are able to articulate local issues.

In 1991, the government divided Hong Kong into nine geographical constituencies which return 18 members to the Legislative Council. In the 1991 election, we can discern two types of candidate running for election. The first type had experience in community action and good connections with the grassroots organizations in their district. This type of candidate has worked at local level for a long time and is deeply involved in community politics. For example, the leader of the HKADPL, Mr. Fung Kin Kee, has been active in the Shamshuipo District and has gained a high reputation and strong support in this district. Another example is that of Mr. Lee Wing Tat and Chan Wai Ip - the leaders of the HKUD, who have both won seats on the District Board several times. This type of candidate can be called the 'communal' type. They simply need to maintain their connections with the local organizations within their constituency to win a seat on the Legislative Council.

In contrast, the second type of candidate consists of those who were more concerned with territory-wide issues, such as advocating the political rights of Hong Kong people. However, because of their involvement in the election on the basis of geographical constituency, they began to become involved in local politics. This type of candidate has been dubbed 'parachutist' by the press since they have no roots in the communities and few connections with grassroots organizations at local level. Among the 18 elected Legislative Councillors, 13 fall into this type of politician. Nine of them are leaders of the HKUD, including Szeto Wah, Man See Cheong, James To, Martin Lee, Lau Chin Shek, Conrad Lam, C.H. Huang, Yeung Sum and C. W. Fung; three are without any affiliation to political parties, including Emily Lau, Andrew Wong and C.W. Tai; and one is a member of Meeting Points, Mr. W.M. Lee.

After the 1991 election, the elected members of the political parties became local leaders in their constituencies. For the 'parachutist' type of politician who has relatively weak connections with the grassroots, it is necessary to forge a stronger link. Despite the establishment of local offices, the relationship between these elected members and the local people is at an embryonic stage. By contrast, the communal type of politician has a strong capacity for mobilization at local level. It is not surprising therefore that in districts where politicians of the communal type have been elected councillor local issues tend to receive more attention, whereas in districts where the parachutist type has been elected local issues are less likely to be the focus of their concerns. We argue that the extent to which politicians are able or willing to aid the grassroots to deal with local issues varies across districts. Its effects can be seen as follows.

First, as has been pointed out, politicians of the 'parachutist' type are adept at dealing with political rights and the 1997 issue, but weak in tackling local problems such as housing, transport and social services.

Moreover, as these party members represent a formal link between the political party and local political groups, local activists are encouraged to contact the politician assigned to their specific constituency area. Given that the majority of party members are uninterested in or have little knowledge of local issues, the likelihood of gaining assistance from the political parties is substantially reduced. For example, in the Kwun Tong district the local leader of the HKUD, Mr. Szeto Wah, has considerable experience and knowledge of education policy and political rights issues, but is not good at dealing with housing issues. Despite his commitment to solving the housing problems in his constituency, he admitted that his knowledge about public housing policy was too limited for him to be of any help. Meeting Points, one of the three pro-democracy political parties, is another case in point. Although it was formerly a pressure group, it has little experience of and few connections with community-based social activists. The manifesto for the MP election campaign in 1991 outlined the principles of its public housing policy, but the majority of its members were not very interested in or able to understand the issues put forward by the housing movement. In an interview in early 1992, the vice-chairman admitted that his party had not clearly worked out the principles of its public housing policy, even if there was ongoing controversy and debate in this respect.

Second, because district and issue based problems require communal skills to handle them, the local leaders of political parties need time to understand the crux of the issues and to learn communal mobilizing skills. In other words, they possess limited knowledge of communal mobilization.

Third, because they are required to simultaneously handle both territory-wide concerns and local issues, local leaders select those issues which they feel competent to deal with. This selection relates to the local leaders' personal experience and interests, and inevitably some issues will be given a lower priority. Although some of the political parties developed district-level offices to improve the efficiency of local leaders, most of these suffered from a shortage of manpower and resources, and their effectiveness in building a connection with the local district was thus thwarted.

To conclude, the political parties vary in terms of their capacity for dealing with housing issues. The prospect of change in the configuration of political power has diverted much of their resources into capturing middle class votes in the coming election. As a result, some housing issues, especially those relevant to the welfare and interests of marginal groups, receive little attention from political parties. In addition, without even a set of basic principles with regard to public housing policy, some of the political parties have not yet developed a systematic way of articulating the problems and issues concerning housing policy or of strengthening their connections with the grassroots. The geographical constituency system also limits the connection between the political party and local interests to only a few local leaders, and makes the chance of articulating local political issues dependent on their personal interests and experience.

Interest and Pressure Groups

In our view, the most salient housing movement organizations in early 1990s continued to be the community-based livelihood concern groups in certain districts and some territory-wide organizations, for instance the PCPHP, the People's Council on Squatter Policy, the Society for Community Organizing (SoCo) and the like.

The livelihood concern groups, such as those in the Tsing Yi, Tuen Mun, and Shamshuipo districts, are very active in local issues. As they are community-based, their effectiveness is largely confined to taking up issues within their local districts.

The PCPHP and SoCo are well developed and organized in articulating political demands concerning housing issues. Recently, SoCo has concentrated on the human rights movement and urban renewal. It largely employs a communal mode of mobilization and emphasises community development. On account of limited manpower and resources, its actions are confined to a few housing issues and districts, for example the single elderly in Tze Wan Shan and urban renewal in Tai Kok Tsui. The PCPHP stands at the forefront of the housing movement and has long been the 'watchdog' of public housing policy. As a political challenger, it also employs a communal mode of mobilization in order to strengthen and develop its connection with local people. In fact, the ATHA issue we study here is the result of its efforts in articulating local grievances. Its activities however, are constrained by limited resources. As the communal mode of mobilization requires considerable manpower to ensure local people's loyalty and commitment, the mobilizing tasks of the PCPHP are to a large extent dependent on assistance from volunteers and university students on placement.[15] Yet such kinds of external assistance tend to be unstable and only very short-term in nature.

The Trade Unionists

Trade unionism in Hong Kong has been weak for a long time. This can be explained by the fragmentation of the trade unions into left-wing and right-wing, the obsolete mobilizing style of the trade unionists and the constraints on their development imposed by the government (Leung and Chiu, 1991; Levin and Chiu, 1993; Levin and Jao, 1988; Ng and Levin, 1983). By virtue of their low degree of activity, trade unionists have paid little attention to housing issues and have seldom criticized public housing policies. Hence, their influence in this respect is very limited. At local level, the trade unions have basically failed to develop any structure for becoming involved in local politics. The failure of the trade unions in local politics and urban movements is due to their political orientation and historical development. One trade unionist, who is also a member of the Chai Wan District Board, explained:

> We have two contrasting views on the issues of involvement in local politics. I belong to the 'young' group, which is more inclined to participate in local politics, so I participated in the election for a seat on the district board. But the 'old' group does not accept this view. They still hold fast to the existing line of action, focusing the task of recruitment on the work place...I admit that we are very weak in community and local issues, we have no good connections or channels to help us understand the situations and the livelihoods of different communities (Miss Chan, trade unionist of the Federation of Trade Unions).

Moreover, there was a low level of membership in the 1970s among the left-wing trade unions, resulting from their initiation of and involvement in some violent incidents in the 1967 riots. Subsequently, much of their efforts and resources have been channelled into re-building the morale of the trade union members. But, this was not achieved by articulating social and political issues. Instead, the trade unions resorted to establishing themselves as social clubs, offering selective incentives like discounts on the purchase of home improvements, electrical appliances, food, and package holidays.

The left-wing trade unionists started to pay attention to local politics when none of their candidates whom they supported succeeded in the 1991 election. To them, this failure was attributable to the lack of a local network and their weak capacity to mobilize the grassroots. In response, they began to focus on public housing policy and general housing issues. However, because of their limited experience and knowledge of public housing issues, they have a long way to go towards developing the trade unions as a strong force in the housing movement.[16]

Social workers

The government has long recognized the political implications of social workers' involvement in community development projects. In 1985 the government disbanded the Community Work Units in the community centres which were run by the Government Social Work Department, and the responsibility for community development was transferred to another government department, namely the City and New Territories Administration Department. This change reflects the government's concern to prevent social workers from becoming involved in community development and promoting community participation.

The other channel for social workers to become involved in local politics is through the Neighbourhood Level Community Development Projects (NLCDP) - the only community development project in the social work profession.[17]

The NLCDP was set up in 1977 by the Committee on Neighbourhood Level Community Development Projects which is composed of representatives of social work agencies and government officials. According to the policy guidelines laid down by this committee, the NLCDP teams have been recruited to serve those areas with target populations ranging from 3,000 to 20,000, and which are identified as having 'special needs requiring more intensive services, e.g. squatter areas, licensed areas, floating population, etc.' (Committee on NLCDP, 1982:1).

Although the social work profession in the 1970s was radical and was able to act as an articulation channel for working class people, the NLCDP as an effective articulation channel for urban movements has been weakened by four factors.

Firstly, both the government and the policy-makers of the social work organizations regard the NLCDP solely as an agency for filling the gaps in social welfare provision. The basic orientation of the NLCDPs is designated as 'service-oriented and social workers of the projects develop programmes with a view to arousing community consciousness and participation' (ibid.:8). This general guideline translates into a number of objectives for the NLCDP teams which are:

1. to identify the needs of the community;
2. to promote interaction among residents;
3. to cultivate 'we-feeling' among residents;
4. to develop leadership;
5 to involve residents in launching activities; and
6. to provide social services.

As Wong (1988) pointed out, neither the government nor the social work profession regard NLCDPs as having any political inclination toward articulating social conflicts by identifying the problems of various public policies or employing social actions to promote the interests of their clients. The nature of the NLCDP is clearly designated by the decision-makers as social services-oriented.

Secondly, some frontline community social workers (CSWs) of the NLCDP teams dislike, and some do not find it necessary to use, violent and confrontational social action. Although there is no clearly stated regulation which prohibits frontline workers from taking social action as a means of advancing the interests of their clients, most of the workers feel that 'their supervisors would prefer the projects not to use the name of the agency for social actions, because this would embarrass the agency' (Yeung, 1987:67). Moreover, it was found that most of the frontline workers of the NLCDP teams believed that Hong Kong had become a prosperous city, and that few people were being deprived of basic necessities. On the other hand, they considered the government to be a very responsive institution in terms of its readiness to tackle social problems and to deliver help. To this kind of worker, there would be no point in using confrontational social action to press for policy change. The CSWs became less radical and as a result, as Yeung concluded, 'if conflict strategies had been popular in Hong Kong in the 1970s, they were now seldom employed' (1987:77).

Thirdly, evidence shows that the social work profession in the community development field has been undergoing a process of depoliticization. As social workers in Hong Kong are either civil servants employed by the Social Work Department, or professionals employed by voluntary agencies (VAs) which are partially funded by the government, the social work profession implicitly avoids being identified as a political force.

The 1980s gave rise to a debate over the possible conflicts of interest of social workers who play the role on the one hand of a professional worker, and on the other a politician. This debate indicated that several CSWs were opposed to the idea of becoming involved in politics. In the main they appeared to accept the view that the professional role of the social worker should be maintained and not be confused with the role of politician. Consequently, the expectation that social workers should serve their clients and act as helpers rather than agitators has been further reinforced (Mok, 1991).

Lastly, the NLCDP teams are set up by different social work organizations. In 1991 there were 51 NLCDP teams organized by 14 social welfare organizations. As the project involves different teams from different organizations, it is difficult for them to form a coalition, especially when the CSWs concerned are not expected to collaborate with other organizations and when communication and collaboration are time consuming. Even if a common issue arises, few communication networks or alliances are formed in order to advance their common interest.

In view of the limited effectiveness of this articulation channel constituted by the NLCDP teams, housing movements turn out to be dependent on the efforts of individual CSW who are more interested in dealing with territory-wide housing issues. Hence the possibility of transforming social grievances and grassroots discontent into a social movement appears to hinge on the interaction between the aggrieved grassroots and individual social workers who are concerned with housing policies.

In this section we have evaluated six possible channels of articulation in relation to housing issues. It can be seen that the current political context to the housing movement is not much more promising now than before. In the stage of pre-democracy, the Housing Authority retained its official tie with the government, and was thereby the target of grassroots' political demands. When the Housing Authority became more independent in the late 1980s, few formal articulation channels were available to the elected councillors of either the Legislative Council or the District Boards to pressurize the Housing Authority. Despite the opening up of the formal political system in the stage of transition to democracy, polity members found few official channels to influence public housing policy. Outside the formal political structure the trade unions are weak. Whether a housing issue is articulated by political party members is largely dependent on the personal interests and experience of individual party members. Moreover, the articulation channel provided by the political parties is district-dependent. In some districts, this channel is very effective, but in others it is not. Under such circumstances, the development of the housing movements relies on pressure groups and interest groups, but the effectiveness of these groups in articulating and sustaining a housing issue is limited by insufficient manpower and financial resources. This situation in fact explains the importance of CSWs in articulating housing issues. As CSWs are employed by social welfare organizations which are in turn backed by the government, they are more resourceful in developing community action and dealing with local issues. Nevertheless, we notice that there are few coalitions in the social work profession involved in organizing the housing movements, and we should avoid overrating the importance of CSWs in general in relation to the housing movement.

To sum up, the development of the housing movement in Hong Kong in the late 1980s and early 1990s has been affected by the closed political structure in relation to housing policy, the changing balance of power of the actors inside and outside the formal political system, and the political orientation of the actors. Our analysis demonstrates the complexities of the political structure and its likely impact on the housing movement as a whole. For convenience, we summarize our findings in Figure 6.1.

Locations in the Political Structure	Actors	Relationships with the target, i.e. the Housing Authority	Responses/Strategies of dealing with housing movements
Polity Members	The Legislative Council with uninterested appointed members and many inexperienced elected members with regard to housing issues	- limited formal power; - limited to consultation and requests for Housing Department officials to attend meetings	- not active in taking up issues; - a small number of political party members are interested in public housing issues, but do not have many connections with the grassroots

158 *Polite Politics*

Locations in the Political Structure	Actors	Relationships with the target, i.e. the Housing Authority	Responses/Strategies of dealing with housing movements
	The District Boards,	- very limited formal power; - only able to ask some middle level officials of the Housing Department to attend meetings	- depends on the degree of activity of the members in different districts and the personal interests of the district boards members
	Political Parties	- elected members in the two formal political institutions can influence the responsible government department	- the possibility of taking up housing issues depends on the personal experience, interests and efforts of some members; - places a high priority on middle class housing issue
Challengers	Interest Groups and Pressure Groups	- no formal relationship, resort to protest and informal connections	- with limited resources, active in different issues, domains and different districts
	Trade Unions	- no formal relationships with the target	- have not been interested in housing issues; - few connections with grassroots defined in terms of housing tenure
	Community Social Workers	- no formal relationships with the target; - the choice of tactics in dealing with the target is dependent on the orientation of the social workers	- strong connections with grassroots; - depends on the orientation and interests of different social work teams

Figure 6.1 Summary of the Political Openness, Orientation Towards Taking up Housing Issues, and the Articulation Strategies of the Actors in Different Articulation Channels in Relation to Housing Movements in the Early 1990s

The ATHA Issue and the Actors in the Political Structure

In the preceding analysis we argued that the Housing Authority is to a very large extent closed to housing movement activists. Because of the limited formal political opportunities for the Legislative Councillors to influence the Housing Authority, the efforts of political party members, pressure groups and social workers outside the formal political system play a crucial role in taking up issues and building up the strength of the grassroots to pressurize the Housing Authority and the Housing Department. In this section we draw on the findings in our fieldwork to examine how the local concern groups of the ATHAs advanced their political demands in such a political context. We argue that the ATHA protesters found it difficult to obtain support from the political actors because the political context was unfavourable to the development of protests initiated by the local concern groups of urban minorities.

In our view it is important to examine how these two local concern groups sought third party support in order to consolidate their own power. As has been discussed, among the existing articulation channels there were very few choices for the two local concern groups. Why was this so? In order to understand this phenomenon, we examine the connections and interactions between the two local concern groups and the actors involved in the channels of articulation. However, we will leave our discussion of the role of social workers and PCPHP volunteers in the protest to chapter 8.

Because the organizers of the two community actions were the social activists of the PCPHP, and the social workers of the Caritas NLCDP team were heavily involved in the protests, they need more detailed examination.

Among the four articulation channels, the trade unions seldom appeared on the agenda of the two local concern groups. Their lack of involvement in local politics resulted in few connections with the grassroots protesters and they rarely served as a channel of articulation. Consequently, the two local concern groups were left with two possible sources of external support: Legislative Councillors and the members of the District Boards, and it was to these targets that lobbying was therefore mainly directed.

The Members of the Legislative Council and the Two Local Concern Groups

Throughout the ATHA protest, the local concern groups attended several meetings with the members of the Legislative Council. The local concern group members did not expect very much from the councillors because experience showed that they would be of little help. As has been pointed out, most of the councillors were not knowledgable about the conditions and problems in the THAs, and their understanding of the situations and demands coming from the grassroots was chiefly derived from information provided by the Housing Department.[18] Not surprisingly, the council members responded to the protesters' questions by referring to the information and explanations provided by officials of the Housing Department. It was apparent that to most of the appointed members, repeating the official line to the representatives of the THA residents would not jeopardise their political position because they are not subject to electoral pressure. The elected party members on the other hand, might feel political pressure from the grassroots. However, as a rule they refer political demands to party members who are knowledgable about public housing policy, their explanation being that the party has specific members who are responsible for housing issues. In our view, these members were largely ignorant in respect of housing issues and this practice reinforces the articulation pattern that, as shown in the previous section, tends to be personal and district-dependent.[19]

The Members of Political Parties and the Two Local Concern Groups

Both concern groups of the Kowloon Bay and the Ping Shek THAs attempted several times to rally the support of politicians. But, as has been argued, the possibility of articulating a housing issue is dependent on the personal interest and orientation of the political party member playing the role of mediator between the political party and the local people. In the Kwun Tong District, Mr. Lee Wah Ming, a member of the Meeting Point, was the first politician who could claim to be informed about the ATHA issue. In April 1990 the residents association held an open meeting and invited Mr. Lee to show his concern and support. Mr. Lee did indicate his personal support of the protest, but after that did not actively assist the protest. In September 1991, both he and Mr. Szeto Wah, a member of HKUD, were running their election campaigns for seats on the Legislative Council. Both were invited to help the ATHA residents in the Kwun Tong District to press for early clearance. However, after showing up at a number of meetings and helping to arrange a meeting between the Kowloon Bay THA concern group and the Housing Department, Mr. Lee ceased to offer assistance to the concern groups in the Kwun Tong District. In 1992 Mr. Szeto was asked to help the Ping Shek THA residents and did visit the THA once, although no further assistance was offered.[20] He had, however, been actively involved in helping public housing tenants affected by the redevelopment project to press for local rehousing. Clearly, he was more inclined to offer help to this kind of tenant than to the ATHA residents. Perhaps, the larger population size of the public housing tenants was more significant to him than the plight of the ATHA residents at the time he was running his campaign for the 1991 election.

We also found that Mr. Szeto Wah was somewhat passive in the sense that he just did what the concern groups asked him to do. He showed little initiative to facilitate greater participation, and discussion about tactics and strategies was non-existent. His low degree of activism in mobilizing the grassroots can be explained by his personal view of his relationship with the CSWs working in the same district.

His assistant explained Mr. Szeto's conception of his role in local issues:

> Wah Suk [Mr. Szeto Wah - D. Ho] does intervene in social issues and projects which have been taken up by social workers. If social workers need our assistance, we are ready to be involved. (Interviewer: But why are you so passive?) Why are we so passive! Mainly because we know there are many social work organizations working in many districts. We want to collaborate with the social workers but we feel that they don't want to develop any close relationship with us. We know the reason. The reputation of councillors like Mr. Szeto Wah is very high. If he became too involved, the residents would depend upon his action and become passive. This would affect the self-development of the residents...Some social workers accept our involvement but some do not...Wah Suk's policy is that if the social workers ask us to help out, we must go to help, if not, we shall not put much of our resources into it...if the kaifongs (the residents) do not ask us to go, we shall not go at all because it is inappropriate and, with our limited resources, a high degree of activism is unfeasible (Interview with a, personal assistant of Mr. Szeto Wah, a member of the Legislative Council in Kwun Tong District).

Another reason for Mr. Szeto Wah's low degree of activism in local issues is his worry about giving false hopes to the residents affected by housing policy. As his assistant explained, when it is uncertain whether protests can bring favourable results, he will not actively take action in mobilizing the grassroots.

Mr. Szeto's personal orientation towards community action derived from the close relationship established between the political rights movement and the housing movement in the pre-democracy stage. Although the two movements diverged in the following period, the activists still thought of each other as 'comrades'. Throughout the protests initiated by the two ATHA concern groups, Mr. Szeto conceived of his relationship with CSWs as that of an ally rather than a competing rival. As a result, they refrained from doing anything that might undermine that alliance. Accordingly, the extent of Mr. Szeto Wah's involvement turned out to be dependent on the local concern groups' initiative to push him to act.

There was another instance indicating the importance of the personal inclination of the Councillors. Mr. Szeto Wah and Mr. Fung Kin Kee were invited to attend an open meeting of the Kowloon Bay THA concern group in September 1991. Mr. Fung's performance at the meeting was strange in that he appeared to adopt the role of a member of the Housing Authority and attempted to explain the relevant clearance and rehousing policies to those present. The concern group members later interpreted his behaviour to mean he was uninterested in their problems, so they did not try to seek his assistance at a later stage of the protest.

Another potential channel for the two THA concern groups to seek assistance from political parties was through Mr. Lee Wing Tak who is the key person in the HKUD with regard to housing issues. As someone who has been very active in dealing with housing problems in the Kwai Chun district, Mr. Lee is very well-informed about housing issues. Consequently the two ATHA concern groups joined the coalition - the Joint Committee of the THA Residents Association - to meet Mr. Lee about the problems in the THAs. When replying to the question about the best way for the THA residents to get their issue onto the agenda of the Legislative Council, Mr. Lee asked the residents of the two THAs to contact the Legislative Councillors in the Kwun Tong districts instead of asking him to take it up, because, as he explained, it was the local councillors' responsibility to take care of local issues.

It appears that the internal arrangement of the political parties unwittingly narrows the range of articulation channels for the THA protesters, presenting the residents with a dilemma. When seeking support from the political parties, residents are asked to contact the Councillors in their local districts.[21] However, on finding that the local district councillor is not knowledgeable about housing issues, the residents are compelled to approach informed members of the political parties, who in turn tend to pass responsibility onto the local district councillors. Unfortunately, this leads the concern groups into a vicious circle of chasing political support.

The Kwun Tong District Board Members and the Two Local Concern Groups

This channel did not provide the concern groups with any promising alliance. We focus on two features of the Kwun Tong District Board so as to illustrate the difficulties which the two THA concern groups encountered in their pursuit of political support.

Firstly, the Kwun Tong District Board is characterized by keen competition between 'pro-government' and 'pro-democracy' wings. In July 1992 the pro-democracy members put forward a motion to establish a special committee on the problems and issues of the ATHAs in the Kwun Tong district. It was hoped that with the formation of such a special committee it would be possible to exert more pressure on the Housing Authority and the Housing Department. But since it was initiated by the pro-democracy wing, the pro-government side regarded it as an opposition tactic for consolidating political power. As the Board was mainly composed of pro-government members, the motion was voted down. Surprisingly, a motion asking the Housing Department to pay more attention to the problem of the ATHAs in the Kwun Tong district was passed in the same meeting. The passing of this motion was intended on the one hand to appease the THA protesters and on the other to avoid the formation of a special committee which would be likely to be dominated by pro-democracy members. Thus, by virtue of the political competition on the District Board, political considerations took precedence over consideration of the welfare of ATHA residents.[22]

Secondly, the constituency areas for the district boards are very small. In the sub-district where Kowloon Bay THA is located, there is one seat on the district board while there are two seats in the area incorporating the Ping Shek THA. In other words, there are only three board members who could offer assistance to the two THA concern groups. Even so, there is no way for the concern groups to gain their support. The small population of THA residents constitute a very small proportion of the constituency. In addition, without seven years' residency in Hong Kong, most of them are not entitled to vote in any political elections. The District Board members can afford to ignore this small element of their constituency. Hence, two out of the three District Board members were uninterested in their demands. The pretexts they gave were interesting. One member said he was too old to be involved in many political issues. Another District Board member criticized the Kowloon Bay THA concern group for involving so few male residents in the protest. He argued that the efforts of the concern group were bound to be in vain when there were no men serving as core members. In the end, only one District Board member offered assistance to the Ping Shek THA concern group by occasionally attending meetings involving the Housing Department and participating in some protests. Although this District Board member was willing to help out, one person's effort did not effect any changes.

The analysis in this section demonstrates the ineffectiveness of the local concern groups in rallying political support from the actors involved in the articulation channels. Our analysis shows that the possibility of obtaining third party assistance was constrained by the formal political structure and by some of the contextual factors, such as the local councillors' personal orientations and knowledge about housing issues. It is our contention that understanding social protest requires more attention to be paid to both the structural features of the formal political structure, contingent and contextual factors, and the political orientations of the actors involved in the political structure. We have shown that since there was limited political opportunity for the ATHA concern groups to build up connections with the polity members, the ATHA concern groups relied on the support of other challengers such as the interest groups and social workers. The relationship between CSWs, interest groups and indigenous organizations will be discussed in the next chapter.

Conclusion

The ATHA issue has been emerging in the context of two changing political processes. The first is that the social movement sector is shifting away from being dominated by a communal mode of mobilization and working outside the formal political system to being characterized by a market mode of mobilization and acting inside the political system. The second process of change is the restructuring of state power by the government. In effect a closed Housing Authority has been established. On the other hand, the increasing openness of the Legislative Council drains resources from housing movements. Difficulties arise from these changes which make it very difficult for working class people to fight their way into the polity.

The analysis in this chapter thus shows that for the ATHA residents, who are of a lower socio-economic class and relatively powerless, the difficulties of securing and sustaining third party support are considerable. Their politically disadvantaged social position also necessitates more external support. Drawing on the insights of our discussion about the political opportunity structure, we have attempted to show the impact of political context on the possibility of powerless groups receiving external political support on the difficulties the powerless groups encounter in the process of protest.

We have looked at the complicated association between political contexts and social protest. In light of our analysis of the structural and contingent (or historical) facets of the political context in which a social protest emerges, there are two questions about urban movements which need more consideration.

First, the analysis of the ATHA protest runs contrary to the expectation that political development (or democratization) enhances the ability of grassroots organizations to gain access to the political decision-making process and influence political outputs. For example, Lui (1984) predicted that the establishment of the District Board system and its consequent effect on the openness of the political structure would bring about more mobilization. In our analysis, the possibility of any increase in terms of mobilizing the grassroots is not only related to the openness of the political system, but is also mediated by state action and some other contingent factors. The formation of the Housing Authority provides an example of one of the ways in which the government keeps its political dominance intact. By granting power to a statutory organization to work on housing policy, it has relinquished much of its responsibility for public housing. However, through its appointment of pro-government people to the Housing Authority the government may count on these 'gatekeepers' to take care of its interests.

Moreover, any increasing mobilization of the grassroots is also contingent on the tactics and strategies of the actors involved in the polity. These factors, however, depend on individual perception, political calculation, personal experience, and the shifting balance of power and political competition at any particular historical conjuncture. Whether a protest will be taken up by the articulation actors is determined by political opportunities in the political structure and the political orientations of the actors within it.

Second, our analysis leads us to rethink the role of urban movements in the process of social change. Urban movements have been seen both as an indicator of an impending crisis of capitalism, and as having the political impetus to effect social change (Castells, 1978). Ceccarelli has pointed out that this view failed to see the possibility that 'urban social movements and the conflicts which accompanied them, far from anticipating a new era, were the expression of the last and most conflictive stage of a process of change and readjustment to it' (1982:264). He further argued that urban movements will eventually fade out when the last conflictive stage has been adequately dealt with by economic reorganization and political reformation. Likewise, it has been pointed out that *regime transition* creates a flourishing of political activity which takes the form of social movements initially, before 'settling down' to the form of political parties' (Pickvance, 1995:134). These arguments not only reveal the role of urban movements in the process of political transition, but also point out the possibility that the state can institutionalize urban movements in order to contain external challenges. The state is not a static entity, but it can act in response to political challenges to contain social and political conflicts. Our case study of the ATHA protest reveals the extent to which the restructuring of the state renders it difficult for marginalized social groups to become involved in the formal political structure.

However, as Fainstein and Fainstein (1974) reminded us, urban political movements remain important in reflecting both the failure of the political parties to articulate the needs of urban minorities, and the failure of the urban agencies, for example the government, social welfare agencies and urban voluntary associations, to represent the interests of the urban minorities. These functions, as shown in our study, seem to be fulfilled by some of the urban movements in Hong Kong.

Since democracy has not provided more political opportunities for the minority groups in Hong Kong to advance their interests, the ATHA concern groups have found it difficult to obtain political support. Consequently, they were forced to take the issue to the street. Working through the formal political structure was unfeasible. Therefore, in order to push for their interests, they needed to consolidate their political power in a context unfavourable to their political actions. When ordinary politics became less feasible, the concern groups had to choose between protests, polite politics and violence. In the following chapters, we turn to explore which strategies were employed during the ATHA protest.

Notes

1. We follow Lipsky's definition of third parties which refers 'both to the reference publics of target groups and, more narrowly, to the interest groups whose regular interaction with protest targets tends to develop into patterns of influence' (1968:1153).
2. For example, policy pertaining to transportation is delegated to the Transport Consultation Committee, medical services to the Hospital Authority, the construction of a new airport to the statutory body known as the Provisional Airport Authority established in April 1990, urban renewal to the Land Development Corporation established in 1988 and education policy to the Education Commission, etc. As far as the provision of public housing is concerned, the Housing Authority is the statutory body responsible for the construction, maintenance and management of all public housing estates. Although the Government Secretary for Transport remains responsible for overall policy formulation, direction and the co-ordination of internal transport matters, the government founded the Transport Advisory Committee which is responsible for advising the Governor in Council on major transport policies and issues. The committee has 17 appointed members, including the chairman and six government officials. Also, the government transferred responsibility for the management and control of public hospitals to the Housing Authority in December 1991. The Housing Authority 'is an independent statutory body established for integrating government and government-assisted hospitals with a view to improving the quality and efficiency of public hospital services by optimising the use of resources, facilitating hospital management reforms and enhancing community participation' (Hong Kong Government, Annual Report, 1993:145). As regards education, the Education Commission is the highest advisory body on education. Its terms of reference include defining the overall objectives of education, formulating policy, recommending priorities for implementation, and coordinating as well as monitoring the planning and development of education at all levels. In 1992 the Commission consisted of 14 members of whom 12, including the chairman, were appointed from outside the government to bear on the issues under review. The two government members are the Secretary of Education and Manpower, who is the vice-chairman, and the Director of Education.
3. The *Far Eastern Economic Review* (7th November 1991) has documented that the Hong Kong Housing Authority has been dominated by influential professionals and businessmen who had a very direct vested interest in the affairs to be decided upon.

4   In late 1992 the Legislative Council endorsed a motion recommending the Housing Authority not to continue its 'double rent' policy. However, the Housing Authority simply ignored this motion. The Chairman of the Housing Authority stated that the authority would take the recommendation into consideration but the policy would not be changed.

5   This is cited from the minutes of a meeting between Mr. Lee Wing Tak, a member of the Hong Kong United Democrats and sub-committee member of the Housing Authority, and the Joint Committee of the Temporary Housing Areas Residents Association on 19th May, 1992.

6   It is not easy to locate the political inclinations of all the members of the Housing Authority in terms of a spectrum ranging from pro-government to anti-government. Noting the risk of wrong characterization, we have identified six members who tend to accept the demands of the grassroots. They are: Mr. Hau Shui Pui, Ms. Leung Wai Tung, Father Burke, Mr. Fung Kim Kai, Mr. Hui Yin Fat and Mr. Pao Ping Wing. There is no evidence to prove our observation of the connections between these six people, but we have an impression of a low degree of unity among them. Moreover, with the exception of Mr. Fung and Father Burke, they began to lose their connections with the grassroots. We have some evidence to support this observation. Mr. Pao was asked by a social activist to give up his membership of the People's Council of Public Housing Policy. Ms. Leung played a very active role in defending the Double Rent Policy. Mr. Hau was closely related to pro-mainland Chinese government groups and seemingly avoided close relations with housing movement activists. Mr. Hui's position has been heavily criticized by social workers for his lack of commitment to protect grassroots' interests. This seems to support McAdam's (1982) argument that political challengers will turn out to be conservative once they get into the political system. In our view, this conservative tendency can frustrate the formation of unity among these representatives of the grassroots.

7   Although the political activists deny this inclination, the slogan 'democracy against Communism' used by the media to describe the implicit political objective of the political rights movement at this moment, seems to point to the heart of the movement.

8   The adoption of a market-managerial mode was necessitated by the intention of rallying more public support for the new political parties, and by the limited resources for the political parties to employ a challenger mode to form connections with various communities. In 1993, as one former staff member of a political party pointed out, with increasing financial resources provided by the government, politicians organized more localized mobilization.

9   The term 'residents association' is employed by Lui (1993) to describe the 'local concern groups' which are mainly formed by grassroots activists. In our view, the term 'local concern groups' is interchangeable with the term 'residents association'.

10 The lack of formal power of the Council vis-a-vis the Housing Authority is reflected in the case of the Double-Rent Policy (the details of this policy have been introduced in chapter 3). In 1992 the Council passed a motion stating its objection to continuing such policy. However, the Chairman of the Housing Authority stressed that the authority would not alter its decision despite the objection of the Legislative Council.

11 Cited from the author's fieldnotes on the meeting between the People's Council of Public Housing Policy and the section in January 1992. The proceedings of the meetings were not taped and so the quotation is only that jotted down by the writer.
12 Housing movement protest actions are normally taken to the Office of the Members of the Legislative and Executive Councils. Meetings are held with the attendance of three or four Legislative members who are responsible for eliciting the protesters' concerns and grievances over public policies. Later, they send a letter replying to all the questions the protesters have asked.
13 For details, see Miners, 1991. Chapter 12.
14 The major cleavage between these two wings is related to the extent of direct election introduced to the Legislative Council. Neither wing opposes democracy, but the pro-government wing argues for a slow pace for the introduction of full direct election to the council.
15 The Council has two full-time organizers and one part-time clerical worker. The Board of Directors is wholly composed of unpaid volunteers who are university lecturers, experienced activists in housing, and members and leaders of local neighbourhood associations. In August 1995, the Council encountered a shortage of financial support and decided not to employ any full-time members of staff in 1996.
16 It was reported by the chief coordinator of the PCPHP that the left-wing trade union federation had sought her assistance in the provision of information, skills and training for its members in 1992. The left-wing trade union in the early 1990s was only a newcomer in the housing movement sector.
17 The details of this project have been discussed in Chapter 4.
18 Mr. Lee Wing Tak provides an insider's observation in support of this view. He said that the voice of the THA residents is very small, and most of the Legislative Councillors, even the members of the Housing Authority, are not able to understand the Temporary Housing Policy (Meeting Minutes, the Joint Committee of the THA Residents' Association, 19th May 1992).
19 The councillors, at a meeting with the grassroots representatives in June 1992, said that the person responsible for housing issues in the United Democrats was Mr. Lee Wing Tak, and any relevant matters should be directed to him. This incident further supports the point that the division of labour within the political parties generates a mode of articulation characterized by person-and-district-dependence.
20 Mr. Szeto was involved again in the Ping Shek THA protest in 1994. However, he simply attended the meetings of local concern groups and arranged meetings with the Housing Department. An informant reported that in one meeting, he asked the protesters to accept the offers by the department. He explained that the 'old' public housing flats allocated to the Ping Shek THA residents were acceptable.
21 The Ping Shek THA concern group invited Mr. Szeto Wah and Mr. Lee Wing Tak to visit their THA. That night, there was an open meeting for the residents. The attitude of Mr. Lee appeared to reflect his individual concerns about the internal division of labour within the political parties. At the beginning of the meeting, Mr. Lee said : 'This is not the Kwai Ching district, so I am only attending the meeting because some of the THA residents have invited me...I can understand the situation of the THA

residents, but I'm sure that Mr. Sze Tao Wah can assist you to advance your interests. As I have a meeting tonight in Kwai Ching, I will have to leave earlier' (Fieldnotes, 16th June, 1992). A more plausible explanation of his attitude can be found in the internal arrangement of the United Democrats. Although he is a member of the Housing Authority, the Kwun Tong district is the constituency in which Mr. Szeto Wah builds up his electoral support. To avoid confusion, Mr. Lee must respect the implicit 'sense of territoriality' of Mr. Szeto Wah. After that, Mr. Lee did not show up at any of the protest activities arranged by the Ping Shek THA concern group.

22 A counterfactual event was the establishment of a special committee in 1994. After the 1994 election, the pro-democracy wing politicians dominated the Kwun Tong District Board and subsequently, upon the request of the ATHA residents, the committee concerning the THA policy was founded.

7 Every Person Counts: The Political Participation of ATHA Residents

Introduction

We argued in Chapter 6 that the local concern groups of the two Aged Temporary Housing Areas (ATHAs) found it difficult to gain access to the polity when third party support was hard to secure. In this situation, the advance of their interests relied on their own efforts and the support of volunteer organizers and community social workers. This chapter addresses the question of the extent to which the local concern groups can mobilize the residents of the two ATHAs, namely the Kowloon Bay and the Ping Shek THAs, to sustain their protests in the context of a political system which marginalizes minority interests and issues. In order to answer this question, we examine the social characteristics of the residents of the two ATHAs, with a specific focus on exploring the factors facilitating or inhibiting the mobilization of residents' support for the ATHA issue. We pose three questions: To what extent is the internal structure of the ATHAs favourable to protest organizations? How can we explain differential participation among residents, i.e. who participates and who does not? To what extent are the local concern groups able to encourage participation?

The characteristics of a social base are important in determining the extent to which a social force is formed, yet this topic has been largely ignored by most students of urban movements. As Lowe pointed out, the nature and characteristics of a social base may 'have the greatest objective potential for a collective response because there are distinct material interests at stake, and are frequently the targets of the policy process' (1985:62). Lowe went further to argue that the degree to which objective potential translates into substantial collective action is associated with a) the form of social relations and integration mechanisms in the community in question and b) the existence of sectoral consumption cleavages. Pickvance (1977), drawing on Rex and Moore's study of housing class mobilization, also argued that the mobilization of urban collective action relies on the absorption capacity of the social relationships and voluntary associations in the community in question. The classical question of how a social base becomes a social force, must then be addressed and answered by reference to the nature and characteristics of the social base.

In section 7.1 we examine the forms of political participation in the two ATHAs in order to depict the opportunities offered to the ATHA residents for participation in political activities. In section 7.2, we present a brief review of two general conceptions of the nature and characteristics of a social base. Although both views consider the social characteristics of a social base to be the principal determinant of potential support for a collective action, one view places more emphasis on individual predispositions while the other stresses the degree of 'groupness' in a community. In this section, we argue that putting more emphasis on individual decisions and less on groupness is more appropriate because, as will be shown, groupness in the two ATHAs is found to be insignificant as a determinant of participation in protest activities.

Sections 7.3 and 7.4 identify the factors determining the extent of the 'mobilization potential' in the Kowloon Bay and Ping Shek THAs respectively. This key concept, which is suggested by Klandermans and Oegema (1987), refers to the likelihood that a group of people will participate in collective action in support of a given social movement. Due to the different situations and development of the two local ATHA protests, our analysis of the mobilization potential of the two ATHA populations will be presented in two sections. In section 7.5, we shall argue that the extent of mobilization potential is related to the rational decisions of the residents. We shall also demonstrate that a high level of mobilization potential does not guarantee a high rate of actual participation. In our view, whether mobilization potential translates into actual political participation depends on mobilization efforts. Simply put, between mobilization potential and actual participation is the intervening variable - 'mobilization effort' - which refers to the strategies and tactics employed by organizers to mobilize participation. Snow *et al.* (1980) draw our attention to the simple fact that mobilization of people to participate in a social movement requires some sort of contact between people and the social movement organization.

Hence, actual participation should be seen as the product of the interplay between mobilization potential and mobilization effort. Drawing on the findings from our intensive interviews and fieldwork observations, we shall argue that limited mobilization effort rather than a low mobilization extent is the major reason for the low degree of actual participation in the ATHAs. Finally, section 7.6 is the conclusion.

Forms of Political Participation in the Two ATHAs

Opportunities for political participation in the two ATHAs are very limited. There is no local political organization in the two ATHAs, unlike the squatter areas where religious groups, mutual aid committees and fire-watch teams are active (Smart, 1992). The most common form of local residents association in Hong Kong is the Mutual Aid Committee. Nevertheless, in 1991 the government failed to organize a Mutual Aid Committee in the Ping Shek THA because of a low rate of response. The Caritas community development project, a social service organization advocating community development, had set up a local residents association in the Kowloon Bay THA which was active until 1985, when the Housing Department announced that the THA was to be cleared.[1] In the case of the Ping Shek THA, a social service agency had operated until 1991, but moved out when the population of residents fell below a preset threshold size.[2]

Throughout the period of the ATHA protest, all participation opportunities for the residents in the two ATHAs were organized by the concern groups which were formed by a small group of local THA residents and volunteer organizers (VOs).[3] These involved three major forms of activities, namely concern group meetings, mass meetings, and petitions and demonstrations. It is difficult to measure the rate of participation in our study because there is only a partial record of attendance in activities. The following description is based on our survey, fieldwork records and observations.

The concern group meeting is typically attended by a small group of residents. This group serves to organize direct actions and mobilization campaigns, and is also the 'think tank' and administrative nucleus of the protest. Not more than a total of 15 residents were involved in each local concern group throughout the protest. This level of participation is higher than in some community actions in the third world, such as Peru where van

Garderen (1989) recorded that in three squatter settlements in Arequipa with a total population of 18,300 people, only 10 to 20 persons were active in neighbourhood associations.

The mass meeting is the second form of protest activity. Both concern groups had organized about ten mass meetings by the end of 1994. Such meetings took place within their THAs, and most of the time the concern groups invited politicians to attend the meetings in order to show to their fellow neighbours external support. On a number of occasions, mass meetings were organized in the form of a press conference, and in the Ping Shek THA the concern group once organized an alternative form of protest, that is, a ceremony celebrating the 18th anniversary of the Ping Shek THA. We found in our fieldwork that mass meetings achieved the highest level of participation of the residents, ranging from 50 to 150 residents. In the Kowloon Bay THA, our survey findings show that until October 1991, about 44% of 115 respondents attended at least one concern group meeting while our fieldwork recorded that 25% of 231 respondents in the Ping Shek THA were involved in meetings. These are relatively high rates of participation. Comparatively, they are higher than the rate of participation in the community development program 'the Mobilization for Youth Experience' in the United States which normally only had about half a dozen parents attending meetings (Kronenfeld, 1969; Pope, 1989). They are also higher than the rate of the British people attending protest meetings in 1985, which is about 15% (Parry et al., 1992:44).

The rate of participation in the third form of protest activity, i.e. petitions and demonstrations, is much lower than that for mass meetings. Our survey shows that 18% of 115 respondents in the Kowloon Bay THA attended at least one protest concerning the ATHA issue. Our fieldwork recorded that the average number of participants was about 15 in the Kowloon Bay THA, and about 10 in the case of the Ping Shek THA. The only exception is the meeting between the Kowloon Bay THA concern group and the members of the Management and Operations Committee of the Housing Authority in November 1991. On this occasion more than 60 residents participated in the petition in front of the meeting venue. In general, the THA concern groups were not able to mobilize a large group of protesters. Their mobilization efforts were less effective than those of the Welfare Rights Movement in the United States which 'could mobilize more than 200 demonstrators on short notice' (Pope, 1989:70); or the urban movement in South Africa which could mobilize several tens of thousands of protesters (Issacs, 1989).

The concern group of the Kowloon Bay THA did organize another form of protest activity. In the period from June to December of 1991, signing and donation campaigns were organized. According to the results of our survey, one-fifth (21%) of the residents (n=115) had donated money to the association. Also, in September 1991, the concern group collected 63 signatures in support of the ATHA protest. We estimated that this was about 22% of the existing households.[4] In comparison with the rate of participation in signing a petition in Hong Kong as a whole, which is 58.2%, this figure shows a low degree of participation (Leung and Lee, 1994).[5]

We notice that the ATHA residents are more likely to participate in mass meetings than in petitions and concern groups. With these findings, it is of interest to us to explore why the rate of participation in meetings is so much higher than in the other forms of protest activity. In this respect, we acknowledge the significance both of the social characteristics of the residents and the mobilization efforts of the concern groups as the determinants of political participation. In the next section, we discuss whether the characteristics of the individual residents or the degree of groupness among the residents is more significant to the residents' participation.

The Social Characteristics of Residents in the Two ATHAs

One of the most debated conceptual issues relating to social movement participation is whether individual characteristics or social relationships are more important in mobilization. The perspective explaining active participation by reference to individual characteristics includes several strands of thought. One theoretical framework, popular in political science, suggests that active participants are those with specific demographic factors, such as those who are male, who have better jobs, higher education and who are married (Kim et al., 1974; Lipset, 1960; Verba and Nie, 1972). A closely related perspective shows how predisposing psychological stress and anxiety motivate movement participants (Geschwender, 1968; Gurr, 1970). Although focusing on individual attributes, Olson (1965) argued that, regardless of predisposing factors such as personal characteristics, political participation is the consequence of rational decision-making by the individuals. Klandermans (1984), while not denying the significance of rational calculation, stressed the individual's evaluation of political efficacy and argued that a high sense of powerlessness is a factor dampening one's motivation to participate.

In contrast, a competing perspective is more concerned with the significance of emergent group norms in relation to participation in a social movement. Insofar as a group has a structured feature that fosters participation, its members are said to be more likely to be involved in collective action. Oberschall (1973) has argued that bloc recruitment (i.e. recruitment when pre-existing groups are incorporated) is more likely to be achieved in a group which has strong social cohesiveness and closely-knit social ties. Wilson and Orum (1966) claimed that social networks prompt political participation. Also, in studies of participation in trade union activities, group characteristics, for example homogeneity of group membership, similarity in ethnicity and work situation, or the status and prestige a group enjoys in the workplace, are found to be critical to the group members' propensity to political participation (Perline and Lorenz, 1970; Shils and Janowitz, 1948; Tannenbaum and Kahn, 1958; Zimmer, 1956). Byrne also found in England's Tyneside that 'in a relatively ethnically homogenous community...with a high level of residential stability, familial and quasi-familial bonds matter a good deal for social action' (1989:160). Calhoun, in his analysis of collective action in nineteenth-century England, pointed to 'the enduring strength of traditional communities which lent concertedness to the social movements which did occur' (1982:213).

It is important to note that this perspective concerning the significance of group characteristics for political participation emphasises the 'social' nature of a group. The key concepts employed to characterize this 'social' nature are group identity, close-knit social networks, group cohesiveness, etc. (Gilbert, 1992; Mueller, 1989). The focus is the extent to which intensive, durable and continuous relationships are found in a social group.

In our view, in respect of political participation, whether it is factors at an individual level or the degree of groupness that matters is an empirical question. We shall demonstrate, based on our fieldwork findings, a low degree of groupness among the ATHA residents, whether expressed in group identity or social networking. We thus argue that it is inappropriate to apply the perspective concerning groupness to the study of political participation in the ATHAs. In the rest of this section, we examine the social characteristics of the ATHA residents in order to substantiate this argument. Our purpose is to justify the use of the perspective stressing factors at individual level in the following analysis.

The two ATHAs we studied show an absence of strong social ties or group norms among the residents. Although daily greeting and chatting are not unusual, daily interaction is restricted to three or four households in the same block. In our 30 interviews in Ping Shek THA, most of the respondents said that they had not interacted much with their neighbours.[6] One-third of the interviewees were not 'familiar' with their neighbours. The other two-thirds of the interviewees, while maintaining that they knew their neighbours well, rarely went out with their neighbours for leisure and seldom talked about their family affairs. Only four interviewees had frequent contacts with their neighbours, such as talking, spending leisure time together and looking after neighbours' flats or children when they were out. Simply put, intensively interacting groups are not evident. Our informal interviews also revealed a similar situation in which most residents of the Kowloon Bay THA seldom approached their neighbours to spend their leisure together.

We can explain this lack of widespread social ties among THA residents by reference to the social characteristics of the residents themselves and the nature of Hong Kong society. The first notable feature of the residents is their restricted opportunities for contact. Most household heads are employed in different areas of the territory, hence work contact, outside or inside the neighbourhood, is very limited. Working people tend to work long hours which eats into their time and energy and leaves them only a small amount of leisure time. During our fieldwork, a mother and her young daughter said that they had talked with their neighbours not more than ten times throughout their four years of residence. Even the members of the concern group in both ATHAs were more like strangers in the initial period of their community action. Their common explanation for this low degree of interaction was lack of time. In addition, as most households move into the THAs on an individual basis, the absence of preexisting social networks creates an obstacle to the building up of social ties.

Secondly, most leisure activity takes place within people's homes and therefore there is little involvement in community life. A majority of the respondents reported that they mainly spent their leisure time at home, watching TV, or going out with their family members. Playing *mahjeuk*, a kind of gambling with tiles, is the most usual form of leisure activity bringing together a group of neighbours. Smart (1992) in his study of squatter areas found it common to see neighbours visiting each other in search of players to fill the table. However, in both ATHAs playing *mahjeuk* was confined to a minority of residents. It appears that neighbours and leisure time partners are clearly distinct, and it is difficult to generate a sense of groupness among the ATHA residents.

The low rate of interaction among the THA residents is associated with the limited numbers of intermediate associations at local level. This reflects one feature of the political participation experience of Hong Kong people. Studies of political involvement at territory-wide level show that only a minority of Hong Kong people have participated in social and political organizations. As revealed in a recent study, only 10% of the respondents were involved in community associations (Leung and Lee, 1994). In comparison, this rate is certainly lower than in the United States and Britain where the rates of participation in community activities are 37% and 17% respectively in the 1970s (Dalton, 1988:47).

The ATHA residents seem to differ little in this regard. In the two ATHAs, few external groups such as religious groups or neighbourhood organizations existed to organize the residents; and residents' dissatisfaction with their living conditions was rarely made public through neighbourhood organizations, as in some areas. A community development team organized by Caritas stopped its services to the Kowloon Bay THA in 1985. The situation in the Ping Shek THA was made worse in 1991 by the departure of the only local social service agency. In a society like Hong Kong where intermediate associations are not as popular as in the United States as a mode of social networking, it is not surprising to see that opportunities for social and political participation are limited.

As Roberts (1973) pointed out, the quantitative extent of social interaction has implications for the quality of social interaction among working class families. The lack of interaction results in a lack of mutual assistance among the THA residents, as reflected by the fact that neighbours were not the recourse for help in case of emergency. In our 30 intensive interviews, only 2 interviewees reported that they had asked their neighbours to take care of their houses when they were out. As shown in Table 7.1, none of the respondents said that neighbours were their first recourse to seeking help whereas 'relying on oneself' remained the most popular form of getting help in an emergency. Eight out of 30 respondents

(27%) said they would rely on themselves to solve any emergency. Seven respondents (23%) said they would turn to their kin and five (17%) to their friends. Six respondents (20%) felt it difficult to get any help.

People to whom respondents turn in case of emergency	Case (Percent)
Rely on oneself	8 (27%)
Relatives	7 (23%)
Cannot find any people who can help	6 (20%)
Friends	5 (17%)
No answer	3 (10%)
No emergency	1 (10%)
Neighbours	0 (0%)
n	30 (100%)

Table 7.1   People to Whom Respondents Turn in Case of Emergency

Source: Author's interview in August 1992

    This lack of interaction means there is little opportunity for residents to organize concerted action to deal with the problems of their living environment. Crime, though not serious, is not unusual in the THAs. Some residents regularly complain about the theft of female underwear, assaults by indecent peepers and their fear of burglars. In addition, fire is another issue of great concern. Two blocks in the Ping Shek THA were destroyed by fires in 1991. Some residents in our informal interviews complained about the authority's indifference to their safety. However, their awareness of crime and other dangers does not translate into collective action. It seems that the lack of interaction among neighbours means they have no opportunity to learn that collective action is a possible way of dealing with their common problems.

    In short, the low degree of groupness among the ATHA residents can be attributed to the lack of social networks or any pre-existing organization which could foster a sense of belonging and group identity. As a result, concerted collective action among the ATHA residents turns out to be difficult. Nonetheless, we note that this argument would be challenged by the proponents of the collective behaviour perspective who contend that a low degree of social cohesion among the residents leads to such a high level of alienation and anxiety that in turn enhances the propensity to participate in collective action (Kornhauser, 1959; Lipset, 1960).

However, even if the THA residents are characterised by the lack of social cohesion, we did not find a high degree of frustration among the 30 respondents; on the contrary, the majority were very satisfied with the social environment of Hong Kong as a whole. In our findings, only 3 respondents (10%) were disappointed with the government or the welfare system and 5 gave no concrete answer, whereas 22 respondents (73%) rated highly the freedom they enjoyed and the low degree of government intervention in social life in Hong Kong. As most of them are refugees from mainland China, their unpleasant experience of the social and economic life in China seems to reinforce their positive appraisal of Hong Kong. As one respondent pointed out:

> I've been here [in Hong Kong] for nine years. Hong Kong people are really of high efficiency in work, but life is too tense. I feel the Hong Kong government is a good administration, better than the Chinese government. No one is checking you all the time. You commit no crime, then, you'll be alright. In mainland China, no matter whether it is big or small issue, some guy is checking you. Moreover, the Hong Kong government gives us no less social welfare. Anyway, the government is fairly good. I can't tell you clearly how good it is, but if you ask me to choose, I go for the Hong Kong government. More freedom here, freedom in thought, and no one is watching you (Mrs. Wong, 42, a Ping Shek THA resident).

It appears that most THA residents adapt successfully to social life in Hong Kong, as indicated by the lack of grievances or disaffection with their lives here. They are atomized and lack internal cohesiveness, but they are not as emotionally disturbed as marginality theorists predict (Perlman, 1977).

To sum up, because of the specific features of the THA residents, we do not consider it useful here to apply the perspective which emphasises groupness as an explanation of the political participation of ATHA residents. Rather, in the next section, we focus on individual variables, namely, demographic characteristics, people's evaluation of political efficacy and their perception of constraints on participation, as factors determining the political participation of the ATHA residents.

To Participate or Not to Participate: A Case Study in the Kowloon Bay THA

In seeking to account for residents' willingness to participate, two separate surveys were conducted in October 1991 in the Kowloon Bay THA and in the Ping Shek THA in the period from May to September 1992. The disadvantage of our analysis, however, is the lack of longitudinal data enabling us to compare the political orientations of the residents at different moments. What we can do is compare and contrast the political orientation of residents of the two ATHAs in order to draw out the factors which can account for political participation. Because of the different stages of development of the two local protests, the analyses of attitudes to participation are reported separately in this section and the next.

In this section, we first present our analysis of the political participation of the residents of the Kowloon Bay THA. We adopt a common framework for this analysis and the analysis in section 7.4. In each case study, the extent of mobilization potential is measured by the indicator 'willingness to participate' which is the dependent variable in our following analysis.

Four dependent variables are used to illustrate the extent of the mobilization potential of the Kowloon Bay THA. The first three are the residents' self-reported willingness to participate in three types of protest activities, namely, meetings, petitions and relatively more radical action (e.g. sit-ins). From this we derive the fourth variable of willingness to participate in protest activities: respondents are categorized as having a 'propensity to participate' if they say that they will participate in any one of the three protest activities. All dependent variables are dichotomous, being categorized into potential participants - those saying they will participate in protest activities - and non-potential participants (hereafter, non-participants) who do not show any willingness to participate.

The residents' willingness to participate in protest activities is accounted for by reference to several factors. In the case of the Kowloon Bay THA, we consider ten factors. The first three factors are the socio-economic characteristics of the respondents, namely gender, age and employment status.[7] As regards employment status, we use the distinction between employed and unemployed (including housewives). In our view, this distinction is more useful than the standard categorization in terms of occupation types since the latter would not provide any clear differentiation of the residents into different subgroups given that most of the employed respondents are manual workers.[8] The fourth factor is the respondents' evaluation of the cause of the community action. It is our contention that a respondent is less likely to participate in community action if he/she does not support the cause. The fifth and sixth independent variables are the objective and subjective interest of the respondents. Objective interest is related to the eligibility of the respondents for public housing flats. Clearance does not necessarily benefit all the residents in the Kowloon Bay THA. According to the prevailing policy, households in which more than half of the members have lived in Hong Kong less than seven years are not eligible for public housing flats. Ineligible households are given a unit in another THA. Since successful protest action may not benefit the ineligible households, it is reasonable for such respondents to think selfishly and to be uninterested in the protest. Also, we should understand the subjective interest of the respondents. Even if a respondent is eligible for public housing flats, he/she may not want to be rehoused in a public housing flat which entails higher rent, and would therefore be unwilling to become involved in the ATHA protest.

The seventh variable refers to perceived constraints on political participation. We take two sub-factors as objective constraints. Time is the first. In the fieldwork, the residents told us they normally got home after six or seven p.m., and some worked shifts and overtime. In some cases, the breadwinners got home at ten or eleven o'clock at night. Working mothers were less likely to have spare time when they had a double responsibility. To many of them, time is a scarce resource. The second perceived constraint is opposition from families and neighbours. Married women in particular encounter objections from their spouses since, in the eyes of some husbands, women are supposed to be responsible for taking care of the children and all the household work, and should not be involved in public issues. Besides, we hypothesize that some encounter objections from neighbours who do not benefit from the protest and show their dislike toward those participating in protest activities. Nevertheless, we argue that the significance of the objections of family members and neighbours depends on whether the respondents take the two groups of people as reference groups. If a resident does not take their views seriously, their objections will not dampen their motivation to participate.

The final three independent variables refer to three distinct aspects of the respondent's perceptions of their political efficacy, namely a) their evaluation of the political effectiveness of their collective effort; b) their estimation of the number of participants and c) the perceived chance of success of their collective action (Klandermans, 1984; Nie et al., 1969; Sallach et al., 1972). The first of these variables reflects the extent to which a resident believes the protest group is likely to be effective. We hypothesize that the more people believe in the political efficacy of collective effort, the more likely they are to be willing to participate in political activity. The second refers to people's evaluation of the solidarity of the group itself (Dunleavy, 1991; Klandermans, 1984). Contrary to Olson, Klandermans argued that 'the willingness to participate in collective action appears to be strengthened by the belief that many others will participate' (1984:591). A belief that there will be a large number of participants seems to indicate a respondent's feeling of solidarity and thus facilitates mobilization (Fireman and Gamson, 1979). The last variable is the estimated chance of success if many residents participate. We hypothesize that people are more likely to be willing to participate if they believe that a large number of protesters increases the probability of success.

Activity	Yes	No
Meeting	56 (75.7%)	18 (24.3%)
Petition	44 (59.5%)	30 (40.5%)
Radical action (e.g. sit-ins)	34 (45.9%)	40 (54.1%)
n = 74[9]	Question asked is 'Would you participate in the following activities organized by the residents association?'	
Willingness to participate in any one type of protest activity	56 (75.7%)	18 (24.3%)
n = 74		
Degree of Militancy		
non-participant	18 (24.3%)	
meeting	9 (12.2%)	
petition	13 (17.6%)	
radical action	34 (45.9%)	
Total	74 (100.0%)	

Table 7.2 Respondents' Mobilization Potential in Protest Activities in the Kowloon Bay THA

Source: Author's survey conducted in Kowloon Bay THA in September 1991

184 *Polite Politics*

We now move on to explore the extent to which these variables affect the Kowloon Bay THA residents' mobilization potential. We first describe the general characteristics of the residents in terms of the dependent and independent variables, and then present the results of our analysis. Sixteen cases in the sample (n=92) with missing values either in the dependent variables or the independent variables, and 2 cases in which the respondents disagreed with the cause of protest are excluded. The sample size is thus reduced to 74.

Extent of the Mobilization Potential

The mobilization potential for the three types of protest activity differ in size. As shown in Table 7.2, attending a meeting is the most acceptable protest activity, with 76% of the respondents saying that they would while 24% said they would not. Regarding petitions, three-fifths (60%) of the respondents said they would participate while 41% said that they would not. When asked if they would participate in more radical activity, 46% said they would while 54% said they would not. In short, residents are more willing to participate in meetings than in petitions and radical actions. We also found that 76% of the respondents said that they would participate in at least one type of protest activity.

One feature of the mobilization potential is that these three activities are in a hierarchical structure: almost all of the respondents who would participants in petitions and radical actions would also be willing to participate in meetings; in turn the majority of residents willing to be involved in radical actions said that they would participate in petitions, but not vice versa.[10]

Another feature is that nearly half of the respondents are willing to participate in radical action (e.g. sit-ins). Although the categorization we used is not strictly comparable with the Guttman scale score Marsh used in his study of British political culture, a comparison gives us a rough idea of the degree of militancy of the Kowloon Bay THA residents. In Marsh's study (1977), 22% of respondents were not willing to participate in any protest, 21% at their most extreme position were willing to participate in petitions but went no further, and 12% were willing to be involved in occupations and blocking traffic. In comparison, the Kowloon Bay THA residents show a relatively higher degree of militancy. As shown in Table 7.2, nearly two-fifths (46%) of the sample were willing to participate in radical action, such as sit-ins at the headquarters of the Housing Authority. Slightly less than one-fifth (18%) said that they were willing to participate in petitions, but not in radical action. Another 12% were willing to participate in meetings, but not in petitions and radical actions. Only a quarter (24%) of the respondents were unwilling to participate in any protest activities. We do not have further information to explain such a high degree of militancy. Based on the data from our fieldwork observation, most residents felt it would be difficult to exert pressure on the Housing Authority through meetings with the officials, whereas protest and radical actions might be relatively effective in arousing both public awareness and the authority's concern.

This analysis raises questions about i) the factors which influence the residents' willingness to participate; ii) those which influence the translation of mobilization potential into actual involvement; and iii) the implications of the type of mobilization potential for the group nature of a protest. We consider the first question here, and the others in sections 7.5 and 7.6.

Factors Affecting Participation Patterns of Kowloon Bay THA Residents

Ten factors are examined to see the extent to which they influence residents' mobilization potential. The characteristics of the respondents described in terms of the independent variables are presented in Table 7.3.

Variable		**Count (percent)**
Sex	Male	35 (47.3)
	Female	39 (52.7)
Age	Mean	43
Employment Status	Employed	47 (63.5)
	Not employed	17 (36.5)
Eligibility for public housing	Yes	61 (82.4)
	No	13 (17.6)

Variable		Count (percent)
Time constraint	No difficulty	30 (40.5)
	Has difficulty	30 (40.5)
	No idea	14 (18.9)
Perceived efficacy of protest	No	15 (20.3)
	Yes	46 (62.2)
	No idea	13 (17.6)
Estimated number of participants	Many	26 (35.1)
	Few	11 (14.9)
	No idea	37 (50.0)
Chance of success	Possible	33 (44.6)
	Little	15 (20.3)
	No idea	26 (35.1)
Type of Housing Wanted	New and Urban	44 (59.5)
	Any urban	18 (24.3)
	No idea and others	12 (16.2)

n = 74

Table 7.3   Characteristics of the Respondents in the Kowloon Bay THA

Source: Author's survey of Kowloon Bay THA residents in September 1991

Socio-economic Characteristics of the Respondents   Slightly less than half (47%) of the respondents are male whereas 53% are female. About two-thirds (64%) of the respondents are employed, and a large proportion of them are manual workers, such as delivery workers, unskilled and skilled workers in manufacturing and construction sectors.[11] The mean age of the respondents is 43.

Respondents' Support for the Cause of the Community Action   All the respondents in this sample are supporters of the protest.[12] This reflects the strong support of the respondents for the cause of the protest. Since this variable has no variation, we shall not include it in the logistic regression analysis.

Eligibility About 18% of the respondents are ineligible for public housing flats.[13]

Types of Housing Expected The demand of the protest at the time of the survey was for rehousing in new public housing flats in the local area. After the announcement of clearance, the Housing Department made it very clear that all the eligible households would be rehoused in Tsueng Kwan O which is located several miles away. A large number of eligible households found this rehousing arrangement unacceptable and insisted on being rehoused in the local area. Our findings indicate that about 60%[14] of the respondents wanted new urban public housing flats, while 24% wanted either new or old urban public housing flats. The rest (16%) includes those who either had not made up their mind, or hoped for public housing flats in non-urban areas.

In order to reduce the number of variables for logistic regression analysis, the variables 'eligibility' and 'types of housing wanted' have been regrouped into one new variable which has three values, namely ineligible, want urban public housing flats, and the last one including 'do not want urban public housing flats' and 'no idea'.

Perceived Efficacy of Protest About three-fifths (62%) of the respondents disagreed with the statement that collective effort was not worthwhile, while only one-fifth (20%) agreed that they were politically powerless. Clearly, a majority of the Kowloon Bay THA residents have a very high degree of confidence in their political power. However, when the respondents were asked how many of their fellow neighbours would participate in protest activities, their confidence was lower. Only one-third (35%) said that there would be many participants while one-seventh (15%) estimated that a few would join. This indicates a moderate degree of solidarity among one-third of the residents. It is interesting to note that half of the residents (50%) did not answer this question. The low response rate reflects the residents' ignorance of their neighbours' behaviour.

The respondents were asked in the study about their estimate of the chance of success. Four-ninths (45%) of them estimated that if many neighbours participated in the protest there would be a high chance of success, but another one-fifth (20%) disagreed. As in the second question, the non-response rate for this question is relatively high - about one-third (35%).

Objective Constraints Objections by family members and neighbours had little impact on residents' willingness to participate. None of the respondents stated that family members' opinions were important to his/her decision. Regarding the neighbours' opinion, no respondents considered that the objection of their neighbours would have influenced their decision about participation. Of the three objective constraints, only time is an important constraint against participation. Two-fifths (41%) said that they had difficulty finding time to support the protest while another two-fifths (41%) did not mention any such difficulty.[15] Hence, only the variable 'time constraint' was included in the logistic regression analysis.

The Analysis of Residents' Willingness to Participate

Here, by means of logistic regression, we attempt to identify the factors contributing to the residents' willingness to participate in the three kinds of protest activities. The dependent variables used to measure this are all dichotomous, and draw a distinction between non-potential participants (i.e. those unwilling to participate) and potential participants (i.e. willing to participate). Table 7.4 presents the results of logistic regressions of participation vs. non-participation on four variables: 1) 'propensity to participate' which identifies those willing to participate in at least one protest activity, 2) participation in meetings, 3) participation in petitions and 4) participation in radical actions.

Every Person Counts: The Political Participation of ATHA Residents 189

Dependent variable/ Independent variable	Propensity to participate (1)	Propensity to participate (1a)	Meeting (2)	Meeting (2a)	Petition (3)	Petition (3a)	Radical Action (4)	Radical Action (4a)
Sex								
Male	-0.38	-0.19	-0.38	-0.19	0.02	0.16	-2.38***	-1.16**
Female	-	-	-	-	-	-	-	-
Age	-0.05*	-0.02	-0.05*	-0.02	-0.01	-0.00	0.02	-0.00
Employment status								
not employed	-1.62*	-1.12*	-1.62*	-1.12*	-0.95	-0.64	-2.40***	-1.27***
employed	-	-	-	-	-	-	-	-
Interest								
ineligible	-1.79		-1.79		-0.83		8.71#	
want urban flats	-0.69	x	-0.68	x	-0.41	x	9.76	x
do not want urban flats	-		-		-		-	
Time constraint								
no idea	-1.99***		-1.99***		-2.27***		-0.45	
no difficulty	2.80***	x	2.80***	x	1.94***	x	2.25***	x
has difficulty	-		-		-		-	
Perceived efficacy of protest								
no idea	-0.58	x	-0.58	x	-0.84	x	-2.50***	
no	-2.28***		-2.28***		-2.55****		-2.77****	x
yes	-		-		-		-	
Chance of success								
no idea	1.13		1.13		0.47		-1.22	
possible	1.21	x	1.21	x	-0.08	x	-1.43	x
little	-		-		-		-	
Estimated number of participants								
no idea	-0.59		-0.59		1.14		1.91*	
many	-1.36	x	-1.36	x	0.64	x	1.17	x
few	-		-		-		-	
N	74	74	74	74	74	74	74	74
R^2	0.42	0.05	0.42	0.05	0.36	0.02	0.41	0.05

Table 7.4 Odds Ratios for Predicting Four Measures of Participation in Protest Activities Among Kowloon Bay THA Residents, Using Two Logistic Regression Models

Figures represent the Beta coefficients for each variable. Participation and non-participation are coded so that positive coefficients indicate that the independent variable is associated with increased odds of being willing to participate relative to the reference group. As age is an interval variable, a positive coefficient indicates that a higher level of age is associated with increased odds of being willing to participate.

Note: x the independent variables not put in the model
- denotes reference group
* $P < 0.20$;   ** $P < 0.10$;   *** $P < 0.05$;   **** $P < 0.01$
\# These figures are not reliable as there is no case of a respondent who did not want urban clearance and was willing to participate in radical action. As there is an empty cell, the calculation is based on a zero.

Source: Author's survey on the Kowloon Bay THA residents' views on the ATHA issue, 1991

Since the sample size is small and there are too many variables in the models, we selected a weak criterion of statistical significance, that is, significance less than 0.20.[16] To start with, our hypotheses are that the socio-economic characteristics of the THA residents are not sufficient to explain participation and that objective constraint and individual estimation of political efficacy are more important. To examine these we compare regressions of the full model, which includes all the independent variables, with a model which includes only socio-demographic characteristics. In Table 7.4, equations 1a, 2a, 3a, and 4a represent the models which only include socio-demographic variables whilst equations 1, 2, 3 and 4 represent the full models. It can be seen that the models including only socio-economic characteristics achieve a value of low R^2 (not more than 0.05) while the full models achieve R^2 between 0.36 and 0.42. (R^2 is a measure of the explanatory capacity of the models). The socio-demographic factors have little independent effect, and the independent variables in terms of interests, objective constraints and political efficacy are more effective at explaining willingness to participate in the ATHA protest. The models including only socio-demographic factors will therefore be ignored in the discussion.

Turning to the full models, we notice that the result of equation 1 is the same as that of equation 2. This is because although the variables 'propensity to participate' and 'participation in meetings' appear to be different, they become identical when measured. This is because propensity to participate separates those willing to participate in any of the three forms of action from those unwilling, and because of the hierarchy among forms of action which means that those willing to participate in meetings are coterminous with those willing to participate in any form of action. As a result, we can discuss these two equations simultaneously.

To clarify the interpretation of logistic regression coefficients, an example can be given. The -1.62 figure in row 3 of Table 7.4 means that those not employed were 1.62 times as likely *not* to be willing to participate in any protest activity, as those who were employed, controlling for the effects of other variables. (The minus sign gives the 'not' interpretation). Hence the greater the divergence of the coefficient from 1, the greater the substantive significance of the independent variable concerned. The figure -0.05 for age indicates that older people are 20 times less likely to be willing to participate than younger people. This relationship is statistically significant at the 0.20 level. In what follows we shall only pay attention to variables which are statistically significant at the 0.20 level or below. Moreover, as explained earlier we focus on equations 1-4 rather than 1a-4a because of their greater explanatory success. For example, equation 1 explains 42% of the variation in the dependent variable which is a sizable amount.

Equations 1 and 2 indicate that 'time constraint', 'perceived political efficacy', 'age' and 'employment status' are good predictors of propensity to participate and willingness to participate in meetings. Respondents who do not feel that they have difficulty finding time to support the protest and those who disagree that they have no political efficacy are more likely to be involved in protest activities and meetings. We also notice that 'age' becomes statistically significant in equation 1 and 2 in the full model (i.e. it reaches the 0.20 level of statistical significance). This means that, by controlling all other independent variables, age has an independent effect on the propensity to participate and willingness to participate in meetings. The negative sign means that 'older' respondents are less likely to be potential participants. Besides this, respondents who have a job are more likely to participate.

While age, employment status, time constraint and perceived political efficacy are better predictors, the results show that sex, interests, estimation of the chance of success and the estimated number of participants are poor predictors of the propensity to participate and willingness to participate in meetings.

As regards willingness to participate in protest and radical action, as shown in equations 3 and 4, time constraint and perceived political efficacy remain better predictors. However, there are some features that need more discussion. First, age is no longer a statistically significant variable which implies that willingness to participate in protest has nothing to do with age. Once again, perceived availability of time and perceived political efficacy are more important than the age of respondents. Sex is another reliable predictor of willingness to participate in radical action; the coefficient -2.38 implies that male respondents are over twice as unlikely to be willing to participate in radical action as women. This is an interesting finding as it is contrary to some literature in which females are found to be less radical (Marsh and Kaase, 1979:107). Thirdly, as shown in equation 4, the coefficient of the variable 'estimated number of participants' in radical action remains statistically insignificant. This shows that the respondents' decision to participate in protest has nothing to do with their estimation about others' decisions. This finding runs counter to the argument suggested by Klandermans (1984) that people's willingness to participate is strengthened by the belief that many others will participate.

Lastly, it is interesting to note that although they do not reach the 0.20 level of statistical significance, the coefficients of the variables 'chance of success' and 'estimated number of participant' in equations 3 and 4 are different from those in equations 1 and 2. The signs of the former variable turn from negative to positive whereas the signs of the latter change from positive to negative. This means that, in respect of meetings, the participants are more likely to be those who believe that they do not have a chance of being successful, and those who estimate that only a few people would participate. As regards petitions and radical actions, those who are pessimistic about the chance of success and those who estimate that many people would participate are more willing to participate. We have no evidence from the survey to explain why the respondents have different perceptions of these two kinds of protest activity. However, some additional information from our informal discussion with the residents at the time of survey shed more light on our findings. At that time, the Housing Department had announced that the THA would be cleared in December 1991, two months from the date of our survey. Many of the residents expressed the view that radical action could make a lot of noise and pressurize the Housing Department and the Housing Authority. Some residents complained that there was little solidarity among their fellow neighbours, otherwise, they could force the government to pay more attention to their demands. It appears that there was a group of residents who thought that radical action is needed when the chance of success is slim and that radical action would bring them favourable results. In contrast, to those who think that they have a chance of success and that only a small group of residents would participate, radical action appears to be neither necessary nor feasible.

To summarize, we can highlight a number of features about the production of mobilization potential among the Kowloon Bay THA residents. First, time constraints and perceived political efficacy are the key variables shaping respondents' willingness to participate in the three types of protest activity. Those who had no difficulty in finding time to participate and who disagreed that they had little political power are more likely to be willing to participate in protest. Secondly, as regards socio-demographic factors, age is a reliable predictor of participation propensity and willingness to participate in meetings, but not in the case of participation in petitions and radical action. Young people are more likely to be willing to participate in meetings. Employed respondents, most of whom are probably breadwinners and household heads, are more likely to participate in meetings and radical action, but we cannot predict willingness to participate in petitions on the basis of employment status. Thirdly, willingness to participate is not a function of objective interest (i.e. eligibility for public housing) and subjective interest (i.e. type of housing wanted). This supports the view that interests do not automatically translate into willingness to participate in collective action and our analysis must capture the 'something more' that is required to motivate residents to participate (Davis, 1991; Dunleavy, 1991). As has been pointed out, we need to consider people's own evaluation of the political power of their collective action as the determinants of their willingness to participate. Lastly, the Kowloon Bay THA residents have a high degree of potential to participate in protest activities, and they are more likely to participate in meetings than in petitions and radical actions. In other words, the ATHA protest in Kowloon Bay THA takes place in favourable conditions for mobilization. We now turn to discuss the mobilization potential in the Ping Shek THA, and to explore whether there is any difference between these two ATHAs.

Participation in the Ping Shek THA

The survey was conducted in the Ping Shek THA in the period from May to June 1992. Before this survey, the local concern group had stopped functioning for six months and the volunteer organizers (VOs) had departed. In April 1992, a new team of VOs contacted some indigenous leaders to start local mobilization again. The VOs intended to do a survey to elicit the residents' opinions on the current THA policy and their willingness to participate in protest activity. At the same time, they intended to inform the respondents about the changes in THA policy through this survey. Hence the survey was conducted in collaboration with the VOs. Simply put, before the survey, there was a lack of local mobilization and the residents were by and large ignorant of the current THA policy. But we should point out that before the survey a team of VOs had been working there for a year and had left the Ping Shek THA at the end of 1991. The political consciousness of the residents may thus have been affected by the mobilization efforts of the VOs before this survey. The results presented here only refer to the political orientations of the residents in May 1992, prior to the mobilization efforts of the new group of VOs who started their work after this survey.

We start our analysis by first delineating the extent of the residents' mobilization potential, and then go on to describe the characteristics of the residents in terms of the same independent variables used in our study of the Kowloon Bay THA residents. There were two changes in the variables in this analysis. As regards the variable of support for the cause of the ATHA protest, we asked the respondents if they wanted early clearance because this was the objective of the protest at the time of our survey, whereas in the case of the Kowloon Bay THA the objective was pressing for local rehousing. Also, unlike the analysis of the Kowloon Bay THA in which the indicator of the variable 'type of housing expected' was subjective interests, the analysis here employs the indicator 'satisfaction with the living conditions' because we hypothesize that dissatisfaction leads to an urge to press for early clearance.

Extent of the Mobilization Potential

Table 7.5 shows the mobilization potential of the Ping Shek THA residents. The proportions of the potential participants in meetings and petitions are very similar to those of the Kowloon Bay THA: about 77% and 51% of the respondents are willing to participate in meetings and petitions respectively, while the comparable figures of the Kowloon Bay THA are 76% and 60%. The extent of mobilization potential for radical action is smaller than in the Kowloon Bay THA, 29% compared with 46%. As regards the propensity to participate, 78% of the respondents are willing to participate in at least one type of protest activity. We also found that modes of participation showed a hierarchical structure in the Ping Shek THA, in the sense that almost all the potential participants of radical actions are also willing to participate in meetings and petitions, and potential participants of petitions are willing to participate in meetings, but not vice versa. There is an even distribution of respondents across the four categories defined in terms of degree of militancy: 22% are non-participants who are not willing to participate in any protest activities, 27% are willing to participate only in meetings, 22% are willing to participate in petitions but not in any radical actions, and 29% expressed a willingness to participate in radical action.

The last figure shows that the residents in the Ping Shek THA are less militant than the residents of the Kowloon Bay THA, 46% of whom said they were willing to participate in radical action.

We now consider which factors determine mobilization potentials in protest activities.

Activity	Yes	No
Meeting	185 (77.4%)	54 (22.6%)
Petition	121 (50.6%)	118 (49.4%)
Radical action (e.g. sit-ins)	70 (29.3%)	169 (70.7%)
n = 239[17]	Question asked is 'Would you participate in the following activities organized by the residents' association?'	
Participate in any one type of protest activity	187 (78.2%)	52 (21.8%)
n = 239		
Degree of Militancy		
non-participant	52 (21.8%)	
meeting	64 (26.8%)	
petition	53 (22.2%)	
radical action	70 (29.3%)	
n	239 (100.0%)	

Table 7.5 Respondents' Mobilization Potential in Protest Activities in the Ping Shek THA

Source: Author's survey conducted in the Kowloon Bay THA in September 1991

Factors Explaining Participation Patterns of Ping Shek THA Residents

In this part, we are concerned with the characteristics of the potential participants and non-participants.

We briefly depict the general features of the respondents in respect of the ten independent variables as presented in Table 7.6, and the results of the logistic regression analysis are presented in Table 7.7. The sample analysis excluded 36 cases with missing values.

Variable		Count (percent)
Sex	Male	159 (66.5)
	Female	80 (35.5)
Age	Mean	42.4
Employment status	Employed	164 (68.6)
	Not employed	75 (31.4)
Eligibility for public housing	Yes	221 (80.4)
	No	46 (16.7)
	No answer	8 (2.9)
Level of satisfaction	Satisfied	50 (20.9)
	Average	109 (45.6)
	Dissatisfied	80 (35.5)
Want clearance	Yes	181 (75.7)
	No	20 (8.4)
	No answer	38 (15.9)
Time constraint	No difficulty	50 (20.9)
	Has difficulty	152 (63.6)
	No idea	37 (15.5)
Perceived efficacy of protest	No	76 (31.8)
	Yes	114 (47.7)
	No idea	49 (20.5)
Estimated number of participants	Many	49 (20.5)
	Few	56 (23.4)
	No idea	134 (56.1)
Chance of success	Possible	67 (28.0)
	Little	106 (44.4)
	No idea	66 (27.6)

n = 239*

Table 7.6 Characteristics of the Respondents in the Ping Shek THA

Note: * There are 275 cases in the full sample. The sample size here is 239 because the cases with missing values in any dependent variables are excluded.

Source: *Author's Survey of the Ping Shek THA residents in September 1991*

Socio-economic Characteristics of the Respondents Two-thirds (67%) of the respondents are male. The mean age is about 43. Two-thirds (67%) of the respondents have a paid job.[18]

Acceptance of the Cause of the Community Action As shown in Table 7.6, 76% of the respondents want the THA to be cleared earlier, 8% hold an opposite view and 16% have no ideas in this respect.

Eligibility Four-fifths (80%) of the respondents' households are eligible for public housing flats, and another 17% are ineligible.

Level of Satisfaction 34% of the respondents were dissatisfied with their living conditions, another 21% expressed satisfaction and 44% showed no strong feeling of satisfaction or dissatisfaction. We hypothesize that dissatisfaction may lead to greater willingness to participate in protest.

Perceived Efficacy of Protest The perceived efficacy of protest is measured in three ways: one's evaluation of the power of the collective effort in which one is involved, of the possibility of success and of the estimated number of participants.[19] About half (48%) of the respondents regarded their collective action as effective in exerting pressure on the Housing Authority whereas 32% of the respondents had a contrary view. Another one-fifth (21%) gave no answer to this question. As for the estimated number of participants, about 23% of the respondents predicted that few of their fellow neighbours would participate in protest activity while another 21% thought that there would be many participants. However, like the Kowloon Bay THA residents, more than half (56%) of the respondents did not answer this question. This means that many residents could not, or did not wish to, contemplate their neighbours' view. We interpret this situation as being due to a low degree of acquaintance and a weak social network among the residents. As to the chance of success, the respondents were pessimistic. Only 28% thought that protest would lead to a favourable result provided that there were many participants; but another 44% of the residents considered that there was little or no chance of winning a concession on this issue. We also note that 28% of the respondents did not answer.

Objective Constraint While 21% of the respondents did not indicate that their decisions about participation depended on the availability of time, 64% maintained that they did have problems in this respect. Like the residents of Kowloon Bay THA, the objections from family members and neighbours did not discourage them from participating. Although 14 respondents said that their family members objected to their participation, and 74 (27%) respondents agreed that their neighbours would oppose their participation, only 6 respondents (2%) in each case would take such objections seriously. Hence, we do not consider that family and neighbours' objections constituted constraints on residents' participation and therefore only the variable 'time constraint' is included in the logistic regression analysis.

The Analysis of Willingness to Participate

We now examine the extent to which the independent variables affect the residents' willingness to participate in protest activities. Because of the absence of data about the political orientation of the residents in previous periods, it is impossible for us to know if there has been any change in the residents' level of grievances and political orientation towards community action and protest activities. The results in Table 7.7 show their political orientation at the time of the survey.

Every Person Counts: The Political Participation of ATHA Residents 199

Dependent variable/ Independent variable	Propensity to participate (1)	Propensity to participate (1a)	Meeting (2)	Meeting (2a)	Petition (3)	Petition (3a)	Radical Action (4)	Radical Action (4a)
Sex								
Male	0.67	0.49	0.77	0.56	0.04	-0.05	0.83***	0.51
Female	-	-	-	-	-	-	-	-
Age	0.01	0.01	0.01	0.01	0.01	0.01	0.01	0.01
Employment status								
not employed	0.16	-0.19	0.32	-0.8	0.10	-0.14	0.24	0.02
employed	-	-	-	-	-	-	-	-
Eligibility								
eligible	0.11	x	0.21	x	-0.11	x	-0.23	x
ineligible	-		-		-		-	
Want clearance								
no answer	-0.73		-0.80		-0.34		-0.24	
no	-0.82	x	-0.75	x	-1.15***	x	-1.44***	x
yes	-		-		-		-	
Level of satisfaction	0.027	x	0.05	x	0.17	x	0.17	
Time constraint								
no idea	-1.55****		-1.43****	x	-0.85	x	-0.83	x
no difficulty	2.77****	x	2.85****		0.87***		0.79***	
has difficulty	-		-		-		-	
Perceived efficacy of protest								
no idea	-0.10	x	0.03	x	0.26	x	-0.41	x
yes	0.87		0.95***		0.57		0.37	
no	-		-		-		-	
Chance of success								
no idea	0.31		0.13		-0.17		0.29	
possible	-0.72	x	-0.84	x	-0.16	x	0.39	x
little	-		-		-		-	
Estimated number of participants								
no idea	0.98***		1.08***		0.27		0.65	
many	1.55***	x	1.69****	x	0.70	x	-0.02	x
few	-		-		-		-	
n	231	231	231	231	231	231	231	231
R^2	0.26	0.02	0.26	0.02	0.11	0.01	0.13	0.01

Table 7.7 Odds Ratios for Variables Predicting Four Measures of Participation in Protest Activities Among the Ping Shek THA Residents, Using Two Logistic Regression Models

Figures represent the Beta coefficients for each variable. Participation and non-participation are coded so that positive coefficients indicate that the independent variable is associated with increased odds of being willing to participate relative to the reference group. As age and level of satisfaction are interval variables, positive coefficients indicate that a higher level of age (or level of satisfaction) is associated with increased odds of being willing to participate.

Note: x refers to variable not put in equation
- denotes reference group
** $P < 0.10$; *** $P < 0.05$; **** $P < 0.01$
Source: Author's survey on the Ping Shek THA residents' view on the ATHA issue, May 1992

Equations 1a, 2a, 3a and 4a represent the models which include only socio-demographic variables. As indicated by the low level of R^2, these variables have very low predictive values. Turning to equations 1, 2, 3 and 4 which represent the full models including all the independent variables in our analysis, we also find that the last two full models concerning the willingness to participate in petitions and radical action have a very low R^2. This means that the models are not useful in understanding the respondents' willingness to participate in these two respects. Hence, we focus only on equations 1 and 2.

Like the results of the analysis of the Kowloon Bay THA residents, time constraint is the best predictor of willingness to participate in meetings. Respondents who do not have difficulties with time are much more likely to be willing to participate, as indicated by the large positive figures in equations 1 and 2. On the other hand, willingness to participate in meetings is associated with the respondents' perception of political efficacy. However, this variable is not significant in equation 1. Such difference in the degree of significance between these two models may be due to the fact that the variable 'propensity to participate' does not have a high degree of overlap with the variable 'willingness to participate in meetings', as it did in the case of the Kowloon Bay THA. Therefore, this variable is not a good predictor of whether the respondents are willing to participate in at least one type of protest activity. The variable 'estimated number of participants' is shown to be a good and strong predicator of propensity to participate and willingness to participate in meetings. This means that respondents who think that many will participate are more willing to participate themselves in meetings. This finding supports the argument suggested by Klandermans that a sense of solidarity is more likely to motivate an individual to participate in protest activities.

As shown in equations 1 and 2, the variables 'sex', 'age', 'employment status', eligibility', 'want clearance', 'level of satisfaction' and 'chance of success' are poor predictors.

These findings provide further evidence for our argument that willingness to participate in protest activities is associated to a much lesser degree with the subjective and the objective interests of the respondents, as reflected in the low level of statistical significance of the variables 'eligibility', 'want clearance' and 'level of satisfaction'. Objective constraint, measured in terms of the availability of time, remains the residents' major consideration.

In comparison with the findings of the Kowloon Bay THA, three features are of interest to us. First, the residents of the Ping Shek THA have a lower level of militancy than that of the Kowloon Bay THA residents. Secondly, the variable 'estimated number of participants' has a strong effect on willingness to participate in meetings. Thirdly, the relatively high levels of R^2 (0.36 and 0.41) achieved by the full models representing the Kowloon Bay THA residents' willingness to participate in petitions and radical action, shown in equations 1 and 2, were not achieved in the analysis of the Ping Shek THA residents, in which the comparable figures are 0.11 and 0.13. This means that the included variables are not useful in explaining the Ping Shek THA residents' willingness to participate in petitions and radical action. These differences between the two ATHAs need more discussion.

We interpret the first two differences by reference to the timing of our survey. At that time, the protest was not a burning issue inside the Ping Shek THA. The first team of VOs had terminated their mobilization campaign more than eight months before the survey. Without the involvement of the VOs, the residents found it difficult to obtain any new information about the THA policy and the development of the ATHA protest in other THAs. To most respondents, therefore, the protest pressing for early clearance was not a focal concern in their daily life. Given that the issue had become less urgent, they did not find it necessary to rely on petitions to voice their demands. However, the residents were willing to participate in mass meetings since they expected to obtain information through mass meetings.

In contrast, the situation of the Kowloon Bay THA is different. At the time we conducted the survey, pressing for local rehousing was an urgent issue when the date for moving out of the area was only two months after the survey. This is the reason why the Kowloon Bay THA residents were more willing to participate in protest activities, as indicated by the high degree of militancy.

As to the second difference that estimated number of participants was a better predicator of participation only in the Ping Shek THA, we also link it to the stage of protest in the Ping Shek THA. The ATHA protest was in its initial stage in May 1992 (i.e. the second volunteer organizer team started their mobilization campaign at that time). At this stage, having a sufficient number of participants seemed to be perceived by the respondents as a precondition for any concerted collective action. In our view, the residents needed a sense of solidarity at the initial stage. This need was reflected in our informal interviews with those respondents who had participated in the ATHA protest in 1991. Most respondents stated that they were reluctant to become involved in the protest and complained that the Ping Shek THA residents were handicapped by a low degree of solidarity. Also, they had considerable doubts about the number of participants recruited by the second round of the mobilization campaign. In the case of the Kowloon Bay THA, in contrast, before the survey, the level of participation in mass meetings increased from about 10 participants to more than 20 in each meeting in an open area. It would seem that the number of participants was no longer an important factor to be considered in this situation but their perceived political efficacy became critical.

Comparing our findings in the Ping Shek THA with those in the Kowloon Bay THA, we argue that respondents' views of political participation are associated with the stage of the protest. When the issue becomes urgent, respondents will put more emphasis on political efficacy whereas in the initial stage, as in the case of the Ping Shek THA, the respondents' willingness to participate is not only associated with their perceived political efficacy but also with the estimated number of participants.

Regarding the differences in equations 3 and 4 between the findings in the Ping Shek and Kowloon Bay THAs - the low levels of R^2 in the case of the Ping Shek THA, our explanation relates to the timing of the survey. As has been pointed out, the mobilization campaign in the Ping Shek THA had stopped for a long period of time, and most residents at the time of the survey knew little about the work of the second volunteer organizer team. Furthermore, little in the way of information was distributed in the community to inform the residents what would be done to press for early clearance. Thus, it is not surprising to see that in the Ping Shek THA the respondents' willingness to participate in protest and radical action was not a result of their calculation of their political efficacy and the estimated number of participants. Looking closely at equations 3 and 4 in Table 7.7, the variables 'time constraint' and 'want clearance' are statistically significant. Despite a low level (about 10%) of the variation explained in the dependent variable, these two variables are associated with respondents' willingness to participate. In other words, those who have time and want the government to clear the ATHA are more likely to participate in protest and radical action. This suggests that the residents' decision in relation to participation in protests and radical action, at this very initial stage of mobilization, may be made in terms of interest and the availability of time, rather than political efficacy and the possible number of protestors. In contrast, the respondents of the Kowloon Bay THA found it difficult to win any concessions from the government, and were therefore willing to become involved in more radical activities. Faced with a situation in which direct action was required, the residents showed greater willingness to invest more time and effort in evaluation their political efficacy.

To sum up, time constraints and the perceived efficacy of protest remain the most important considerations in relation to willingness to participate in protest activities. Moreover, because the Ping Shek THA was at a different stage of protest from that of the Kowloon Bay THA, the variable 'estimated number of participants', an indication of a sense of solidarity, was also an important factor determining the respondents' willingness to participate in meetings. We also note that the residents take different factors into consideration at different stages of the protest. Hence, by paying attention to the dynamics of the protest we can make more sense of the statistical patterns recreated through our models. We shall return to this point.

In sum, in our analysis, time constraint is shown to be a very important determinant of the willingness to participate in protest. We wonder why time constraint plays such a critical role in this respect and why the non-participants are not willing to reschedule their daily time-table in order to allow more time for participation in protest. It is necessary for us to further explore what made the residents attach such a low priority to protest participation.

Further Discussion About the Features of the Mobilization Potential of the ATHA Residents

Two features of the mobilization potential of both ATHAs need more discussion. The first is related to the fact that more residents are willing to participate in meetings than in petitions and radical action; the other concerns time constraint as a determinant of non-participation.

In order to understand the first feature, we need to discuss the nature of mass meetings in both THAs. We observed that participation in mass meetings did not indicate a high degree of commitment, nor did it necessarily reveal one's dissatisfaction with the government. Some residents attended mass meetings to see what was going on, or to get some updated information about the current THA policy. Most attenders stood on the fringe of the meeting place, folding their arms and staying for only half an hour. Making a speech was very rare. By contrast, participation in protest and radical action involves the loss of a day's wages and travelling a long way to the site of protest. These activities entail a much higher cost than participation in mass meetings. Hence it is not surprising to see that more residents are willing to participate in mass meetings.

Also, it is interesting to note that non-participants are more likely to have difficulty finding the time to participate in protest activity. However, why do the non-participants not sacrifice some of their working time or leisure time in order to make more room for participation?

Our survey contains no relevant data as to how the respondents attach priority to different activities. In order to answer this question, we draw on our findings from 16 intensive interviews conducted in the Kowloon Bay THA and 30 in the Ping Shek THA.[20] Of the 16 Kowloon Bay THA residents, 8 were non-participants and 8 were participants; among the 30 respondents of the Ping Shek THA, 6 did not support the protest, 12 had participated in at least one meeting organized by the concern groups, and 12 were non-participants. In order to understand people's reasons for non-participation, we only focus on the 20 non-participants in both ATHAs.

In Table 7.8, we categorize the 20 respondents supporting the protest in terms of the reasons they gave for non-participation. Four respondents who are ineligible for public housing felt they had no reason to participate since early clearance brings them no benefits. The 4 elderly respondents are over sixty-five and are sick. They said that they were not able to go out late at night to attend the meetings. One respondent could not speak Cantonese well and was unable to communicate with her neighbours. All these respondents had obvious difficulties in participating in protest activities.

Main reason for non-participation	Kowloon Bay THA	Ping Shek THA
Ineligible for public housing	2	2
Aged/sickness	3	1
Communication problems	1	0
Other	2	9
Total	8	12

Table 7.8   Reason for Non-participation in Protest Activities by THA

Source: Author's intensive interviews in the Kowloon Bay and Ping Shek THAs, in September 1991 and July - Oct 1992 respectively

Among the rest of the respondents (11 out of 20) whom we grouped into the 'other' category, 9 work full-time. We found two reasons why the non-participants proclaimed that they lacked time to participate in protest. One is the insecurity of income from work which demands that a higher priority be given to work than other activities. Two respondents were subject to such a constraint. One respondent is a subcontractor employing three workers to help him in interior decoration work. He agrees with the use of more radical action to pressurize the government. But when he was asked to participate he said he had no time to do so. As he explained: 'I am different from those working for a big company. When I have a job, I have got to work hard. Sometimes we have to wait a long time to get a contract' (Mr. Tsang, 40, Ping Shek THA resident).

The second reason for lack of time is associated with an orientation held by some non-participants, namely a belief that 'one gets what one deserves'. The residents do not attribute their relatively poor living conditions to government policy. On the contrary, they blame themselves. One respondent who illustrates this orientation said that:

> I feel that Hong Kong has a strong sense of fairness, we can compete on the basis of a fair game. If you have the ability, you get the right to choose. How can the government arrange it for you, there are many people, not only you. It is impossible for the government to please everybody. The government is just like a family, it is good to make every member happy. But this is impossible. There must be one or two people dissatisfied with it. Yes, there are demands,

but the government has limited capacity. There is no solution. Hong Kong is good, you can go anywhere and it gives you a lot of chance to choose. You can accept, or you don't. I feel that everyone has an equal chance. I understand that I have low qualifications. If you have the qualifications, you deserve what you get. Unfortunately, I did not fight for it when I was young.... Now, I accept what I get. The Hong Kong government has given us a lot of chances. It gives me no welfare, and I never ask it to give me any. I just ask it to clear this THA and give me a flat. The government has not interfered with me. If you get rich, you can live better. I feel satisfied if no one interferes in my life (Miss Yau, 43, a Ping Shek THA resident, employed and single)

This respondent explained her own situation by her lack of qualifications and a belief that the rules of the game were fair. Although dissatisfied with her living conditions and wanting to move to public housing flats, she felt that it was important to take one's chance and work hard in Hong Kong. It appears that relying on one's own efforts and grasping any opportunity available are the ways to survive in Hong Kong. The drive to earn more through individual effort is particularly intense among those having a family. One respondent stays in his THA for one or two days a week when he is off from his work in mainland China. He came to Hong Kong 15 years ago, and now likes living in Hong Kong. The only thing he is dissatisfied with is his inability to afford a decent accommodation unit. He said, 'I blame myself for not being able to buy my house. Many people came to Hong Kong later than I did, but they bought their own house' (Interview with Mr. Leung, 41, with a wife and one child). He does not blame the government because in his view the government has to consider many factors before taking action; instead he attributes the residents' powerlessness to their lack of solidarity. We can see that he has little confidence in collective action and blames himself for not being able to earn more in order to achieve better living conditions. In the face of keen competition in the urban environment, he resorts to hard work in pursuit of more income for a better future.

As is illustrated in these cases, individual solutions take precedence over collective action. Non-participants have little sense of political efficacy, and also feel that what one gets is what one deserves. In their view, one should be aware of and grasp the chance in Hong Kong for personal betterment. Hence, they give higher priority to work than to participation in communal activity.

The analysis in this section has drawn out the determinants of the extent of mobilization potentials, but it gives us little to go on with regard to the relationship between mobilization potential and actual participation. The next section will explore such a relationship.

Mobilization Potential and Actual Participation

In this section, we discuss the factors that determine actual involvement.

Unfortunately, in the case of the Kowloon Bay THA, we had no opportunity to conduct another survey to explore how willingness to act was translated into action because the ATHA was cleared two months after our survey. Although we have data about the participation experience prior to the study, we cannot use this data to explore whether willingness to participate determines future actual involvement. Nonetheless, we can examine the process of translating mobilization potential into actual mobilization on the basis of data collected in the Ping Shek THA.

As regards the actual involvement in the Ping Shek THA, we use participation in meetings as one of the indicators of actual participation. In order to discover the level of actual involvement, we checked the attendance records of two mass meetings and five concern group meetings within the seven months following the survey. Participation in petitions is not used as this action was not publicized, and therefore except for the concern group members, few other residents knew petitions were taking place.

As shown in Table 7.9, 58 out of 186 potential participants, that is 31%, actually participated in meetings. There is little comparable research to indicate whether this is a high percentage. If we compare this result with the findings by Oegema and Klandermans (1994) of a signing campaign in which 70% of potential participants turned up, the rate of actual involvement in the Ping Shek THA is somewhat low; but it is higher than that of the 1983 Peace Demonstration against the deployment of cruise missiles in the Hague which mobilized 5.3% of the mobilization potential (Klandermans and Oegema, 1987).

208 *Polite Politics*

	Potential participant of mass meeting Count (%)
Had participated	58 (31.2)
Had not participated	126 (68.8)
Total	186 (100.0)

Table 7.9 Rate of Actual Participation in the Ping Shek THA

Source: Author's survey in September 1991 and data from the attendance record of meetings from May to December 1992

Variable		Count (percent)
Sex	Male	37 (63.8)
	Female	21 (36.2)
Age	Mean	44
Employment Status	Employed	38 (65.5)
	Unemployed	20 (34.5)
Eligibility	Yes	49 (84.5)
	No	7 (12.1)
	No answer	2 (3.2)
Want clearance	No answer	5 (8.6)
	No	2 (3.4)
	Yes	51 (87.9)
Level of satisfaction	Satisfied	7 (12.1)
	Average	25 (43.1)
	Dissatisfied	26 (44.8)
Time constraint	No idea	3 (5.2)
	No difficulty	20 (34.5)
	Has difficulty	35 (60.3)
Perceived efficacy of protest	No	14 (24.1)
	Yes	34 (58.6)
	No idea	10 (17.2)
Estimated number of protesters	Many	15 (25.9)
	A few	14 (24.1)
	No idea	29 (50.0)
Chance of success	Possible	22 (37.9)
	Little	23 (39.7)
	No idea	13 (22.4)

n = 58

Table 7.10 Characteristics of the Actual Participants in the Ping Shek THA

Source: Author's survey of the Ping Shek THA residents in September 1991

As shown in Table 7.10, of those actually involved in meetings, 64% are male and 37% are female. The mean age of these participants is 44. Most participants (66%) are employed and 85% are eligible for public housing flats. Slightly less than nine-tenths (88%) want early clearance. These characteristics are similar to those of the respondents in the full sample as shown in Table 7.6. The degree of satisfaction is lower than that revealed in the full sample: more respondents (45% in comparison with 36% in the full sample) are dissatisfied with their living environment. As regards time constraints, three-fifths voiced such a difficulty while 35% did not. Slightly less than three-fifths (59%) disagree that they are politically powerless and 24% agree. It appears that actual participants are more confident of their political power. In the full sample, only 48% disagree with the statement that they are politically powerless. About one quarter (24%) of actual participants, similar to the figure (23%) in the full sample, estimate that only a few residents would be participants. By contrast, actual participants are more likely to believe that many residents will participate (26% in comparison with 21% in the full sample). Actual participants are likely to be those with more confidence about the chance of success (38% compared with 28% in the full model). However, 40% are very pessimistic.

In short, compared to the characteristics of the respondents in the full model, the actual participants are more likely to be those with a stronger desire to have the THA cleared, a higher level of dissatisfaction, more confidence in their political power and a greater belief in the chance of success, and a belief that more residents will participate in protest activities.

We apply the same model used in the analysis of willingness to participate to explore whether the factors at individual level can account for the translation from mobilization potential to actual involvement. Table 7.11 displays the results of the logit regression analysis. The low degree of R^2 indicates the inadequacy of the model in accounting for actual participation. Such a result may be related to some situational factors at the time of conducting the survey. Up till then, there had been no mobilization campaign organized by the VOs, and therefore there were few opportunities (e.g. meetings and protest activities organized by the VOs) for the respondents to consider whether they would participate in the ATHA protest. But when mobilization campaigns were under way, the respondents knew more about the objectives and the activities of the local concern groups. The respondents' decisions about actual participation were thus

210 *Polite Politics*

influenced by the mobilization campaigns. We argue that the translation of mobilization potentials to actual involvement does not rely solely on factors at individual level. Our suggestion is that in order to determine how mobilization is achieved, mobilization efforts should be taken into consideration. Hence we go on to discuss this issue.

Variable		Participation (1)	Participation (1a)
Sex	Male	-0.39	-0.34
	Female	-	-
Age		0.01	0.00
Employment status	Employed	0.06	0.14
	Unemployed	-	-
Eligibility	Yes	-0.27	
	No	-	x
Want clearance	No answer	-1.38***	
	No	-2.06***	x
	Yes	-	
Level of satisfaction		0.12	x
Time constraint	No idea	-0.99	
	No difficulty	0.43	x
	Has difficulty	-	
Perceived efficacy of	no idea	-0.03	
protest	yes	-0.15	x
	no	-	
Estimated number of	no idea	-0.37	
protesters	many	0.20	x
	a few	-	
Chance of success	no idea	0.05	
	possible	0.31	x
	little	-	
n		186	186
R^2		0.12	0.01

Table 7.11 Models Predicting Actual Participation in the Ping Shek THA Protest Activities

Figures represent the Beta coefficients of each variable. Participation and non-participation are coded so that positive coefficients indicate that the independent variable is associated with increased odds of being willing to participate compared with the reference group. As age and level of satisfaction are interval variables, positive coefficients indicate that a higher level of age is associated with increased odds of being willing to participate.

Note: x   refers to variable not put in equation
       -   denotes reference group
    ** $P < 0.10$; *** $P < 0.05$; **** $P < 0.01$

Source: *Author's Survey of the Ping Shek THA residents in September 1991*

Oegema and Klandermans (1994) have argued that the actual involvement of potential participants is associated with whether they are targeted by 'mobilization effort' and became motivated to participate and overcome the barriers against participation. 'Mobilization effort' refers to a range of activities by the mobilization agent. Recent studies, while acknowledging the necessity for the study of mobilization effort, have paid little attention to the study of the actual process of mobilization but have remained reliant on survey findings to illustrate the 'translation process' (Klandermans and Oegma, 1987; Oegema and Klandermans, 1994). It is our contention that for the purpose of examining the translation process, we need to look closer at the process, and in particular at how the mobilizing agents develop and implement the mobilization strategies.

We focus on three aspects of the mobilizing strategy employed by the local concern group mobilization agents in the Ping Shek THA, namely a) targeting the potential participants, b) motivating them and c) overcoming the barriers which the targeted people encounter.

Targeting the Potential Participants

One of the most important issues concerns the scope and intensity of the mobilization effort. At the initial stage of the mobilization campaign in the Ping Shek THA, the VOs distributed a leaflet informing the residents about the current THA policy in April 1992. This was followed by a survey through which the VOs had their first contact with the Ping Shek THA residents. The survey did not specifically mention that there would be a concern group working for the demand of early clearance, but the VOs took this opportunity to explain THA policy and to explore the residents' attitude towards pressing for early clearance. Two weeks later, a mass meeting was organized. The promotion of this mass meeting was through a limited number of posters. The VOs carried out a more intensive promotion campaign on the day of the mass meeting. Two hours before the mass meeting, the VOs announced the place and time of the meeting using a loudspeaker. They walked around the THA so as to ensure full coverage. The VOs also contacted all the residents who had in the survey shown willingness to participate. The mass meeting aimed at explaining the current situation of the ATHA and THA policy. At the meeting, the VOs took down the names, addresses and telephone numbers of everyone present. Immediately after the meeting, they compiled a list of names on the basis of the attendance record. The second meeting was scheduled later and the VOs informed those residents on the list. A few days before the meeting, the VOs contacted the residents again and made sure that everyone knew where and when the meeting was to be held. At the second meeting, the objectives and the form of protest were discussed and decided. After that, contact between the activists and the residents was confined to those whose names were on the list. This contact network was used continually until eight months later when another mass meeting was organized in order to recruit new members.

During this period, there were three ways for the residents to receive information from the activists involved in mobilization. First, they learned that the first meeting was to be held by hearing an announcement two hours before the meeting. Second, activists knocked on the doors of those who had shown willingness to participate in the survey. The final way of becoming informed was through attendance at the first meeting and having one's name and address recorded on the attendance sheet.

It can be seen that the scope of the mobilization effort was quite wide at the initial stage in which the survey and the public announcement covered the whole THA. However, its intensity was not high enough since such mobilization strategies were only employed twice throughout the eight months. Furthermore, in the later stage, both the scope and intensity of the mobilization effort declined because the VOs only targeted those whose names were on the list. However, the VOs took no action to contact those who had shown willingness to participate in protest activities but not shown up at the first meeting. In other words, if one missed the chance to put one's name on the list, one received little information directly from the concern group. We argue that such a mobilization strategy is ineffective because of its narrow scope and low intensity.

Theoretically, potential participants would also be approached through a mobilization campaign involving friends and neighbours. However the VOs found it difficult to get through to most residents in a community like the two ATHAs which are characterized by weak and loose-knit social ties. As has been pointed out, there was no preexisting neighbourhood organization in the two ATHAs, and hence information was difficult to disseminate. In addition, the VOs found it difficult to activate the weak social networks for recruitment. We also discovered that there was little trust among the residents. Two concern group members were reluctant to talk with their fellow neighbours about their involvement in the protest because they were upset by gossip describing them as power-seekers and trouble makers. Another member also disliked doing any direct face-to-face promotion and door-knocking, explaining that she was afraid of being blamed as a trouble-maker. Suffice it to say that the absence of social networks limits the flow of information among the ATHA residents.

The Arousal of Motivation

The literature on participation in social movements highlights the use of hard (or material) and soft incentives to maintain and increase motivation (Knoke and Adams, 1990; Muller and Opp, 1986; Oberschall, 1973; Olson, 1965; Opp, 1986; Opp and Roehl, 1990). Soft incentives refer to self esteem, sociability, felt obligations, and moral injunctions to civic duty (Knoke and Adams, 1987; Mitchell, 1979). We have little information on the effectiveness of using hard (or material) incentives to arouse motivation, since the VOs were unable to try this strategy since they had too few resources to provide any hard incentive. The VOs in both ATHAs tended to employ soft incentives to encourage motivation. At the mass meetings, the concern group members criticized the government and stressed the rights of ATHA residents to decent housing. However, this strategy was only applied to the participants in meetings and the members of the concern groups, rather than to all the potential participants who had expressed their willingness to participate.

Removing Barriers Against Participation

As Klandermans and Oegema (1987) pointed out, this strategy requires knowledge of barriers and the resources to remove them. The VOs were aware of the problem of the limited time residents had to participate in protest. Hence, mass meetings were always held at nine o'clock at night. Nonetheless, they were helpless to remove other barriers, such as the fact the residents were too tired after work, mothers were engaged in heavy housework, etc.

In summary, the translation of mobilization potential into actual participation was held back by the mobilization strategy which was of narrow scope and low intensity, which made limited use of hard and soft incentives, and proved unable to remove barriers against participation. The mobilization effort found it difficult enough to achieve a high rate of realization of mobilization potential in respect of participation in meetings, let alone participation in petitions and radical action. Furthermore, we have examined the issue about the lack of mobilization effort in recruiting participants in petitions.

Conclusion

We start by answering the three questions we posed at the outset. The first question concerned the extent to which the internal structure of the ATHAs was favourable to protest organization. We found that the presence of loose-knit social ties was an obstacle to effective recruitment. Without any preexisting ties between residents and organization at neighbourhood level, the VOs found it difficult to make 'en bloc recruitment' possible.

However, there was a high mobilization potential in both ATHAS, in particular almost three-quarters of the residents were willing to participate in mass meetings. This is a highly favourable condition for a mobilization campaign. We found that the ATHAs were somewhat unique, in that the mobilization potential of the residents was higher than that of the public housing estates where comparable figures are 10% in respect of issues involving estate management and 25% for issues concerning rent policy (Ho et al., 1993).[21] These findings, also, contradict the results of most political culture studies in Hong Kong which describe Hong Kong people as characterized by political apathy and deference (Lau, 1982), and run counter to some literature depicting working class people as being characterized by fatalism. Hence, we argue that the extent of mobilization potential of the THA residents is high and most of them are not politically passive.

Second, how can we explain who participates and who does not? This depends on the interplay of mobilization potential and mobilization efforts. Non-participation is firstly related to people's unwillingness to participate. We found that a low perceived efficacy of protest and time constraints were the determinants of reluctance to participate. Our findings indicate the importance of rational assessments of political effectiveness in decisions about political participation. As regards the meaning of time constraint, we discovered that non-participants attached a higher priority to work and sought individual solutions to their poor living conditions rather than collective action. Some non-participants attributed their problem to personal failure. This reflects the way the keen competition in urban life in Hong Kong fosters a belief that makes people less likely to identify an external agent (e.g. the government) as the cause of personal problems (Ferree and Miller, 1985). Another reason for non-participation is related to the answer of the third question about the extent to which the local concern groups are able to mobilize participation.

This is that the mobilization effort was limited. The concern group in the Ping Shek THA did not maintain a mobilization campaign of a sufficiently wide scope and high intensity. The low level of actualization of mobilization potential was also associated with the limited use of incentives and an inability to overcome the residents' barriers against participation. In this chapter, we have not explored the reasons why the concern groups employed such a limited mobilization strategy. We shall come back to this in the next chapter.

Above all, we have argued against the view that dissatisfaction and grievances are the cause of participation in collective action. Instead, we have emphasized the gap between discontent and mobilization potential, and between the mobilization potential and actual involvement, and have seen how mobilization effort is the link as to the translation. However, we have also noted that the timing of the surveys affected the data collected. The recency of mobilization efforts by activists and the proximity of clearance were shown to be important in interpreting the survey data.

Finally, our discussion of the ATHA protest has a number of limitations. First, in respect of the factors influencing residents' mobilization potential, less than half of the variance was explained by the regression equations, hence there is much room for further work to account for how people decide to participate in collective action. Second, in our discussion we treated participation and non-participation as a 'once and for all' decision, whereas in reality, it is not. Those who participate once may change their mind and lose interest in participation. Questions such as how a protest group can maintain its supporters' interest and motivation, and why some participants give up have not been addressed. Third, we remain ignorant of how the mobilizers organize a protest with the people who have no preexisting social networks and a low degree of social cohesion. It is true that, as Mullins (1987) pointed out in his study of an urban movement in Brisbane, social cohesion is not a necessary condition for mobilization, but successful mobilization needs a 'broader social base, specifically the way it [is] linked to a great range of other contradictions' (1987:365). This raises the question of how the ATHA protest could spread its protest activity in order to build up links with other social forces? Finally, we found a moderately high degree of militancy among the residents in both THAs (46% in the Kowloon Bay THA and 29% in the Ping Shek THA).[22] In this chapter, we have not entered into a discussion of why such a tendency does not translate into actual protest activities or why the ATHA protest remains polite. Also, we have mentioned the limited mobilization campaign to motivate residents to participate in protest action. But, why was this so? These questions will be answered in the next chapter.

Notes

1   The scheduled clearance was cancelled later, but the project did not resume its work in the Kowloon Bay THA.
2   The minimum population size to justify the work of a community social work team is 3,000 people.
3   See chapter 4 for the characteristics of the volunteer activists, and the types and frequency of the protest activities organized by the two concern groups.
4   It is difficult to obtain an exact figure for the number of residents living there at that moment. According to the official data as at April 1991, there were 447 eligible households and 59 which were ineligible. An official of the Housing Department stated that in April 1991 there were 185 households which they were unable to contact and he believed that such residents were living outside the THA. Moreover, by September, we estimate that about 40 households had moved out, and subsequently there were about 281 households in Kowloon Bay THA at that time. Given that there were 60 household members participating in protest activities, the estimated rate of participation is about 22 % of the total number of prevailing households.
5   This figure is not strictly comparable with the rate of participation in the signing campaign in the ATHA protest because in our study the ATHA respondents were asked if they had participated in that particular campaign whereas in Leung and Lee's study the respondents were asked whether they had participated in 'any signing campaign in the past.' In the latter survey, the question was about the participation in any protest, not any specific protest, therefore it should have inflated the number of respondents who had participated in protest activities.
6   The sample of interviews was selected randomly by computer. One hundred and twenty addresses were generated. The first period of interviews were targeted at 30 ouseholds, and only 12 successful interviews were returned. Cases were categorized as unsuccessful after the interviewer had visited the household three times without success or found a vacant unit. Additional households were then put on the interview list. The

response rate for this survey is quite low at 25%. We obtained 30 successful cases and 90 were unsuccessful. This low response rate was largely because of vacant flats.

7. Respondents' education level is not included in the analysis. Most respondents received their education in mainland China in the late 1960s and 1970s when the Cultural Revolution was at its peak. It is difficult for us to assess the meaning of education level when the education system has been undermined entirely. One respondent told us that she attended Middle Three but had not learnt anything throughout her three years in the middle school. Owing to unreliable data about education level, we do not take it into consideration in our analysis.

8. For details about the socio-economic characteristics of the respondents, see Chapter 5.

9. In our survey, the sample size is 115. We dropped 23 cases in the analysis because these respondents had received offers from the Housing Department and were going to move to Tseung Kwan O. We believe that their acceptance of the offer affects their willingness to participate and their perception of the issue, and have therefore not included these cases. The sample size is reduced from 92 to 74 after we exclude those cases with missing values.

10. No respondents in our survey replied that they would participate in petitions and radical actions but would not participate in meetings. Among the 36 respondents who said that they would participate in radical action, all of them gave an affirmative reply to the question about participation in meetings and only 4 said that they would not participate in petitions.

11. For details about the socio-economic characteristics of the THA residents, see chapter 5.

12. Only three (2.6 %) out of 115 respondents disagreed with the demands of the associations. Another one-seventh (16 %) did not answer this question. After the cases of those who had accepted the offer of rehousing by the Housing Department were excluded, the sample size fell to eighty. In this sample, 98 % of the respondents supported the cause of the protest, i.e. pressing for local district rehousing. Only 2 respondents did not accept the cause of the protest. As there are only 2 cases of non-supporters, they are excluded from the following analysis.

13. According to the official data, there were 122 ineligible households (17.3 % of the total) (Hong Kong Housing Authority, File Code: HD(C) 5/397/91). The differences between our survey and the official findings is small.

14. The total number of respondents in our survey is 115 of which 17 cases are ineligible. The question about the expected type of housing is only applicable to those eligible households.

15. After excluding those cases with missing values, the sample size in this analysis becomes 261.

16. This convention has been used by Fernandez and McAdam (1989). See also Lincoln and Zeitz, 1980; Rao and Miller, 1971.

17. Thirty-six cases with missing values are excluded.

18. Employment status refers to whether a respondent has a paid job or not. Unlike the political participation surveys concerning the class positions of the respondents, we tend

to accept that class position is less important as a differentiator in our study as most respondents were engaged in manual work in the manufacturing and construction sectors. We argue that a paid job is more important because it indicates that the respondent is a breadwinner and has more power in the family.

19   Another aspect is shown in the respondents' evaluation of their own participation. As Klandermans (1984) argued, one would hesitate to become involved in protest activities if one's involvement was considered unimportant. Nevertheless, most of the Ping Shek THA residents seem to be able to overcome this constraint. The findings in the survey indicate that over 70% of the respondents think of their involvement as important, while only around 9% regard their support as unimportant. Our questionnaire posed this question in a specific way. The respondents were asked whether they thought of their participation as important, and the respondents could answer yes, no or no idea. But another dimension was added to this question. As it was usual for the respondents (as we found out in our pilot test) to say 'yes' but to add that there is no time, our interviewer would mark this reply at the same time. Therefore, this question indicates two aspects. The first concerns the respondents' evaluation of their own contribution to the protest. The second indirectly shows whether the respondents subjectively perceived that time is a constraint against their participation. In our analysis, we decided to employ this question as an indication of the second aspect, namely, time constraint, on the grounds that few respondents answered that their participation was unimportant. Twenty-four (9%) out of 275 respondents said that their participation was unimportant, 16 of which (6%) did not support the concern group.

20   During the fieldwork period, many households had moved out, leaving about 200 - 250 households. We were not able to construct an exact sample frame for sampling, so we employed random sampling to choose interviewees. We first selected 35 blocks and then randomly selected one household for interview. Fifteen successful interviews were returned, and the response rate is 43%. The failure cases were largely because of vacant flats. We found that the sample was biased towards having more female and older persons. Even though we conducted our interviews in the late evening, i.e. after 9 p.m., most respondents said that the young and male family members usually came back after midnight. We could not find any alternative way of contacting the younger members. For this reason, we should interpret very cautiously the findings of our interviews. For the sampling method for the interview in the Ping Shek THA, see note 6.

21   The survey was conducted in order to examine the tenants' views and opinions on the Hong Kong Housing Society which is one of the statutory organizations responsible for the provision of public housing in Hong Kong. The sample size is 964. The question asked in the survey was: 'Please indicate the most likely way you would choose to express discontent with issues about estate management?'. Another question with the same wording is about rent policy. The respondents can choose: 'staff of Housing Society', 'media and councillors', 'tolerate' and 'collective action'.

22   Marsh's findings are not strictly comparable with our figures because of his use of a different number of items and measuring methods. However, if we take the item

'occupation and blocking traffic' as equivalent to our item 'radical action', the tendency of THA residents to take militant action is much higher than that of British people. Whereas only 19% of British people are willing to go so far as militant action, the figure for the Kowloon Bay THA and the Ping Shek THA residents reached 46% and 29% respectively.

8 The Mobilization Process: External Organizers, Local Leaders and the Choice of Strategies

Introduction

In Chapter 2, we categorized movement actions into four types, namely orderly politics, polite politics, protest and violence. The first type, 'orderly politics' is considered to be an institutionalized action while the other three are non-institutionalized actions. In chapter 6 we argued that there were limited political opportunities available to the Aged Temporary Housing Area protesters. Given the difficulty they faced in gaining access to the formal political structure, protesters were obliged to adopt non-institutionalized actions to fight for their interests. In order to take non-institutionalized actions, the local concern groups encountered three issues concerning (a) the maintenance of the concern groups themselves, (b) participation mobilization, and (c) the choice of strategy. In this chapter, how the local concern groups deal with these issues is the main focus.

As has been pointed out in the previous chapters, there were few attempts to mobilize participation in order to build up mass base support. Also, polite politics strategy was the dominant form of strategy adopted. In this chapter, we want to explore the factors determining these features of the local concern groups. Was the limited mobilization effort due to the low emphasis placed on building up a mass social movement by the mobilization agents, or were there structural constraints which restricted the alternatives open to the concern groups? Whether the use of polite politics strategy was a choice by the mobilization agents, or due to external constraints which prevented these agents from carrying out their chosen strategies?

To understand the choice of mobilization strategy, we focus on the orientations and interpretations of the mobilization agents' situation, and the constraints they face. The next section starts with an examination of the three major mobilization agents in local concern groups, namely, the community social workers (CSWs), the volunteer organizers (VOs) and the indigenous leaders, with specific focus on their *social positions, degree of commitment*, and *orientations toward local protest*. We should stress that the composition of the organizers, including the VOs and the CSWs, of the concern groups studied here is not typical of local protest groups or neighbourhood associations in Hong Kong. Unlike other protest groups which are only made up of paid CSWs and lay leaders, VOs are involved in these concern groups.

In this chapter, we examine in turn the actors involved in mobilizing local residents into action (section 8.1), the role of mobilization agents in creating and sustaining local concern groups (section 8.2), the interaction between these actors and the formulation of mobilization strategies and tactics (section 8.3), and the success or failure of the local mobilization and protest (section 8.4).

The Mobilization Agents

In chapter 6 we pointed out that the VOs and the CSWs were the most likely sources of agents who would act as agitators in the ATHA protest. In chapter 7 we also argued that both were critical to the formation and the development of the local concern groups in the absence of indigenous leaders who would be able to independently articulate the ATHA issue. In such circumstances, the ATHA protest involved two kinds of external mobilization agents, namely the CSWs, and the VOs who are recruited by pressure groups. This section examines the character of these two types of external mobilization agents and the indigenous leaders.

In the ATHA protest, the two local concern groups were each composed of three types of agents: VOs, CSWs and indigenous leaders. VOs were unpaid and had no roots in the ATHAs where they were involved in mobilization and organization tasks. CSWs were paid staff of a social work organization and could command organizational resources to assist the THA residents in a designated THA. Indigenous leaders were those who were residing in a THA and were continuously involved in the ATHA protest activities. The difficulty in giving a concrete definition of indigenous leaders lies in the lack of a clear criterion to distinguish leaders from those who are involved in protest activities on an irregular basis. In our analysis, indigenous leaders refer to those ATHA residents who participated in concern group activities for at least two months.

The VOs and the CSWs joined the ATHA protest at different moments. The initial mobilization tasks were carried out by the Caring Groups for the THA Policy (CGTP) whose major objective is to organize the ATHA residents to pressurize the Housing Department to tackle the appalling living conditions in the THAs. (This pressure group consisted of paid social workers who were interested in the analysis of THA policy, and whose main function was to provide information to the THA residents). As regards the ATHA issue, a survey in 18 ATHAs conducted in 1990 revealed that in 10 ATHAs more than half of the respondents were dissatisfied with their living conditions and wanted early clearance. In particular, of the Kowloon Bay THA residents, 72% of the respondents wanted early clearance and in the case of Ping Shek THA, 62% had the same desire.

The evidence of the residents' demand for early clearance provided the CGTP with a basis on which to launch community action. The CGTP aimed to mobilize the THA residents to form their local concern groups in order to arouse the public and the government's awareness of the ATHA issue. Subsequently it organized several small teams to serve those ATHAs where there were no community social work teams of the Neighbourhood Level Community Development Projects (NLCDP) in order to avoid conflict with NLCDP teams.[1] Later a staff member of the People's Council on Public Housing Policy (PCPHP)[2] decided to work in four ATHAs, namely Lai Chi Kok, Kowloon Bay, Ping Shek and Hong Ning Road THAs, and the Council established the Small Cross-District Alliance team to coordinate the mobilization and organization tasks for the last three ATHAs.[3]

Five VOs were involved in the initial stage of mobilization in the Kowloon Bay THA. They started in April 1990 and recruited six residents to be the indigenous leaders. A local concern group for the ATHA issue was set up later. After two months only two VOs continued to be involved in local mobilization, one was the author and the other was a social work student in his final year of study in a post-secondary college.[4] One month later, a CSW, Mr. Han, joined the volunteer organizer team and worked in his spare time as a VO. Since he was an experienced CSW, Mr. Han took the role of chief organizer. During this period, the local concern group consisted of the VOs and the indigenous leaders. The composition changed in late 1990 after the involvement of the paid CSWs. In late 1990, Mr. Han applied to the Community Section of the Council of Social Service for the establishment of an NLCDP team to work in the Kowloon Bay THA. The application was approved and the job was assigned to Cooperative, the social work organization that Mr. Han worked for as a paid CSW. The NLCDP team consisted of a team supervisor (Mr. Han), one team leader and one social work assistant, and was responsible for providing services to the residents there. Since 1991, two types of external agents have thus been working in the Kowloon Bay THA, namely the paid CSWs and the VOs. Both worked with the indigenous leaders until the local concern group dissolved in January 1992, at the time when the ATHA protest in this THA terminated.[5]

Despite the unbroken involvement of the CSWs and the VOs, the indigenous leadership in the Kowloon Bay THA was characterized by a high turnover rate. From the beginning, the Kowloon Bay THA concern group had certain formal organizational roles: it had a committee that consisted of a chairperson, a vice-chairperson, a secretary, a recreational secretary and four coordinators. After a couple of months, the chairperson, two secretaries and one coordinator withdrew and left four members to try to maintain the functioning of the concern group. Later, four new members were recruited. One male resident who had experience in social protest was also recruited by the VOs. During the period from April 1990 to June 1991, three men and six women were involved in the concern group. In July 1991, the membership changed entirely because of an internal conflict. Except for one couple, all the previous members left the concern group while seven new members joined, including two men and five women.

In the Ping Shek THA, local mobilization was initiated by two VOs in May 1990. They organized the first local concern group which consisted of ten residents and focused on pressing for early clearance. By the summer of 1991, the VOs departed and the concern group dissolved. There had not been any ATHA protest until the arrival of the second team of VOs in May 1992. The new team consisted of the author and six people who were paid staff of different social work organizations. They knew that there were no social workers assigned to the area, and therefore decided to continue the mobilization campaign in this ATHA. However their involvement was very unstable. Table 8.1 shows the period of involvement and the reasons for departure of the VOs in the Ping Shek THA.

Volunteer organizer	Period of involvement	Reason for departure
A	May 1992 - August 1992 June 1993 - April 1994* (very inactive in this period)	study abroad
B	May 1992 - April 1994*	
C	May 1992 - August 1993	study abroad
D	May 1992 - August 1993	study abroad
E (the author)	May 1992 - September 1992 April 1993 - April 1994*	study abroad
F	May 1992 - March 1993	personal reason
G	May 1992 - August 1992	personal reason

Table 8.1 Period of Involvement of the Volunteer Organizers in the Ping Shek ATHA Protest, May 1992-April 1994

Note: * The fieldwork ended in April 1994.

Source: Author's fieldwork

A community social work team (i.e. an NLCDP team) became involved in the Ping Shek THA in January 1993 because of the expansion of the social work organization - Hong Kong Christine Service. This organization was allowed to work in the Ping Shek THA by the government and its terms of reference were to meet the needs of the residents in the Ping Shek and Shun Lee THAs.[6] The team consisted of one team leader and two social work assistants. All were involved in the ATHA protest till the end of our fieldwork.[7]

The first local concern group of the Ping Shek THA was composed of about six to eight members.[8] It lay idle in early 1992 because of the departure of the VOs. In May 1992, with the assistance of the new volunteer organizer team, a group of residents, including six women and five men, re-formed the concern group but its membership was unstable. Only one man and three women remained actively and continuously involved in the concern group. In October 1993, they recruited seven active members (five women and one man).

After a brief description of the three types of mobilization agents, the question will be raised of how the agents interpret the meaning of the ATHA protest. In understanding recruitment to social movements, much attention is given to the characteristics of those being recruited (Gerlach and Hine, 1970). In our view, this overlooks an important aspect of recruitment, that is, the motivation, the commitment and the interpretation of the aims of the protest of those who do the recruiting, i.e. the mobilization agents. No less important are the social positions of these agents which may influence their incumbent's interpretation of the situation. Here we outline the characteristics of the mobilization agents of the ATHA protest and show that the mobilization agents' interpretation of the situation is associated with their social positions. The following analysis of the mobilization agents is based on the data collected from our fieldwork and interviews.

Volunteer Organizers

In April 1990, the author and a social work student approached a staff member of the PCPHP and expressed their willingness to become involved in a local housing protest. The author's intention was to study a locally-based social action, while the student wanted to have some experience of community development work. Whereas the author had personal (and academic) reasons for being involved, the social work student was solely motivated by his sympathy with the disadvantaged people in the ATHAs. As he explained, he just wanted to help the ATHA residents to obtain better living conditions. Both seemed to have a simple and clear rationale of their involvement in the ATHA protest. As far as Mr. Han (mentioned above) was concerned, he said that he felt responsible for the Kowloon Bay THA residents. He had been a member of the community social work team in the Kowloon Bay THA before 1985. His team left the THA in 1985 and after that the CSWs paid little attention to the residents even though the THA was still there. His personal sense of guilt led him to join the volunteer organizer team. It appears that the VOs' personal motives had nothing to do with any consideration of material return or non-material benefits such as social status and reputation, since it was clear to them that no material benefit could be gained from their involvement. Also, we found that none of these VOs had any relationship with political parties and political ideology was not a key factor crucial to their involvement.

One intriguing feature of the VOs is the relationship between Mr. Han and the other two VOs. The two VOs disagreed with Mr. Han's view that organizers should strictly refrain from any directive action, and avoid influencing the clients. Their differing interpretations of the role of organizer in community action created tension.

To understand the roots of their conflict, we should explore their different orientations toward the ATHA issue. The term orientations is understood, as Roberts suggested, 'as those dispositions to act that emerge from the conscious effort of individuals to make sense of their past experiences and to mould their futures in accordance with these interpretations' (1973:296). One's dispositions to act may be associated with one's experience, knowledge and personal preference. Also, we should not lose sight of the means by which the VOs can explain and justify their action and performance. As Roberts pointed out, any external agents, when getting involved in community organizations, are strangers to the people in the community. Hence, it is necessary for them to justify their existence, involvement and performance. For example, as members of a CSW team which is officially assigned to a THA, the CSWs can easily justify their involvement in a THA. But, as part of the social work profession and paid staff members of social work organizations, the CSWs are accountable to the profession and to their superiors in the organization. Their performance should be in conformity with the rules set by the profession and their social work organizations. We can see that one's disposition is not only associated with one's experience, education and personal preference; it is also related to one's social position.

Mr. Han, as an experienced CSW, was inclined to interpret his involvement in the ATHA protest from a social worker's point of view. Despite taking the role of a VO, his action continued to be dictated by his self-conception as a social worker. For example his commitment to not directing clients is part of the traditional social work role. He saw his involvement largely as an attempt to complete his unfinished work in the Kowloon Bay THA.

The two VOs by contrast were neither social workers nor experienced in community action. They simply saw themselves as new learners ready to help out. Whereas Mr. Han cherished the non-directive principle because he considered himself to be a CSW, the VOs perceived themselves as independent helpers. Most important, the VOs wanted to achieve a successful mobilization of residents, and hopefully, a concession from the government. Such desire was not only a matter of personal preference, but is also related to the VOs' social positions. Success in mobilization and securing a victory would prove the VOs' ability and their significance. So unlike Mr. Han who saw himself as a social worker and needed to observe the principle of being 'non-directive', the two VOs wanted to do more and get things done. We can see that different social positions led to these different interpretations of their roles. Accordingly, conflicts arose when Mr. Han imposed on the team his interpretation of the role of organizer which differed from that of the VOs. In 1991, the main issue between the VOs and the CSWs was their working relationship. Two meetings were held, in which the CSWs attempted to persuade the VOs to depart while the latter insisted on staying in the Kowloon Bay THA. No solution was reached, cooperation ended, and conflicts between the two groups continued.[9] However, the CSWs were to a large extent dominant in meetings and agenda setting because they insisted on being the chief organizers in the team.

In the case of the Ping Shek THA, none of the seven VOs had a political background. They had full-time paid jobs as CSWs in other THAs. Their involvement began through a joint meeting organized by a committee of THA residents associations, in which the CSWs learnt that the worsening conditions in many ATHAs were being ignored by the government. They subsequently formed a VO team to mobilize the ATHA residents to fight for better living conditions. Working in the same profession and having known each other, they had a very good social relationship. Their interpretation of their roles in the protest was different from that of Mr. Han in the Kowloon Bay THA. As VOs, they did not think that they had to strictly observe all the rules set by the social work profession, especially the non-directive principle. However, simultaneously, as CSWs and VOs, they were confused about when and to what extent they could deviate from the non-directive principle. When we discuss their forms of involvement in the concern group, we can see how this confusion shapes their behaviour.

As in the Kowloon Bay THA, the CSWs disliked the involvement of the VOs. They saw the involvement of other external agents as an intervention into their area, i.e. the area for which the CSWs were responsible. There were some arguments between the two groups and their working relationship was not good.

In short, we see that the VOs had neither political nor calculative motives for their involvement. No political ideology served as a framework governing their behaviour, or as a conceptual framework to interpret issues. They were highly committed to offering help to the ATHA residents. There was a better relationship among the Ping Shek VOs, than in the case of the Kowloon Bay THA. With little experience in taking the organizer role, none of the VOs, except Mr. Han, possessed any pre-conception about the nature and direction of the ATHA protest. Moreover, since they were not part of the paid staff of any organization, they were not responsible to any superior. It is thus reasonable to say that they considered themselves to be accountable to both the ATHA residents to whom they offered assistance, and to their conscience.

Community Social Workers

Following the above analysis, we examine the motivation, commitment, and interpretations of the role and situations of the CSWs. As the paid staff members of a social work organization, the CSWs were clearly not self-motivated to engage in the ATHA protest. This raises the question of what factor drives the CSWs to work for the ATHA residents.

The social position of the CSWs was different from that of the VOs. They were paid staff of social work organizations and were responsible for the designated community. But their terms of reference were not clearly specified. Frontline CSWs in Hong Kong enjoy a very high degree of autonomy because the Committee of the Community Development of the Hong Kong Council of Social Services lays down few objectives apart from simple and abstract principles requiring the CSWs to provide social services to the deprived. Neither the mobilization of THA residents to protect their rights nor teaching the residents the importance of concerted collective action is included in the list of responsibilities.[10] Community social work in Hong Kong is entirely different from the 'Maximum Feasible Participation' and the Community Action Program that were advocated in the United States with an emphasis on shifting service coordination towards citizen participation (Greenstone and Peterson, 1976; Marris and Rein, 1967; Moynihan, 1969). As pointed out in Chapter 6, collective action was discouraged by the social work profession in the 1980s. This does not mean, however, that CSWs are entirely prevented from organizing collective action. Since there are no strict rules against advocating collective action, the CSWs can exercise their discretion as to the extent of their involvement. In other words, whether the CSWs advocate social protest is dependent on their personal orientations and interpretations of situations. Their evaluation of the significance and effects of concerted collective action also matters. Our analysis must be sensitive to these aspects.

The CSWs in the Ping Shek THA appeared to be less committed to the ATHA issue than their counterparts in the Kowloon Bay THA. Before 1993, the CSWs had been working in an ATHA - the Shun Lee THA - where the local concern group had not been involved in any protest action concerning the ATHA issue. The team leader explained in a meeting with other CSWs that this lack of action was because of the unreadiness of the residents, in the sense that the residents were not prepared to organize any social protest. However, it is strange to see that the CSWs did not undertake any training in that THA to enable the residents to launch such action. Another team member pointed out in an interview that the team leader was lazy and not keen on protest activity.[11] When serving the Ping Shek THA, the CSWs were reluctant to deal with emerging issues in the THA. For example, in June 1993, the Housing Department announced the clearance date of part of the Ping Shek THA. The VOs urged the CSWs to consider whether it was necessary to explore the extent to which the residents were dissatisfied with the rehousing arrangement, but no action was taken by the CSWs.

In our view, the low commitment among the CSWs in the Ping Shek THA was generated by the discordant relationship between the two groups of organizers. The tension between the CSWs and VOs was evident in an argument after a demonstration held on the day of Governor Chris Patten's visit to the Ping Shek THA in June 1993. On that day the Shun Lee THA residents participated in the petition and were well prepared with banners and colourful slogans. By contrast, the Ping Shek THA concern group received little advice from the CSWs. In the face of the concern group members' criticism, the community social workers explained that everything had been organized by the Shun Lee THA residents themselves. The VOs were critical of this explanation. They argued that even though the tactics were worked out by the Shun Lee THA residents, the CSWs should have instructed the Ping Shek THA residents to organize similar actions in protest. Our interpretation of the inaction of the CSWs was that it resulted from the overt competition between the two groups of organizers. Since the CSWs were unhappy about working with the VOs, they put more effort into the Shun Lee THA and less in the Ping Shek THA in order to avoid creating any chance for the VOs to claim credit.

By contrast, the commitment of the CSWs in the Kowloon Bay THA seems to have been higher than that of their counterparts in the Ping Shek THA. They devoted more time to building personal ties with the residents and issued a number of leaflets about the ATHA protest to the residents. Nevertheless, despite a high degree of commitment, the CSWs were gradually burnt out by the heavy workload of providing social services to the THA residents. With limited time and manpower, the CSWs in the Kowloon Bay THA were unable to take care of all the residents' needs. As one CSW said in an interview, he had little time to deal with the huge volume of daily work. The increasing caseloads prevented him from assisting the local concern group. In addition, since everything seemed to be changing rapidly and was out of their control, the CSWs found it difficult to think through any strategy or tactics of the protest.[12]

Nevertheless, although they had a higher degree of commitment, all the CSWs of the Kowloon Bay THA observed the CSW's non-directive principle and were reluctant to play the leadership role in the local concern group. They were also somewhat pessimistic. One CSW said: 'The THA residents were fighting for an impossible dream' (Informal interview, Mr. Lip, a CSW team leader). As a consequence, the CSWs spent a lot of effort in organizing meetings, publishing leaflets and providing services, but they refrained from leading the ATHA protest.

In spite of a difference between the CSWs in the two ATHAs in terms of their degree of commitment, their orientations toward local issues were similar. They neither interpreted the ATHA issue in the context of ethnic and class conflict, nor attempted to ideologize or theorize this issue by relating it to the deeper level of social structure. Both had a tendency to consider the rise of ATHAs to be simply a result of a shortage of public housing flats.

After an examination of the orientations of the CSWs and the VOs, we can discern their similarity and differences. First of all, neither the VOs nor the CSWs had connections with political parties or a deep commitment to any ideology. Secondly, the CSWs, occupying the specific social position of social workers, considered themselves to be responsible for their clients - i.e. the THA residents. Thus, even if not committed to the cause of the ATHA protest, they considered themselves to be obliged to provide assistance to the local concern groups and were not allowed to hand their tasks to other external organizations, such as politicians and VOs. The VOs by contrast did not occupy the same social positions as the CSWs, and thereby enjoyed a higher degree of autonomy. Thirdly, due to their acceptance of the 'non-directive' principle of social work, the CSWs refrained from playing any role as formal leaders in the protest. By contrast, the VOs were not CSWs and therefore were free to decide their roles in the protest. To sum up, our comparison of the two groups of organizers shows that different social positions entail different role interpretations, which in turn generate competition and conflicts.

Indigenous Leaders

The reasons for the participation of the indigenous leaders are discussed in the next section which focuses on the maintenance of the local concern groups. Here we simply present a brief account of the characteristics and levels of involvement of the indigenous leaders.

We have defined the indigenous leaders as those who participated in concern group activities for at least two months, and therefore our discussion here does not include those who participated in the concern groups for a short period of time. During the four years of the ATHA protest, altogether about 20 people in the Kowloon Bay THA and 25 people in the Ping Shek THA took an active part in the local concern groups. However, the turnover rates in both THAs were high. Table 8.2 shows the number of active concern group members in the two ATHAs. We should point out that as their involvement was somewhat unstable, what is presented here is a rough description of the indigenous leaders' level of involvement.

Name of THA	Period	Number of indigenous leaders in the concern group
Kowloon Bay	May 1990 - Jul 1990	12
	Aug 1990 - Jun 1991	9
	Jul 1991 - Jan 1992	9*
Ping Shek	Jun 1990 - Aug 1991	8
	May 1992 - Apr 1993	11**
	May 1993 - Aug 1993	4
	Sep 1993 - Apr 1994#	10

Table 8.2 Level of Involvement of the Indigenous Leaders in the Kowloon Bay THA and the Ping Shek THA, April 1990-April 1994

Note: * Except a couple, all of them are new members.
  ** Only three members were involved in the concern group in the first period.
  # Our fieldwork ended in April 1994.

Source: Author's fieldwork

The majority of the concern group members in the two ATHAs had similar social backgrounds, organization affiliations and political consciousness. Like most THA residents, most concern group members had not finished secondary education, but there were two exceptions: one woman who was a medical practitioner in mainland China and another woman who was a college graduate.[13] Of those with a full-time job, most were manual workers, skilled or unskilled, in factories or in the construction sector. But one vice-chairperson of the Kowloon Bay THA concern group was a self-employed trader and one active member in the Ping Shek THA was a salesman. Most of their household incomes in 1991 were not more than HK$10,000.

Political activity seemed to be a new experience to all of the concern group members. Few had experience in local politics and community action, or belonged to any voluntary organizations. Only one woman in the Ping Shek THA concern group had been active in trade union activities and was enthusiastic about helping her fellow neighbours; another woman had been involved in a squatter protest ten years before.

Surprisingly, as we saw in Chapter 7, spatial proximity did not lead to strong social networks among the THA residents. Most concern group members were not acquainted with other members before the first concern group meeting, and throughout the protest, they did not develop strong friendship ties.

In this section, we have examined the motivation, commitment, social positions and the role interpretations of the CSWs and the VOs. The CSWs considered themselves to be the organizers of the ATHA residents, but since they observed the 'non-directive' principle, they had limited involvement in leadership. The VOs were self-motivated activists but inexperienced in leading a social protest. Due to their different role interpretations, the working relationship between the CSWs and VOs is characterized by tension and competition. The indigenous leaders lacked experience and their levels of involvement were unstable. In the next section, we shall ask how such a locally-based protest group can maintain itself as the centre of the local protest, especially in an internal context characterized by unstable involvement and internal competition.

The Creation and Maintenance of the Foundation of ATHA Protest: The Local Concern Groups

As we pointed out in the previous section, in practice the local concern groups had a high turnover, and in Chapter 7 we found a low level of participation in various forms of protest activity. In view of these features, there arise a question of how the local concern groups are created and sustained. We shall emphasize the mobilization efforts of the organizers, i.e. the CSWs and the VOs, and in particular the reasons for the indigenous leaders' participation. We first examine what the organizers' mobilization efforts have achieved, and then proceed to explore the reasons for the participation of the indigenous members.

The Achievements of the Mobilization Agents

The major contribution of the organizers to the ATHA protest can be seen in three respects: organizing activity, sustaining the groups and training the members.

Organizing Activity The organizers are important to the continuity of the ATHA protest. Since the concern group members seldom took the initiative to call meetings, the organizers arranged meetings and kept in touch with the concern group members.[14] The 'door knocking' method, though time-consuming, was very effective. Prior to meetings, the organizers knocked on the doors of those residents whose names were on a membership list and asked them to attend. This gave the concern group members a sense of obligation to participate. Also, the organizers had actively developed a relationship with the concern group members to create more trust among them.

The importance of the organizers was revealed by the fact that when they were inactive, the concern groups no longer functioned. In the summer of 1991, the Ping Shek THA concern group collapsed after the two VOs departed. In the Kowloon Bay THA, the concern group frequently became inactive when the VOs did not initiate any meetings or activities.[15]

Maintenance of the Concern Group Members The VOs continually persuaded the concern group members that collective effort was possible and necessary to gain victory. Their emotional support encouraged the concern group members to stay and fight on. When concern group members were pessimistic about their neighbours' motivation to participate, the organizers arranged mass meetings to recruit members. In mid-1991, the concern group in the Kowloon Bay THA became disoriented and dispirited when the clearance date was announced. The CSWs organized a mass meeting to recruit new leaders, and the VOs invited social activists to attend their mass meeting so as to show third party support for the residents. A similar situation occurred in the Ping Shek THA. In September 1993, only four members remained involved in the Ping Shek THA concern group. They complained about the lack of support from their neighbours, and were ready to wind up the concern group. The organizers responded to this crisis by organizing a mass meeting from which about 10 residents were recruited.

It is clear that the organizers served as facilitators and were able to provide emotional support for the concern groups. They continually reinforced the belief among the concern groups that their collective efforts could have an impact. But we should point out that the organizers were able to maintain the functioning of the local concern groups, but were unable to mobilize a large membership. We will come back to this later.

Training the Concern Group Members Since most concern group members were inexperienced in protest activity and ignorant of the organizational structure of the Housing Department and the Hong Kong Housing Authority, the organizers had to provide information, explanations and analysis of THA policy. The organizers were of great help in training members to acquire the skills of letter writing, poster design and making contact with the press throughout the protest. With training, group members became more confident in taking responsibility for organizational tasks.

The Reasons for the Participation of the Indigenous Leaders

With the help of the mobilization agents, the concern groups were able to remain in existence. However, in our view, the mobilization efforts were not able to ensure the continued participation of the indigenous leaders; therefore only some members stayed, and some 'exited'. Furthermore, the local concern groups did not place emphasis on internal mobilization, and subsequently most of the potential participants were never converted into actual participants. To explore the reasons for participation and non-participation in the concern groups, we examine three types of resident, namely those indigenous leaders who participated in the concern groups for a longer period, those who 'exited', and finally reasons for few mobilization campaigns.

Those Who Participate Continuously Apparently, the paramount reason for the participation of the concern group members was to press for early clearance. Their primary political motivation had nothing to do with 'the prospect of jobs, payment for participation, access to services, or political power for oneself or one's ethnic group' - the reasons found in some cases of political participation of lower socio-economic groups (Kramer, 1969). It was quite clear to the concern group members that there was little possibility of getting these things from their participation in community action in Hong Kong. The political situation in Hong Kong is marked by an absence of patron-client relationships which bring material benefits and political power to local leaders (Mainwaring, 1987, 1991; Roberts, 1973; Wolf, 1966). The CSWs have discretion to decide the ways of providing services and task priority, but unlike caseworkers, they have no influence concerning the provision of personal benefits. Accordingly, the concern group members could not obtain any material benefits from being a local leader or having connections with the CSWs. Opportunistic involvement in the local concern group was thus discouraged since local politics had no connection with the social welfare and political systems.

The concern group members were in fact committed to the cause of the ATHA protest, but their motivation was undermined by doubts about their political efficacy. The lack of support from their fellow neighbours generated some degree of pessimism among them. As one active member claimed:

> Our concern group may be useful. Although many things are decided by the government, the concern group can influence it, can exert pressure on it... I feel our action is not very successful, the neighbours did not support it nor did they show solidarity. Now we cannot get any satisfactory accommodation units (Interview with Ms. Cheung, a Kowloon Bay THA concern group member).

Another young woman held a similar view, she said:

> Hong Kong people have few opportunities to express their views, so once you get it, you have to take it and fight for your interests. The government just takes everything for granted, never caring for the feelings and preferences of the *kaifongs* (neighbours), so we have to fight on. The residents association is useful... But our neighbours are only concerned with their own business (Interview with Ah Yuk, an active Kowloon Bay THA concern group member).

Despite this, their pessimism was to a certain extent counteracted by their view that collective effort was necessary to win concessions from the authority. This attitude seems to support Oliver's argument that active members are more likely to accept the belief that 'if they want something done they will have to do it themselves' (Oliver, 1984:609). Most concern group members expressed this view in interviews. They explained that their problem should be solved by themselves and nobody could take their place. Their involvement was thus sustained by a sense of responsibility for their own situation.

But obviously such a sense of personal responsibility still needs continual support and encouragement. This raises the question of what sustains the concern group members' motivation for participation. There are two answers. A sense of responsibility is the first element which can reinforce participation. A member continues to participate when explicitly or implicitly, formally or informally, being recognized as a lay leader. Having received recognition from one's fellow members, he (or she) becomes more willing to accept responsibility and take initiatives. This is shown in the case of the vice-chairperson of the first committee of the Kowloon Bay THA concern group. She continued to be involved in the concern group even though she was purchasing a flat from the Home Ownership Scheme[16] and was due to move out shortly. She explained that although involvement brought her no benefit, as the vice-chairperson, she had to be responsible for her neighbours until she moved out.[17] In the Ping Shek THA, two of the four active concern group members were due to be rehoused in 1993 by virtue of the first partial clearance. They remained active, however, as they believed that their withdrawal would lead to the termination of the concern group.

The second reinforcing element is the existence of reference groups. One type of reference group is the organizers. About half of the active concern group members were moved by the commitment and altruistic attitude of the organizers, in particular the VOs, because they knew that the organizers were not potential beneficiaries but were involved in fighting for the residents' interests. One active concern group member said that her participation was entirely due to her appreciation of the enthusiasm and altruistic behaviour of the organizers. Similarly, another member of the Kowloon Bay THA concern group said:

> I don't know why I come out and continue to participate. I was asked by the social workers to participate. I saw that they got no benefits from this action, but they are still very active, so I came out. At first, I was very dependent on the social workers, but now I am getting better (Ms. Wong, an active member of the Kowloon Bay THA concern group).

The lay leaders also served as a reference group. Two active members explained their persistent involvement in terms of the perceived commitment and dedication of their vice-chairperson who served as a role model, instilling them with a sense of support and confidence.

To sum up, some concern group members were influenced by their indigenous leaders, and some were impressed by the organizers' effort. It is not easy to say which factor has more impact on the residents. Our analysis has illustrated that the concern group members' recognition and appreciation of the organizers was the impetus behind their involvement in protest activities. Yet we do not want to imply that the local groups succeeded in building up a very strong political group. Throughout the protest, both groups suffered from a high turnover in group membership. We now turn to discuss this issue.

The 'Exit' Cases Given that the participation of the concern group members is maintained by emotional and affective factors, such as their appreciation of the altruistic attitude of the organizers, the question arises as to whether the members can sustain their motivation to participate in collective action when there are other solutions to their housing needs. There are four weaknesses inherent in the local concern groups that encourage people to exit from participation.

The first is the lack of solidarity within the concern groups. In the small concern groups which suffer from a lack of material incentives and coercive sanctions, the organizers are bound to appeal to shared values and collective responsibility to persuade and induce residents to serve as local leaders (Brown & Hosking, 1986; Douglas, 1983; Etzioni, 1975; Janis & Mann, 1977; Knoke and Prensky, 1984). However, moral appeal is not accompanied by legal or formal sanctions against members using personal and individual solutions to deal with their problems. Members often leave when individual methods can improve their situation. In the case of the ATHA protest, all the THA residents, including the concern group members, could either participate in collective action or attempt to move out of the ATHA through individual effort. Apart from protest, they could apply for rehousing through the waiting list, purchase flats from the Home Ownership Scheme or apply for 'trawling'. It is not uncommon to find 'exit' cases among those who participated in protest activities but departed when individual solutions became more promising. One woman explained clearly the reason for her 'exit' from participation:

I knew the concern group members very well. I've participated in their activities. But now the Housing Department have allowed me three times to select a flat. Although I'm not very happy with the flats, I don't want to be involved in the protest any more, since I'm worried that the department will say I'm going too far and demanding too much. I'm worried that they won't allow me to choose any more. Next time, I would choose those flats in Tsing Yi district. I feel that I already have more chance to choose, so that I don't want to participate. Now I don't think the concern group can go any further, since not many residents are supporting them (Interview with Mrs. Wong, a Kowloon Bay THA resident).

We also found that the vice-chairperson of the Kowloon Bay THA concern group purchased a flat from the Home Ownership Scheme and did not wait to be rehoused upon clearance. There were four other 'exit' cases among the Kowloon Bay THA concern group members who took the opportunity of trawling to move to public housing estates. This shows that residents leave the concern group once they are offered an alternative solution.

The second weakness of the concern groups is related to the divisive tactics of the government. Faced with the increasing frequency of protest activities in the ATHAs, the government has usually offered a special rehousing scheme - officially known as 'trawling' - to allow the residents of some designated THAs to apply for 'old' urban public housing flats.[18] This tactic is effective in giving the press and the public the impression that the Housing Department is very responsible and responsive to the demands of the ATHA residents.[19] For example, the Housing Department announced a new round of trawling specially for the Ping Shek THA residents three days before the visit of the Hong Kong Governor, Mr. Chris Patten, in June 1993. This created the image that the department really cared about the ATHA residents. The Housing Department also deliberately adopted this tactic to undermine the leadership of the THA concern groups. Having identified the active concern group members, the Housing Department granted them some privileges in order to urge the leaders to move out of the present THA. The chairman of the first committee of the Kowloon Bay THA concern group is a case in point. Although ineligible for public housing, he was allocated a better unit in Tsing Yi THA shortly after the protest started.

The experience of Mr. Lee, an active member of the Ping Shek THA concern group, is intriguing. He was asked to attend an interview for rehousing which he had not applied for. We believe that this 'mistake' reflects the tactics of the officials of the Housing Department to weaken the concern group by rehousing some of its members. The first chairperson and two very active concern group members of the Kowloon Bay THA, along with two concern group members in the Ping Shek THA, were all rehoused through the trawling scheme in 1990 and 1992 respectively. However, we are not arguing that people become involved in the concern group in the hope of receiving priority treatment from the Housing Department. None of the members knew this to be a government tactic before their involvement.

The third source of weakness is the perceived ineffectiveness of collective action which has a dampening effect on the confidence of the concern group members. It is usual to hear the concern group members complaining about the low level of participation in the protest and their powerlessness vis-a-vis the authorities. When they heard about the victories won by other ATHAs, the concern group members were upset and attributed their failure to the low level of participation and the indifference of the mass media and the politicians. This perceived ineffectiveness then reduced the motivation of some members to participate.[20] Among the eleven interviewees who have participated in the Ping Shek THA protest (none of whom had participated in the group for more than two months), eight considered that the concern group was ineffective. Their pessimism is clearly illustrated by one interviewee's comment on the efficacy of the concern group:

> You can't say what is fair. It is difficult to discuss the government policy. It's useless to talk about it. The chance of getting concessions by talking to the government is slim, unless we can invest a lot of manpower and resources. A few people can't make an impact. I know there is a concern group. I went there frequently. I wouldn't go if I had got to work. They are quite good, but achieve no welfare. No effect, just a few people, can't make much noise. Leading you nowhere. It's useless to struggle on the basis of a few people's support. But I don't know why there are so few people involved in the concern group. Perhaps, because many people have moved away (Interview with Mr. Ng, 40, a Ping Shek THA resident).

It was difficult for people to find a very clear reason for the low number of participants, but what they saw in reality was that there were only a few participants. This creates a vicious circle. Participants withdraw when they see a small number of participants, and when other participants see the smaller number of participants, they too leave. This is similar to Klandermans's argument that 'collectively, expectation about the behaviour of others can work as self-fulfilling prophecies. If a movement organization fails to convince people that others will participate, people are less motivated to join the movement and the prediction that few people will participate becomes reality' (1988:183).

Lastly, the lack of time is an obstacle to residents' participation. Most working residents with jobs went home at seven or eight o'clock in the evening. They usually joined the group meetings at nine, but left before eleven. This short duration of participation seemed insufficient to develop a strong sense of solidarity among the participants. Moreover, in order not to lose their daily wages, they were unwilling to participate in any day-time protest activities. Most housewives had to take care of their children. Some were involved on an irregular basis because of helping their children finish their homework. In short, work and housework responsibilities lessened the chance for the active concern group members to stay and as a result, their involvement was sporadic.

Rreasons for Little Internal Mobilization Efforts By internal mobilization efforts we mean the activities aimed at attracting the residents to become involved in the concern groups and protest activities.

We first argue that the low level of mobilization effort was a result of the strategic calculation of the CSWs, the VOs and the concern group members. Although both concern groups drew heavily their own residents to create support for the protest, most efforts by the concern groups were spent on organizing direct actions instead of internal mobilization.

To the VOs and the CSWs, organizing direct action was understood as a chance to train the indigenous leaders to organize themselves and to be independent. In particular, the CSWs expected that internal mobilization would be organized by the indigenous leaders once they were fully trained. In the case of the Kowloon Bay THA, the CSWs were also reluctant to recruit more residents to become involved in the concern group. The chief organizer explained that the THA was transitory in nature and there was no point in developing the THA as a neighbourhood group with a large membership base. The CSWs considered the local concern group to be functioning well as a forum for the expression of residents' demands to the authority, and believed it was not necessary to invest time and energy in internal mobilization. Therefore, they avoided initiating internal mobilization campaigns.

It is true that the indigenous leaders could, theoretically, expand the membership base by extending the cause of protest (i.e to develop a multi-issue protest). But they thought that this would divert attention to other issues, or that the government would deal with other demands in order to avoid tackling the ATHA issue. The VOs conceded to this idea because they did not have enough time and resources to deal with other issues. The CSWs also had their own priorities. Other issues, such as family problems, poor hygiene and the lack of public lighting, were considered to be within the CSWs' scope of responsibility, therefore they were keen to prevent the VOs and the concern groups from taking an interest in these subjects. Hence it is understandable that throughout the protest, none of the three parties - the VOs, the CSWs, or the concern group members - put issues other than early clearance on the agenda of the concern groups.

The concern group members were also reluctant to take advantage of the occurrence of some critical events to mobilize their neighbours. There were opportunities for them to mobilize the residents when the officials of the Housing Department promised to attend meetings within the THAs. The local concern group members, however, argued that the residents might be too concerned with their own issues and not concentrate on the ATHA issue, and that a larger group would not allow a thorough discussion about the ATHA issue between the officials and the leaders. For such reasons, the concern groups did not make use of opportunities to organize mobilization activity.

On some occasions, the lack of a common interest rendered internal mobilization difficult. The Ping Shek THA concern group faced this situation at the time of the announcement of the partial clearance of their THA. An internal split emerged among two groups of members. Since partial clearance only affected half of the residents, those concern group members whose units were not included in the clearance schedule thought that issues arising from rehousing were not their concern. They argued that directing the concern group to deal with the rehousing issue was a betrayal of those who were unaffected but who needed the support and assistance of the concern group. Some other group members thought that to neglect issues arising from partial clearance was unfair to those affected. The VOs wanted to establish a new concern group to take up new issues but they lacked the time and resources for this task. The CSWs said that they had to wait until there was a clear indication of the residents requesting their assistance in respect of rehousing issues. Finally, the concern group reached a stalemate and decided to continue to press for clearance in one go, rather than taking up the issues arising from clearance.[21]

The concern group members felt the need to mobilize the THA residents' participation, particularly when most of the indigenous members complained that they lacked neighbours' support. On some occasions, the concern groups organized internal mobilization campaigns. However, in our view, it was difficult for the local concern groups to achieve this.

Theoretically, the local concern group could maintain a stable inflow of participants by internal mobilization in order to expand the membership base of the local concern group. But we argue that objective constraints lead to the small size of the local concern groups.

For this purpose of analyzing objective constraints, we follow Roberts' suggestion that four types of internal resources are considered to be necessary to encourage activism in neighbourhood associations, namely commitment, orientation, availability and resources (Roberts, 1973). Commitment is engendered if a) most of the social relationships that serve the residents in their daily life are located in or near its neighbourhood; and b) when the neighbourhood presents the best and only feasible way of coping with residential problems. Orientation means that the activists recognize the value of organizing others. The other two factors refer to the availability of time and to monetary resources for participation.

As shown in our analysis, neither the CSWs nor the VOs were able to mobilize internal resources. Both found it difficult to heighten the residents' commitment in a context where the social relationships among the THA residents were loosely-knit, and the local concern groups, in the absence of concessions gained from the government, were unable to persuade their fellow neighbours that concerted collective action was the best and only feasible way of coping with their problems. We also saw that the organizers were unable to change the residents' perception that collective action was ineffective. While they provided continual support and encouragement to the indigenous leaders, they failed to mobilize any immaterial resources such as moral appeal, or material resources such as better rehousing flats or selective incentives, to counter the government's tactics of partial clearance and selective rehousing.

Besides, although the organizers knew that the availability of time was a critical factor in political participation, neither the CSWs nor the VOs were able to help out. As regards finances, the activities organized by the local concern groups did not require much in the way of monetary resources. Therefore, even though the organizers' donation campaigns were successful, money was found to be a less critical factor. In fact, at the end of the protest, there was a surplus of monetary resources.

Theoretically, the organizers could create an image that the residents' concerted action was effective by mobilizing external resources, such as the support of third parties, through building up interorganizational, horizontal and vertical, links. Before examining the interorganizational links, we should identify those which are available for the local concern groups to build on and then proceed to the question of whether the mobilization agents are able and willing to build.

It was difficult for the concern groups to build up vertical links with political parties since, as was pointed out in Chapter 6, the political parties and the members of the formal political structure were uninterested in local THA issues. Regarding horizontal links, the local concern groups could establish coalitions with other local concern groups. In the case of the Kowloon Bay THA, the VOs joined a committee called the Small Joint District Committee concerning the ATHA issue. But this committee lasted for only three months because of the VOs' lack of time to organize an independent coalition.

There is a coalition called Joint Committee of THA Residents' Association (JCTRA). This is composed of the CSWs and the representatives of local concern groups in THAs, and its aim is to scrutinize the development of THA policy. Although the CSWs encouraged the representatives of local THA concern groups to be the leaders of this committee, in practice they took up the leadership role because of the high turnover of the representatives. The CSWs found it difficult to develop this committee into a coalition leading the local concern groups. Local representatives' involvement in both this coalition and local concern groups led to competition for time and energy. We found that most local representatives tended to give priority to local concern groups. Moreover, since the committee aimed to deal with all the issues arising from THA policy, some local representatives were uninterested in issues concerning the benefits of other THAs. The 'self-interests' of the local representatives created problems in building up a sense of solidarity for the coalition. Since this coalition failed to serve as an umbrella organization for the local concern groups, the CSWs in turn found it difficult to mobilize support from the coalition in order to give the local residents a strong sense of support from third parties. The VOs on the other hand, could not help in this respect since they were excluded by the CSWs from the coalition. As a result, they were unable to mobilize any external resources through interorganizational linkages. In other words, neither type of external mobilization agent was able to mobilize resources to strengthen the political power of the local concern groups.

In short, while the resource mobilization theorists emphasize the importance of the external mobilization agents to the maintenance of protest groups, we found that the organizers in the ATHA protest encountered a lot of constraints on mobilizing internal and external resources to sustain the local concern groups.

In this sub-section, we have examined the internal mobilization of the local concern groups. We come to the conclusion that the local concern groups was affected by the high turnover rate of membership and the lack of internal mobilization. The difficulty in maintaining the local concern groups was the result of the lack of moral appeal or material incentives for the members and organizers to deal with 'exit' cases and to counter the government's tactics. The inflow of new members was not sustained because strategic calculations discouraged them from investing resources in internal mobilization. While attempting to mobilize participation, they encountered the difficulties in maintaining the local concern group, including the existence of objective constraints and the different strategic calculations among the organizers in respect of organizing more internal mobilization.

All in all, this section has shown that organizers are important to the formation of the concern groups since without their initiative the concern group members would be unable to operate effectively. Moreover, their involvement imparts to the concern group members a sense of solidarity and belief in collective action. However, the organizers are unable to sustain a belief in the efficacy of concerted collective action when there is little indication of its success. Consequently some members develop a sense of defeatism and back out. The organizers are also unable either to persuade back those members who can find individual solutions to improve their living conditions, or to deal with the government's tactics of rehousing the indigenous leaders of the concern groups. Above all, there is no steady inflow of members because of the limited mobilization effort.

In Chapter 6 we showed the lack of support from other political parties and in Chapter 7 the absence of a stable membership base. In this social and political context, how did the ATHA protesters formulate strategies to progress their campaign in order to pressurize the authorities? In the next section, we examine the process of strategy formulation and discuss the protesters' reaction to such an unfavourable context.

Strategy Formation

We classify the different forms of strategy into four types: 'orderly politics', 'polite politics', 'protest' and 'violence'. Orderly politics refers to those actions which work through both formal and informal channels in the political institutions. Polite politics are those actions making political demands known or evident by visible and invisible means outside the political structure. The essential characteristic of this kind of strategy is that it does not disrupt prevailing social routines and political structures. By contrast, protest refers to those actions which are aimed at disrupting the current social arrangements. These include rent strikes, sit-ins, non-cooperation, blockades, illegal occupation and swamping telephone lines. Violence refers solely to actions which physically damage or destroy property.

In Chapter 5, we emphasized that polite politics is the major form of strategy employed by the ATHA protest. In this section we explore why polite politics is the dominant form of strategy and why disruptive protest and violence are seldom employed in the ATHA protest despite the moderate militancy among the ATHA residents as measured by survey questions described in Chapter 7. We first examine the power positions of the mobilization agents, their preferred strategies and the power struggle in the local concern group. The aim of this analysis is to identify the dominant actors in the process of strategy formation, and link their preferences to the strategy adopted. Following this is an analysis of actual strategy formation within the local concern groups.

As has been pointed out, the CSWs cherish the 'non-directive' principle and believe that organizers should take a low profile throughout the protest.²² They interpret their role in social protest as that of facilitators, providing information and resources to train and educate their clients in order to enable them to improve their living conditions. They do not regard themselves as the type of social organizer advocated by Alinsky, who serves as an agitator agitating to the point of conflict. This role interpretation leads to a self-limiting attitude among the CSWs.

In practice, the CSWs, though trying hard not to assume the leadership role in the concern groups, were compelled to take up such role. It cannot be denied that the CSWs possessed more skills, knowledge, information and better connections with external organizations than local residents. On account of their position, the CSWs were more likely to 'acquire power to the extent that people rely on them because (typically) they have provided better (more useful) pictures [analysis of situation] than other members of the group' (Morley and Hosking, 1984:73). Besides, the indigenous leaders were very reluctant to do written work, like preparing the agenda, or writing minutes and letters to the authority. They thought that they were not capable of working out strategies either. This leads to a paradox. Despite trying not to take the residents' place, the CSWs found it necessary to set the agenda for the concern groups. Usually, the CSWs in the Kowloon Bay THA held pre-meetings among themselves to set the agenda for each meeting and sometimes they worked out possible strategies for the concern groups to discuss. This indirectly led to the dominance of the CSWs in the local concern groups. In short, the CSWs in the Kowloon Bay THA implicitly took up the leadership role.

By contrast, there is little evidence to prove that the CSWs in the Ping Shek THA observed the 'non-directive' principle. In practice, however, they did nothing more than act as facilitators, giving information and explaining current policy. Their low level of involvement in leadership stemmed from the fact that they were not very committed to the ATHA protest, and therefore they simply carried out the decisions passed at the meetings.

The VOs in the Kowloon Bay THA did not endorse the non-directive principle. The two VOs felt it was inevitable that they and Mr. Han (another VO, but one who observed the non-directive principle) would become the leaders because the THA residents were not experienced in protest activity and were unable to invest too much time and energy in collecting information. In late 1990, the two VOs competed with Mr. Han for the role of the chairperson of meetings, and there was conflict between them. After the arrival of the NLCDP team in 1991, the CSWs became dominant. But this does not mean that the influence of the VOs was reduced. The tactic the VOs used to influence the concern group members was by means of personal contact. They visited the group members so as to persuade them to accept their ideas. A special tactic they adopted was to invite a THA resident to attend the meetings. This particular THA resident who had previous experience in a housing protest was convinced that the CSWs and VOs should play an active part in leadership. Therefore, the resident introduced the VOs' ideas at the meetings. Subsequently, conflicts arose between the CSWs and the VOs, with the CSWs trying but failing to force the VOs to give up their role.

The VOs in Ping Shek THA, who were trained CSWs (except the author), also accepted the non-directive principle at the early stage of the protest, so they avoided doing a lot for the residents. However in the course of the protest they came to the conclusion that this principle was too restrictive to provide adequate assistance to the concern group. Increasing doubt about this principle allowed them to do more in place of the residents. They came to play the executive role and were involved in activities such as writing letters to newspaper editors, making posters, painting slogans on walls, setting the agenda, writing the minutes and formulating strategies.

The CSWs in the Ping Shek THA, however, were unable to compete with the VOs because the VOs had built up a good relationship with the concern group members. The CSWs had tried but failed to take the role of chairperson of group meetings.[23] Put simply, the VOs were dominant in the concern group of the Ping Shek THA.

Hence we can see that the local concern groups are not unified bodies, but are characterized by competition and conflict between the CSWs and the VOs. We have also illustrated the power positions of the CSWs and the VOs in the local concern groups. However, this raises the question of what it is about the nature of the organizational context which allows the CSWs or the VOs to play a dominant role. Two factors seem important.

The first is related to the social positions of the VOs and the CSWs. Both groups had more access to resources and information. On the surface, it was the active indigenous leaders who led the concern groups. In fact, it was the VOs and the CSWs who set the agenda and chaired meetings. This left the indigenous leaders with only a veto power to influence decisions. Most of the indigenous leaders considered themselves to be less informed and tended to accept the advice and instructions of the VOs and the CSWs, and were to a large extent dependent on the assistance of the organizers throughout the protest. We did not find that the protest served a successful training function or produced local leadership.

The second factor is that the concern groups had no formal organizational structure. Both the VOs and the CSWs were influenced by the idea of participatory democracy. Accordingly they saw the concern group as a training ground and emphasized participatory democracy in the sense that authority should be minimized and collective decision-making was important. Informed by this ideal, decision-making involved all participants in each individual meeting, with the organizers attempting to remain neutral. In other words, neither of the local concern groups had a formal leadership. In addition, because of the high turnover among the indigenous leaders, the VOs and the CSWs were obliged to chair meetings in order to maintain continuity between meetings.

Given the dominance of the CSWs and the VOs, the process of strategy formation appeared to be largely shaped by their preferences and interpretations of the situation. To see how this happens, we move on to explore the process of strategy formation in the two concern groups. In general, we argue that since there is room for the organizers, i.e. the CSWs and the VOs, to assume a dominant role in the concern groups, their interpretation of the situation and their personal preferences determine the choice of strategies of the concern groups. We shall show that shifts in strategies reflect changes in the power positions of the CSWs and the VOs, and changes in the political context.

The analysis of strategy formation in the two ATHAs is kept separate since their characteristics and trajectories vary. We shall compare and contrast them in the final part of this section.

Strategy Formation in the Kowloon Bay THA Concern Group

Three periods can be distinguished in the Kowloon Bay THA protest in terms of the main strategies employed. They are:

1) from May 1990 to March 1991 - polite politics
2) from April 1991 to August 1991 - polite politics and orderly politics
3) from September 1991 to December 1991 - polite politics with a few disruptive protest actions

In our view it is the organizers' preference which dictates the choice of strategy in each period. Hence changes in strategy can be accounted for by reference to the competition between the VOs and the CSWs. In the first period, before the involvement of the CSWs, the executive role of the concern group was mainly implicitly assumed by the VOs, and the choice of strategy was largely determined by their preferences. As Kleidman argues, these 'preferences and choices are shaped by their [the organizers] purposes, career, and other interests. They are also affected by their goals, values, assessments of strategic options and choices, and the tactical repertoire they draw upon and perhaps change' (1994:267). At that time, the VOs were influenced by the Chairman and the coordinator of the PCPHP who were experienced activists and protesters. The VOs learned from these two people, and employed petitions and demonstrations to start the ATHA protest. Basically, most activities fell into the category of 'polite politics'. They included sending letters to the government and the press, and making petitions to the politicians. This type of strategy was employed because both the indigenous leaders and the organizers tended to think that this sort of action would not provoke much criticism from the media and the public. It also appeared that polite politics were more 'legitimate' and 'appropriate', in the sense that these actions conveyed an image of being rational and less radical. Furthermore, these actions required less time and resources to organize. At this stage, the conflicting interpretation of the role of organizer between the VOs and the CSWs did not exist because the CSWs were not yet involved. Moreover, Mr. Han also agreed to the use of this strategy.

In the second period, after the involvement of two CSWs, the strategy became more 'orderly'. This change started at a meeting held in April 1991, after the announcement of the clearance date of the ATHA. At the meeting, which discussed the next step for the protest, the participants deliberated as to how and when a demonstration to the relevant departments should take place. But when the CSWs proposed the idea of asking for a meeting with the Clearance Section of the Housing Department, this suggestion was accepted by the members. Throughout the second period, the CSWs organized meetings with the department in the hope of talking the officials into granting the ATHA residents the right to choose their rehousing location.

This change of strategy was the result of the increasingly dominant role of the CSWs. On the basis of their work roles, the CSWs perceived themselves, and were perceived by the government, as legitimate helpers of the disadvantaged residents. Accordingly, through their official connections with the Housing Department, they preferred to work within the established system. By contrast, the VOs rejected the strategy of orderly politics, since they considered it to be allowing too much room for the Housing Department to deal with the protesters. They thought that closed negotiations in a meeting room would prevent the wider public from becoming aware of the issue. Meetings and negotiations were felt to be less ineffective in exerting pressure on the authority relative to direct social action. Nevertheless, the VOs failed to influence the concern group to accept their arguments.

The indigenous leaders regarded working through the established system as a chance to talk face-to-face with the authority. As long as they remained dependent on the authority to provide them with public housing flats, they were afraid of making things worse by taking militant action. Hence they preferred orderly politics.

Unfortunately, in June 1991, most leaders were disappointed when they found that lobbying and meetings had not brought them any concessions. The critical moment emerged at the end of June 1991 as follows. An active member thought that their action was too weak to exert any pressure on the Housing Department. He discussed with the CSWs whether it was possible to do something more militant. The CSWs disagreed because they did not think the protest had a high chance of success. One CSW, though sympathetic to the idea of protest, regarded it as an impossible dream and thought that the residents would not be able to gain anything from the government. Another CSW persuaded the leaders not to go any further and eventually had a row with a concern group member who reported that:

> I rang Ms. Y [a CSW] and asked her if she could write a letter for us to the Housing Department and the Public Relations Department of the Police to complain about the poor social order and the poor hygiene in our THA. She refused and asked me to do it. She just gave me the telephone number. She also said that she did not understand why the neighbours did not move to Tsueng Kwan O. She said everyone could live there, so she didn't understand why this group of neighbours wouldn't. She said that even though all of us keep struggling, other people would not support us (Interview with Mrs. Lau, Kowloon Bay THA, an active concern group member).

After an argument with the CSW, this member contacted the VOs to discuss possible alternative forms of action. The VOs also shared the view that disruptive action might be feasible, and subsequently they encouraged the member and her husband to contradict the CSWs, and to propose a meeting to elect new committee members. To avoid an open dispute with the members, the CSWs agreed to organize an election in September, 1991. As a result, a new committee was founded and new members were recruited. On the other hand, the VOs invited the Chairman and the coordinator of the PCPHP to attend a meeting and give advice to the concern group. At the meeting, a decision about making a petition to the Housing Authority was made.

The protest subsequently moved into the third period when the concern group presented a petition at the open meeting which resulted in a confrontation between the protesters and officials of the Housing Authority. In this confrontation, the CSW just stood aside and watched. The confrontation forced the authority to arrange a meeting for the Kowloon Bay THA representatives. As this incident was reported by the media, the THA residents seemed to be aware of their political power and more residents participated in the ensuing meetings and petitions.[24]

In this period, the impatience of the concern group members drove them to take the issue to the street again. They became more militant and appeared to be more willing to adopt disruptive action. Rather than using the strategy of 'orderly politics' and 'polite politics', some disruptive actions were taken. The indigenous members began writing slogans on the wall of the THA. More participants showed up at the protest actions, such as a demonstration to the Housing Authority in October 1992 which involved more than 60 participants. However, neither further disruptive protest action nor 'violence' became the dominant form of strategy in this period. This does not mean that the concern group members were reluctant to try more militant actions. Indeed, some members in mass meetings suggested the use of disruptive actions, such as a continuous phone-in aiming at blocking the telephone lines of the Housing Authority, or sending chain letters to pressurize the authority. Nevertheless, these suggestions received scant attention from the CSWs. On the contrary, the CSWs remained pessimistic about their chances of success and discouraged the use of disruptive protest strategies. The CSWs even dissuaded the concern group members from continuing their action. In the minutes of one meeting, a VO reported that:

A kaifong [a concern group member] rang Mr. Liu, at the Housing Department. Mr. Liu angrily criticised the kaifong, and said if they wanted to live in good flats they should move back to mainland China. He refused to meet the kaifong. The CSW asked the kaifongs to pay attention to the attitude of the Housing Department, and see if the department officials had changed their attitude. The worker also asked the kaifongs to face reality, and consider whether there was a sufficient supply of new flats in local districts... The CSW thought that the Housing Department had become tough. But the kaifongs disagreed since they knew that the Housing Department had offered people new flats in urban areas, and this implied the department was less tough. But the CSW still asked the kaifongs to consider the situation thoroughly before making their decisions. The CSW pointed out that the kaifongs had taken many actions but there was no change in the policy. The CSW asked the kaifong what they had achieved if the authority changed nothing...the CSW said that the kaifongs were entertaining a false hope (Minutes of a meeting held on 10th December, 1991).

With the departure of one VO in this period, the other VO was not able to challenge the views of the CSWs.[25] Since the CSWs kept trying to discourage the concern group from continuing their action, the concern group became inactive. Some concern group members left and the local protest became disorganized.

This case illustrates the dominant roles of the CSWs and the VOs, and the importance of the power struggle between them for the choice of strategy. When the VOs were in a strong position, the concern group members' belief in disruptive action was reinforced and was reflected in the choice of strategy. When the CSWs became dominant, their preference for 'orderly' action dictated the strategy.

Strategy Formation in the Ping Shek THA Concern Group

We divide the trajectory of the Ping Shek THA protest into two periods in terms of the dominant strategies which the concern group employed:[26]

1) from May 1992 to May 1993   - polite politics
2) from June 1993 to April 1994   - polite politics with a few disruptive protest actions

In the first period from May 1992 to May 1993, the concern group mainly organized non-institutionalized protest activities such as petitions, demonstrations and sending letters to newspaper editors. This sort of action was intended to make the wider public aware of the residents' collective feelings and grievances. Like its counterpart in the Kowloon Bay THA, the non-institutionalized actions employed in this period were largely 'polite' in the sense that they were essentially peaceful and courteous. The concern group had attempted 'orderly politics' by explicitly trying to build up connections with political parties and local politicians. As illustrated in Chapter 6, it failed to secure the politicians' involvement. The concern group held a number of meetings with officials of the Housing Department, but the outcomes always upset the members.

In order to gain wider support from the media and the public, the dominant VOs seemed to follow an irregular sequence of activities. First, with the assistance of the VOs, the concerned group organized mass meetings, recruited members, sent letters to the press and the Housing Department, made contacts with the politicians, waited for replies from the politicians and the officials, held a meeting with the Housing Department, and then waited for the reply again. After the group received the authority's denial of early clearance, the same sequence of actions started again. In our view, the VOs learned this strategy pattern from their own and their colleagues' experience. As Kung has pointed out, the choice of strategy in the urban protests of Hong Kong was to a large extent determined by the historical practices which 'constitute the basis of reference for the forms of action to be adopted within a specific context' (1984:120). The VOs drew on all the forms of action which were commonly adopted by social activists and protesters in other areas.

In the second period of the protest, more disruptive protest activities were organized in addition to polite politics. In July 1993, the concern group achieved little success even though they had undertaken lobbying, petitions, meetings and demonstrations. One active member at that time insisted that it was necessary to organize a sit-in or sleep-in to pressurize the Housing Authority. With the support of the VOs, the concern group members began painting slogans on the wall during the summer of 1993. They even attempted to organize a rent strike in August 1993, but this did not take place. It is interesting to note that despite the similar composition of mobilization agents in the two THAs, a rent strike - a disruptive action - was planned only in the Ping Shek THA. In order to understand this difference, it is important to examine the strategy preference of the mobilization agents and the decision-making process within the concern group.

As has been pointed out, the VOs in the Ping Shek THA concern group were more dominant in agenda setting and decision-making than in the Kowloon Bay THA. The VOs had been involved in the concern group for more than half a year before the involvement of the CSWs, and had gained the trust and acceptance of the indigenous leaders. By contrast, the CSWs found it difficult to gain credibility or establish good links with the leaders. Some group members were critical of the performance of the CSWs since they felt that the CSWs were not very committed. One active member regularly complained that the CSWs were lazy and only cared about the issues in the Shun Lee THA. The support from the indigenous leaders enabled the VOs to play a critical leadership role. Their role was equivalent to the CSWs in the Kowloon Bay THA, and gave them power in agenda setting and chairing meetings. Until April 1994, the VOs remained in power. Besides this, not being required to account for their actions to any superiors, the VOs enjoyed a high degree of autonomy in organizing protest actions. In the course of the protest, the VOs became increasingly dissatisfied with bureaucratic procedures in handling the ATHA issue, and thereby became more committed to organizing direct actions.

However, besides painting slogans on the wall of the THA which eventually irritated the Housing Department officials, rent strikes and other disruptive protest actions were not carried out. It appeared that the strategy preference of the VOs and some concern group members did not entirely determine the choice of strategy. As will be shown, apart from the personal preferences of the mobilization agents, the veto power of other members, the availability of political support and the changing political climate played a part in determining the protesters' choice of strategy.

The lack of more disruptive action can be explained firstly by the reluctance of some of the group members. At one meeting, a VO suggested that it was ineffective to press for early clearance by lobbying and negotiation, and that it was possible for the concern group to exert direct pressure on the new Chairperson of the Housing Authority. This strategy access point became critical. At that time the new chairperson, recognizing the gap between the Housing Authority and local leaders, had carried out a series of visits and meetings with the local politicians and indigenous leaders in order to create a better relationship between the Housing Authority and the local social forces. The VOs proposed to organize a sit-in at the office of the Chairperson. One group member disliked this strategy. She said, 'We are rational people. I don't want to do anything which makes people think that we are too radical. We are also polite people, and would not do anything like that'. Interestingly, this member had initiated and carried out the painting of slogans on the wall. It is indeed enlightening to see that the concern group members did not accept some kinds of disruptive action. In the course of the second period, one group member insisted that it was necessary to organize sit-ins and sleep-ins to put more pressure on the authority. The members' reaction to this suggestion was very ambiguous. They made fun of it in order to sidestep discussing this suggestion. The members' power of veto seemed to be the main factor discouraging the VOs from organizing the sit-ins.

The failure to carry out the rent strike proposed by the VOs was not only due to the veto power of the group members. The concern group members agreed to carry out a rent strike on the condition that this action would be supported by most of their fellow neighbours. This shows that they needed the neighbours' support to organize more militant action. Their confidence in using militant action was affected by fear of criticism, and uncertainty of the results and the response of the wider public. Hence, two ways were suggested for exploring the level of neighbours' support. One involved asking the neighbours to post a slogan on their wall in order to show their support; and the second was to do a survey. The concern group members chose the first method because, as they explained, they felt that in the process of doing a survey they would be humiliated in a face-to-face situation by those who did not accept the cause of the protest. This further shows that the concern group members had little confidence in gaining their fellow neighbours' support. Moreover they invited a protester from another area to talk about his experience of a rent strike. After these activities, however, the indigenous leaders remained dubious about the support of their fellow neighbours and the wider public.

In fact, at that time, there was a further deterrent to radical action: the political climate was unfavourable to it. On 25th March 1993, a demonstration to the Governor, in which some THA residents were involved, took place at the entrance to Governor House. There being a confrontation with the police, the protesters finally decided to block the road in front of Governor House. As a result, twenty-five protesters were arrested. Public reaction as revealed in the media was very discouraging.

The protesters were severely criticized for undermining the social and public order of Hong Kong. Within the social work profession, this action was interpreted as an illegitimate action and as a result of the fact that a few social workers influenced their clients. Some members of the Ping Shek THA also found this type of action risky and too radical.

Consequently, the rent strike was not carried out since the concern group members found it difficult to gauge the number of supportive residents and because of the risk involved. Meanwhile, the Chairperson of the Hong Kong Housing Authority at that time decided to visit the Ping Shek THA, and subsequently diverted the concern group's attention from a rent strike to making petitions to the Chairperson.

In comparing the situations in the two ATHAs, we found that the strategy of polite politics was the dominant form of action in both. However, the Ping Shek THA concern group appeared to be more likely to try disruptive protest actions. This tendency can be explained by the dominance of the VOs in the Ping Shek THA who were more autonomous and were willing to adopt disruptive action when polite politics became less promising. The experience in the Ping Shek THA also shows that subjective preference is insufficient to shape the use of strategy. We notice that objective constraints play a part in this respect. The Ping Shek THA concern group had tried to organize a rent strike but this plan failed in practice due to the lack of support from fellow neighbours and the unfavourable political climate at the time.

In this section, we have analyzed the decision-making process in the local concern groups. We have also highlighted the importance of the involvement of external agents to mobilization and strategy formation. Our findings support the argument suggested by the resource mobilization theory that external agents are critical to the emergence and development of protest activities. However, we have also drawn attention to factors which the theory ignores, that is, the orientation and interpretation of the actors involved, and the internal dynamic which shapes the decision-making process and the choice of strategy. An unfavourable political climate for the use of disruptive protest action gives less support to the actors and militant action is less likely to be taken. Our analysis however raises an interesting question. It has been argued that disruptive action is necessary for powerless social groups to win any concessions (Piven and Cloward, 1977). Without violence and disruptive actions, it is interesting to explore whether the ATHA protesters could achieve any concessions. This is the focus of our discussion in the next section.

Success or Failure of the Local Mobilization and Protest

At the time of writing up this thesis in October 1995, the Housing Department had cleared the Ping Shek THA in September 1995. However, at the time of the fieldwork ended in April 1994, the Ping Shek THA concern group was still struggling for early clearance. In assessing the success and failure of the Ping Shek THA protest, we confine our attention to its achievement or failure in our fieldwork period. As regards the Kowloon Bay THA concern group, the government announced the clearance schedule in April 1991, and the ATHA was finally cleared in March 1992.

There are three criteria for our evaluation of the success or failure of the local ATHA protests: the benefit gained by the protesters such as concessions won from the Housing Department, the impacts of this protest on the participants and the impact on society. The second criterion concerns whether the protest can provide the participants with a new experience in social conflict which trains and prepares them to become engaged in social issues subsequently. As Mueller pointed out, a social movement is regarded as successful when the participants are trained in one social movement, and become a manpower resource for a second movement phase (Mueller, 1988). Because the results of the two local protests differ, our discussion of their success or failure will be separated. We first discuss the case of the Kowloon Bay THA.

The first measure of success is the scale of the concessions granted to the two ATHAs. This depends on what we count as concessions.

In the case of the Kowloon Bay THA, the petition was for early clearance and rehousing in the same district. It is a fact that the Kowloon Bay THA residents succeeded in winning early clearance but failed to push the government into granting local rehousing. The Housing Department gave the official reason for the clearance of the Kowloon Bay THA as 'non-development clearance', that means clearance which is not for any development purpose. This is unusual because, as the official of the Housing Department explained, 'under the existing THA clearance policy, THAs would only be cleared when the sites were required for development.'[27] Also, according to an official document, the Kowloon Bay THA had not been due for clearance until 1993/94 or 1994/95. An official document wrote: 'In view of their age and the structural conditions and at the residents' request, [this THA was] slotted into the 1991/92 clearance programme...'[28] On several occasions, officials of the Housing Department claimed that the clearance was due to the pressure from the Kowloon Bay THA residents.

This raises an interesting question about the genuine reason for the early clearance of the Kowloon Bay THA. Was the change in the clearance schedule due to the residents' request as the official document stated, or to other reasons? Without any insider's view on this issue, our interpretation of the reason is somewhat speculative. In our view, the Housing Department tended to clear a THA only when the land which it occupied was needed by another department. In the case of the Kowloon Bay THA, it appeared that the land was not claimed back by another department. In 1993 the land remained undeveloped. All the evidence suggests, therefore, that the role of the protesters was critical and the ATHA was cleared because of the residents' pressure.

In respect of the objective of local rehousing, most residents were eventually rehoused in Tseung Kwan O and not more than 10 households were rehoused in the same district. Rehousing in Tseung Kwan O, according to the rehousing policy, was regarded as conforming to the current policy at that time because the district was classified as an extended urban area. Clearly the ATHA protest failed to obtain the right to rehousing in the Kwun Tong district or in the districts which the residents preferred. Although there was no change in policy, one interesting result is that 10 households, including some concern group members, were rehoused in the Kwun Tong District. Does this imply that the protesters won a partial concession from the authority?

As one social worker said in an interview, 'the Housing Department has prepared some new flats for those who insisted on not moving into the New Territories. The department will not change the policy. The new urban flat is officially said to be earmarked for and allocated to compassionate and other deserving cases'. Some of these flats would be offered to those, for whatever reason or by whatever means, who are unwilling to move to the designated estates' (Interview with Mr. Cheng, a CSW). This means that the Housing Department prepared some urban public housing flats for rehousing those who refused to move out if the

Housing Department did not allocate them their preferred flats. In this case, the collective action of the Kowloon Bay THA concern group failed to change the rehousing policy, but some households were able to win concessions from the Housing Departments when they refused to move out. However, we do not consider such action as collective as it was not planned by the concern group. They just coincidentally insisted on not moving out, and finally won the concession from the authority.

But we notice that the protest of the Kowloon Bay THA had a negative consequence on the ensuing ATHA protest. Before November 1991, local rehousing had been the Housing Authority's policy. The Kowloon Bay THA residents were not offered local rehousing simply because the Housing Authority disregarded the rehousing policy on the grounds that there were insufficient local new public housing flats to rehouse them. In November 1991 the Housing Authority ended the local rehousing policy which made the Ping Shek THA protest more difficult since it removed the legitimacy of its request for rehousing in the same district.

The aims of the Ping Shek THA concern group were early clearance, clearance in one go and local rehousing. In practice, the concern group won early clearance of this ATHA but failed to obtain clearance in one go. A partial clearance was announced in June 1993 and 15 blocks were designated for clearance in early 1994. A few months later, the Housing Department promised to clear the remainder in 1995. This means that more blocks were to be cleared earlier than the date set out in the original clearance schedule. According to an earlier official document, only 8 blocks were to be cleared in 1993/1994, 17 blocks in 1994/1995 and the remaining 26 blocks in 1995/1996.[29] The promised clearance of the Ping Shek THA appeared to be earlier than the date set in the earlier tentative clearance plan. This can be regarded as a success for the protest.

However, we should treat this argument with caution. Pickvance has pointed out that 'there is a danger that the research-worker tends to attribute too much causal influence to the actions of the movement organization and insufficient influence to the actions of the authority' (1976:202). Hence, the motivations of the government should be taken into consideration. In our view, the reason for the change of the clearance schedule was related to the social and political situation at the time. The Governor Mr. Chris Patten, in his first annual address to the Legislative Council in 1992, promised to rehouse almost three-quarters of the people in the existing THAs by 1997. In April 1993, the Housing Department set up a special THA clearance section which was said to be for the purpose of speeding up the THA clearance. There is little information to explain why the Governor proposed to speed up THA clearance. In our view, this change can be accounted for by the following reasons. In 1993 the governor faced a delicate situation in which the Chinese government had severely criticized the political reform policy initiated by Mr. Chris Patten. In order to win more support from the Hong Kong people, the Governor tackled the issues concerning the disadvantaged people. Speeding up the clearance of the ATHA can be seen as part of this tactic. However, this interpretation may risk underestimating the impacts of collective action initiated by the ATHA residents. We would argue that the ATHA protest might have created a very negative image of the government since the ATHA protest showed to the wider public that the government had neglected the living conditions of the THA residents. In our view, when the Governor tried to build up an image of a responsible government, the ATHA issue became one of the issues it focused on. Therefore, the positive outcome of the Ping Shek THA protest in respect of pushing for early clearance can be seen as the result of the interplay between the political priorities of the Governor and the Ping Shek THA protest itself.[30]

The Ping Shek THA concern group failed to secure clearance in one go. However, the bringing forward of the date for the clearance of the remaining part of the THA indicates that the authority was making a concession to the residents. Besides this, the authority offered new urban public housing flats to the residents affected by the second clearance in 1995. In spite of the initial refusal to grant rights for residents to be rehoused in urban areas, a majority of the residents affected by the second stage of clearance were rehoused in urban areas. Since this took place after the fieldwork, we have collected little evidence to explain the success of the residents in this respect. One resident however pointed out that the reason was the availability of new flats. Most of these flats had been earmarked for rehousing public housing tenants affected by the redevelopment programme, but many of the tenants refused to accept them which left more new flats in the Kwun Tong District.

The second and third criteria for evaluating the ATHA protest are in terms of its effects on subsequent protest. We distinguish two types of impact of the ATHA protest, namely the nurturing of grassroots political leadership, and the creation of public awareness of the poor living conditions of the residents in ATHAs.

As regards the impact on the indigenous leaders, neither of the two local protests was able to train local leaders at the time of writing this thesis. Few grassroots political leaders played a role in subsequent protests. It was said that the Chairman of the Kowloon Bay second core group had participated in a neighbourhood association in the public housing estate he moved to. But this is the only case. On the other hand, we notice that most concern group members never came back to visit their 'comrades' in the THAs after moving out. This seems to indicate they had a low degree of commitment to the concern groups. However, some of the leaders of the Ping Shek THA had a good relationship with the CSWs. In September 1995 four leaders participated in a protest against the termination of the Neighbourhood Level Community Development project. We do not have any more information to examine how far and how long the indigenous leaders were involved in this protest. But this indicates that the indigenous leaders were more likely to be concerned with social issues and more willing to take part in social actions.

It is somewhat difficult to measure the extent to which THA conditions have won public attention. The ATHA protest activities in 1993 received coverage from some newspapers but TV news showed little interest in them. Politicians did not show much more interest in the articulation of the THA residents' interests after three years of protest either. Issues concerning THAs were not articulated as important social problems in the election campaigns in 1995, as shown in the candidates' manifestos. An ATHA protest was initiated by the concern group of the Kai Cheung THA in the summer of 1995 but its protest actions were ignored by politicians. Above all, in September 1995 the Housing Authority announced that 13 THAs would be retained for rehousing squatters, rather than four THAs as planned. In other words, the existing residents were forced to tolerate the deteriorating living conditions for a longer period. This change in the clearance schedule did not, however, attract politicians' concern. The involvement of politicians in issues concerning THAs remained limited.

To conclude, the two local mobilizations were successful in pressing for early clearance, but they failed to change the local rehousing policy. The Ping Shek THA concern group faced more difficulties in fighting for its members' interests because the authority had cancelled their rights to local rehousing in September 1991, and the government used the tactic of partial clearance to contain residents' grievances. In the face of these changes, the protesters failed to realize their aim of pressing for clearance in one go.

They succeeded in pressing for early clearance and local rehousing because they were able to exert pressure on the government, and because the Governor needed to win more political support from Hong Kong people in the face of harsh criticism from the Chinese government about his political reform plans. The reason for the success of the Ping Shek THA in pressing for early clearance is thus to a certain extent different from the case of the Kowloon Bay THA.

Conclusion

The aim of this chapter has been to explain the choice of strategies. We found that both ATHA protest groups used polite politics and a few disruptive protest actions. Two factors were highlighted in order to explain such a choice of strategy, namely the actors' preferences and the internal context which allowed the use of a certain strategy.

As regards the actors' preference, we studied three types of mobilization agent, namely the VOs, the CSWs and the indigenous leaders. We argued that the VOs and the CSWs were the critical actors in determining the choice of strategy, and that the choice reflected the power struggle within the local concern groups, and their organizational structure. We found that the CSWs were dominant in the Kowloon Bay THA, whereas the VOs were more powerful in the Ping Shek THA. Hence the powerful mobilization agents' preference in terms of strategy to a large extent determined the use of polite politics. The CSWs, being informed by their professional ideology, tended to favour orderly and polite politics. The CSWs, as members of the social work profession, had better access to the formal political structure, and this encouraged them to favour orderly politics. Polite politics was also accepted by the CSWs because they considered this kind of action to be a training opportunity for the residents to learn to be independent. This thought is in line with the philosophy of community social work in Hong Kong. In addition, the CSWs tended to discourage the indigenous members from using disruptive protest actions.

In the Ping Shek THA the VOs were more dominant than the CSWs. They had no strategic access to the formal political structure, unlike the CSWs in the Kowloon Bay THA. They tended to favour polite politics and disruptive protest action. However, they encountered the veto power of the residents when they tried to persuade the residents to use disruptive protest action. Some concern group members did not accept disruptive actions such as sit-ins and the illegal occupation of the offices of the chairperson of the Housing Authority. However, members did accept rent strikes and painting slogans on walls. But the proposed rent strike was not carried out. This was due to the lack of perceived support from the neighbours, rather than due to the objections of the CSWs and other concern group members.

This lack of support for protest action is not due to the low mobilization potential of the other residents. As was pointed out, the residents of both THAs had a high mobilization potential. But we note that the mobilization potential was higher in the Kowloon Bay THA than in the Ping Shek THA. Therefore, though we argue that the lack of actual participation in protest activities in the Kowloon Bay THA was to a large extent due to the lack of internal mobilization, as shown in our analysis, in the case of the Ping Shek THA, the lack of actual participation was not only related to the lack of internal mobilization but was due to the lower mobilization potential.

We also noted a more frequent use of polite politics than protest politics in the Kowloon Bay THA than was the case in the Ping Shek THA. This difference has been explained by reference to the internal conflicts within the two local concern groups. Since the CSWs in the Kowloon Bay THA, who favoured polite politics, were in a more powerful position than the VOs, more polite politics were adopted, whereas in the Ping Shek THA protest politics were more frequent because the VOs who favoured protest politics were more powerful.

Besides, we have pointed out that both concern groups found it difficult to maintain the membership of the concern groups due to government tactics and the existence of other feasible solutions to people's housing needs. On the other hand, none of the mobilizing agents were willing to invest resources to mobilize more residents, partly due to constraints on the mobilizing agents themselves. These two factors led to the absence of a large membership base. In the face of limited actual participation, the indigenous members' confidence and perceived political efficacy were hard to sustain. In this situation, disruptive actions were difficult to organize because they needed more manpower and political support from the residents. Disruptive action such as painting slogans on the walls were carried out since this kind of action only needed a minimum of resources and support, while a rent strike required more. Given that disruptive action was difficult to organize, violence was completely excluded.

Our analysis of the ATHA protest seems to support the argument suggested by the Fainsteins who argued that 'neighbourhood organizations... suffer from all the conditions that circumscribe groups whose members are united only by their common occupation of a nonsovereign territory: narrowness of issues, part-time leadership, cross-cutting cleavages, individual geographical mobility, and few financial resources' (1985:203). There is no doubt that such difficulties hinder a neighbourhood organization from winning concessions from the opponents and effecting policy change. However, in our analysis other factors also help explain the failure of such political action; in particular the internal dynamic of the protest organization, interacting with features of the political context.

Both local concern groups appear to have been partly successful and partly failures. Both groups secured change in clearance policy and some residents were able to obtain rehousing in their local district. It is true that they succeeded in pressing for early clearance and local rehousing for their fellow neighbours, and the 'noise' they made in the political system did exert pressure on the authority. However, their action was not sufficient to secure any change in policy. In addition to their efforts, their success in winning concessions was also related to a contingent factor, that is, the governor's political tactic to win the support of the Hong Kong people in the face of the mounting challenge from the Chinese government to the governor himself. From 1993 onwards the government has attempted to build up an image of a governor who is responsible to the people, and therefore the government payed more attention to the livelihoods of the poor. Moreover, what concessions the protesters obtained were not granted as rights but as a result of bureaucratic discretion. The government kept intact the policy of rehousing residents in extended urban areas and the New Territories. In our view, the government remained powerful and was able to selectively respond to the grassroots' demands.

This chapter has focused on the internal dynamics of the local concern groups. In the next chapter, we shall relate our discussion of the character and orientation of the actors and the 'polite' character of mobilization at local level to the social and political context of Hong Kong in the 1990s. We shall draw on our findings and discussion in Chapters 3 to 8, in order to present a picture which shows the significance of local protest for the political development of Hong Kong.

Notes

1. For details about how an NLCDP team is assigned to a specific THA, see Chapter 5.
2. The PCPHP is a pressure group whose main concerns are about public housing policy in Hong Kong. It mainly provides information and assistance in policy analysis for the grassroots. It consists of two full-time and two part-time staff members. Although the PCPHP is an umbrella organization and the CGTP is one of its sub-committees, a full-time staff member of the former participates in the CGTP as a member.
3. This coalition was formed for information exchange among the organizers involved in the three THAs. It held only a few meetings. Since it did not organize any protest action, we do not analyze this small coalition.
4. Two out of the three volunteer organizers who left the Kowloon Bay THA include a staff member and the chairperson of the PCPHP. Their involvement was to help the author and the social work student to start mobilization work. Another volunteer organizer was an experienced indigenous leader. He left because of lack of time.
5. The team leader resigned in October 1991.
6. The Shun Lee THA is located in the Kwun Tong District, and is not far away from the Ping Shek THA. Since the population of the Ping Shek THA was not over 3,000, the NLCDP team had to concentrate on providing services to another THA.
7. Our fieldwork ended in April 1994. At the time of writing this thesis, the Ping Shek THA and Shun Lee THA local concern groups had become inactive.
8. The Ping Shek local concern group was not a residents association. It had no formal organizational structure and was not officially registered as a formal organization.
9. There were a number of meetings between the volunteer organizers and the paid community social workers to work out a solution to enhance their cooperation and to reduce internal conflicts. Both parties knew that allowing the conflict to appear in public would affect the solidarity of the local concern groups.
10. Social workers whom we interviewed supported this view. For details, see Chapters 5 and 6.
11. In 1993, the CSW team began to mobilize residents to participate in action concerning the ATHA issue. It seemed that the team leader and the team member had changed their mind. However, as another team member explained, this was because her teammate needed to do a project on social participation as part of his social work degree, and therefore became active in the ATHA protest. The interview was conducted after the interviewee had resigned from her job. It is difficult to assess the validity of the interviewee's interpretation of the motives and commitment of her team leaders and members in respect of the ATHA protest. Therefore, we should be cautious about accepting her interpretation as proof of the low commitment of the community social workers.

12   The team leader of the CSWs said in an interview that they found it difficult to have the time and energy to deal with the increasing caseloads, and consequently they had little time to help the indigenous leaders to organize protest activities.
13   For a description of the demographic characteristics of the THA residents, see Chapter 5.
14   The concern group members seldom took the initiative to call a meeting. In January 1994, it seemed that the concern group members became more active. A member of the Ping Shek THA called a meeting two weeks after their protest action to the Hong Kong Governor. She was impatient with the inaction of the organizers who had not taken any further action.
15   The case of Hong Ning Road THA suggests this argument. Its local concern group became completely inactive in 1992 when there was no VO involved in mobilization and organization tasks.
16   For details about the Home Ownership Scheme, see Chapter 4.
17   Another example was the member who became very active after being elected as a vice-chairperson of the Kowloon Bay THA concern group.
18   The number of trawling exercises were recorded as follows. In 1990, there was one trawling for the Kowloon Bay THA in 1990, and another one in February 1991. For the Ping Shek THA, there was one in July 1992 and another one in June 1993. Such an effort of the Housing Department undermined the credibility of the THA protest. Often the trawling exercise was announced a few days before some politicians were to visit the ATHAs. This gave the politicians fewer points to attack.
19   Many reporters asked the ATHA protesters why they were not willing to move to the public housing estates offered by the Housing Department. Although the protestors kept telling the press that they were entitled to be rehoused in the same district when they were evicted by clearance, most of the reporters were not convinced of the protestors' views. On many occasions, the reporters argued that moving to the public housing estates in the New Territories did no harm to the ATHA residents. Moreover, they considered the estates to be of good quality and environment. Seemingly, the reporters agreed more with the Housing Department's view than the residents.
20   In May 1992, the VOs failed to persuade three previous concern group members to reform the concern group for the ATHA issue. These members were upset by their powerlessness and the difficulties in dealing with the Housing Department.
21   An active member declined 11 offers of public housing flats from the Housing Department and was dissatisfied with the allocation policy. Her case was not discussed by the concern group. Although at the later stage of the protest there were grievances and complaints about the rehousing policy, the local concern groups did not show any interest in this respect.
22   As is reflected in one instance, the chief organizer in the Kowloon Bay THA discouraged the VOs from revealing some news and information pertaining to the THA. His justification was that the concern group members were capable of finding out the information for themselves if they needed it. He also discouraged the VOs from becoming involved in any formal meeting between the Housing Department and the

concern group members. They on the other hand, thought of the meetings as a training place for the development of the concern group members' skills in negotiation and bargaining.

23 In December 1992, the CSW team leader asked the VOs to leave the Ping Shek THA, or to let the CSWs act as leaders of the concern group. The VOs refused to accept this request and continued to play the leadership role.

24 This action was somewhat dramatic. A group of protestors were knocked up by the staff of the Housing Department and finally led to a sit-in inside the Headquarters of the Housing Authority. After a couple of hours of the sit-in, the Housing Authority conceded and promised to hold a meeting to solve the protesters' problem.

25 The author left Hong Kong in October 1991. Another VO joined the concern group. She was a student in her first year of study in social work. As a new VO, she could not suggest anything going against the views of the VOs. Another VO stayed in the concern group but was unable to challenge the dominance of the CSWs.

26 Our fieldwork ended in April 1994 but the concern group in the Ping Shek THA continue to function until August 1995. Our analysis does not cover the protest from May 1994 to August 1995.

27 *Notes of Meeting of the Legco Panel on Housing held on Monday 24 May 1993.* Legco Paper No. 3596/92-03.

28 Hong Kong Housing Authority, *Memorandum for the Housing Authority and the Management and Operations Committee. Location of Rehousing of Urban Clearees.* Paper No.: HA 58/91 MOC 114/91. 29 October, 1991.

29 Hong Kong Housing Department. *Clearance Programme of THAs/CAs For 1991/1992 - 1992/1993 and Long Term THAs/CAs Clearance Forecast 1993/1994 1995/1996 (As at 7.7.92).*

30 Two events reveal the impacts of the officials at the higher echelon of the Hong Kong Government. A few months after Chris Patten's visit, the Choi Chuk THA was included in the clearance schedule of the following year. A similar sequence of events happened in the case of the Kai Lok THA whose clearance date was announced after the visit of the new Chairperson of the HKHA.

9 Conclusion

This chapter draws together the main contributions of our study of the Aged Temporary Housing Area protest. In section 9.1, we present an overview of the contributions of each chapter, summarize our answers to the four questions we posed in Chapter 2, and highlight the evolution of the protest over time. Section 9.2 will discuss the theoretical implications of our analysis, with a personal note about our reflections on our methodology and the extent to which we achieved the original aims of this study. We also suggest an agenda for future research in the field of urban movements. Section 9.3 is a more speculative discussion about the future of ATHAs within Hong Kong and Chinese housing policy, the future of urban movements and the position of external organizers.

Summary of the Argument

The objectives of this study were to examine an urban protest in Hong Kong, with specific attention to its origin, its development and its role as a viable form of collective action for advancing the interests of the grassroots. We sought to show the complexities of mobilizing the social base into an active social force, the intricacies of the relationship between the political context and an urban movement, and the strategy employed by the state to demobilize or even repress urban movements. These are topics which the new urban sociology paradigm has ignored.

In this section we provide an overview of the contributions of each chapter, give answers to the four questions we posed in Chapter 2, and summarize our argument about the evolution of the movement over time.

Overview of the Contributions of Each Chapter

Our analysis started with a critical review of the classical perspective on collective action, the resource mobilization theory, the political process model and the social construction perspective. We came to the conclusion that we needed to combine the last three theoretical frameworks into an integrated multilevel approach to the study of social movements, focusing on the political context, the inputs from mobilization agents, the conflicts among the mobilization agents, and the reactions of the movement target, i.e. the government. This approach in our view makes a substantial advance on much previous work in the social movement field.

Chapter 3 is an overview of the political system and the housing movement in Hong Kong. We argued that in the 1970s, which we defined as the pre-democracy stage, the colonial regime took two measures to deal with the possible detrimental effects on its rule of the two riots which occurred in 1966 and 1967: the provision of more social services and public goods (such as better housing, environmental improvements and communal amenities), and the establishment of a new local administrative system. These measures subsequently attracted the attention of community activists. Community protest actions were characterized by the predominant use of non-conventional methods and confrontational stances. Housing movements in this stage played a critical role in mounting a challenge to the dominance of the colonial regime.

In the next stage, which refers to the stage of transition to democracy from 1981 to 1992, the government opened up the polity with the establishment of the District Boards and the introduction of direct elections into the Legislative Council. In response to such changes, pressure groups were thriving and many grassroots political leaders assumed a significant role in the government-sponsored political structure. However, the subsequent expansion of pressure group politics drew in leaders from local levels, and most of their attention shifted from local issues to those at territory-wide level. Having entered into the government-sponsored political structure, more politicians believed that confrontational methods and the mobilization of a mass base would be less influential than lobbying and working through the formal political system. In addition, the 1997 issue became the dominant issue on the political agenda in the polity, and politicians put greater political effort into pressing for further political reform towards democratization of the formal political structure. As a result, the connection between the pressure groups and the local concern groups in community politics was weakened. Most important, in the 1980s the needs and interests of some urban minorities were ignored by the government, politicians and local leaders.

Chapter 4 examined the policy situation in respect of public housing provision in order to show the extent to which the housing needs of some urban minorities were ignored by the government. We first described the structure of housing provision and public housing policy in Hong Kong. We found that it was difficult for Hong Kong people to purchase their own homes. In the late 1980s the escalating property prices outpaced the rate of salary increases. On the other hand, since the 1980s the Housing Authority has sought to increase the provision of public housing flats for sale, though there was a shortfall in the production of public rental flats in the early 1990s. We argued that this shortfall was the result of the government's attempt to withdraw from involvement in the provision of public housing. Due to the shortfall, the housing needs of some social groups in Hong Kong were ignored. We identified three types of urban minorities, including single-person households, the squatters and the ATHA residents, whose housing needs were largely ignored by the prevailing public housing policy. The Aged Temporary Housing Area protest which we studied here was also related to the shortfall in the provision of public rental housing. The link between the shortfall and the protest was examined in detail in Chapter 5.

Having sketched the context, in Chapter 5 we described the origin and development of the ATHA issue, and in particular the key mobilization agents involved in the protest over this issue, namely the indigenous leaders, the community social workers (CSWs) and the voluntary organizers (VOs). We identified five main features of the ATHA protest. Firstly, due to the lack of involvement of politicians, the key external mobilization agents involved in this protest were the CSWs and the VOs. Secondly, the size of the protest groups was small in terms of their membership base, and they mainly took the organizational form of territorially-based local concern groups. Thirdly, they lacked interorganizational links with other social protest groups, and the input of resources came mainly from the CSWs and the VOs. Fourthly, in spite of a small membership base and a high turnover of group membership, the local concern groups were able to survive the protest for two years in the Kowloon Bay THA and four years in the Ping Shek THA. The last feature was the predominance of the polite politics strategy. We used a typology which classified movement strategies into four types, namely 'orderly politics', 'polite politics', 'disruptive protest' and 'violence'. Polite politics refers to action through formal and informal channels within the formal political institutions. Chapters 6 to 8 sought to explain these features of the ATHA protest.

In Chapter 6, we examined the political context in the early 1990s and highlighted three key aspects of it. First of all, the Housing Authority - a statutory body with no democratic participation - provided few formal political channels for the ATHA residents to press for their interests. Secondly, the 1997 issue drew much of the attention of the politicians and the ATHA issue was thus ignored. Thirdly, as most of the politicians were concentrating on issues concerning political reform, the CSWs and the VOs became the only actors with influence on the trajectory of this protest.

Chapter 7 put forward an explanation for the key features of the ATHA protest, in particular the moderate level of mobilization potential, the fact that more residents were willing to participate in meetings than in protest and radical actions, and the small size of its membership base measured in terms of actual participation in protest activities.

In order to account for the moderate level of mobilization potential, we examined the internal structure of the ATHAs to see if there were factors facilitating political participation. While there were theoretical frameworks to suggest that emergent group norms and close-knit social ties facilitate political participation, strong social norms and ties were absent in the ATHAs. We explained this by reference to the residents' restricted opportunities for contact, their limited opportunity for organizing concerted action, and the limited number of intermediate associations at local level for promoting interaction among neighbours.

Having shown that group norms and social ties were not the factors facilitating political participation, we focused on individual variables, including demographic characteristics, subjective and objective interests, residents' evaluation of political efficacy and both the subjective and objective constraints against participation.

We found that the socio-economic variables, namely sex, age, and employment status, were not strongly associated with political participation, and neither were the objective interests (i.e. eligibility for rehousing in public housing flats) nor the respondents' estimation of the chance of success. Objective constraints (i.e. the availability of time to attend protest activities) and the perceived political efficacy of their concerted action were found to be the major factors determining participation. Besides this, we found that there were two factors which were determinant in one case but not in the other: a sense of solidarity (i.e. the estimated number of participants) was significant in the case of the Kowloon Bay THA, while subjective interests (i.e. wanting early clearance) were significant in the

Ping Shek THA. We found that the significance of some factors was related to the specific timing and context of the protest. This alerts us to the possibility that some determining factors of political participation are context-sensitive or context-specific.

In order to explain the higher extent of mobilization potential in respect of participation in meetings than in protest and radical actions, we made reference to the importance of the availability of time and the nature of meetings in the ATHAs. First, since they were held within the THAs, most residents found that attending meetings was less time-consuming and second, they could obtain information about the latest changes in THA policy at meetings. By contrast, protest activities took place in other districts and were more time-consuming, and hence were less attractive to most of the residents.

The last feature of the political participation of the ATHA residents was the small membership base of the ATHA protest. In spite of a moderate extent of mobilization potential in relation to participation in meetings, few participated in the protest activities organized by the two local concern groups. In order to explain who actually participated and who did not, we analyzed the interplay of mobilization potential and mobilization efforts. We found that although a majority of the residents were willing to participate in protest activities, the concern groups did not maintain a mobilization campaign of sufficiently wide scope and high intensity. In view of these specific characteristics of the mobilization campaign, we sought to analyze how the local concern groups decided their protest and mobilization strategies in Chapter 8.

Chapter 8 explained how the local concern groups maintained themselves in spite of a small membership base, and how the local concern groups made decisions in relation to the strategies adopted. We focused in particular on the reasons for the dominant use of polite politics. In considering the internal dynamics of the local concern groups, we stressed the strategy preferences of the actors involved who were the community social workers (CSWs), the volunteer organizers (VOs) and the indigenous leaders.

Regarding the CSWs, we examined their characteristics with specific attention to their social positions as paid social workers. Their involvement was not due to their personal commitment to the cause of the ATHA protest, but because of their duties as paid staff members of social work organizations. They were thus accountable to their superiors rather than the

ATHA residents. Due to this social position, the CSWs tended to accept the non-directive principle cherished by the social work profession, and hence avoided taking a leadership role in the local concern groups. By contrast, the VOs were self-motivated and committed to the cause of the ATHA protest. Without any commitment to the non-directive principle, they sought to provide more instruction and assistance to the indigenous leaders. We argued that because of different interpretations of their role in the local concern groups, tensions arose between the CSWs and the VOs which subsequently affected the extent of internal mobilization.

In the case of the Kowloon Bay THA, the VOs were less powerful than the CSWs, and their influence was thus reduced. Decisions about mobilization strategy were largely influenced by the CSWs. In the case of the Ping Shek THA, by contrast, the VOs were powerful and could promote internal mobilization campaigns. However, due to the fact that they had limited time and manpower to organize mobilization activities, internal mobilization campaigns were not frequently organized.

As regards the indigenous leaders, their lack of experience and knowledge about mobilization and organizing protest activities led to their dependence on the two types of mobilization agent (i.e. the CSWs and the VOs). In addition, while they all knew that mobilization of their fellow neighbours would strengthen their ability to pressurize the government, they tended to downplay internal mobilization because they were worried that if the numbers of participants expanded this might divert attention from the early clearance issue to some other personal problems and concerns.

Apart from the fact that the different interpretations of the actors involved influenced the extent of internal mobilization, we noted that the high turnover of the residents was a difficulty threatening the survival of the local concern groups, and the CSWs, the VOs and the indigenous leaders sought to organize as many protest activities as possible to keep the concern groups alive and active. We argued that their efforts to maintain the concern groups almost exhausted the CSWs, the VOs and the indigenous leaders.

In short, the limited attempts at internal mobilization were due to different interpretations about the need to organize mobilization campaigns and to the limited availability of resources.

In Chapter 8, we also explained the predominance of polite politics throughout the protest, especially in the Kowloon Bay THA. As shown, the strategy preference of the most powerful mobilization agents to a large extent determined the use of polite politics. In the Kowloon Bay THA, the CSWs who preferred polite politics were more powerful than the VOs, and thus the local concern group adopted the polite politics strategy. In the Ping Shek THA, in contrast, the concern group were more likely to try disruptive action since the VOs who preferred using such protest action were more powerful. However, we found that strategy preference was not the sole determining factor. Another factor that should be taken into consideration is whether the indigenous leaders accepted the use of disruptive activities. We found that the indigenous leaders gave up a rent strike to pressurize the government because they found little support from their fellow neighbours and the wider public. In short, our analysis showed that the use of strategy must be explained by reference to the strategy preference of the most powerful actors within a protest group, the perceived support of the members and the current political climate.

Answers to the Four Questions Posed

We now draw on our findings to answer the four questions posed in Chapter 2. These were:

1. Why do some groups of Hong Kong people stand outside the formal political system to advocate or defend their interests in an era in which democracy has been introduced into the political system?
2. How does a social base develop into a social force and what strategies has the social force adopted to exert pressure on the political authority?
3. What effects can such an urban movement bring about?
4. What is the nature of the political system in Hong Kong as revealed by urban politics?

The Reasons for the Existence of Some Social Groups in Hong Kong Using Non-institutionalized Strategies in Order to Advocate or Defend Their Interests in an Era in Which Democracy has been Introduced into the Formal Political Structure The origin of the ATHA protest was explained by reference to three factors, namely the marginalization of the housing needs of the ATHA residents by the prevailing public housing policy, the involvement of the CSWs and the VOs, and the political context in the early 1990s.

We traced the source of the marginalization of the housing needs of these urban minorities in Chapter 4. Our analysis showed that public housing policy in the 1980s was oriented toward reducing the resources invested in public rental housing provision, while re-commodification of public housing became the dominant trend. The increasing production of Home Ownership Scheme flats clearly showed that the government had shifted resources away from public rental housing provision to the construction of flats for sale. As a result, with a shortage of rental public housing flats, the housing needs of some social groups were not catered for adequately. This was true of squatters, single-person households and those living in ATHAs.

Advocates of the new urban sociology regard the shortage of urban facilities as a product of contradictions within the urban structure in the capitalist mode of production and as a factor which subsequently generates urban movements. However our analysis repudiates this mechanistic framework and instead emphasizes the specific features of the political context and the involvement of external organizers.

We focused on the political context in order to examine the extent to which it is related to the rise of the ATHA protest. We showed that while the political system was geared toward a more democratic political structure in the early 1990s, the government simultaneously restructured political institutions by the establishment of statutory bodies in order to defend its political dominance. With the establishment of statutory bodies, the colonial regime remained dominant in the decision-making concerning social issues, such as education, health services and housing. While it is true that the grassroots representatives had more access and opportunity to secure positions inside the formal political structure, their power to influence social policies remained minimal since decisions on social policy were transferred to statutory bodies where democracy did not exist. As shown in our study, the limited access to decision-making within the Housing Authority prevented the ATHA protesters from expressing their discontent and pursuing their grievances through institutionalized means, and consequently they used non-institutionalized means to demand government attention to their housing situation.

However, we did not argue that this political exclusion and the lack of politicians' concern were sufficient conditions for the rise of the ATHA protest, but that the involvement of the CSWs and the VOs was equally important.

The origin of an urban protest, in our view, is strongly associated with the active intervention of external organizers, particularly in cases involving people who lack experience and knowledge about protests. The mobilization agents involved in the ATHA protest proved their importance as agitators in the initial period of the ATHA protest. They assisted the indigenous leaders in organizing mass meetings, protest activities and local concern groups in order to gain public awareness. By contrast, among other groups who were dissatisfied with prevailing public housing policy, such as squatters and single-person households, there were few protest groups or political actions to press for their demands when external mobilizers were not present. Similarly, the residents of the Hong Ning Road THA, who formed an active group in 1990 when VOs were involved, stopped functioning one year later when the VOs had departed. This evidence strongly suggests that deprivation alone is not sufficient to generate collective action and that the intervention of mobilization agents is crucial.

How the Social Base of the ATHAs Develops into a Social Force The form of the social force and the strategies employed to develop a social force are the main foci of our study. As has been pointed out, the ATHA protest is characterized by its small-scale, its territorial-base, the limited input of resources from organizational links and the community, and the dominant use of polite politics. Our objective is to explain these features and the trajectory of the ATHA protest.

We explained the character and development of the ATHA protest by reference to the following key variables: the specific features of the political context in the 1990s, the characteristics of the ATHA residents, the interpretation of the situation by the mobilization agents, and the internal conflicts of the local concern groups.

The first feature of the ATHA protest we sought to explain was its small membership base. Our account of this feature is based on the findings reported in Chapters 6 and 7. As resource mobilization theory suggests, participation in a social protest can be expanded by three types of modes of resource acquisition - the market mode, the organizational mode, and the communal mode. Our findings showed that the protesters mainly used the communal mode of resource acquisition. The mobilization agents and the indigenous leaders of the two ATHA local concern groups never attempted to adopt the market mode in order to expand their membership base beyond the THAs. The lack of use of this mode reflected the belief of the mobilization agents that the ATHA protest should be originated by the local THA residents, and that the membership base was necessarily confined to the THA residents. On the other hand, throughout the protest, the organizational mode was employed but links were only forged with social work organizations and pressure groups, as shown in their relationships with the CSWs and the VOs. In Chapter 6, we examined the political context and found that the specific political context at that moment meant that politicians were uninterested in the political claims of the ATHA protesters. The local concern groups were not able to form organizational links with political parties or with trade unions either. Consequently, the ATHA issue only attracted the attention of the CSWs and the VOs. Turning to the input from organizational links with the CSWs and the VOs, we found that only non-material resources such as training and leadership were supplied, but not manpower. Therefore the expansion of the membership base for the ATHA local concern groups mainly depended on the use of the communal mode of resource acquisition.

In Chapter 7, we sought to understand why little use of the communal mode of resource acquisition occurred in mobilizing the residents.[1] We argued that the small membership base, as reflected in the low rate of actual involvement of the ATHA residents in protest activities, was associated with limited mobilization efforts in using the communal mode of resource acquisition. To explain the low participation rate, we examined three factors identified by previous writers as determinants of political participation: the degree of groupness, the extent of mobilization potential of the ATHA residents, and the effects of mobilization effort.

We first examined the degree of groupness or communalism of the two ATHAs. We found that the ATHA neighbourhoods were characterized by infrequent contact and little social interaction. Also, there were few local organizations working to tackle the problems which the ATHA residents encountered. In sharp contrast to the black immigrant communities in Britain studied by Rex and Moore (1965) who found that existing organizations largely absorbed most of their grievances and discontents, the low level of actual involvement of the ATHA residents in the protest could not be explained by the absorptive capacity of any neighbourhood associations. Rather, our findings seem to support the argument that the loose-knit social ties in the ATHAs did not constitute a favourable condition for political mobilization. We found that there was little en bloc recruitment in the ATHAs; and the lack of preexisting social networks rendered difficult the formation of a sense of solidarity for sustaining collective action.

We moved on to analyze the mobilization potential which refers to the likelihood that a group of people will participate in collective action. There has been a widely accepted view that Hong Kong people are politically apathetic and alienated. For example, Lau and Kuan (1988) conclude that 'political involvement by the Hong Kong Chinese is still quite low, even though they are aware of, and have become accustomed to, some new influence tactics which contain an element of political confrontation. Hong Kong Chinese are still plagued by feelings of powerlessness, cynicism and alienation' (1988:103). In this view, the lack of political activism is strongly related to the attitudes of Hong Kong people. But our findings did not support this culturalist interpretation of low political activism. We found that the residents' willingness to participate in protest activities was relatively high. Our findings contradict the results of many political culture studies in Hong Kong which conclude that Hong Kong people are culturally predisposed to be politically inactive. On the contrary, we found that the reasons for the THA residents' unwillingness to participate were less associated with the cultural factor (i.e political apathy) than with constraints such as the lack of time. We also found that the perceived inefficacy of protest was highly associated with the unwillingness to participate in protest. But we are not sure whether the residents' perception of inefficacy is culturally predisposed or situationally specific. Further research is needed to look into the root of this political attitude of the THA residents.

In order to achieve a better explanation of the low level of actual participation of the ATHA residents despite the high level of mobilization potential, we stressed the interplay of mobilization potential and mobilization effort. We argued that little mobilization effort was invested in social mobilization. With limited use of incentives and scant attention to mobilization campaigns, most residents who were willing to participate were not informed by the protesters, and subsequently had little chance to show their support through actual participation.

This finding led us to explore the factors underpinning the limited mobilization effort. We asked why there was limited mobilization effort in motivating the ATHA residents to participate. We were interested in how the local concern groups, together with the external mobilizing agents (i.e. the CSWs and the VOs), designed their mobilization strategies. We then shifted our attention to the choice of strategies. The analysis of this aspect also sought to account for another feature of the ATHA protest, i.e. the dominant use of the polite politics strategy. These two aspects of the ATHA protest were the foci of Chapter 8.

Before proceeding to analyze the process of the choice of strategy, we examined in chapter 8 the organizational situation in order to situate the process of choice of strategy within the specific internal context of the local concern groups. Our analysis focused on three aspects of the two local concern groups in the ATHA protest. Firstly, we examined the character and strategic preference of the external mobilization agents and the indigenous leaders. Secondly, we explored the social relationships within the local concern groups. Lastly, we focused on the actual process of choice of strategies.

Our examination of the characteristics of the mobilization agents sought to explore their strategic preference. This aspect has been largely ignored by students of social movements, as reflected in the general literature on this topic. We argue that tracing the strategic preferences of mobilization agents sensitizes us to the link between the pattern and characteristics of an urban movement on the one hand, and the characteristics, political orientations and strategy preferences of the mobilization agents on the other.

In the case of the ATHA protest, the CSWs were inclined to interpret their involvement as social workers responsible for training the ATHA residents to become indigenous leaders and supplying resources which the residents needed. Interpreting their role as social workers, the CSWs conformed to the 'non-directive' principle and therefore avoided taking up the leadership role. On the other hand, in respect of strategic preference, the CSWs were more inclined to advise the ATHA protesters to use institutionalized means for expressing their grievances and demands, since they were able to obtain access to the formal political structure. By contrast, the VOs were not accountable to any social work superiors and thus did not observe the 'non-directive' principle. Also, since they lacked any access to the formal political structure, they were less likely to favour the orderly politics strategy and were more likely to support non-institutionalized means. As a result, the rise in conflict between the CSWs and the VOs was due to their different interpretations of their roles in the ATHA protest and their different preferences regarding strategy. As regards the orientation of the indigenous leaders, their limited experience in social protest made them dependent on the advice provided by the CSWs and the VOs, and they were therefore less influential in the decision-making process.

Despite the internal tension between them, both the CSWs and the VOs were important to the maintenance of the local concern groups, just as resource mobilization theorists argue. They were of great help in training and giving support to the indigenous leaders. The continuous involvement of the indigenous leaders was largely due to their recognition and appreciation of the CSWs and the VOs. Nevertheless, the external mobilization agents failed to maintain a large membership base. We found a high turnover rate among the local concern groups. Some group members left because of a lack of confidence in the efficacy of collective action. Others departed when they found individual solutions to improving their living conditions. Moreover, the government's tactics of rehousing the indigenous leaders and partial clearance led to the departure of some of the indigenous leaders.

Surprisingly, although there were difficulties in reducing the turnover rate of the indigenous leaders, we found that the local concern groups were somewhat reluctant to do more in terms of internal mobilization. There were several reasons for this.

Firstly, the CSWs expected to enable the indigenous leaders to initiate internal mobilization activities by themselves. Secondly, the VOs lacked resources such as time and manpower for internal mobilization. Thirdly, the indigenous leaders were reluctant to mobilize their fellow residents since they were worried that if too many participants became involved they would introduce additional issues and the objective of pressing for early clearance and local rehousing would be edged off the agenda.

Without support from politicians and the ATHA residents, how did the ATHA protesters pressurize the government? In chapter 8, we examined the internal dynamics of the local concern groups in respect of their choice of strategy. Our main finding was that the strategy of polite politics was the dominant form of protest action employed by the two local concern groups. In order to account for this, we examined the process of choice of strategy with specific reference to the political context, the strategy preferences of the actors and the internal dynamics of the local concern groups.

We found that the local concern groups were unable to work through the channels of orderly politics, since, as illustrated in Chapter 6, polity members were uninterested in the ATHA issue. The infrequent use of orderly politics was mainly due to the limited formal channels available to the ATHA protesters. Meetings with the Housing Authority were held merely because the CSWs had formal connections with the officials of the Housing Authority. Hence, only when the CSWs became powerful vis-a-vis the VOs within the concern groups were meetings with officials organized.

In relation to the choice of the three other types of strategy, the power positions of the different actors within the local concern groups were critical. We found that when the CSWs, who preferred using polite politics, were powerful, the local concern groups were more likely to adopt the strategy of polite politics. By contrast, when the VOs were most powerful, disruptive protest strategies were employed. But we found that the use of the disruptive protest strategy was not as frequent as the use of polite politics because of the objections of indigenous leaders. In particular, some indigenous leaders felt this kind of strategy was inappropriate since the political climate was not favourable to the use of disruptive action. Moreover, the indigenous leaders objected to using disruptive protest strategy when there was little political support from their neighbours. Hence the strategy of polite politics became the dominant form of protest action.

In short, our findings indicate that in considering the character of a social protest, it is important to consider the actors' strategy preference, the internal dynamics among the actors, and the social and the political contexts in which the social protest operates.

The Success or Failure of the ATHA Protest Our evaluation of this protest was based on three criteria, namely the benefits gained by the ATHA protesters, its impact on the participants and its impact on society.

Both ATHA protests were successful in obtaining early clearance, but they failed to get their challenging idea of a right to local rehousing incorporated into government policy. In terms of the second and third criteria, neither local protest succeeded. The indigenous leaders, at the time of writing this thesis, had not participated in other neighbourhood associations. But their participation in this protest seems to have increased their awareness of their power and potential to challenge the government. We cannot provide any detailed information about the extent of such a change, but our informal interviews with the indigenous leaders after the protest revealed the leaders' increased confidence in their political efficacy.[2]

As regards the impact of the protest on society, we found that the ATHA issue received little attention from the politicians and the media despite the ATHA protest.

Understanding the Nature of Urban Politics in Hong Kong on the Basis of Our Study of the ATHA Protest As reflected in our study, the grassroots groups in Hong Kong are influenced by government policy, strategies and tactics in three respects, namely, in their relationship with the political level, in their relationships with external social actors, and in neighbourhood relations among the grassroots people.

In the first respect, limited formal channels were available to the grassroots to influence decision-making. While Hong Kong is stepping into an era in which democracy has been introduced into the formal political system, the grassroots find it difficult to advance their interests concerning the distribution of urban facilities such as housing. The government responded to the challenges of the grassroots by restructuring the formal political system by the establishment of statutory bodies which exclude grassroots representatives from the decision-making process. Also, the use of partial clearance and granting new flats to the indigenous leaders were tactics used by the government to achieve demobilization.

The government also exerts power on the relationship between the grassroots and intermediary associations. Since grassroots protesters lack formal access to the political system, they seek to organize and mobilize support within the social domain in order to exert pressure on the government. However, the social domain is hardly free of government influence. The formal intermediate structure which could serve to articulate the interests of the grassroots is to a large extent controlled by the government. For example, the Mutual Aid Committee system and the traditional neighbourhood associations - the 'Kaifong Associations' - are subject to close scrutiny by the government. On the other hand, the government allows CSWs to deal with the grievances arising from inadequate urban services and thus to serve as mechanism of social control.

The grassroots people frequently interact with the CSWs and are more likely to be subject to the influence of the social work profession. In the case of the ATHA issue, we found that the involvement of external mobilization agents was important because most of the grassroots people lacked the skills and experience of protest activities. But the problem is that the external mobilization agents were not necessarily committed to the cause of the protest and that their ideology and preferences influenced the trajectory of the protest. In our view, as shown in our analysis of the ATHA protest, the CSWs exercised their power in the direction of using polite politics strategy and the grassroots people did not feel able to act independently of the influence of the CSWs.

At the neighbourhood level, social groups find it difficult to constitute a strong social force to act on the government. Typically they are small, locally-based neighbourhood concern groups which are subject to the power of the government and the CSWs. Advocates of resource mobilization theory have pointed out that the survival of an urban movement depends on whether horizontal and vertical integration is developed, i.e. links with other community organizations or with extra-community organizations (Pickvance, 1976). Nevertheless, as shown in the case of the ATHA local concern groups, neither form of integration was achieved. Without strong integration, either vertical or horizontal, the local concern groups were bound to be overdependent on the assistance and resources supplied by the CSWs and the VOs. We wonder whether it will be possible for the urban protest groups in Hong Kong to develop their autonomy in the urban political sphere in the future, and to what extent they can construct a free space for the cultivation of democratic consciousness and ideas which challenge government power in the various policy domains.

In short, urban politics in Hong Kong is characterized by a colonial regime which exercises dominance through the establishment of statutory bodies, through the weak system of interest intermediation for the articulation of the grassroots' interests, and through the lack of an extensive network for the housing movement to form a strong social force. Our findings thus reveal how the government exercises power over the social forces originated by the grassroots.

Having answered the four questions, we summarize our analysis of the evolution over time of the ATHA protest.

A Summary of the Evolution of Two Local ATHA Protest Groups

The ATHA protesters attempted to mobilize both external and internal resources such as participants, organizations, skills and experience in order to win concessions from the government. Facing constraints constituted by the prevailing political context, the local concern groups found that the available resources and political support were insecure. In our view, the development of this protest was the result of the interactions between the protest groups and the forces impinging on them. In this part, we seek to delineate the evolution of the ATHA protest. We distinguish four stages: the formation of local concern groups, the mobilization of potential supporters, organizational stability or transformation and the ending of the local concern groups.

The Formation of Local Concern Groups The ATHA protest began with the VOs taking the initiative in the mobilization of the ATHA residents to form their own local concern groups. The VOs were influential at this stage since the ATHA residents, who lacked skills and experience in protest activities, needed their assistance. In both the Kowloon Bay and Ping Shek THAs, they mobilized the THA residents by way of mass meetings in which they identified and recruited the residents with the greatest willingness to participate in protest activities. After that, briefing sessions took place in order to explain to the members the government structure and the policy-making mechanisms in relation to public housing policy. One of the core issues in these sessions was to identify the root cause of the existence of ATHAs. The government was thus identified as being responsible for the poor living conditions of the ATHAs, and the cause and goals of the ATHA local concern groups were then decided. At this stage, the VOs played the leadership role, and were influential in the decisions made in respect of the organizational forms and goals of the local concern groups.

The Mobilization of Potential Support Once the local concern groups had been established, the VOs and the active members had two tasks: making claims to the government and mobilizing support for their cause from neighbours, politicians and the media. Unlike the suggestion of the resource mobilization perspective that movement leaders adopt the strategy which maximizes the benefits of movement members, the VOs in our case deployed the protest strategies which they were accustomed to employ in other protest actions. As we pointed out in Chapter 8, they learned these strategy patterns from their own and their colleagues' experience. In both ATHAs, the VOs agreed to organize press conferences and make protests to the Housing Authority and the District Boards in order to carry out the two tasks. They sought to raise public awareness about the problems of the ATHAs and the government's indifference to the poor living conditions. This series of protest actions was the first move to pressurize the government. We found that there was a sequence of actions: organizing press conferences, sending letters to the media; making petitions and demonstrations to politicians and the relevant government departments; and waiting for a reply from the departments. If there was no positive reply, another round of protest activities was started.

We noticed that after the first wave of protest, the Ping Shek THA local concern group differed from the Kowloon Bay THA group in choosing a protest activity aimed at mobilizing potential supporters. As we pointed out in Chapter 8, the choice of mobilization strategy was associated with the internal dynamics of the local concern groups.

In the case of the Kowloon Bay THA, the CSWs had been involved and were powerful in the local concern groups from 1991. They insisted on using institutionalized means. By contrast, the VOs involved in the Ping Shek THA concern group preferred to use more non-institutionalized means, and were able to convince the concern group members to organize relatively more innovative protest activities, such as the 18th Anniversary of the Ping Shek THA which was used to goad the government about the fact that it had allowed the existence of 'temporary' housing areas for more than 18 years. Moreover, because of the arrival of the new Governor Chris Patten in 1992 who appeared to be more concerned with the problems of the disadvantaged people, more demonstrations took place at the entrance of Governor House. In other words, because of the involvement of the VOs and the specific historical conjuncture, the members of the Ping Shek THA were able to organize different forms of protest activity from those organized by the Kowloon Bay THA concern group.

However, the concern groups came to an impasse when the series of protest actions gained no concessions from the government nor support from politicians and the media. The reason for their failure to win concessions was related to the fact that the housing problems of the urban minorities in Hong Kong received less attention than issues linked to political reform. On the other hand, the government rehoused some of the leaders through the trawling exercise which led to a high turnover of membership and contributed to the impasse.

Organizational Stability or Transformation The essential feature of the third stage of the ATHA protest was related to how the local concern groups reacted to their earlier failure in winning concessions and the high turnover of membership. We found three kinds of reactions to the organizational dilemma.

In the case of the Kowloon Bay THA, by virtue of the lack of both political support from the politicians and concessions from the government, many active members were disappointed and became unwilling to organize protest activities. In early 1991, a sense of pessimism prevailed among the members of the local concern group in the Kowloon Bay THA. In April 1991, however, the Housing Authority announced the clearance date of the Kowloon Bay THA. This unexpected concession from the government served as a stimulus which subsequently attracted more residents to participate. It also led the concern groups to start a new wave of negotiations with the officials of the Housing Department in respect of the rehousing location. Consequently, the local concern group was able to sustain the protest until July 1991 when the group members were disappointed again with the government's reluctance to rehouse them in the urban area. At that time, the development of the Kowloon Bay THA protest was shaped by the internal conflict between the VOs and the CSWs. The VOs wanted to use more non-institutionalized means to pressurize the government whereas the CSWs considered the prevailing strategies were to be viable. Finally, with the support of some group members, the VOs won the argument. A new committee was consequently formed and new members joined the group. Since the new members accepted the use of demonstrations rather than only negotiations to exert pressure on the Housing Authority, the concern group was transformed into a group using more non-institutionalized means. With a new membership composition, the strategy adopted was changed. This revealed how the tactics and strategies of a protest group are strongly associated with the composition of the group.

As regards the Ping Shek THA, we found that the low morale of the local concern group members was also due to a sense of pessimism among the concern group members about their political effectiveness. When the VOs departed from the first concern group in late 1991, the group members were reluctant to continue their actions and finally the group stopped functioning. In short, this protest group was unable to overcome the organizational dilemma.

A second concern group was formed in the Ping Shek THA in May 1992. After one year of operation, it faced the same impasse: winning no concessions from the government, gaining limited support from politicians, and achieving only a low participation rate among the residents. In view of this situation, the active members considered that they lacked support from their neighbours. Since only four members of the Ping Shek THA remained active in July 1993, the group members decided to dissolve the local concern group. As has been pointed out, the VOs and the CSWs were significant in maintaining the local concern groups in this period. They persuaded the active members to stay and devoted more resources into mobilizing participants.

Being powerful in the local concern group, the VOs were also able to convince the group members to adopt more radical types of action, such as painting slogans and rent strikes, to mobilize both internal and external support. A mass meeting took place prior to the rent strike in order to gauge the number of supportive residents, and the active members painted slogans on the walls of the THA blocks. Moreover, at that time, the ATHA won a partial success. The Housing Authority announced a partial clearance of the THA. But this change led to growing dissatisfaction among the concern group members, who wanted clearance of the whole area. The concern group then set off a new round of protest activities pressing for clearance in one go. In short, the revival of the local ATHA protest was due to three factors, namely the involvement of the VOs, the successful mobilization of the ATHA leaders, and the changing THA clearance policy.

The Termination of the Local Concern Groups In the period from September to November 1991, the Kowloon Bay THA concern group was active in organizing protest activities since the clearance date was set by the Housing Authority for December 1991. Many residents and active concern group members felt it necessary to do more in order to exert pressure on the Housing Authority. However, at this later stage of the protest, some members considered it futile to fight with the government which they saw as too tough to be won over. Most importantly, after a series of protest activities, they felt they were running out of innovative and powerful means to pressurize the government. In addition, without the support of the CSWs, some members accepted the Housing Authority's offer and were ready to move out. This sense of pessimism finally led to the termination of the local concern groups.

The Ping Shek THA concern group remained active until the end of our fieldwork (i.e. April 1994). In early 1994, the concern group organized demonstrations and petitions in order to press for clearance in one go. But many VOs departed in 1994 and only the CSWs were still involved in the protest. We realized that in 1995 the CSWs and some active members were able to sustain the operation of the local concern group. However, the group had shown no specific changes in terms of the strategies adopted or in its organizational form. In June 1995, the Housing Authority announced the clearance of the rest of the ATHA blocks and the local concern group stopped functioning.

By the time the ATHA protest ended, the claims and ideas of this protest were neither incorporated into government policy nor accepted by the wider public. Some specific benefits had been won by the residents in the two areas but the ATHA protest failed to achieve the granting of rights to local rehousing to ATHA residents affected by clearance. We also found little evidence of the wider public's acceptance of the rights of the ATHA residents to early clearance and local rehousing. We therefore argue that the ending of the ATHA protest was not due to the protesters effecting changes in clearance policy, but was a result of the specific concessions granted by the government to the ATHA residents.

In this part, we have explained the evolution of the ATHA protest by making reference to three factors: the involvement of the CSWs and the VOs, the internal dynamics of the local concern groups and the contingent factors impinging on the protest groups.

In the next section we shall discuss the theoretical implications of our study.

The Theoretical and Methodological Implications of this Study

The contribution of our study of an urban protest in contemporary Hong Kong to the wider literature has two aspects: theoretical and methodological.

Theoretical Contribution

First, we argued in Chapter 2 that an integrated approach was needed to the study of the origin, development and effects of social movements. We also pointed out that different theories relate best to different levels of analysis. The political process model speaks to the macrolevel of political structure and context; the resource mobilization theory addresses issues at the mesolevel of organization and resources; and the social construction perspective relates to the microlevel of grievance formation and identity. We argued that an improved theoretical framework was necessary which explored the links across these levels of analysis. We therefore proposed an integrated approach to social movements in which the three levels of analysis are linked and some key factors highlighted, including the political context, the availability of resources, the actors' interpretation of the situation, their preference regarding strategies and the internal dynamics of the protest group.

Our study of urban movements depends on a particular conceptualization of the political context. This can be shown in three respects. First, in understanding the link between the formal political structure and the rise of social movements, our analysis is not only concerned with the openness and effectiveness of the Hong Kong Government but also focuses on the strategy of the state for containing external pressure. In Lui's (1984) study, the origin of non-institutionalized social action was explained by reference to the degree of openness of the government. The political system was regarded as closed when there was an absence of popularly elected councillors. Lui argued that where the formal political structure is constituted by appointed councillors rather than popularly elected representatives, 'such a form of polity is likely to direct the discontented people to tackle their problems by means of non-institutional action' (1984:187). However, we found that even though popularly elected councillors could now be found in the Legislative Council, the political system was not necessarily open. As shown in our analysis, the government on the one hand used democracy to incorporate politicians into the formal political structure, but on the other, shifted decision-making to other parts of the state where democracy did not exist. This created an image of democratic government while protecting the power and dominance of the government, and restricted the chance for grassroots representatives to become involved in negotiations with the decision-makers. It was this aspect of the political context that led to the exclusion of the ATHA residents from the decision-making process, and their consequent need to resort to non-institutionalized means to press for their interests.

Secondly, in addition to the structural aspects of the political system, we emphasize the role of historical and contingent factors in the political context, namely the current political issues and the balance of power among political parties. Our analysis showed that in the early 1990s the major political cleavage in Hong Kong was between pro-democracy and anti-democracy wings. Moreover, it was the debate about political reform before 1997 which attracted most attention among the politicians. The popularly elected councillors were heavily engaged in these debates and consequently issues concerning the political demands of urban minorities were given a lower priority on their agenda. Thus, difficulty in gaining access to the political structure for the ATHA protesters was not only due to the undemocratic statutory bodies but was also related to the fact that politicians were more concerned with political reform generally than with the political demands of the ATHA residents. It was this political condition which led to the use of non-institutional means of protest by the ATHA protesters.

Thirdly, we have emphasized the link between the political context and the possible external mobilization agents interested in a specific social movement. In our view, the question of who is interested in a social movement is contingent on the balance of political power and the historical situation of the society in question. For example in the United States, professional social movement activists are crucial when there are sufficient resources to fund them. By contrast, in Latin America where economic resources are insufficient to support an independent social movement profession, social movement activists mainly come from the preexisting intermediary associations, just as in Brazil, where external agitators are those from Catholic based communities, and when the state increasingly penetrates into the social terrain, women come out to protest in the interests of their families (Bruneau, 1980; Gay, 1990; Jaquette, 1989). In addition, the specific characteristics of the political system in Latin America, e.g. the patron-client ties, also attract political party members to local protests (Stokes, 1991). In Hong Kong, we learned from the ATHA protest that the involvement of the CSWs and the VOs in this protest was strongly related to the fact that they had been involved in the housing movement since the 1970s. Besides this, the lack of other mobilization agents interested in the political issues concerning the urban minorities was associated with the dominance of the 1997 issue and political reform on the politicians' agenda.

Our view is that the link between political context and the character of social movements is mediated by the actors whose values and strategic preferences can influence the trajectory of social movements. Unlike the advocates of the concept 'political opportunity structure' who emphasize a direct link between the political context and the strategy adopted by a social movement, we suggest that the link is mediated by the mobilization agents whose values, characteristics, social positions and strategy preference need close inspection.

To sum up, the reasons for our examination of the political context are (1) to specify the political opportunity and constraints which a social movement encounters; and (2) to identify the external mobilization agents who are interested in becoming involved in the social movement in question.

The second level in our integrated approach is the organizational level: the focus here is on the importance of social movement organizations in resource mobilization. Rather than examining the organizational structure of social movements, we focus on the resources which could be mobilized by the mobilization agents, including non-material resources (e.g. manpower, knowledge and skills) as well as material resources (e.g. money). We would highlight that in the study of social movements generally, little attention has been devoted to the nature and characteristics of the actors involved. In our view the identity of mobilization agents is specific to different political contexts. It is necessary to situate the ATHA protest in its socio-political context in order to understand how, and the extent to which, the mobilizing agents involved in a movement are helpful in mobilization.

One of the strengths of our integrated approach is that the levels of resource inputs contributed by different external mobilization agents are emphasized. This subject has not received sufficient attention from the advocates of resource mobilization theory who attach great importance to external assistance. Some studies in Hong Kong have also failed to address this theoretical issue. Lui (1984) in his study of urban protest argued that the expansion and intervention of social work agencies led to a supply of organizational resources to working class people which subsequently led to housing protests. And in his study of squatter clearance, Smart found that 'the availability of social workers who know how to organize protests to gain media attention and public support, and the importance of the media in Hong Kong's unique political structure have played a major part in making the protests of squatters more effective in recent years' (1992:194). These two studies emphasized the contribution of CSWs in supplying resources such as organizing skills and connections with the media, in order to raise public awareness and to elicit the support of the media and third parties. However, these studies were merely concerned with the positive impacts of the external agents, and did not give sufficient attention to their negative impacts.

In contrast, we have argued that it is necessary to specify what resources the protesters need and what resources the external mobilization agents can offer. In order to specify what resources a social movement organization needs, we distinguished between two types of resources, namely resources for the maintenance of the protest organization and those for organizing actions for exerting pressure on opponents and/or rallying support from third parties (Turner and Killian, 1987; Lipsky, 1968). Regarding the resources for maintenance, for example, Roberts (1973) suggested four types of internal resource which were necessary to encourage activism in neighbourhood associations, namely commitment, orientation, availability and monetary resources. Commitment is engendered if a) most of the social relationships that serve people in their daily life are located in or near the neighbourhood; and b) when the neighbourhood presents the best and only feasible way of coping with residential problems. Orientation means that the activists recognize the value of organizing others. The other two factors refer to the availability of time and to monetary resources for participation.

As regards external resources, we suggest that two aspects need more consideration. The first is the interorganizational links, vertical or horizontal, which a social movement can be involved in and second, the contents of the inflows of resources through these linkages. We stress that our focus is not on the quantitative level of the inflows of resources, but on whether the resources brought in meet the demands of the protesters in question. Put simply, what is crucial is whether 'appropriate' resources are available. This raises a question about how to determine what resources are 'appropriate' to a social movement. In our view this is an empirical question and can only be identified and examined through research.

We also argued that resource mobilization theory pays little attention to the social positions and orientations of the external mobilization agents. In contrast, our study showed that the values and strategy preferences of the external agents had a strong influence on the trajectory of the ATHA protest. Resource mobilization theory is largely asocial in the sense that it does not take into account the social origin of the external mobilization agents. However, we argue that social origins determine people's values, interpretations and orientations. As Schwartz *et al.* pointed out, 'insofar as the leaders of a social movement come from different social origins than their followers, they may also bring to the organization orientations which reflect the interests and attitudes of their social group' (1981:25). This enables us to show that even if external mobilization agents have resources at their disposal, their values and interpretations will govern their choice of resources. Hence they may not supply all the resources which are available to them.

Our study also showed that internal conflicts between subgroups within a social movement exist due to the external mobilizers' different values and interpretations of the situation. The VOs and the CSWs were in two different positions and their interpretations of their roles in the ATHA protest largely shaped their choice of strategy. Whereas the VOs were more willing to use radical action, the CSWs were reluctant to go so far as to break their connections with the established system.

In our view, the identity of the actors is important but, unlike the advocates of the social construction perspective who consider shared identity to be a precondition of strategic action, we argue that there is a plurality of identities within a social movement. In order to understand the character and the trajectory of a social movement, it is necessary to shed light on the interactions between actors who have different identities.

We noted that the analysis of the actors' interpretation of the situation is not sufficient to account for the character and trajectory of a social movement. Instead, as Johnston and Klandermans pointed out, apart from an emphasis on the cultural aspect, 'theoretical advance comes from incorporating what we know about the role of organizations, material resources, and social structure with culture' (1995:21). Our study illustrated a possible means of such incorporation. We first examined the resources that the actors could offer, and their ideological preferences, and then proceeded to examine the interplay among these actors. At the same time we took into account the available resources, the organizational situation and the actors' interpretation of the wider political context in order to show that actions are simultaneously influenced by all these factors. In our view the study of social movements must pay attention to political contexts, the organizational situation, the characteristics of the actors, the actors' interpretation of the situation, and the interplay among the actors in practice.

Methodological Contribution

Turning to the methodology of the present study, its distinctive feature has been participant observation. Although this method has been used by several students of social movements in western societies, our study is the first to use it in Hong Kong. In their studies of urban movements, Lui (1984) and Kung (1984) collected information about the mobilization process through interviews. Because of the shortage of written information on the mobilization process, their analyses relied on the interviewees' ability to recall past events. However, this method involves a considerable loss of information about the process of choice of strategy, and the internal conflicts and interaction patterns between the actors involved. In the course of our participation in protest actions, debates in meetings, informal discussions and in the actual social life of the participants, we recorded their speeches, feelings, interpretations of the situation, actions and observed behaviour. After that, through interviews we asked the actors to give an account of their behaviour. This approach gave us particular insights into the thinking of the actors. The information we obtained throughout our involvement in the process of mobilization and protest action enabled us to draw up a general descriptive account of the trajectory of the social movements and our interviews enabled us to make sense of the interviewees' understandings of their actions. By doing so, we were able to go beyond the provision of a descriptive account of the behaviour involved. The advantage of this methodological approach is particularly clear in our study of the link between the action and the meaning system of the CSWs and the VOs.

Limitations and Scope for Future Research

After a discussion of the theoretical and methodological contribution of our study, we will now indicate some of its limitations. Three limitations relate to our methodological approach. First, it was difficult for us to ensure that our interpretation of the meanings behind actions was correct. In respect of the interviews, when we asked the actors to give a personal account of their behaviour, we were aware that these are to some degree situationally determined and subject to the selective processing which is largely dependent on the cues given by the interviewer to the interviewee (Johnston and Klandermans, 1995).

Secondly, as a participant observer, the author found it easy to take sides in debates. This certainly caused tension with other subgroups in our study such as the CSWs. Although good social relationships were established between the author and the indigenous leaders, it was not easy to maintain a relationship of trust with the CSWs. Hence, due to the problem of partisanship, we cannot be sure about the extent to which the views of the CSWs were correctly revealed through our interviews.

Thirdly, since our research is based on a case study of a single type of urban movement, we make no claim to generalize from our findings to the housing movement in Hong Kong as a whole. Equally, since the two local concern groups were located in the same district, we cannot know whether factors at district level, such as the power configuration within a specific district board, or the number of social groups competing for public housing in a district, etc., shape the character and trajectory of protest actions. A further study in another district would be necessary in order to assess the importance of factors at district level.

Besides these methodological limitations, there were a number of issues which we did not examine thoroughly in this thesis but which should be put on the research agenda for the future.

First, we have shown the importance of the involvement of the CSWs, but we did not go further to explore the cultural values of the social work profession. Our case study showed that the CSWs had a particular interpretation of their roles in local protest and that this influenced their choice of strategy. If these CSWs are representative of their profession, it is possible that there is a social work culture which has a significant impact on the rise and fall, and the general character of urban movements in Hong Kong.

Second, we have not examined the relationship between the state and the social work profession. We cannot say whether the principles cherished by the CSWs today are the products of an ideological strategy adopted by the state, or whether they are the products of the academic training of the social work profession.

Thirdly, we did not give enough attention to the attitudes of the indigenous leaders to their participation, and in particular how participants deal with their new identity as protest participants. As Foweraker (1995:45-60) pointed out, the social identity of a participant is not exclusive. A participant of a social movement remains a woman, a worker or a housewife. Therefore, participation in protests leads to competition for time and energy. The question of how protest participants deal with multiple identities and how we can link this to our understanding of participation and non-participation poses a challenge to social movement theories.

Finally, we suggest that more comparative research on urban movements is necessary. Since the present analysis is based on one protest, we are not in a position to say whether the trajectory and character of an urban movement varies with the nature of the issue. Further studies of protest over other urban issues may offer the answer. Comparative study may also be helpful in examining protest over other political issues. Although our analysis reveals the lack of interest of politicians in respect to one demand by urban minorities, politicians may be interested in issues other than housing. A comparative study could give us information about the link between the nature of the issue and the reaction of the politicians. Also, by comparing similar organizations and movements across nations, it is possible to detect the impact of a specific political context on social movement mobilization. We believe that comparative research not only gives us insight into the relative degree of importance of the factors at different levels of analysis, but also provides more information for us to expose our theoretical framework to challenge. Suffice it to say, the aim of continuing research is to achieve a 'reconstruction of existing theory' (Burawoy, 1991).

Future Development of the ATHA Protest

We conclude with a discussion about the development of the ATHAs, and the housing movement after 1997 when Hong Kong is subject to a new political context and to Chinese housing policy.

We know that the THAs will continue to play a role within Chinese housing policy. In mid-September 1995, the government announced that thirteen THAs were to be retained although the Governor had previously promised to demolish all THAs by 1996. The reason for this change in THA policy, as the government officials explained, is to meet the heavy demand for temporary accommodation in the next two years, particularly from mainland China.[3] This change of policy resulted in an eruption of violence during a visit by the Governor to a THA two weeks after the announcement. Is the THA residents' anger likely to intensify now that the government has broken its promise? It turned out that there were few social actions undertook by ATHA residents in the late 1990s. The fact that there was little grievances among THA residents could be explained by a number of factors that inhibit the rise of THA protests.

On the basis of our study, we would argue that the incidence of protests over the THA issue is strongly associated with two factors: whether political parties are willing to put the THA issue on the political agenda, and the involvement of CSWs and VOs. It will also be important to see the reaction of the new government of the 'Special Administrative Region' (as Hong Kong will be described after 1997) to urban movements and whether the government will increase the supply of public housing flats.

In the light of the above considerations, we arrive at a very pessimistic conclusion. First, the new SAR government established on July 1 1997 has been a more repressive government which is likely to abhor social movements initiated from the bottom. In mid-October 1995, the legal subgroup of the Preliminary Working Committee - the Beijing-appointed think-tank on Hong Kong's future - proposed the deletion of six articles in the Bill of Rights and the reinstatement of six ordinances which had previously been deleted due to their violation of the Bill of Rights. This proposal would affect laws protecting human rights, civil liberties and freedom of speech and may finally emasculate the Bill of Rights.[4] In late October 1995 the Chinese government admitted that this proposal was in line with its policy. This indicates that social movements has have a very hard time since 1997. However, until 2000, there had no testing case to illustrate the extent to which many of the Hong Kong peoples' rights to enjoy freedom of speech, petition and demonstration will be removed.

In the late 1990s, the roles and functions of the CSWs and the VOs need more attention. In the case of the ATHA protest, the VOs were recruited by the pressure group - the Hong Kong People's Council on Public Housing Policy. However, this pressure group has been on the brink of collapse because of financial problems. It was unable to obtain sponsorship from overseas religious organizations, and was rejected by the Community Chest - a voluntary association which collects donations and distributes them to grassroots organizations - as 'too radical'.[5] The Council now trys very hard to keep its original role of providing housing rights activism, but its limited resources could not support it to take up the role as a radical pressure group on housing policy will give up its function of training volunteer organizers.

The situation of the CSWs is somewhat similar to that of the Council. In September 1995 the government proposed to terminate its support for their programmes - the Neighbourhood Level Community Development Projects - due to budget cuts. Despite a series of protests by the CSWs against this proposal, the government has not shown any intention of changing its mind. Many CSWs ended their role in local politics, and the urban minorities found it difficult to organize their protests, particularly when there were so few intermediary associations working at neighbourhood level as in Hong Kong.

We seem to be somewhat disappointed about the development of the housing movement in Hong Kong in the late 1990s. However, in view of the more repressive government in future and, most important, the fact that the protest groups tend to use polite politics, we have little grounds for expecting that the local protest groups will be able to exert sufficient pressure on the political system in order to win concessions.

Notes

1   We are not convinced that the local concern groups failed to mobilize the residents. On the contrary, given the considerable obstacles we described, the level of mobilization which the local concern groups achieved was quite considerable. What we are concerned with is why the local concern group members and the external mobilizers were reluctant to expend more resources on mobilization.
2   We interviewed three former indigenous leaders of the Ping Shek THA concern groups. All of them admitted that their protest led to an earlier clearance of their THAs.
3   See South China Morning Post, September 29 1995.
4   See South China Morning Post, October 18 1995.
5   See South China Morning Post, October 5 1995.

Appendix 1

Methods

This appendix aims to delineate the methods adopted in this study. Our study involves three levels of analysis, namely the political context, the internal structure of the Aged Temporary Housing Areas, and the internal dynamics of the local concern groups. In the following sections, we describe the different methods adopted to collect data about each level.

The Analysis of the Political Context

Our analysis at this level was based on data collected from two sources, namely official documents and interviews. The analysis of the institutional structure of the polity (e.g. the relationship between the government and the Housing Authority) was based on unpublished official documents, the annual reports of the departments concerned, and the minutes of the District Board meetings. Besides this, we interviewed twenty-four people including political party members, social workers, trade unionists and politicians, as shown in Table A1.1.

Category	Number of interviewees	Comments
Political party member	7 (2)*	Four were the candidates for the 1991 Legislative Council Election, whose constituency area was the Kwun Tong District
		Three were members of three political parties, namely the Meeting Point, the Hong Kong Democratic United and the Hong Kong Association for Democracy and People's Livelihoods
Politician	9	Three were members of the Kwun Tong District Board
		Six were members of the other District Boards
Social worker	4	Two were staff members of a social work organization which was regarded as more radical than the conventional social workers
		Two were involved in ATHA protests
Trade unionist	2	Both were staff members of the Federation of Trade Unions
Social activists	2	One was the Chairperson and the other was a paid staff member of the People's Council on Public Housing Policy

Table A1.1 Distribution of Interviewees

Note: * We had a well established relationship with two staff members of the Hong Kong Democratic United and several formal and informal interviews were conducted with them. But we did not regard them as interviewees since the interviews were not conducted in accordance with our interview schedule.

Source: *Author's fieldwork*

We used different sampling methods to select the interviewees. The interviews were guided by a semi-structured, open-ended questionnaire.

I. Personal Particulars: age, sex, education, occupation

II. Interviewee's retrospective view on his/her experience of political participation

   a. kind of social/political activity involved in
   b. party alignment
   c. membership of public bodies (either elected or appointed)
   d. strength of ties with the political groups in which the interviewee was involved
   e. personal involvement and experiences in housing protests
   f. interviewee's account of the historical development of local politics in general and the housing movement in particular

III. Interest Articulation

   a. what kind of issue is their main concern?
   b. what is the most important issue which he/she is dealing with at the time of interview?
   c. the reason for giving high priority to this issue
   d. whose interests does the interviewee claim to represent and for what reasons?
   e. a brief account of the involvement of the interviewee's organizations in local politics and the housing movement, and their main concerns
   f. an evaluation of the performance of their organizations in solving housing issues and protecting and advancing the interests of the people whom they claim to represent

IV. Interviewee's view on the prevailing social and political situation in Hong Kong

   a. the extent to which Hong Kong can be regarded as a fair society
   b. what are the current social problems in Hong Kong?
   c. what problem needs to be dealt with immediately? why?

d. which social groups do the interviewees think need the interviewees' assistance?
e. how do the interviewees interpret their role in relation to these problems?
f. Does the interviewee think that the housing problem in Hong Kong is an issue to which the interviewees need to pay attention? Why?

V. Personal views on the housing policy performance of the Hong Kong Government

a. whether the Hong Kong Government performed satisfactorily in the provision of public housing to Hong Kong people?
b. the interviewee's personal evaluation of public housing policy in Hong Kong
c. the priority of the social groups which should be allocated public housing flats in Hong Kong, including those on the waiting list, public housing tenants affected by redevelopment schemes, THA tenants, one person and two persons families, compassionate cases, the elderly and those households suffering overcrowding in the private housing sector.
d. the interviewee's understanding of the ATHA issue
e. the frequency, duration and intensity of actions which aim to help the ATHA residents
f. any solution suggested to solve the ATHA problem?

VI. Specific topic

(for elected District Board (DB) members/Legislative Council (Legco) candidates)

1. the social groups the interviewees think of as their major supporters in the DB and the Legislative Council elections
2. the strategy they used to gain people's support
3. the ways they understand the interests and preferences of their supporters?

(for appointed DB members)

1. the social groups the interviewees think that they should help as DB members
2. how and why the interviewees identify this/these group(s) as their target group?
3. how the interviewees know the preferences of their target groups?

(for social activists)

1. the social groups the interviewees are concerned with
2. how and why they identify this/these group(s) as a priority
3. how the interviewees understand the preferences of the group they are concerned with

(for social workers)

1. the social groups the interviewees are concerned with
2. the strategies they adopted to help the people
3. an historical account of the development of community social work in Hong Kong
4. the difficulties in advocating community participation
5. the relationships between political parties, pressure groups and local community groups

(for all interviewees)

1. the interviewees' assessment of the effectiveness of the District Board in helping people who lack housing resources
2. their assessment of the effectiveness of the Legislative Council in helping people who lack housing resources

As regards the political party members, four candidates for the 1991 Legislative Council Election were selected. They were involved in the 1991 election campaign in the Kwun Tong District from where two candidates would be returned to the Legislative Council. They were also members of four political parties. One was a member of a political party which advocated the Trotskyist political ideology, another was a member of a small socialist political party. The third was a key figure among Leftists in Hong Kong - a general term which refers to those people with pro-Chinese government attitudes. The fourth was a member of the Hong Kong Democratic United. The interviews with these people sought to explore the political parties' orientations towards housing movements, the historical trajectory of their involvement in local politics, and in particular their attitudes towards the issues concerning the Aged Temporary Housing Areas (ATHAs).

In order to discover the three major political parties' policy concerning public housing in general, and THA policy in particular, we interviewed members of three important political parties, including Meeting Point, the Hong Kong Democratic United, and the Hong Kong Association for Democracy and People's Livelihoods. All of them were the spokesperson of their party and were responsible for housing issues and policy.

We also interviewed local politicians in the Kwun Tong District. Three local politicians (i.e. the District Board members) were interviewed because their constituency included the Ping Shek and Kowloon Bay districts. In order to understand the extent to which the internal dynamics within the Kowloon Tong district differed from those in other District Boards, six local politicians on other District Boards were randomly selected. We firstly selected six District Boards out of the 19 (i.e. the total number of District Boards in Hong Kong), and randomly chose one from the membership list of each District Board. These interviews sought to explore the local politicians' views about housing issues in Hong Kong, the ways in which District Boards deal with the issues arising from THA policies, and the internal dynamics of the District Boards in these districts.

The aim of interviewing social workers was two-fold. The first was to collect data about the historical development of community social work in Hong Kong and the other was to discover the strategies adopted in the protests concerning THA policy. Two community social workers had been involved in community politics and adopted relatively 'radical actions' such as blockades, sit-ins, etc. Most importantly, they were experienced community social workers and we could ask them a brief historical account of community social work in Hong Kong, their interpretation of the prevailing political context and particularly their experience of a THA protest. The third and fourth community social workers were selected since they were involved in an ATHA protest in 1989.

In order to look at the involvement of the trade unionists, we interviewed two staff members of the Federation of Trade Unionists which has been widely regarded by the media and politicians as the key representative of the Leftists in Hong Kong. There was another federation which represented the interests of the Taiwan government, namely the Hong Kong and Kowloon Trade Union Council. We learned the views of its Chairperson through our attendance at a meeting with the grassroots representatives; therefore no interview with him was conducted.

Social activists in our study refer to the members and staff members of pressure groups on public housing policy. We interviewed one paid staff member and the Chairperson of the Hong Kong People's Council on Public Housing Policy (PCPHP). This pressure group was established in the mid-1970s with a specific concern with public housing policies. There has been another less active pressure group, namely the Association for Public Housing Tenants. Since it was at its embryonic stage in the early 1990s and had not been involved in any local protests, we decided not to interview any members of this pressure group.

The Analysis of the Internal Structure and the Mobilization Potential of the ATHAs

We have conducted three questionnaire surveys. The first survey was conducted in the period from May 1991 to July 1991. Its objective was to explore the demographic characteristics and residents' attitudes towards delayed clearance and the living environments of three ATHAs, including the Kowloon Bay, the Ping Shek and the Hong Ning Road THAs. The second and third surveys were conducted in October 1991 and May 1992 in the Kowloon Bay and the Ping Shek THAs respectively. We sought to examine the residents' attitudes to the clearance policy and their propensity for political participation.

The First Questionnaire Survey

It involved three teams of volunteer interviewers. Each team was composed of six to eight interviewers, all of whom were social workers, either holding a social work diploma or a social work degree. A briefing session was held to train the interviewers, and the author was also involved in the survey as both interviewer and field instructor.

The first section took place in the Kowloon Bay THA and the last was in the Ping Shek THA. This survey was administered by the author of this thesis. We adopted an all-population sampling approach to cover all the households in the three ATHAs. It was impossible to construct a sampling frame because the Housing Department did not provide any information about the household characteristics of the THA residents, and because there were a lot of households holding tenancy but not living in the ATHA. Therefore it was impossible for us to know in advance the exact number of households within each THA. We thus attempted to interview all the households we could contact. We encouraged the interviewers to interview the head of household, and if they could not contact the household head, the spouse of the household head was the second choice.

In total, 782 valid questionnaires were completed, of which 417 were from the Kowloon Bay II & III THA, 112 from the Hong Ning Road THA and 253 from the Ping Shek THA. Another 8 questionnaires were regarded as invalid at the checking stage. The number of registered households in 1991 were 738 in the Kowloon Bay THA, 757 in the Ping Shek THA and 236 in Hong Ning Road THA. In other words, we interviewed 57%, 33% and 48% of the total households in the Kowloon Bay, the Ping Shek and the Hong Ning Road THAs respectively. Those not interviewed were mainly households that the interviewers were unable to contact after three visits, including 203 cases in the Kowloon Bay THA, 183 cases in the Ping Shek THA and 91 cases in the Hong Ning Road THA. There were 477 cases of non-contacts and 20 cases of refusal. The overall no-response rate (including non-contact and refusals) was 38%. On average interviews took about twenty-five minutes.

The questions asked in the survey were related to five themes which are listed as follows (for the questionnaire see Appendix 3):

a. level of satisfaction
b. social background of the household members
c. the household's history of applying for rehousing
d. preferences regarding rehousing date and location
e. attitudes towards political participation in neighbourhood associations

The Second Questionnaire Survey

It was conducted in the Kowloon Bay THA to explore the residents' political attitudes and the extent of political participation. The questionnaire used is contained in Appendix 4. Two groups of interviewers, each consisting of five members, carried out the survey in October 1991. The author was unable to participate in this survey because he was studying in England. However the questionnaire was designed and the field work organized by the author. The fieldwork was administered by a volunteer who was a social work diploma holder. She had been trained by the author in the first survey and was therefore an experienced field instructor.

As in the case of the first survey, we were unable to construct a sampling frame in advance. Because of limited time and resources, we employed the 'x + 3' formula. The interviewer was required to randomly choose one household from one block to conduct the first interview and then the household three units away from the first was chosen for interview. We aimed to interview half of the total households. The household heads were the targeted respondents, but if they were not available, the spouse of the household head was interviewed. If the interviewer was not able to interview the household head or spouse, the interviewer could accept another member of the household as the respondent, but only if the member interviewed was involved in decision-making about rehousing.

We knew from the official data that there were 506 households living in the Kowloon Bay THA in April 1991. By September 1991, we estimated that about 225 households had been moved out. Hence there were about 281 households in the Kowloon Bay THA. We finally contacted 248 households after one month of fieldwork. Only 115 questionnaires were returned. There were 20 cases of refusal and 113 cases of non-contact. About 15% of the failure cases were due to refusal. The non-response rate was 54%. In our analysis of the political participation of the residents, we cut down the sample from 115 to 92, since 23 households had accepted rehousing offers from the Housing Department. We believe that their acceptance of offers affected their willingness to participate in protest activities and their perception of the issues. Therefore these cases are not included in our analysis. The 92 cases were further reduced to 74 after the exclusion of cases with missing data.

The questions asked in this survey are listed below (for details, see Appendix 4):

a. situation regarding flat allocation
b. experience of participating in the ATHA protest
c. personal views on the current THA policy
d. mobilization potential of the interviewee
e. willingness to participate in protest activities
f. perception of the views of their family members and neighbours on their participation or non-participation
g. personal particulars: age, sex, household size, length of residence in Hong Kong and in the THA

The Third Questionnaire Survey

It took place from May to June 1992. This survey was administered by the author of this thesis. Six volunteer organizers of the Ping Shek THA local concern groups were involved in this survey as interviewers. They were trained in a brief session a week before the commencement of the survey. All of them were holders of the social work diploma and had knowledge of social research. Since we had no exact number of the current households in the Ping Shek THA, we adopted an all-population sampling approach, trying to interview all the households in this THA. The registered number of households in 1991 was 757. But we estimated that during the survey there were only about 440 households living in the Ping Shek THA since most households had been rehoused. Cases were categorized as unsuccessful after the interviewers had visited the households three times without success or if a flat was found to be vacant. Finally, 275 successful interviews were returned, there were 35 cases of refusal, 320 non-contact cases and 20 questionnaires were regarded as invalid at the checking stage. The non-response rate was 55%. About 90% of the unsuccessful cases were because of vacant flats. The response rate of this survey was 63%. The targeted respondents were the household heads or their spouses.

The questions asked in this survey are listed below (for further details, see Appendix 5):

a. social background of the respondents
b. satisfaction level in respect of living conditions
c. knowledgability of the respondents about current THA policy
d. preferences concerning the date of clearance and rehousing location
e. experience of participating in the ATHA protest

f. personal views on THA policy
g. the mobilization potential of each interviewee
h. their perception of the views of their family members and neighbours about their participation or non-participation
i. personal particulars: age, sex, household size, length of residence in Hong Kong and in the THA
j. characteristics of the respondents' family members

We also conducted intensive interviews in the Ping Shek and the Kowloon Bay THAs (15 and 30 respectively) in order to collect data about the structure of social relationships among the THA residents. The interviews in the Kowloon Bay THA were conducted from September to October 1991. As the THA was due to be cleared in December 1991, we had limited time to conduct the interviews. Therefore, we chose a small sample of 20 people, selected randomly from each block of the THA. Due to the lack of sampling frame in advance, we used random sampling. We first selected 35 blocks and then randomly selected one household from each block for interview. With the assistance of one volunteer organizer, we obtained interviews with 16 residents, with encountered 2 refusal cases and 18 failure cases which were mainly vacant flats. The non-response rate (including refusal and non-contacts) was 56%. We found that the sample was biased towards having more female and older persons. Even though we conducted our interviews in the late evening, i.e. after 9 p.m., most respondents said that the young and male family household heads usually came back after midnight. We could not find any other way of contacting the younger household heads. For this reason, we should interpret very cautiously the findings of the intensive interviews. All the interviews took place inside the respondents' THA units, and the average time was about one hour. All the interviews were tape-recorded for subsequent analysis.

The intensive interviews with the Ping Shek THA residents were conducted in August 1992. The author of this thesis administered these interviews and a female volunteer organizer was also involved. The presence of the volunteer organizer was important, since most of our respondents were female and we found that female respondents were reluctant to talk with a male interviewer.

The sample of interviews was selected randomly by computer. We first generated the block number and then the unit number. One hundred and twenty addresses were obtained. The first interview period targeted thirty households, but only twelve successful interviews were returned. Cases were categorized as unsuccessful after the interviewer had visited the households three times without success or found a vacant unit. All the non-response cases were due to vacant flats. Additional households were then added to the interview list. We obtained 30 successful cases and 90 were unsuccessful. The 25% response rate for this survey was quite low, largely because of vacant flats. About 80% of the interviewees were the household heads or their spouses, and the rest were the parents of the household heads. All interviews were tape-recorded and later transcribed for analysis.

The questions asked in these intensive interviews are listed below:

a. their views on early clearance
b. their views on the performance of the local concern groups
c. duration, intensity, and frequency of their participation in the local concern groups
d. the reasons for their participation (or non-participation)
e. their experiences in participating in the ATHA protest
f. the perceived political efficacy of concerted action
g. their relationships with their fellow neighbours
h. ways of spending their leisure
i. ways of getting assistance in case of emergency
j. their views on the current political situation in Hong Kong
k. their views on the performance of the Hong Kong government
l. their general views on the nature and character of Hong Kong people
m. their personal evaluation of social life in Hong Kong
n. their evaluation of the differences in social life between Hong Kong and mainland China

We also conducted more than 30 interviews on the site of the protest activities. A social work student was employed to interview the participants in meetings. The questions asked concerned the evaluation of the political efficacy of their concerted actions, the reasons for their participation, and their evaluation of the performance of the local concern groups and their fellow neighbours. The major findings of these interviews were recorded in field notes.

The Analysis of the Dynamics of the Local Concern Groups

The author started his extended participant observation in April 1990 and ended it in April 1994. Undertaking the role of volunteer organizer, we could follow the activities of the local concern group closely. Apart from recording our observations, we conducted more than 50 extensive, open-ended formal and informal interviews with the participants, the indigenous leaders, the volunteer organizers, and the community social workers. Most of the last three categories were interviewed several times in order to obtain information about their changing perceptions and evaluation of the protest, and their perceptions about their roles in the decision-making process in relation to the choice of strategy. All the formal interviews were tape-recorded, and informal interviews were recorded in field notes. Through these informal interviews, we aimed to 'have a general idea about a matter of interest and desire to be more certain of the insiders' perspective' (Jorgensen, 1989:88).

The author was also involved in a number of meetings organized by the Joint Committee for the THA Residents' Associations (JCTRA) in order to see the extent to which the local concern groups were able to build up their own coalition. Eight interviews were conducted; the interviewees included three indigenous leaders involved in the JCTRA and five community social workers whom we identified as key figures in this coalition in different periods. All the interviews were tape-recorded. The average length of interviews was one and a half hours. The questions asked in these interviews are listed below:

a. the objectives of this coalition
b. its organizational structure
c. the frequency and duration of the participation of the indigenous leaders
d. the issue priority in different periods
e. the activities organized in order to press for the early clearance of the ATHAs
f. the relationships between the indigenous leaders and the community social workers involved in this coalition
g. their personal interpretations of the role of community social workers and the indigenous leaders within the coalition

h. a brief account of action taken to advance the interests of the THA residents
i. the characteristics of the decision-making process within the coalition

We were also able to have access to the minutes of the JCTRA held between 1991 and 1994. These documents provided us with sufficient information to examine the internal dynamics of this coalition.

The strategy of extended participant observation gave rise to a number of methodological issues and will be discussed in Appendix 2.

Appendix 2

A Personal Reflection on Methodology

This study of the local concern groups in two Aged Temporary Housing Areas adopted both quantitative and qualitative research methods. We needed to use qualitative methods for the following reasons.

a. we had little knowledge about the operation of any local concern groups in Temporary Housing Areas, and therefore needed to be involved in the groups in order to observe and record the operation of this kind of local concern group. Furthermore there was little empirical material concerning the local concern groups in Hong Kong.
b. we found it difficult to collect data about the actual decision-making process within the concern groups through interviews, because we found that the interviewees only gave reasons for the decisions they made, rather than describing the dynamics and actual process. In my view the study of natural settings within the ATHAs can provide us with more information about the internal processes of the local concern groups.
c. perhaps because of some cultural habits, the interviewees tended to avoid talking about conflicts between members, and we were therefore not able to capture the tensions within the local concern groups. On the other hand, the community social workers disliked disclosing too much information about their relationships with the indigenous leaders, or as we found in our fieldwork, they reported on how they thought they should behave rather than their behaviour in practice. Hence, we decided to adopt participant observation to collect data about internal tensions and conflicts within the natural settings of the local concern groups.

In order to collect data and information regarding the actual decision-making process within the local concern groups, the author participated in the groups as a volunteer organizer, and took part in meetings, protest activities, and mobilization campaigns. At some meetings, the author also prepared the agenda and took minutes. At the site of protest activities (such as mass meetings and protest activities), we talked with the THA residents about their views on the efficacy of their activities. Informal interviews were also conducted with other volunteer organizers and the community social workers involved in the ATHA protest. Findings from all these interviews were recorded after the fieldwork. Through participant observation, we sought to discover how the participants made sense of their behaviour and how they performed in a natural setting.

We acknowledge that participant observation has been criticized as unscientific, entirely personal and full of bias, and raises a vast range of methodological issues (Denzin and Lincoln, 1994). First of all, this method has been criticized for the fact that participant observation researchers are unable to meet one of the important methodological rules of qualitative research, which requires the researcher to record as fully as possible the respondent's verbatim answers and to record in detail what the researcher observed, because in practice it is impossible to observe everything and record everything the researcher observes. Hence the data collected is largely the result of the researcher's personal choice and judgement about the importance of what is observed. Secondly, participant observation is seen as vulnerable to distortion by the researcher's idiosyncratic interpretation and manipulation. Thirdly, the actors involved may behave differently due to the presence of the researcher, and the involvement of the researcher may influence the events to be studied. The fourth issue posed by participant observation is the problem of partisanship. In view of these criticisms, it is important to point out the extent to which they have been met by the author of this thesis.

Difficulties in Observing and Recording

We admit that there are difficulties in observing and recording as fully as possible in fieldwork, especially in a community where some residents who were involved in the protest were somewhat mistrustful of outsiders. We found it difficult to use a tape-recorder and/or write a lot of notes in the presence of the indigenous leaders. Our analysis was hence largely based on notes jotted down after the meetings, rather than verbatim. Also, it was difficult to ask as many questions as the researcher wished. Without any idea as to the intentions of the researcher, some participants were not willing to report their views in detail. These difficulties in the fieldwork may affect the reliability and accuracy of our reconstruction of social phenomena. However, in this study such methodological difficulties were unavoidable.

With regard to the criticism that the 'raw data' collected through participant observation is largely the result of the researcher's idiosyncratic choice and judgement, our reaction cannot be given in detail here due to lack of space. But we argue that the methodological rule requiring researchers to objectively describe reality and to be free of any personal values and idiosyncratic preferences is based on a positivist conception of science, which has been challenged by proponents of various schools of thought, from Popper's critical rationalism to the proponents of postmodernism (see Guba, 1990; Richardson, 1994; Vidich and Lyman, 1994). We share the view that a researcher cannot examine reality in an 'innocent' manner, or serve simply as a mirror reflecting 'reality out there'. We agree with Guba and Lincoln that 'it now seems established beyond objection that theories and facts are quite *interdependent* - that is, that facts are facts only within some theoretical framework' (original italics, 1994:107).

Interpretation of Data is Vulnerable to Researcher's Distortion and Manipulation

Various proponents of participant observation have sought to increase and demonstrate the validity of the method, and have suggested a number of measures. Baker recommended that 'field researchers should sensitize themselves to the way in which theories shape perceptions. In practical terms, this may require sharing initial findings with colleagues, especially with those who operate from different assumptions' (1988:246). Fantasia suggested that we could conduct interviews with the people under study in order to discuss the researcher's interpretations of the flow of events and the actors' performance. He argued that the quality of interpretations would be improved if they had all been confirmed independently by the actors present in the events under study.

It is true that these measures may provide us with a chance to gain more insight into how the actors give meanings to their activities. So, the author presented the findings to the volunteer organizers, the community social workers and the indigenous leaders in order to see the extent to which the findings revealed how the actors reflected on their experience of involvement in the protest. Nevertheless, in our view, neither Baker's nor Fantasia's suggestions offer us a clear criterion for identifying one interpretation as more acceptable than other. Sharing findings with colleagues may lead us to view the actors' behaviour from different perspectives but it does not imply that a better interpretation can be obtained. On the other hand, we are not convinced that we need to adopt the view that an interpretation is valid only when both the researcher and the actors under study agree, because the researcher's interpretation can justifiably be different from those of the actors when the former views the latter's behaviour from a theoretical perspective.

The Actors Involved may Act Differently Due to the Presence of the Researcher, and the Involvement of the Researcher Influences the Events to be Studied

The author took several measures to avoid influencing events. Any involvement in discussions was kept to the minimum. However, as a participant observer and a volunteer organizer, the author in some situations could not avoid offering opinions. For example, the indigenous leaders at the meetings asked for the author's advice. Moreover, it was apparent that involvement in discussions gave the indigenous leaders the impression that the author was committed to the course of the protest and really wanted to offer assistance to them. In other words, a certain degree of participation increased people's trust in the author.

The author's presence in fact influenced the ATHA protest in various ways. The nature of this influence depends on:

a. whether the researcher is known to be a researcher by all those being studied, or only by some, or by none
b. how much, and what, is know about the research and by whom
c. what sorts of activity are or are not engaged in by the researcher in the field, and how this locates her or him in relation to the various conceptions of category and group membership used by participants
d. what the orientation of the researcher is; how completely the

researcher consciously adopts the orientation of insider or outsider
e. the reactions of the other actors to the researcher

The reason for the researcher's involvement (i.e. conducting research on a locally-based social protest group) was not disclosed to the indigenous leaders, whereas all the volunteer organizers and the community social workers engaged in the local ATHA protest knew that the author was doing a thesis on the ATHA protest for a Ph.D. degree. The latter group did not however know the theoretical perspective the author was adopting or the aspects of the protest being observed. Since they lacked a clear idea about what the author was doing, the community social workers were suspicious about the genuine reason for the author's involvement. One community social worker even suspected that the author would produce something which was detrimental to the local concern groups, such as disclosing the weaknesses of the concern group to the government. The lack of trust between the author and the community social workers therefore led to tension and conflict. This subsequently gave rise to some phenomena which might not occur in another setting where volunteer organizers were absent. First, the dominance of the community social workers, especially in the Kowloon Bay THA, was challenged. Second, the trajectory of the protest was likely to be shaped not only by the strategy preference of the community social workers, but also by that of the author. Third, there were conflicts between the local indigenous leaders and the community social workers. As shown in Chapter 8, with the support of the author and other volunteer organizers, the indigenous leaders were more confident in having a contrasting view to that of the community social workers, and even challenged the community social workers at meetings. We admit therefore that the presence of the author led to different actions and reactions between the indigenous leaders and the community social workers involved in the protest.

Regarding the sort of activities which were or were not engaged in by the author in the field, the author had better access to the activities organized by the local concern groups than to the community social workers' meetings. The author built up trust and cooperative relationships with the residents in the two ATHAs. These relationships were also critical for improving the quality of data (Johnson, 1975; Jorgensen, 1989). Throughout the protest, the author was involved in most of the local concern group meetings and protest activities. First-hand information about the feelings and reactions of the participants could be collected. In contrast, because of lack of trust between the author and the community social workers, the former was not able to attend any of the latter's team meetings. Therefore, the author had little information about how the decision-making process among the community social workers.

Most importantly, this exclusion reinforced the author's self-concept as a volunteer organizer rather than a member of the community social work team. It also had important implications for the author's interpretation of reality. Jorgensen stated that '[R]elations with people in the field are interconnected with the participant observer's self-concept. How you imagine yourself influences how you relate with insiders, and in turn this influences people's reactions to you. Your self-concept affects participant role performances, data collection, and other aspects of the research' (1989:79-80). Having a self-concept as a volunteer organizer, the author tended to interpret the activities of the community social workers as being manipulative of the local concern groups. This further reinforced the tensions between the author and the community social workers.

Another reason reinforcing the author's self-concept as a volunteer organizer is related to the method of entering the field. It is true to say that gaining entry to the field is the very first problem which social researchers face (Jorgensen, 1989). We faced little difficulty in entering the field. At the initial stage of mobilization, the Chairperson and a staff member of the People's Council on Public Housing Policy (PCPHP) were involved. They were renowned for their commitment to advancing the interests of public housing tenants, and for their efforts in criticizing the public housing policy. Most residents had heard of them and even knew their faces. On their first visit to the Kowloon Bay THA, residents approached them and talked about their personal problems concerning their difficulties in adding new members to their tenancy agreement or splitting their tenancies. The author was introduced to the residents as one of the volunteer organizers of the PCPHP. Hence the residents seldom questioned the involvement of the author and other volunteer organizers. Having the trust of a few key people in the field, the author's role as a volunteer organizer was accepted by the residents. As a result, we found it easy to discuss with the chairperson and two vice-chairpersons of the local concern group in the Kowloon Bay THA their views on the political context and the possibility of winning concessions from the government.

Despite the advantages of my involvement in the local concern groups, the fact that I entered the field with the assistance of the PCPHP did have an impact on the research. Upon reflection, the author considers that having close contact with the staff members of the PCPHP influenced his strategy preferences. The PCPHP staff members were experienced housing movement activists and preferred using non-institutionalized means. Due to their experiences, they distrusted the government, politicians and political party members, and hence accepted the view that only grassroots' collective action could effect some kind of change in housing policies. The author was influenced by this view and subsequently acted in a way which was not acceptable to the community social workers.

In fact, the author found that his presence had a great impact on the reactions of the other actors in the THAs. As shown in Chapter 8, the presence of the author gave the indigenous leaders some kind of emotional support. In addition, because of the author's advice, a rent strike was put on the agenda of the local concern group meeting in the Ping Shek THA. The author also helped to build up and sustain a connection between the local concern groups and the PCPHP. Regarding the internal relationships among the volunteer organizers, the critical role of the author needs to be spelled out. At the initial stage of the Ping Shek THA protest, the volunteer organizers, who were community social workers in other THAs, were committed to the non-directive principle. Their behaviour and modes of thought were akin to those of the community social workers in the Ping Shek THA. However, after many discussions with the author, they became convinced of the necessity of giving more instruction and assistance to the indigenous leaders. The conflict with the community social workers in the Ping Shek THA was in fact the result of the VOs' changed attitude towards the 'non-directive' principle.

The Problem of Partisanship

Since the author had a different strategy preference from the community social workers, tensions arose between the community social workers and the author. Put simply, the author was confronted with the question of partisanship in the fieldwork. However, as Fantasia (1988) argues, this is inevitable when the research is taking place in a conflictual context. But the author found that this methodological issue turned out to be a dilemma which requires a researcher to decide whether the use of participant observation is worthwhile. One of the disadvantages of partisanship is that it leads to the closing off of some research areas. In this study, for example, the author found it difficult to gain access to the community social workers' side. On the other hand, due to active involvement in the conflict, the researcher may discover things which might not be revealed in a situation where the researcher is not present. For example, we would not have known that the community social workers are opposed to the involvement of other external agencies (e.g. volunteer organizers). Another advantage of being a participant observer is that the researcher's active involvement in a situation can lead to the acquisition of data which a 'purist' observer would not be able to obtain. For example, at one meeting the researcher suggested the use of a rent strike (a strategy which none of the indigenous leaders had mentioned at meetings) in order to see the reactions of the actors to the use of radical action. This methodological strategy was used by Garfinkel to expose the implicit foundations of common social understandings, and proved to be appropriate for finding out unspoken elements in personal meaning structures.

In this section, we have spelled out the extent to which the author influenced the 'natural settings' in the two ATHAs, and argued that the findings of this study should not be dismissed as unscientific. It is true to say that the active involvement of the researcher may influence the natural settings under study, but on the other hand, this strategy can help the researcher to collect data which other methods would find difficult to obtain. Hence we consider the use of such a methodological strategy (i.e. active involvement) as a matter of choice. In a conflictual context where the question of partisanship is unavoidable, taking sides may facilitate entry into the field, but at the same time may close off some areas of investigation. Fantasia has argued that to solve this question the researcher must 'consider the costs and benefits beforehand' (1988:251). In addition, in our view, the quality of the data collected by this methodological strategy could be improved by the researcher having a higher degree of self-awareness about the extent to which he or she influences the natural settings. What we can do is to examine closely our held beliefs and try to free ourselves from their influence. By describing carefully the extent and types of influence which researchers bring in may also help readers to understand the context of the study from which data are derived. Of course, the accuracy, the validity of the findings and the reliability of the interpretation must be assessed by the reader.

Appendix 3

Survey on the Tenants' Preferences in the Temporary Housing Areas in the Kwun Tong District

Case No: _____
Name of THA: _____
House No: _____
Area: _____

I. Level of Satisfaction

1. Are you satisfied with your living condition?

    ☐ yes, satisfied (answer Q.3)
    ☐ no, dissatisfied (answer Q. 2)
    ☐ no comment, it is better than being homeless (answer Q.3)
    ☐ no answer (answer Q.3)

2. With which aspects of your living conditions do you feel dissatisfied? (can give more than one answer)

    ☐ public order
    ☐ environment and hygiene
    ☐ the building structure
    ☐ living space
    ☐ others (please state) _____

II. **Household Information** (please record all members' information)

3.

Relationship	Sex	Age	Occupation (and location of work)	Years in THA	Years in Hong Kong
Interviewee					

4. Before you moved to this THA, where did you live?
   _____ district

5. What kind of housing had you lived before moving into this THA?

   ☐ Squatter
   ☐ Temporary Housing Areas
   ☐ Private Housing
   ☐ Public Housing

6. Why did you move to this THA?

   ☐ Squatter Clearance
   ☐ Splitting household
   ☐ Demolition of Private Housing
   ☐ Natural Disaster
   ☐ Others (please state): _____

III. Special Scheme of Resettlement

7. Have you applied for the special resettlement scheme to Junk Bay last year?

    ☐ Yes (answer Q.8)
    ☐ No (answer Q.11)
    ☐ I didn't know there was a special resettlement scheme last year (answer Q.12)

8. Is your application successful?

    ☐ successful (answer Q.9)
    ☐ unsuccessful (answer Q. 10)
    ☐ have not received any reply (answer Q. 12)

9. When will you move to your new home? (answer Q. 15)

    ☐ I don't know
    ☐ soon
    ☐ half a year later
    ☐ have given up (if the respondent gives this answer, go to Q.15)
       (Reason: _____)

10. Do you know the reason for your failure?

    ☐ one person and two persons families
    ☐ over the income limit
    ☐ have the problems of adding new member/split household/illegal occupants
    ☐ the majority of the members are ineligible for public housing
    ☐ others (please state) : _____

11. Why have you not applied for special resettlement to Junk Bay? (only those who have not applied for this scheme should answer this question)

    ☐ waiting for clearance
    ☐ unsatisfactory location
    ☐ inconvenient for children going to school
    ☐ one person and two persons families are not allowed to apply
    ☐ over the income limit
    ☐ have the problems of adding new member/split household/illegal occupants
    ☐ the majority of the members are ineligible for housing
    ☐ others (please state) : _____

IV. Preferences

12. If the Housing Authority clears the THA where you are living now and moves you to the Junk Bay, do you agree to demolishing your THA?

    ☐ yes (answer Q. 14)
    ☐ No (answer Q. 13)
    ☐ No answer/Don't know (answer Q.13)

13. If you still want the Housing Authority to improve your living conditions, what are your views on the following options? (read out each option)

	Agree	Disagree	Don't know
A. clear the THA and rehouse the tenants in the public housing estates nearby	☐	☐	☐
B. re-build a THA on the same area	☐	☐	☐
C. no clearance, only major renovation	☐	☐	☐
D. only need better management	☐	☐	☐
E. others (please state) : _____			

13a. Of the above options, which one would you prefer most? (only applies to those who gave more than one answer in Q.13)

    _____

14. If you are offered a choice of rehousing location which district would you choose?

    (i)_____district
    (ii) second choice:_____

15. Do you know there is a neighbourhood association _____(the name of the association)?

    ☐ yes (answer Q. 16)
    ☐ no (answer Q. 18)
    ☐ no answer (answer Q. 18)

16. Do you think they can improve the living quality on your behalf?

    ☐ yes (answer Q. 18)
    ☐ no (answer Q. 17)
    ☐ don't Know/no comment (answer Q. 18)

17. Why?

    ☐ don't know what they are doing
    ☐ they have never consulted me
    ☐ they are only concerned with their own interest
    ☐ others (please state) : _____

18. If the organization needs help, are you willing to join?

    ☐ yes
    ☐ no
    ☐ no answer

19. If the organization wants to fight for your benefits, what do you want them to do? (can give more than one answers)

    ☐ speed up the clearance process
    ☐ improve the public order of the district
    ☐ press for more social services
    ☐ help you to apply for split household/adding new members/ registration of illegal occupants
    ☐ others : _____

20. What is your total family income?

    ☐ < 1,500
    ☐ 1,500 - 3,000
    ☐ 3,000 - 4,000
    ☐ 4,000 - 5,000
    ☐ 5,000 - 6,000
    ☐ over 6,000
    ☐ no answer

21. Have you planned to purchase a unit from the Home Ownership Scheme?

    ☐ yes
    ☐ no
    ☐ no answer

Appendix 4

Survey on Kowloon Bay THA Residents' Attitudes to "Same District Rehousing" Policy

Case No.: _____
Interviewer: _____
Village No: _____

A. **Flat allocation:** ☐ Have the key   ☐ Have not get the key

1. How many times did the Housing Department offer you a flat?

    ☐ none (answer Question 4)
    ☐ once
    ☐ twice
    ☐ three times
    ☐ more than three times
    ☐ don't know/no answer (answer Question 4)

2. Location of the flat offered : (please circle 'new' or 'old' flats)

    Name of the estate

First time :	_____	(new/old)
Second time:	_____	(new/old)
Third time :	_____	(new/old)
Fourth time:	_____	(new/old)

    88 ☐ not applicable
    99 ☐ no answer

3. What are the most important reasons for not accepting the offers (please tick) : (can give more than one answer as to the second important reason, use X)

First time

First time	Second time
01 ☐ location is not suitable	01 ☐ location is not suitable
02 ☐ old flat	02 ☐ old flat
03 ☐ too small	03 ☐ too small
04 ☐ bad design	04 ☐ bad design
05 ☐ has not decided	05 ☐ has not decided
06 ☐ other: _____	06 ☐ other: _____
07 ☐ view and floor are unacceptable	07 ☐ view and floor are unacceptable
08 ☐ no answer	08 ☐ no answer
09 ☐ inapplicable	09 ☐ inapplicable
Third time	Fourth time
01 ☐ location is not suitable	01 ☐ location is not suitable
02 ☐ old flat	02 ☐ old flat
03 ☐ too small	03 ☐ too small
04 ☐ bad design	04 ☐ bad design
05 ☐ has not decided	05 ☐ has not decided
06 ☐ other: _____	06 ☐ other: _____
07 ☐ view and floor are unacceptable	07 ☐ view and floor are unacceptable
08 ☐ no answer	08 ☐ no answer
09 ☐ inapplicable	09 ☐ inapplicable

4. Have you thought about your location preference?

    00 ☐ no
    01 ☐ yes, new flat and in urban area
                   (please state the location: _____)
    02 ☐ yes, in urban area and not too old flat
    03 ☐ in urban area, old or new flats
    04 ☐ not in urban areas and new flats
                   (please state the location: _____)
    05 ☐ not in urban areas, not too old flats
    06 ☐ new flats, any location
    99 ☐ no answer

B. Personal Participation

I want like to ask you something about your views on pressing for local rehousing.

1. Do you know what the Kowloon Bay residents' concern group is pressing for?

    00 ☐ wrong answer
    (answer: pressing for rehousing in new urban public housing flats)
    01 ☐ right answer
    02 ☐ no answer/don't know

2. Have you ever participated in any protest activities organized by the residents' concern group?

    a) Meeting   00 ☐ no   01 ☐ yes   02 ☐ don't know/no answer
    b) Petition   00 ☐ no   01 ☐ yes   02 ☐ don't know/no answer
    c) Donation   00 ☐ no   01 ☐ yes   02 ☐ don't know/no answer

3. Do you agree with the cause of the protest: the rehousing of those residents, who are reluctant to move to the Tseung Kwan O districts, to the new public housing flats in urban areas?

    00 ☐ do not agree
    01 ☐ agree
    02 ☐ no idea/no answer

4. The Housing Department proclaimed that since there was a shortage of public housing flats in urban areas, they were forced to move the residents to the Tseung Kwan O district. Do you accept this argument?

    00 ☐ no
    01 ☐ yes
    02 ☐ don't know/no knowledge about it
    99 ☐ no answer

5. The Housing Department proclaimed that the 'old' flats were new and clean. Do you agree with this?

   00 ☐ not agree
   01 ☐ agree
   99 ☐ don't know/no idea

6. Someone said that if everyone is unwilling to move to extended urban areas such as the Tseung Kwan O district, then all Hong Kong people will concentrate in the urban areas and their living conditions get worse. Do you agree?

   00 ☐ not agree
   01 ☐ agree
   99 ☐ don't know/no idea

7. If there is a concern group which asks you to participate in their protest activities, because your support is very important to them. Do you regard your participation as an important indication of showing your support to the concern group?

   01 ☐ important, and I did participate
   02 ☐ important, but do not have time
   03 ☐ not important, because there are other people/other reason
   04 ☐ not important, because I do not support them
   05 ☐ important, but have difficulty. Reason: _____
   99 ☐ no answer/ don't know

8. If someone says that there is no need to support the concern group since it is difficult to win concessions from the Housing Department about the issue of local rehousing. Do you agree?

   01 ☐ agree
   02 ☐ not agree
   99 ☐ don't know/no idea

9. If the concern group organizes a petition, according to your estimate, how many residents will participate?

   01 ☐ few
   02 ☐ some
   03 ☐ many (about 30-40 people)
   04 ☐ a large group (more than 40 people)
   99 ☐ don't know/no answer

10. If there are many people participating in a petition to the Housing Department, what is the possibility of success on the issue of local rehousing?

    01 ☐ a great chance
    02 ☐ possible
    03 ☐ little chance
    04 ☐ definitely impossible
    99 ☐ don't know/no answer

C.

1. If you participate in the concern group, do your **husband/wife/family members** support you?

   01 ☐ no
   02 ☐ yes
   03 ☐ don't know/no answer
   04 ☐ inapplicable

2. If you participate in the concern group, do your fellow neighbours dislike you?

   01 ☐ no
   02 ☐ yes
   03 ☐ don't know/no answer

Appendix 4 333

3. If you do not participate in the concern group, do your family members blame you for not caring about issues concerning your family?

   a) family members
       00 ☐ no 01 ☐ yes 99 ☐ don't know 88 ☐ inapplicable
   b) neighbours
       00 ☐ no 01 ☐ yes 99 ☐ don't know 88 ☐ inapplicable

4. Do you think that the opinions and the support of (a)/(b) are the important factors influencing your decision about participating in the local concern group?

   a) family members
       00 ☐ no 01 ☐ yes 99 ☐ don't know/no answer
       88 ☐ inapplicable
   b) neighbours
       00 ☐ no 01 ☐ yes 99 ☐ don't know/no answer
       88 ☐ inapplicable

5. Will you participate in the following activities organized by the local concern group?

   a) meetings   00 ☐ no 01 ☐ yes 99 ☐ don't know/no answer
   b) petitions   00 ☐ no 01 ☐ yes 99 ☐ don't know/no answer
   c) take a day-off,
       and have a meeting with the Housing Department
                         00 ☐ no 01 ☐ yes 99 ☐ don't know/no answer
   d) a more radical action
       (such as a sit-in) 00 ☐ no 01 ☐ yes 99 ☐ don't know/no answer

D.

1. Sex : 01 ☐ Male 02 ☐ Female 99 ☐ no answer

2. Age : _____ 99 ☐ no answer

3. Number of family members: _____

4. Eligibility for public housing flat:
   00 ☐ no 01 ☐ yes 99 ☐ no answer

5. Interviewee: i) Occupation: _____ ii) Position: _____

E. Interviewer's Observation (not apply to the interviewees)

1. Do you think that the interviewee knows about the performance of the local concern group?

   01. ☐ very familiar
   02 ☐ familiar
   03 ☐ not familiar
   04 ☐ very not familiar
   99 ☐ don't know/no answer

2. Do you think that the interviewee is a key person within the decision making process of his/her family?

   00 ☐ yes
   01 ☐ no
   99 ☐ don't know/no answer

3. Note: (please report your observation about the following aspects of the interviewee)

   a) reasons for being unwilling to move to Tseung Kwan O.
   b) reasons for not participating in the local concern group?

Appendix 5

Survey of the Living Conditions of the Ping Shek THA

Case No.: _____
Block No.: _____
House No.: _____

I. Background Information

1. How many years have you lived in this THA? _____ years

2. On which district did you live before you moved into this THA?
   _____

3. Which type of housing did you live before moving into this THA?

   01 ☐ squatter/stone house   04 ☐ private housing
   02 ☐ THA   05 ☐ other : _____
   03 ☐ public housing
   99 ☐ don't know/no answer   88 ☐ inapplicable

4. Why did you move to this THA?

   01 ☐ clearance of squatters   04 ☐ clearance of private housing
   02 ☐ clearance of THAs   05 ☐ natural diaster
   03 ☐ splitting households   06 ☐ other (please state: _____)
   99 ☐ don't know/no answer   88 ☐ inapplicable

5. We would like to ask your views on the following aspects of your living condition. You can say very satisfied (1), satisfied (2), average (3), dissatisfied (4), very dissatisfied (5), or no idea (8).

   Please fill the blanks in column 1-5, 8 or 9.

	1	2	3	4	5	9	8
a) transport	☐	☐	☐	☐	☐	☐	☐
b) social order	☐	☐	☐	☐	☐	☐	☐
c) hygiene and environment	☐	☐	☐	☐	☐	☐	☐
d) recreation facilities	☐	☐	☐	☐	☐	☐	☐
e) housing structure	☐	☐	☐	☐	☐	☐	☐
f) housing management	☐	☐	☐	☐	☐	☐	☐
g) neighbourhood	☐	☐	☐	☐	☐	☐	☐
h) living space	☐	☐	☐	☐	☐	☐	☐

6. What are your views on overall living conditions in this THA?

   01 ☐ satisfied 03 ☐ it is good to have a place to live
   02 ☐ average 04 ☐ not satisfied
   99 ☐ no answer/ don't know

II. Eligibility for Public Housing Flats

7. How many people are living in your THA unit? _____ people

8. Are you (or your family members) eligible for public housing flats?

   01 ☐ yes ------------------------------ (answer question 10)
   02 ☐ no ------------------------------ (answer question 9)
   03 ☐ don't know ---------------------- (answer question 10)
   99 ☐ no answer ---------------------- (answer question 10)

9. (only ask those who are ineligible for public housing flats)

    Reasons for ineligibility:

    01 ☐ insufficient eligible members
    02 ☐ over income ceiling
    03 ☐ illegal households
    04 ☐ household head living here for less than one year
    05 ☐ household head living in Hong Kong for less than 7 years
    99 ☐ no answer/don't know
    88 ☐ inapplicable

III. Information Received by the Residents

10. Do you know the date of clearance?

    01 ☐ yes, the government said this THA would be cleared next year
    02 ☐ the THA policy was changed, and this THA will be cleared later
    03 ☐ yes but the interviewee gave a wrong answer (right answer: 94/95 or 95/96)
    04 ☐ don't know
    05 ☐ no answer

* if the interviewee does not know that the clearance has been delayed, please explain the policy change

(FOR THOSE INELIGIBLE HOUSEHOLDS, ANSWER QUESTION 14)

11. Do you know that the government has changed the THA policy, and thus you will be moved to an extended urban areas (such as the Tsueng Kwan O, Shatin, Tsuen Wan and Tsing Yi districts etc.)?

    01 ☐ yes   99 ☐ no answer
    02 ☐ no   88 ☐ inapplicable

12. Do you believe the government's explanation that because there are insufficient public housing flats in urban areas, the government is forced to move you to an extended area upon clearance?

   01 ☐ yes
   02 ☐ no need to say believe or not just conform to what the government says
   03 ☐ no
   99 ☐ no answer
   88 ☐ inapplicable

13. When the Housing Department demolishes this THA, and moves you to the estates in the extended urban areas (i.e. the Tseung Kwan O, and Shatin), do you think that this policy is acceptable?

   01 ☐ yes
   02 ☐ no
   03 ☐ no idea/don't know
   99 ☐ no answer
   88 ☐ inapplicable

IV. Interviewee's Preference

14. Do you want this THA to be cleared earlier?

   01 ☐ yes (answer question 15) (ineligible interviewee answer question 20)
   02 ☐ it is good to have a place to stay, so no point in considering clearance or not clearance (answer question 15) (ineligible interviewee answer question 20)
   03 ☐ no (answer question 16)
   04 ☐ don't know (answer question 15) (ineligible interviewee answer question 20)
   99 ☐ no answer (answer question 15) (ineligible interviewee answer question 20)

* (please explain the THA policy to the ineligible interviewees that they are entitled to moving to other THAs with better facilities and living condition)

15. If you move to an extended urban area (such as Tseung Kwan O, Shatin etc.) do you want to have early clearance?

    01 ☐ yes   04 ☐ don't know
    02 ☐ no   99 ☐ no answer
    03 ☐ depends on situation   88 ☐ inapplicable

(move on to Question 17)

16. (only ask the interviewees who answered "no")

    Why don't you want to move? (can give more than one question)

    01 ☐ low rent   05 ☐ ineligible for public housing
    02 ☐ easy to access to   (answer question 20)
         public transport   06 ☐ other (please state) _____
    03 ☐ get used to this place
    04 ☐ easy for the children
         to go to school

(those interviewees who are ineligible for public housing flats, move on to question 20)

17. If the Housing Department offers you a large flat, are you willing to move to the Tseung Kwan O district?

    01 ☐ yes   03 ☐ depends   99 ☐ no answer
    02 ☐ no   04 ☐ don't know   88 ☐ inapplicable

18. If the Housing Department offers you a large flat, are you willing to move to the estates in the New Territories (such as Tai Po, Ma On Shan)?

    01 ☐ yes   03 ☐ depends   99 ☐ no answer
    02 ☐ no   04 ☐ don't know   88 ☐ inapplicable

19. In the following arrangements, which one measure do you want the Housing Department to adopt? (read out items 1 - 6)

    01 ☐ clearance, move the residents to the public housing in the same district
    02 ☐ clearance, move the residents to the public housing which has been existing for less than 10 years
    03 ☐ clearance, move the residents to Tseung Kwan O
    04 ☐ clearance, move the residents to the New Territories
    05 ☐ no clearance, carry out a large-scale refurbishment
    06 ☐ no action is needed
    07 ☐ no idea/don't know
    99 ☐ no answer
    88 ☐ inapplicable

(move on to question 21)

20. (only ask the interviewees who are ineligible for public housing flats)

    If the Housing Department demolishes this THA, where do you want to be rehoused?

    01 ☐ THA in the New Territories   99 ☐ don't know/no answer
    02 ☐ THA in urban areas   88 ☐ inapplicable
    03 ☐ other (please state): _____

21. If you have the right to choose the rehousing location, where do you want to be rehoused?

    a) First choice: _____ district
    b) Second choice: _____ district

(For those interviewees who are ineligible for public housing flats, move on to question 25)

22. Do you think that the extended urban areas (e.g. Shatin, Tsuen Wan, Tseung Kwan O) are suitable for your family?

    01 ☐ yes ------------------ (go to question 24)
    02 ☐ no ------------------ (go to question 23)
    03 ☐ don't know ---------- (go to question 25)
    99 ☐ no answer ------------ (go to question 25)
    88 ☐ inapplicable -------- (go to question 25)

23. Why is it unsuitable? (can give more than one answer)

    01 ☐ far away from workplace/children's school
    02 ☐ is required to adapt to a new community
    03 ☐ no idea about the communal facilities there
    04 ☐ other (please state) _____
    88 ☐ inapplicable
    99 ☐ no answer/no idea/don't know -------> (move to question 25)

24. Why is it suitable? (can give more than one answer)

    01 ☐ living here for a long time, and need to be cleared
    02 ☐ nothing specific
    03 ☐ good location
    04 ☐ other (please state) _____
    99 ☐ no answer/no idea/don't know --------> (move to question 25)
    88 ☐ inapplicable

25. Do you plan to purchase a Homeownership Scheme flat?

    01 ☐ yes   02 ☐ no   99 ☐ no answer/ don't know

(For those interviewees who are ineligible for public housing flats, answer question 33)

V. Trawling Exercise

26. Have you applied for rehousing through trawling?

    01 ☐ yes (answer question 27)
    02 ☐ no (answer question 32)
    03 ☐ no idea about the trawling exercise (answer question 33)
    88 ☐ inapplicable
    99 ☐ no answer/don't know (answer question 33)

27. How many times have you applied through trawling?
    _____ times

28. Which districts do you want? _____ district

    88 ☐ inapplicable

29. Is your application successful?

    01 ☐ yes   (answer question 42)
    02 ☐ yes, had not accepted the offer   (answer question 30)
    03 ☐ no   (answer question 31)
    04 ☐ have not received a reply   (answer question 33)
    99 ☐ don't know/no answer   (answer question 33)
    88 ☐ inapplicable   (answer question 33)

[from 30 - 32, if the answer is yes use 1, no use 0, inapplicable use 8]

30. Why did you decline the offer? (could give more than one answer)

    a) ☐ unsuitable location
    b) ☐ the flats is on a floor which is undesirable
    c) ☐ the view is unsuitable
    d) ☐ too little space
    e) ☐ the flat is too old
    f) ☐ other (please state): _____

(move to question 33)

Appendix 5 343

31. What are the reasons for the failure in applying for rehousing through trawling? (could give more than one answer)

    a) ☐ one-person, two-person household
    b) ☐ over the income ceiling
    c) ☐ have problems in adding new members in tenancy/splitting household/illegal tenancy
    d) ☐ insufficient members who are eligible for public housing
    e) ☐ other (please state: _____)
    f) ☐ don't know

(move on to question 33)

32. Why do you not apply for rehousing through trawling? (could give more than one answer)

    a) ☐ wait for clearance
    b) ☐ unsuitable rehousing location
    c) ☐ not suitable for children
    d) ☐ over the income ceiling
    e) ☐ have problems in adding new members in tenancy/splitting household/illegal tenancy
    f) ☐ other (please state): _____
    g) ☐ don't know/no answer

VI. Residents' Attitude Towards Political Participation

(We would like to know the residents' views on the establishment of a local concern group. This group aims to pressurize the government to look into the living conditions of the THA residents)

33. If there is a concern group which asks you to participate in their protest activities, because your support is very important to them. Do you regard your participation as an important indication to show your support?

    - 00 ☐ important, and I did participate
    - 01 ☐ important, but participation depends on the availability of time
    - 02 ☐ important, but do not have time
    - 03 ☐ not important, because there are other people/other reason
    - 04 ☐ not important, because I do not support them
    - 05 ☐ other (please state: _____)
    - 99 ☐ no answer/ don't know
    - 88 ☐ inapplicable

34. If someone says that there is no need to support the concern group since your involvement may not contribute much to the success of pressing for early clearance. Do you agree?

    - 01 ☐ agree
    - 02 ☐ not agree
    - 99 ☐ no idea/no answer
    - 88 ☐ inapplicable

35. If the concern group organizes a petition, according to your estimate, how many residents will participate?

    - 01 ☐ few
    - 02 ☐ some
    - 03 ☐ many (about 30-40 people)
    - 04 ☐ a large group (more than 40 people)
    - 99 ☐ don't know/no answer
    - 88 ☐ inapplicable

36. If there are many people participating in a petition to the Housing Department, what is the possibility for getting success about the issue of local rehousing?

    01 ☐ a great chance
    02 ☐ possible
    03 ☐ little chance
    04 ☐ definitely impossible
    99 ☐ don't know/no answer
    88 ☐ inapplicable

37. Will you participate in the following activities organized by the local concern group?

    a) meetings   01 ☐ no   02 ☐ yes
                         99 ☐ don't know/no answer
    b) petitions   01 ☐ no   02 ☐ yes
                         99 ☐ don't know/no answer
    c) take a day-off,
       and have a meeting
       with the Housing Department
                         01 ☐ no   02 ☐ yes
                         99 ☐ don't know/no answer   88 ☐ inapplicable
    d) a more radical action
       (such as a sit-in)
                         01 ☐ no   02 ☐ yes
                         99 ☐ don't know/no answer

38. If you participate in the concern group, do your **husband/wife/family members** support you?

    01 ☐ not support
    02 ☐ not support, but will not oppose to the interviewee's involvement
    03 ☐ yes
    99 ☐ don't know/no answer
    88 ☐ inapplicable

39. If you participate in the concern group, do your fellow neighbours dislike you?

    01 ☐ no
    02 ☐ yes
    03 ☐ depends on the nature of the protest activities
    99 ☐ don't know/no answer

40. If you do not participate in the concern group, do your family members blame you for not caring about issues concerning your family?

    01 ☐ no
    02 ☐ yes
    03 ☐ don't know
    99 ☐ don't know
    88 ☐ inapplicable

41. Do you think that the opinions and the support of (a) (b) is important to your decision about participating in the local concern group?

    a) family members

    01 ☐ no
    02 ☐ yes
    99 ☐ don't know/no answer
    88 ☐ inapplicable

    b) neighbours

    01 ☐ no
    02 ☐ yes
    99 ☐ don't know/no answer

VII. Personal Particulars of the Interviewee

42. Have you participated in any protest activity to fight for your interests?

    01 ☐ yes, in mainland China
    03 ☐ yes, in Hong Kong
    03 ☐ yes, in Hong Kong and Mainland China
    02 ☐ no
    05 ☐ forgot/no answer

43.

Name	Relationship	Sex	Age	Occu.	Posit.	Location of work	Years in HK	Years in THA

Telephone No.: _____

Note: _____

Name of Interviewer: _____

Bibliography

Aberle, David. (1965), 'A Note on Relative Deprivation Theory as Applied to Millenarian and Other Cult Movements', in Lessa, W. and Vogt, E. (eds.), *Reader in Comparative Religion: An Anthrological Approach,* New York: Harper and Row.

Alexander, Jeffrey. (1989), 'Action and Its Environment', in Jeffrey Alexander et al., (eds.), *The Micro-Macro Link,* California: University of California Press.

Alvarez, Sonia E. (1990), *Engendering Democracy in Brazil: Women's Movements in Transition Politics,* Princeton, N.J.: Princeton University Press.

Ambrecht, Biliana C.S. (1976), *Politicizing the Poor: The Legacy of the War on Poverty in a Mexican-American Community,* New York: Praeger Publishers.

Arendt, Hannah. (1951), *The Origins of Totalitarianism,* New York: Harcourt, Brace.

Ash, Roberta. (1972), *Social Movements in America,* Chicago: Markham.

Aveni, Adrian. (1978), 'Organizational Linkages and Resources Mobilization: The Significance of Linkage Strength and Breadth', *The Sociological Quarterly.* Vol.19 (Spring), pp.185-202.

Bailis, Lawerence Neil, (1974), *Bread or Justice: Grassroots Organizing in the Welfare Rights Movement,* London: Lexington Books.

Baker, Therese L. (1988), *Doing Social Research,* New York: McGraw-Hill Book Company.

Barkan, Steven E., Steven F. Cohn and William H. Whitaker. (1993), 'Commitment Across the Miles: Ideological and Microstructural Sources of Membership Support in a National Hunger Organization', *Social Problems,* Vol.40(3), pp.362-73.

Barkan, Steven E. (1986), 'Interorganizational Conflict in the Southern Civil Rights Movement', *Sociological Inquiry,* Vol.56(2), pp.190-209.

Barkan, Steven E. (1979), 'Strategic, Tactical and Organizational Dilemmas of the Protest Movement Against Nuclear Power', *Social Problems,* Vol.27(1), pp.19-37.

Barnes, Samuel H. and Max Kaase, *et al.* (1979), *Political Action: Mass Participation in Five Western Democracies,* London: Sage.

Bennett, Vivienne. 'The Evolution of Urban Popular Movements in Mexico Between 1968 and 1988', in Escobar, Arturo and Sonia E. Alvarez, (eds.), *The Making of Social Movements in Latin America: Identity, Strategy and Democracy,* Boulder: Westview Press.

Bolton, Charles D. (1972), 'Alienation and Action: A Study of Peace Group Members', *American Journal of Sociology,* Vol.78, pp.537-61.

Bonacich, Philip, Gereld H. Shure, James Kahan, and Robert J. Meeker. (1976), 'Cooperation and Group Size and the Free-Rider Problem', *Journal of Conflict Resolution,* Vol.20, pp.687-706.

Bowen, D., Elinor Bowen, Sheldon Gawiser and Louis H. Masotti. (1968), 'Deprivation, Mobility and Orientation Toward Protest of the Urban Poor', in Masotti, L. and Bowen D. (eds.), *Riots and Rebellion: Civil Violence in the Urban Community,*.Hills, CA: Sage.

Boyte, Harry C. (1980), *The Backyard Revolution: Understanding the New Citizen Movement,* Philadelphia: Temple University Press.

Breines, W. (1989), *Communities and Organization in the New Left* (2nd edition), New Brunswick, N.J.: Rutgers University press.

Breines, W. (1980), 'Community and Organization: The New Left and Michels' Iron Law', *Social Problems,* Vol.27, pp.419-429.

Bristow, R. (1989), *Hong Kong's New Town: A Selective Review,* Hong Kong: Oxford University Press.

Broom, Leonard. (1959), 'Social Differentiation and Stratification', in Robert K. Merton, Leonard Broom and Leonard S. Cottrell (eds.), *Sociology Today,* New York: Basic Books.

Brown, M.H. and D.M. Hosking (1986), 'Distributed Leadership and Skilled Performance as Successful Organization in Social Movements', *Human Relations,* Vol.39(1), pp.65-79.

Bruneau, Thomas C. (1980), 'The Catholic Church and Development in Latin America: The Role of the Basic Christian Communities', *World Development,* Vol.8, pp.535-544.

Burawoy, Michael (1991), 'Reconstructing Social Theories', in Burawoy, Michael et al., (eds.), *Ethnography Unbound: Power and Resistance in the Modern Metropolis,* Berkeley: University of California Press.

Burdick, John (1992), 'Rethinking the Study of Social Movements: The Case of Christian Base Communities in Urban Brazil', in Escobar, Arturo and Sonia E. Alvarez (eds.), *The Making of Social Movements in Latin America: Identity, Strategy and Democracy,* Boulder: Westview Press.

Burstein, Paul, Rachel, L. Eivwohner and Jocelyn, A. Hollander (1995), 'The Success of Political Movements: A Bargaining Perspective', in Jenkins, J. Craig and Bert Klandermans (eds.), *The Politics of Social Protest: Comparative Perspective on States and Social Movements,* Mineapolis: University of Minnesota Press.

Byrne, D. (1989), *Beyond the Inner City,* Milton Keynes: Open University Press.

Calhoun, C.J. (1982), *The Question of Class Struggle: The Social Foundations of Popular Radicalism During the Industrial Revolution*, Oxford: Oxford University Press.

Canel, Eduardo (1994), 'Democratization and the Decline of Urban Social Movements in Uruguay: A political-Institutional Account', in Escobar, Arturo and Sonia E. Alvarez (eds.), *The Making of Social Movements in Latin America: Identity, Strategy and Democracy*, Boulder: Westview Press.

Carden, Maren Lockwood (1989), 'The Institutionalization of Social Movements in Voluntary Organization', *Research in Social Movement, Conflict and Change*, Vol.11, pp.143-161.

Carden, Maren Lockwood (1978), 'The Proliferation of a Social Movement: Ideology and Individual Incentives in the Feminist Movement', *Research in Social Movements, Conflicts and Change*, Vol.1, pp.179-196.

Carden, Maren Lockwood (1974), *The New Feminist Movement*, New York: Russell Sage Foundation.

Castells, M. (1988). 'Public Housing and Economic Development in Hong Kong', in Castells, M. et al. (eds.), *Economic Development and Housing Policy in the Asian Pacific Rim: A Comparative Study of Hong Kong, Singapore, and Shenzhen Special Economic Zone*, Berkeley: Institute of Urban and Regional Development, University of California at Berkeley, Monograph 37.

Castells, M. (1985), 'Commentary on C G Pickvance's - The Rise and Fall of Urban Movements...', *Environment and Planning D: Society and Space*, Vol.3, pp.31-53.

Castells, M. (1983), *The City and the Grassroots*, London: Edward Arnold.

Castells, M. (1978), *City, Class and Power*, London: Macmillan.

Castells, M. (1977), *The Urban Question: A Marxist Approach*, London: Edward Arnold.

Castells, M. (1976), 'Theoretical Propositions for an Experimental Study of Urban Social Movements', in Pickvance, C.G. (ed.), *Urban Sociology: Critical Essays*, London: Tavistock Publications.

Castells, M., Lee Goh and Reginald Y.W. Kwok with Top Lap Kee. (1988), *Economic Development and Housing Policy in the Asian Pacific Rim: A Comparative Study of Hong Kong, Singapore, and Shenzhen Special Economic Zone*, Berkeley: Institute of Urban and Regional Development, University of California at Berkeley, Monograph 37.

Ceccarelli, Paolo (1982), 'Politics, Parties and Urban Movement: Western Europe', in Norman I. Fainstein and Susan S. Fainstein (eds.), *Urban Policy Under Capitalism*, Beverly Hills: Sage.

Chamberlin, John R. (1978), 'The Logic of Collective Action: Some Experimental Results', *Behavioral Science*, Vol.23(6), pp.441-445.

Chan, H. (1979), 'The 'Old' and 'New' Middle Class in Hong Kong', *Meeting Point Review*, (September), *Hong Kong: Meeting Point* (in Chinese).
Chan, K.W. (1992), 'Privatization Versus Socialization: Solving the Housing Problems in Hong Kong', Paper Presented in the *Conference on Residential Housing in Hong Kong*, jointly organized by the Department of Business Studies, Hong Kong Polytechnic and the Department of Economics, The Chinese University of Hong Kong.
Chau, L.C. (1989), 'Labour and Labour Market', in Ho, H.C.Y. and Chau, L.C. (eds.), *The Economic System of Hong Kong*, Hong Kong: Asian Research Service.
Cheung, A.B.L. and Louie, K.S. (1991), *Social Conflicts in Hong Kong: 1975-1986: Trends and Implications*, Hong Kong: Hong Kong Institute of Asia-Pacific Studies, The Chinese University of Hong Kong.
Cheung, L. (1979), 'The New Middle Class', *Meeting Point Review* (September), Hong Kong: Meeting Point. (in Chinese).
Chui, Y.F.A. (1986), *An Exploration into the Elements Affecting Strategy Formation of a Public Interest Group: A Case Study on the People's Council on Squatter Policy*, Unpublished M.S.W. Dissertation, University of Hong Kong, Hong Kong.
Chui, Wing-tak and Lai On-kwok (1994), *Research Report on Patterns of Social Conflicts in Hong Kong in the Period 1980 to 1991*. Unpublished report. Hong Kong: Centre of Urban Planning and Environment Management, University of Hong Kong.
Clarke, Susan E. and Margit Mayer (1986), 'Responding to Grassroots Discontent: Germany and the United States', *International Journal of Urban and Regional Research*, Vol.10(3), pp.401-417.
Cohen, Jean (1985), 'Strategy or Identity: New Theoretical Paradigms and Contemporary Social Movements', *Social Research*, Vol.52(4), pp.663-716.
Collier, David, (1976), *Squatters and Oligarchs: Authoritarian Rule and Policy Change in Peru*, Baltimore, Md.: Johns Hopkins University Press.
Committee on Neighbourhood Level Community Development Project.
Conover, P.J. and Virginia Gray (1983), *Feminism and the New Right: Conflict Over the American Family*.
Curtis, Russell L. Jr. and Louis A. Zurcher. Jr. (1973), 'Stable Resources of Protest Movements: The Multi-Organizational Field', *Social Forces*, Vol.52(3), pp.53-61.
Curtis, Russell L. Jr. and Louis A. Zurcher, Jr. (1971), 'Voluntary Associations and the Social Integration of the Poor', *Social Problems*, Vol.18, pp.339-357.
Dahl, Robert (1982), *Dilemmas of Pluralist Democracy*, New Haven: Yale University Press.

Dalton, Russell J. (1995), 'Strategies of Partisan Influence: West European Environmental Groups', in Jenkins, Craig J. and Bert, Klandermans (eds.), *The Politics of Social Protest: Comparative Perspectives on States and Social Movements,* Minneapolis: University of Minnesota Press.

Dalton, Russell J. (1988), *Citizen Politics in Western Democracies: Public Opinion and Political Parties in the United States, Great Britain, West Germany, and France,* Chatham, New Jersey: Chatham House Publishers, Inc.

Davies, James C. (1969), 'The J-curve of Rising and Declining Satisfactions as a Cause of Some Great Revolutions and a Contained Rebellion', in Graham, Hugh Davis and Ted Robert Gurr (eds.), *Violence in America: Historical and Comparative Perspective,* Washington, D.C.: U.S. Government Printing Office.

Davies, S.N.G. (1989), 'The Changing Nature of Representation in Hong Kong Politic', in Cheek-Milby K. and Mushkat, M. (eds.), *Hong Kong: The Challenge of Transformation,* Hong Kong: Centre of Asian Studies, University of Hong Kong.

Davies, S.N.G. (1977), 'One Brand of Politics Rekindled', *Hong Kong Law Journal,* Vol.7, (Jan.), pp.44-80.

Davis, John Emmeus (1991), *Contested Ground: Collective Action and the Urban Neighbourhood,* Ithaca: Cornell University Press.

Dearlove, J. (1973), *The Politics of Policy in Local Government,* Cambridge: Cambridge University Press.

Delgado, Gary (1986), *Organizing the Movement: The Roots and Growth of ACORN,* Philadelphia: Temple University Press.

Della Seta, Piero (1978), 'Notes on Urban Struggles in Italy', *International Journal of Urban and Regional Research,* Vol.2, pp.303-329.

Denzin, Norman K. and Yvonna S. Lincoln. (1994), 'Introduction: Entering the Field of Qualitative Research', Denzin, Norman K. and Yvonna S. Lincoln (eds.), *Handbook of Qualitative Research,* Thousand Oaks: Sage Publications.

Donati, Paolo R. (1984), 'Organization Between Movement and Institution', *Social Science Information,* Vol.23, pp.837-859.

Dore, R. and Mars, Z. (eds.) (1981), *Community Development,* Croom Helm and Unesco.

Douglas, T. (1983), *Groups: Understanding People Gathering Together,* London: Tavistock.

Downey, Gary L. (1986), 'Ideology and the Clamshell Identity: Organizational Dilemmas in the Anti-nuclear Power Movement', *Social Problems,* Vol.33(5), pp.357-373.

Duffhues, Ton and Albert Felling (1989), 'The Development, Change and Decline of the Dutch Catholic Movement', *International Social Movement Research,* Vol.2, pp.95-117.

Dunleavy, Patrick (1991), *Democracy, Bureaucracy and Public Choice*, New York: Harvester Wheatsheaf.
Dunleavy, Patrick (1980), *Urban Political Analysis*, London and Basingstoke: Macmillan Press.
Eckstein, S. (1990), 'Poor People Versus the State and Capital: Autonomy of a Successful Community Mobilization for Housing in Mexico City', *International Journal of Urban and Regional Research*, Vol.14(2), pp.274-296.
Eckstein, S. (1977), *The Poverty and the Revolution: The State and the Urban Poor in Mexico*, Princeton: Princeton University Press.
Eisinger, Peter K. (1973), 'The Conditions of Protest Behaviour in American Cities', *Americal Political Science Review*, Vol.67, pp.11-28.
Etzioni, Amitai. (1975), *A Comparative Analysis of Complex Organizations*, (Revised Edition), New York: Free Press.
Eyerman, R. (1992). 'Modernity and Social Movements', in Haferkamp, Hans and Neil J. Smelser (eds.), *Social Change and Modernity*, Berkeley: University of California Press.
Fainstein, Norman I. and Susan S. Fainstein (1985), 'Economic Restructuring and the Rise of Urban Social Movements', *Urban Affairs Quarterly*, Vol.21, pp.187-206.
Fainstein, Norman I. and Susan S. Fainstein (1982), *Urban Policy Under Capitalism*, Beverly Hills: Sage.
Fainstein, Norman I. and Susan S. Fainstein (1974), *Urban Political Movements*, Englewood Cliffs, N.J.: Prentice-Hall.
Fantasia, Rick (1988), *Cultures of Solidarity: Consciousness, Action, and Contemporary American Workers*, Berkeley: University of California Press.
Fernandez, Roberto M. and Doug McAdam (1989), 'Multiorganizational Fields and Recruitment to Social Movements', *International Social Movement Research*, Vol.2, pp.315-343.
Ferree, Myra Marx (1992), 'The Political Context of Rationality: Rational Choice Theory and Resource Mobilization', in Morris, Aldon D. and Carol McClurg Mueller (eds.), *Frontiers in Social Movement Theory*, New Haven and London: Yale University Press.
Ferree, Myra Marx and Beth B. Hess (1985), *Controversy and Coalition: The New Feminist Movement*, Boston: Twayne Publishers.
Ferree, M. and F.D. Miller (1985), 'Mobilization and Meaning: Toward an Integration of Social Psychological and Resource Perspectives on Social Movement', *Sociological Inquiry*, Vol.55, pp.38-61.
Fireman, B. and William A. Gamson (1979), 'Utilitarian Logic in the Resource Mobilization', in Zald, Mayer N. and John D. McCarthy (eds.), *The Dynamics of Social Movement*, Cambridge, MA: Winthrop Publishers, Inc.

Fisher, Robert and Joseph Kling (1993), 'Introduction: The Continued Vitality of Community Mobilization', *Mobilizing the Community: Local Politics in the Ear of the Global City,* Newbury Park, California: Sage Publications.
Flanagan, William G. (1993), *Contemporary Urban Sociology,* Cambridge: Cambridge University Press.
Folin, Marino (1979), 'Urban Struggles: A Critical Commentary on the Article by Della Seta', *International Journal of Urban and Regional Research,* Vol.3, pp.81-86.
Foweraker, Joe (1995), *Theorizing Social Movements,* London: Pluto Press.
Frankland, E. Gene and Donald Schoonmaker (1992), *Between Protest and Power: The Green Party in Germany,* Boulder: Westview Press.
Freeman, Jo. (1979), 'Resource Mobilization and Strategy: A Model for Analyzing Social Movement Organization Actions', in Zald, Mayer N. and John D. McCarthy (eds.), *The Dynamics of Social Movements,* Cambridge, Massachusetts: Winthrop Publishers, Inc.
Freeman, Jo (ed.) (1983), *Social Movements of the Sixties and Seventies,* White Plains, N.Y.: Longman Inc.
Freeman, Jo (1973), 'The Origins of the Women's Liberation Movement', *American Journal of Sociology,* Vol.78, pp.792-811.
Friedland, R. (1982), *Power and Crisis in the City,* London: Macmillan.
Frohlich, N., Hunt, T., Oppenheimer, J. and Wagner, R.H. (1975), 'Individual Contributions for Collective Goods: Alternative Models', *Journal of Conflict Resolution,* Vol.19, pp.310-329.
Frohlich, N. and J.A. Oppenheimer (1970), 'I Get by with a Little Help from Friends', *World Politics,* Vol.23, pp.104-120.
Fung, H.L. (1994), 'Parliamentary Politics and Social Work', in Chau, W.S. (ed.), *New Theories of Social Work,* Hong Kong: Commercial Press Ltd. (in Chinese).
Gale, Richard P. (1986), 'Social Movements and the State', *Sociological Perspectives,* Vol.29(2), pp.202-240.
Gamson, William A. (1992), 'The Social Psychological of Collective Action', in Morris, Aldon D. and Mueller, Carol McClurg (eds.), *Frontiers in Social Movement Theory,* New Haven and London: Yale University Press.
Gamson, William A. (1989), 'Reflections on the Strategy of Social Protest', *Sociological Forum,* Vol.4(3), pp.455-467.
Gamson, William A. (1987), 'Introduction', in Zald, Mayer N. and John D. McCarthy (eds.), *Social Movements in an Organizational Society: Collected Essays,* New Brunswick: Transaction Books.
Gamson, William A. (1975), *The Strategy of Social Protest,* Belmont, California: Wadsworth Publishing Company.
Gamson, William A. and Schmeidler, E. (1984), 'Organizing the Poor', *Theory and Society,* Vol.13(40), pp.367-385.

Garner, R.A. and Zald, M.N. (1985), 'The Political Economy of Social Movement Sectors', in Suttles, G. and Zald, M.N. (eds.), *The Challenge of Social Control: Citizenship and Institution Building in Modern Society: Essays in Honor of Morris Janowitz,* N.J.:Norwood.

Gay, Robert (1990), 'Community Organization and Clientelist Politics in Contemporary Brazil: A Case Study from Suburban Rio de Janeiro', *International Journal of Urban and Regional Research,* Vol.14(4), pp.648-666.

Gelb, Joyce and Marian Lief Palley (1982), *Women and Public Policies,* Princeton, New Jersey: Princeton University Press.

Gerlach, Luther P. and Virginia H. Hine (1970), *People, Power, Change: Movements of Social Transformation,* Indianapolis and New York: Bobbs-Merrill Company, Inc.

Geschwender, James A. (1971), 'Civil Rights Protest and Riots: A Disappearing Distinction', Geschwender, James A. (ed.), *The Black Revolt,* Englewood Cliffs, N.J.: Prentice-Hall.

Geschwender, James A. (1968), 'Explorations in the Theory of Social Movements and Evolutions', *Social Forces,* Vol.47, pp.127-135.

Geschwender, James A. (1967), 'Continuities in the Theories of Status Consistency and Cognitive Dissonance', *Social Forces,* Vol.46, pp.160-171.

Giddens, Anthony. (1984), *The Constitution of Society,* Cambridge: Polity Press.

Gilbert, Alan and Ward, Peter (1984), 'Community Participation in Upgrading Irregular Settlements', *World Development,* Vol.12(9), pp.913-922.

Gilbert, David (1992), *Class, Community, and Collective Action,* Oxford: Clarendon Press.

Godwin, R. Kenneth and Mitchell, Robert C. (1984), 'The Implications of Direct Mail for Political Organizations', *Social Science Quarterly,* Vol.65, pp.829-839.

Goering, John M. (1978), 'Marx and the City: Are There Any New Directions for Urban Theory?' *Comparative Urban Research,* Vol.6(2,3), pp.76-85.

Goldstone, Jack (1980), 'The Weakness of Organization: A New to Look at Gamson's The Strategy of Social Protest', *American Journal of Sociology,* Vol.85, pp.1017-1042.

Granovetter, Mark (1973), 'The Strength of Weak Ties', *American Journal of Sociology,* Vol.78, pp.1360-1380.

Greenstone, David and Peterson, Paul E. (1976), *Race and Authority in Urban Politics,* Chicago: University of Chicago Press.

Grofman, B.N. and Muller, E.N. (1973), 'The Strange Case of Relative Gratification and Potential for Political Violence: The V-Curve Hypothesis', *American Political Science Review,* Vol.67, pp.514-539.

Guba, E.G. (1990), 'The Alternative Paradigm Dialog', in Guba, E.G. (ed.), *The Paradigm Dialog,* Newbury Park, C.A.: Sage Publications.

Guba, E.G. and Lincoln, Yvonna S. (1994), 'Competing Paradigms in Qualitative Research', in Denzin, Norman K. and Lincoln, Yvonna S. (eds.), *Handbook of Qualitative Research,* Thousand Oaks: Sage Publications.

Gurney, J.N. and Tierney, K.J. (1982), 'Relative Deprivation and Social Movements: A Critical Look at Twenty Years of Theory and Research', *The Sociological Quarterly,* Vol.23, pp.33-47.

Gurr, Ted Robert (1970), *Why Men Rebel,* Princeton, NJ.: Princeton University Press.

Habermas, Jurgen (1985), *Theories of Communicative Behaviour,* English Translation, 2 volumes, Boston: Beacon Press.

Haines, Herbert M. (1984), 'Black Radicalization and the Funding of Civil Rights: 1957-1970', *Social Problems,* Vol.32, pp.31-43.

Hannigan, John A. (1985), 'Alain Touraine, Manuel Castells and Social Movement Theory', *The Sociological Quarterly,* Vol.26(4), pp.435-454.

Harloe, Michael (1977), *Captive Cities: Studies in the Political Economy of Cities and Regions,* Chichester: John Wiley & Sons.

Hasson, Shlomo (1993), *Urban Social Movements in Jerusalem: The Protest of the Second Generation,* Albany: State University of New York Press.

Heisler, B.S. and Hoffman, L.M. (1989), 'Threats to Homes' as Grievance: Targets and Constituencies', *Research in Social Movement, Conflicts and Change,* Vol.11, pp.55-72.

Hengchen, Bernard and Christian Melis (1980), 'Contribution to the Study of Brussels Urban Social Movements', *International Journal of Urban and Regional Research,* Vol.4, pp.116-126.

Henig, Jeffrey R. (1982), *Neighbourhood Mobilization: Redevelopment and Response,* New Brunswick, NJ.: Rutgers University Press.

Henig, J.R. (1982a), 'Neighbourhood Response to Gentrification: Conditions of Mobilization', *Urban Affairs Quarterly,* Vol.17(3), pp.343-358.

Hertz, Susan Handley (1981), *The Welfare Mothers Movement: A Decade of Change for Poor Women?* Lanham: University Press of America. Inc.

Hirsch, Eric L. (1986), 'The Creation of Political Solidarity in Social Movement Organizations', *The Sociological Quarterly,* Vol.27(3), pp.373-383.

Ho, D.K.L. (1993), *Tenants' Views and Opinions on Hong Kong Housing Society: A Summary Report, A Survey Report Submitted to Hong Kong Housing Society,* Hong Kong: Department of Applied Social Studies, Hong Kong Polytechnic University.

Ho, D.K.L. (1989), 'The Political Economy of Public Housing in Hong Kong: A Sociological Analysis', Unpublished *M.Phil. Thesis,* Hong Kong: The Sociological Department, the University of Hong Kong.

Ho, H.C.Y. (1989), 'Views on Hong Kong's Past Growth and Future Prospects', Ho, H.C.Y. and Chau, L.C. (eds.), *The Economic System of Hong Kong*, Hong Kong: Asian Research Service.

Ho, L.S. (1992), 'Privatisation of Public Housing: An Analysis of Proposals and A Suggested Alternative', Paper presented in the *Conference on Residential Housing in Hong Kong*, jointly organized by the Department of Business Studies, Hong Kong Polytechnic and the Department of Economics, The Chinese University of Hong Kong.

Ho, S.Y. (1986), 'Public Housing', in Cheng, J.Y.S. (ed.), *Hong Kong In Transition*, Hong Kong: Oxford University Press.

Ho. Y.P. (1986), 'Hong Kong's Trade and Industry: Changing Patterns and Prospects', in Cheng, J.Y.S. (ed.), *Hong Kong In Transition*, Hong Kong: Oxford University Press.

Hobsbawm, E.J. (1984), 'Should Poor People Organize?' in Hobsbawn, E.J., *Worlds of Labour*, London: Weidenfeld and Nicolson.

Hong Kong Council of Social Services (1986), *Report on New District Organizations*, Community Development Division, Working Group on District Dynamics, (July).

Hong Kong Council of Social Services, Community Development Division (1985), *Report of the Working Group on Future of Neighbourhood Level Community Development Project*.

Hong Kong Council of Social Services, Community Development Division, (1984), *The 1985 Five Year Plan Review Process*.

Hong Kong Council of Social Services (1976), *Community Development Position Paper*, Memograph copy.

Hong Kong Justice of Peace Commission (1979), *The Land of Hong Kong: So Precious*, Hong Kong: Hong Kong Justice of Peace Commission.

Issacs, Arnold H. (1989), 'Crossroads: The Rise and Fall of a Squatter Movement in Cape Town, South Africa', in Schuurman, Frans and van Naerssen Ton (eds.), *Urban Social Movements in the Third World*, London: Routledge.

Janis, I.L. and Mann, L. (1977), *Decision Making: A Psychological Analysis of Conflict, Choice and Commitment*, London: Collier-Macmillan.

Janssen, Roel (1978), 'Class Practices of Dwellers in Barrios Populares: The Struggle for the Right to the City', *International Journal of Urban and Regional Research*, Vol.2, pp.145-159.

Jao, Y.C. (1979), 'Hong Kong as a Regional Financial Centre: Evolution and Prospects', in Leung, Chi-Keung, et al (eds.), *Hong Kong: Dilemmas of Growth*, Occasional Papers and Monograhps, No.45, Hong Kong: Centre of Asian Studies, Hong Kong University.

Jao, Y.C., Levin, David A., Ng, S.H. and Sinn, E. (eds.) (1988), *Labour Movement in a Changing Society: The Experience of Hong Kong,* Hong Kong: Centre of Asian Studies, University of Hong Kong.

Jaquette, Jane (ed.) (1989), *The Women's Movement in Latin America: Feminism and the Transition to Democracy,* Winchester, M.A.: Unwin Hyman.

Jenkins, J. Craig (1995), 'Social Movements, Political Representation, and the State: An Agenda and Comparative Framework', in Jenkins, J. Craig and Bert Klandermans (eds.), *The Politics of Social Protest: Comparative Perspectives on States and Social Movements,* Minneapolis: University of Minnesota Press.

Jenkins, J. Craig (1985), *The Politics of Insurgency: The Farm Worker Movement in the 1960s,* New York: Columbia University Press.

Jenkins, J. Craig (1983), 'Resource Mobilization Theory and the Study of Social Movements', *Annual Review of Sociology,* Vol.9, pp.527-553.

Jenkins, J. Craig (1983a), 'The Transformation of a Constituency into a Movement: Farmworker Organizing in California', in Freeman, J. (eds.), *Social Movement in the Sixties and Seventies,* N.Y.: Longman Inc.

Jenkins, J. Craig (1979), 'What is to be Done? Movement or Organization', *Contemporary Sociology,* Vol.8, pp.222-228.

Jenkins, J. Craig and Bert Klandermans (eds.) (1995), *The Politics of Social Protest: Comparative Perspectives on States and Social Movements,* Minneapolis: University of Minnesota Press.

Jenkins, J. Craig and Charles Perrow (1977), 'Insurgency of the Powerless: Farm Workers Movements, 1946-1972', *American Sociological Review,* Vol.42(2), pp.249-268.

Johnson, J.M. (1975), *Doing Field Research,* New York: Free Press.

Johnson, Larry R. and William A. Johnson (1974), *Protest by the Poor: The Welfare Rights Movement in New York City,* Lexington, Massachusetts: Lexington Books.

Johnson, Nevil (1982), 'Accountability, Control, and Complexity: Moving Beyond Ministerial Responsibility', *Quangos in Britain: Government and the Networks of Public Policy-making,* London and Basingstoke: The Macmillan Press Ltd.

Johnston, Hank (1980), 'The Marketed Social Movement: A Case Study of the Rapid Growth of TM', *Pacific Sociological Review,* Vol.23, pp.333-354.

Johnston, Hank and Klandermans, Bert (1995), 'The Cultural Analysis of Social Movements', in Johnston, Hank and Klandermans, Bert (eds.), *Social Movements and Culture,* London: UCL Press.

Jorgensen, Danny L. (1989), *Participant Observation: A Methodology for Human Studies,* Newbury Park: Sage Publications.

Judkins, B.M. (1983), 'Mobilization of Membership: The Black and Brown Lung Movements', in Freeman, J.(ed.), *Social Movement in the Sixties and Seventies,* N.Y.:Longman Inc.

Kaplowitz, Stan A. and Bradley, J. Fisher (1985), 'Revealing the Logic of Free-Riding and Contributions to the Nuclear Freeze Movement', *Research in Social Movements, Conflicts and Change,* Vol.8, pp.47-64.

Katzenstein, Mary Fainsod and Mueller, Carol McClurg (eds.) (1987), *The Women's Movement of the United States and Western Europe,* Philadelphia: Temple University Press.

Katznelson, I. 1981. *City Trenches: Urban Politics and the Patterning of Class in the United States.* New York: Pantheon.

Keung, J. (1985), 'Government Intervention and Housing Policy in Hong Kong: A Structural Analysis', *Third World Planning Review,* Vol.7(1), pp.23-44.

Killian, L.M. (1984), 'Organization, Rationality and Spontaneity in the Civil Rights Movement', *American Sociological Review,* Vol.49, pp.770-783.

Kim, Jae-on, Nie, Norman H. and Verba, Sidney (1974), 'The Amount and Concentration of Democratic Participation', *Political Methodology,* (Spring), pp.105-132.

King, A. (1981), 'The Administrative Absorption of Politics in Hong Kong: With Special Emphasis on the City District Officer Scheme', in King, Ambrose Y.C. and Rance P. Lee (eds.), *Social Life and Development in Hong Kong,* Hong Kong: Chinese University of Hong Kong.

Kitschelt, H. (1991), 'Critique of the Resource Mobilization Approach', in Rucht, Dieter (ed.), *Research on Social Movements: The State of the Art in Western Europe and the USA,* Boulder, Colorado: Westview Press.

Kitschelt, H. (1986), 'Political Opportunity Structures and Political Protest: Anti-Nuclear Movements in Four Democracies', *British Journal of Political Sciencem,* Vol.16(1), pp.57-85.

Kitschelt, H. (1985), 'New Social Movements in West Germany and the United States', *Political Power and Social Theory,* Vol.5, pp.273-324.

Klandermans, Bert (1992), 'The Social Construction of Protest and Multiorganizational Field', in Morris, Aldon D. and Carol McClurg Mueller (eds.), *Frontiers in Social Movement Theory,* New Haven and London: Yale University Press.

Klandermans, Bert (1991), 'New Social Movements and Resource Mobilization: The European and the American Approach Revisited', in Rucht, Dieter (ed.), *Research on Social Movements: The State of the Art in Western Europe and the USA,* Boulder, Colorado: Westview Press.

Klandermans, Bert (1989), 'Introduction: Social Movement Organizations and the Study of Social Movements', in Klandermans, Bert (ed.), *International Social Movement Research,* Vol.2, pp.1-20.

Klandermans, Bert (1988), 'The Formation and Mobilization of Consensus', *International Social Movement Research,* Vol.1, pp.173-196.

Klandermans, Bert (1986), 'New Social Movements and Resource Mobilization: the European and the American approach', *International Journal of Mass Emergencies and Disasters, Special Issue: Comparative Perspectives and Research on Collective Behaviour and Social Movement*, Vol.4, pp.13-37.

Klandermans, Bert (1984), 'Mobilization and Participation: Social Psychological Expansions of Resource Mobilization Theory', *American Sociological Review*, Vol.49, pp.583-600.

Klandermans, Bert and Dirk Oegema (1987), 'Potentials, Networks, Motivations, and Barriers: Steps Towards Participation in Social Movements', *American Sociological Review*, Vol.52, pp.519-531.

Kleidman, Robert (1994), 'Volunteer Activism and Professionalism in Social Movement Organization', *Social Problems*, Vol.41(2), pp.257-276.

Knoke, D. (1989), 'Resource Acquisition and Allocation in U.S. National Associations', *International Social Movement Research*, Vol.2, pp.129-154.

Knoke, David (1988), 'Incentives in Collective Action Organizations', *American Sociological Review*, Vol.53, pp.311-329.

Knoke, David and Richard E. Adams (1987), 'The Incentive Systems of Associations', *Research in the Sociology of Organizations*, Vol.5, pp.285-309.

Knoke, David and Prensky, David (1984), 'What Relevance do Organization Theories have for Voluntary Association?' *Social Science Quarterly*, Vol.65, pp.3-20.

Knoke, David and Wright-Isak, Christine (1982), 'Individual Motives and Organizational Incentives', *Research in the Sociology of Organizations*, Vol.1, pp.209-254.

Kornhauser, William (1959), *The Politics of Mass Society*, Glencoe, IL: Free Press.

Kramer, Ralph M. (1969), *Participation of the Poor*, Englewood Cliffs, N.J.: Prentice Hall.

Krause, L.R. (1988), 'Hong Kong and Singapore: Twins or Kissing Cousins', *Economic Development and Cultural Change*, Vol.36(3), pp.S45-S66.

Kriesi, H. (1992), 'Support and Mobilization Potential for New Social Movements: Concepts, Operationalizations and Illustrations from the Netherlands', in Diani, Mario and Eyerman, Ron (eds.), *Studying Collective Action*, London: Sage Publications.

Kriesi, H. (1991), 'The Political Opportunity Structure of New Social Movements: Its Impact on their Mobilization', Discussion paper FS III 91-103, Wissenschaftszentrum Berlin.

Kriesi, H. (1989), 'The Opportunity Structure of the Dutch Peace Movement', *West European Politics*, Vol.12, pp.295-312.

Kriesi, H. and Van Praag, P. Jr. (1987), 'Old and New Politics', *European Journal of Political Research*, Vol.15, pp.319-346.

Kronenfeld, Daniel (1969), 'A Case History of a Block Association', in Harold H. Weissman (ed.), *Community Development in the Mobilization for Youth Experience,* New York: Association Press.

Kung, J.K.S. (1984), 'The Struggle for a Hospital: A Contextual Analysis of an Urban Social Movement in Hong Kong', Unpublished *M.Phil. Thesis,* Department of Anthropology and Sociology, University of Queensland.

Kung, P.Y. (1987), 'An Exploration into the Educational Needs of the Resident Leaders', Unpublished *M.S.W. Dissertation,* Social Work Development, University of Hong Kong.

Lagana, Guido, Mario, Pianta and Anna, Segre (1982), 'Urban Social Movements and Urban Restructuring in Turin, 1969-76', *International Journal of Urban and Regional Research,* Vol.6(2), pp.223-245.

Lau, K.Y. (eds.) (1991), 'Housing', *The Other Hong Kong Report,* Hong Kong: The Chinese University Hong Kong Press.

Lau, K.Y. (1989), 'The Development of Public Housing Policy', in Cheng, J.Y.S. (ed.), *Hong Kong In Transition,* Hong Kong: Joint Publishing (HK) Co. Ltd. (In Chinese)

Lau, P.K. (1986), 'Economic Relations Between Hong Kong and China', in Cheng, J.Y.S. (ed.), *Hong Kong In Transition,* Hong Kong: Oxford University Press.

Lau, S.K. (1982), *Society and Politics in Hong Kong,* Hong Kong: Chinese University Press.

Lau, S.K. (1981), 'The Government, Intermediate Organizations, and Grass-Roots Politics in Hong Kong', *Asian Survey,* Vol.XXI, No.8, (August).

Lau, S.K. and Kuan, H.C. (1988), *The Ethos of the Hong Kong Chinese,* Hong Kong: The Chinese University Press.

Lau, S.K. and Kuan, H.C. (1986), 'The Changing Political Culture of the Hong Kong Chinese', in Cheng, J.Y.S. (ed.), *Hong Kong In Transition,* Hong Kong: Oxford University Press.

Lau, S.K. and Kuan, H.C. (1985), *The 1985 District Board Election in Hong Kong: The Limits of Political Mobilization in a Dependent Polity,* Centre for Hong Kong Studies, Occasional Papers No.8, Hong Kong: Institute of Social Studies, The Chinese University of Hong Kong.

Lau, S.K. and Louie Kin-sheun (1993), *Hong Kong Tried Democracy: The 1991 Elections in Hong Kong,* Hong Kong: Hong Kong Institute of Asia-Pacific Studies, The Chinese University of Hong Kong.

Lawson, Ronald (1984), 'The Rent Strike in New York City, 1904-1980: The Evolution of a Social Movement Strategy', *Journal of Urban History,* Vol.10(3), pp.235-258.

Lawson, R. (1983), 'A Decentralized But Moving Pyramid: The Evolution and Consequences of the Structure of the Tenant Movement', in Freeman, J. (ed.), *Social Movements of the Sixties and Seventies,* N.Y.: Longman Inc.

Lee, James (1992), 'From Social Rented Housing to Home Ownership: The Dilemma of Housing Policy in the Nineties', Paper presented in the *Conference on Residential Housing in Hong Kong*, jointly organized by the Department of Business Studies, Hong Kong Polytechnic and the Department of Economics, The Chinese University of Hong Kong.

Lenski, Gerhard (1954), 'Status Crystallization: A Non-vertical Dimension of Social Status', *American Sociological Review*, Vol.19, pp.405-413.

Leung, B.K.P. (1990), 'Power and Politics', in Leung, Benjamin K.P. (ed.), *Social Issues in Hong Kong*, Hong Kong: Oxford University Press.

Leung, B.K.P. and Chiu, Stephen (1991), *A Short History of Industrial Strikes and the Labour Movement in Hong Kong, 1946-1989*, Social Science Occasional Paper 3, Hong Kong: Department of Sociology, University of Hong Kong.

Leung, C.B. (1990), 'Problems and Changes in Community Politics', in Leung, Benjamin K.P. (ed.), *Social Issues in Hong Kong*, Hong Kong: Oxford University Press.

Leung, C.B. (1986), 'Community Participation: The Decline of Residents' Organizations', in Cheng, J.Y.S. (ed.), *Hong Kong In Transition*, Hong Kong: Oxford University Press.

Leung, C.B. (1982), 'Community Participation: From Kai Fong Association, Mutual Aid Committee to District Board', in Cheng, J.Y.S. (ed.), *Hong Kong in the 1980s*, Hong Kong: Summerson (HK) Educational Research Centre.

Leung, S.W. and Lee, M.K. (1994), *Democratisation without Participation: The Emergence of Spectator Political Culture in a Transitional Polity*, Unpublished Research Report.

Leung, W.T. (1993), 'Housing', in Choi, Po-king and Ho, Lok-sang (eds.), *The Other Hong Kong Report, 1993*, Hong Kong: The Chinese University Press.

Leung, W.T. (1983), 'The New Town Programme', in Chiu, T.N. and So, C.L. (eds.), *A Geography of Hong Kong*, Hong Kong: Oxford University Press.

Leung, W.T. (1980), 'Hong Kong's New Town Programme', in Leung, C.K. et al. (ed.), *Hong Kong: Dilemma of Growth*, Occasional Papers and Monograhps, No.45, Hong Kong: Centre of Asian Studies, Hong Kong University.

Levin, D. and Chiu, Stephen (1993), 'Dependent Capitalism, A Colonial State, and Marginal Unions: The Case of Hong Kong', in Frenkel, Stephen (ed.), *Organized Labor in the Asia-Pacific Region: A Comparative Study of Trade Unionism in Nine Countries*, Ithaca, N.Y.: ILR Press.

Levin, D. and Jao, Y.C. (1988), 'Introduction', in Jao, Y.C., Levin, David A., Ng, S.H. and Sinn, E. (eds.), *Labour Movement in a Changing Society: The Experience of Hong Kong*, Hong Kong: Centre of Asian Studies, University of Hong Kong.

Levine, Sol. and White, Paul E. (1961), 'Exchange as a Conceptual Framework for the Study of Interorganizational Relationships', *Administrative Science Quarterly*, Vol.5, pp.555-601.

Lin, T.B. and Ho, Y.P. (1982), 'The Past Experience, Present Constraints, Future Course of Industrial Diversification in Hong Kong', Cheng, J.Y.S. (ed.), *Hong Kong in the 1980s*, Hong Kong: Summerson Eastern Publishers and Ltd.

Lincoln, J.R. and Zeitz, G. (1980), 'Organizational Properties from Aggregate Data: Separating Individual and Structural Effects', *American Sociological Review*, Vol.45, pp.391-408.

Lipset, Michael and Wolin, Sheldon (1965), *The Berkeley Student Revolt*, New York: Doubleday Anchor.

Lipset, Seymour Martin (1960), *Political Man: The Social Bases of Politics*, New York: Doubleday.

Lipsky, M. (1968), 'Protest as a Political Resource', *American Political Science Review*, Vol.62, pp.1144-1158.

Lipsky, M. and Levi, Margaret (1972), 'Community Organization as a Political Resource', in Hahn, Harlan (ed.), *People and Politics in Urban Society*, Beverly Hills, California: Sage Publication Press.

Liu, W.T. and Duff, R.W. (1972), 'The Strength in Weak Ties', *Public Opinion Quarterly*, Vol.36, pp.361-366.

Lo, Clarence Y.H. (1992), 'Communities of Challengers in Social Movement Theory', in Morris, Aldon D. and Carol McClurg Mueller (eds.), *Frontiers of Social Movement Theory*, New Haven and London: Yale University Press.

Lo, Clarance Y.H. (1982), 'Countermovements and Conservative Movements in the Contemporary U.S', *Annual Review of Sociology*, Vol.8, pp.107-134.

Lo, Shiu-Hing (1988), 'Decolonization and Political Development in Hong Kong: Citizen Participation', *Asian Survey*, Vol.XXVIII(6), pp.613-629.

Lofland, John (1991), *Polite Potesters: The American Peace Movement of the 1980s*, Syracuse, N.Y.: Syracuse University Press.

Lofland, John (1985), *Protest: Studies of Collective Behaviour and Social Movements*, New Brunswick and London: Transaction Publishers.

Lowe, Stuart (1986), *Urban Social Movements: The City After Castells*, London: Macmillan.

Lui, P.K., Wong, Y.C. and Ho, K.L. (1994), *Report of Survey on Rehousing Preference of Households Living in Temporary Housing Areas*, Hong Kong: Hong Kong Housing Authority.

Lui, T.L. (1993), 'Two Logics of Community Politics: Residents' Organizations and The 1991 Election', in Lau, Siu-kai and Louie Kin-sheun (eds.), *Hong Kong Tried Democracy: The 1991 Elections in Hong Kong*, Hong Kong: Hong Kong Institute of Asia-Pacific Studies, the Chinese University of Hong Kong.

Lui, T.L. (1984), 'Urban Protests in Hong Kong: A Sociological Study of Housing Conflicts', Unpublished *M. Phil. Thesis*, Hong Kong: Department of Sociology, University of Hong Kong.

Ma, Stephen Fook-tong (1986), *Urban Neighbourhood Mobilizations in the Changing Political Scenes of Hong Kong*, Unpublished *Master Dissertation* of Social Sciences in Urban Studies, University of Hong Kong, Hong Kong.

Maguire, Diarmuid (1995), 'Opposition Movements and Opposition Parties: Equal Partners or Dependent Relations in the Struggle for Power and Reform?' in Jenkins, Craig J. and Klandermans, Bert (eds.), *The Politics of Social Protest: Comparative Perspectives on States and Social Movements*, Minneapolis: University of Minnesota Press.

Mainwaring, Scott (1991), 'Politicians, Parties, and Electoral Systems: Brazil in Comparative Perspective', *Comparative Politics*, Vol.24(1), pp.21-43.

Mainwaring, Scott (1987), 'Urban Popular Movements, Identity and Democratization in Brazil', *Comparative Political Studies*, Vol.20(2), pp.131-159.

Marger, Martin N. (1984), 'Social Movement Organizations and Response to Environmental Change: The NAACP, 1960-1973', *Social Problems*, Vol.32, pp.16-30.

Marris, Peter and Rein, Martin (1967), *Dilemmas of Social Reform: Poverty and Community Action in the United States*, New York: Atherton.

Marsh, A. (1977), *Protest and Political Consciousness*, Beverly Hills and London: Sage.

Marsh, Alan and Kaase, Max (1979), 'Background of Political Action', in Barnes, Samuel H. and Kaase, Max *et al.*, *Political Action: Mass Participation in Five Western Democracies*, London: Sage.

Marwell, Gerald and Pamela, Oliver (1984), 'Collective Action Theory and Social Movement Research', *Research in Social Movements, Conflicts and Change*, Vol.7, pp.1-27.

Marx, Gary T. and Wood, James (1975), 'Strands of Theory and Research in Collective Behaviour', *Annual Review of Sociology*, Vol.1, pp.363-428.

Mayer, Margit (1991), 'Social Movement Research and Social Movement Practice: The U.S. Pattern', in Rucht, Dieter (ed.), *Research on Social Movements: The State of the Art in Western Europe and the USA*, Boulder, Colorado: Westview Press.

Mayer, M. (1990), *Theoretical Assumptions in American Social Movement Research and Their Implications*, Paper for the World Congress of Sociology.

McAdam, Doug (1986), 'Recruitment to High-rish Activism: The Case of Freedom Summer', *American Journal of Sociology*, Vol.92, pp.64-90.

McAdam, Doug (1982), *Political Process and the Development of Black Insurgency 1930-1970*, Chicago and London: The University of Chicago Press.

McAdam, Doug, McCarthy, John D. and Zald, Mayer N. (1988), 'Social Movements', in Smelser, N. (ed.), *Handbook of Sociology*, Newbury Park: Sage.

McAdam, Doug and Paulsen, Ronnelle (1993), 'Specifying the Relationship Between Social Ties and Activism', *American Journal of Sociology*, Vol.99(3), pp.640-667.

McCarthy, John D., Britt, David W. and Wolfson, Mark (1991), 'The Institutional Channeling of Social Movements in the Modern State', *Research in Social Movements, Conflict and Change*, Vol.13, pp.45-76.

McCarthy, John D. and Zald, Mayer N. (1987), 'The Trend of Social Movements in America: Professionalization and Resource Mobilization', Zald, Mayer N. and McCarthy, John D. (eds.), *Social Movements in an Organizational Society: Collected Essays*. New Brunswick: Transaction Books.

McCarthy, John and Zald, Mayer (1977), 'Resource Mobilization and Social Movement: A Partial Theory', *American Journal of Sociology*, Vol.82, pp.1212-1241.

McKeown, Kieran (1987), *Marxist Political Economy and Marxist Urban Sociology: A Review and Elaboration of Recent Developments*, London: MacMillan Press.

McPhail, Clark (1971), 'Civil Disorder Participation: A Critical Examination of Recent Research', *American Sociological Review*, Vol.36, pp.1058-1073.

Melucci, Alberto (1989), *Nomads of the Present*, in Keane, John and Mier, Paul (eds.), London: Hitchinson Radius.

Melucci, Alberto (1988), 'Getting Involved: Identity and Mobilization in Social Movements', in Klandermans, Bert et al.(eds.), *From Structure and Action: Comparing Movements Across Cultures, International Social Movements Research*, Vol.1., Greenwich, CT.: JAI Press.

Melucci, Alberto, (1985), 'The Symbolic Challenge of Contemporary Movements', *Social Research*. Vol.52(4), pp.789-816.

Melucci, Alberto (1984), 'An End to Social Movements?' *Social Science Information*, Vol.23, pp.819-835.

Melucci, Alberto (1980), 'The New Social Movements: A Theoretical Approach', *Social Science Information*, Vol.19(2), pp.199-226.

Miners, N. (1991), *The Government and Politics of Hong Kong* (Fifth edition), Hong Kong: Oxford University Press.

Mitchell, C. (1983), 'Case and Situation Analysis', *The Sociological Review*, Vol.31, pp.187-211.

Mitchell, Robert C. (1979), 'National Environmental Lobbies and the Apparent Illogic of Collective Action', in Russell, Clifford S. (ed.), *Collective Decision Making*, London: John Hopkins University Press.

Mok, Bong-ho (1991), *Influence Through Political Power: The Emergence of Social Workers as Politicians in the Recent Political Reform in Hong Kong*, HKIAPS Reprint Series No.3, Hong Kong: Hong Kong Institute of Asia-Pacific Studies, The Chinese University of Hong Kong.

Molotch, Harvey (1970), 'Oil in Santa Barbara and Power in America', *Sociological Inquiry*, Vol.40, pp.131-144.

Morley, Ian E. and Hosking, D.M. (1984), 'Decision-making and Negotiation: Leadership and Social Skills', in Gruneberg, M. and Wall, T. (eds.), *Social Psychology and Organizational Behaviour*, Chichester: John Wiley and Sons Ltd.

Morris, A. (1984), *The Origins of the Civil Rights Movement: Black Communities Organizing for a Change*, New York: Free Press.

Morris, A. (1981), 'Black Southern Student Sit-in Movement: An Analysis of Internal Organizations', *American Sociological Review*, Vol.46, pp.744-767.

Morris, Aldon D. and Mueller, Carol McClurg (eds.) (1992), *Frontiers in Social Movement Theory*, New Haven and London: Yale University Press.

Morris, A. and Herring, C. (1987), 'Theory and Research in Social Movements: A Critical Review', in Long, S.P. (ed.), *Annual Review of Political Science*, Vol.2, pp.137-198.

Mottl, Tahi L. (1980), 'The Analysis of Countermovements', *Social Problems*, Vol.27(5), pp.620-635.

Moynihan, Daniel P. (1969), *Maximum Feasible Misunderstanding*, New York: Free Press.

Mueller, Carol McClurg (1992), 'Building Social Movement Theory', in Morris, Aldon D. and Mueller, Carol McClurg (eds.), *Frontiers in Social Movement Theory*, New Haven and London: Yale University Press.

Mueller, Carol McClurg (1989), 'Collective Consciousness, Identity Transformation, and the Rise of Women in Public Office in the United States', in Katzenstein, Mary Fainsod and Mueller, Carol McClurg (eds.), *The Women's Movement of the United States and Western Europe*, Philadelphia: Temple University Press.

Muller, E.N. (1980), 'The Psychology of Political Protest and Violence', in Gurr, T.R. (ed.), *Handbook of Political Conflict, Theory and Research*, New York: Free Press.

Muller, E.N. (1972), 'A Test of a Partial Theory of Potential for Political Violence', *American Political Review*, Vol.66, pp.928-959.

Muller, Edward N. and Opp, Karl-Dieter (1986), 'Rational Choice and Rebellious Collective Action', *American Political Science Review*, Vol.80, pp.471-488.

Mullins, Patrick (1987), 'Community and Urban Movements', *Sociological Review*, Vol.35, pp.347-369.

Nelson, Joan M. (1977), *Access to Power: Politics and the Urban Poor in Developing Nations*, Princeton, N.J.: Princeton University Press.
Ng, S.H. and Levin, D. (eds.) (1983), *Contemporary Issues in Hong Kong Labour Relations*, Hong Kong: Centre of Asian Studies, University of Hong Kong.
Nie, N.H., Poweel, G.B. Jr. and Prewitt, K. (1969), 'Social Participation and Political Participation: Developmental Relationships I', *American Political Science Review*, Vol.63, pp.361-378.
O'Brien, David (1975), *Neighbourhood Organization and Interest-Group Processes*, Princeton University Press.
O'Brien, David (1974), 'The Public Goods Dilemma and the 'Apathy' of the Poor Toward Neighbourhood Organization', *Social Service Review*, Vol.48(2), pp.229-244.
Oberschall, A. (1980), 'Loosely Structured Collective Conflict: A Theory and an Application', *Research in Social Movements, Conflicts and Change*, Vol.3, pp.45-68.
Oberschall, A. (1978), 'The Decline of the 1960s Social Movements', *Research in Social Movement, Conflict and Change*, Vol.1, pp.257-289.
Oberschall, A. (1973), *Social Conflict and Social Movement*, Englewood.
Oegema, Dirk and Klandermans, Bert (1994), 'Why Social Movement Sympathizers Don't Participate: Erosion and Nonconversion of Support', *American Sociological Review*, Vol.59, pp.703-722.
Offe, Claus (1985), 'New Social Movements: Changing the Boundaries of Institutionalized Politics', *Social Research*, Vol.52, pp.817-868.
Oliver, Pamela E. (1989), 'Bringing the Crowd Back In: The Nonorganizational Elements of Social Movements', *Research in Social Movement, Conflicts and Change*, Vol.11, pp.1-30.
Oliver, Pamela (1984), 'If You Don't Do It, Nobody Else Will: Active and Token Contributors to Local Collective Action', *American Sociological Review*, Vol.49, pp.601-610.
Oliver, Pamela (1983), 'The Mobilization of Paid and Volunteer Activists in the Neighbourhood Movement', *Research on Social Movement, Conflict and Change*, Vol.5, pp.133-170.
Oliver, Pamela (1980), 'Rewards and Punishments as Selective Incentives for Collective Actions: Theoretical Investigation', *American Journal of Sociology*, Vol.85, pp.1356-1375.
Oliver, Pamela E. and Marwell, Gerald (1992), 'Mobilizing Technologies for Collective Action', in Morris, Aldon D. and Mueller, Carol McClurg (eds.), *Frontiers in Social Movement Theory*, New Haven and London: Yale University Press.
Olson, Mancur (1965), *The Logic of Collective Action: Public Goods and the Theory of Groups*, Cambridge, MA: Harvard University Press.

Opp, Karl-Dieter (1988), 'Grievances and Participation in Social Movement', *American Sociological Review,* Vol.53, pp.853-864.

Opp, Karl-Dieter (1986), 'Soft Incentives and Collective Action: Participation in Anti-nuclear Movement', *British Journal of Political Science,* Vol.16, pp.87-112.

Opp, Karl-Dieter and Roehl, Wolfgang (1990), 'Repression, Micromobilization and Political Protest', *Social Forces,* Vol.69(2), pp.521-547.

Pahl, R.E. (1989), 'Is the Emperor Naked? Some Questions on the Adequacy of Sociological Theory in Urban and Regional Research', *International Journal of Urban and Regional Research,* Vol.13(4), pp.711-720.

Parenti, Michael (1970), 'Power and Pluralism: A View from the Bottom', *Journal of Politics,* Vol.32, pp.501-530.

Park, R.E. (1952), *Human Conditions,* Glencoe, IL: Free Press.

Parry, Geraint, George Moyser and Neil Day (1992), *Political Participation and Democracy in Britain,* Cambridge: Cambridge University Press.

People's Council on Squatter Policy (1991), 'Newsletter of the Council' (January).

People's Council on Squatter Policy (1991a), 'Newsletter of the Council' (May).

Perline, Martin M. and Lorenz, V.R. (1970), 'Factors Influencing Member Participation in Trade Union Activities', *American Journal of Economic and Sociology,* Vol.29, pp.425-438.

Perlman, Janice E. (1977), *The Myth of Marginality: Urban Poverty and Politics in Rio de Janeiro,* Berkeley: University of California Press.

Perrow, Charles (1979), 'The Sixties Observed', in Zald, Mayer N. and McCarthy, John D. (eds.), *The Dynamics of Social Movements,* Cambridge, Massachusetts: Winthrop Publishers, Inc.

Petras, James and Zeitlin, Maurice (1967), 'Miners and Agrarian radicalism', *American Sociological Review,* Vol.32, pp.578-586.

Pickvance, C.G. (1995), 'Social Movements in the Transition from State Socialism: Convergence or Divergence', in Maheu, Louis (ed.), *Social Movements and Social Classes: The Future of Collective Action,* London: Sage Publications Ltd.

Pickvance, C.G. (1986), 'Concepts, Contexts and Comparison in the Study of Urban Movements: A Reply to M Castells', *Environment and Planning D: Society and Space,* Vol.4:???.

Pickvance, C.G. (1985), 'The Rise and Fall of Urban Movements and the Role of Comparative Analysis', *Society and Space,* Vol.3, pp.31-53.

Pickvance, C.G. (1977), 'From 'Social Base' to 'Social Forces': Some Analytical Issues in the Study of Urban Protest', in Harloe, Michael (ed.), *Captive Cities: Studies in the Political Economy of Cities and Regions,* Chichester: John Wiley & Sons.

Pickvance, C.G. (1976), 'On the Study of Urban Social Movements', in Pickvance, C.G. (ed.), *Urban Sociology: Critical Essays,* London: Tavistock Publications.

Pinard, M. and Hamilton, R. (1989), 'Intellectuals and the Leadership of Social Movements: Some Comparative Perspectives', *Research in Social Movements, Conflicts and Change,* Vol.11, pp.73-107.

Piven, Frances Fox (1975), 'Low-income People and the Political Process', in Piven, Frances Fox (ed.), *The Politics of Turmoil,* New York: Pantheon.

Piven, Frances Fox and Cloward, Richard A. (1977), *Poor People's Movement,* New York: Pantheon.

Pope, Jacqueline (1989), *Biting the Hand that Feeds Them: Organizing Women on Welfare at the Grass Roots Level,* New York: Praeger.

Porta, Donatella Della and Rucht, Dieter (1995), 'Left-Libertarian Movements in Context: A Comparison of Italy and West Germany, 1965-1990', in Craig, Jenkins, J. and Klandermans, Bert (eds.), *The Politics of Social Protest: Comparative Perspectives on States and Social Movements,* Minneapolis:

Portes, Alejandro (1971), 'On the Logic of Post-factum Explanation of the Hypothesis of Lower-class Frustration: The Cause of Leftist Radicalism', *Social Forces,* Vol.50, pp.26-44.

Preteceille, E. (1986), 'Collective Consumption, Urban Segregation, and Social Classes', *Society and Space,* Vol.4, pp.145-154.

Pryor, E.G. (1983), *Housing in Hong Kong,* (second edition), Hong Kong: Oxford University Press.

Rao, P. and Miller, R.L. (1971), *Applied Econometrics,* Belmont, CA.: Washington.

Rear, J. (1971), 'One Brand of Politics', in Hopkins, K. (ed.), *The Industrial Colony,* Hong Kong: Oxford University Press.

Rex, J. and Moore, R. (1967), *Race, Community and Conflict,* London: Oxford University Press.

Rich, Richard C. (1980), 'The Dynamics of Leadership in Neighbourhood Organizations', *Social Science Quarterly,* Vol. 60(4):570-587.

Richardson, Laurel (1994), 'Writing: A Method of Inquiry', in Denzin, Norman K. and Lincoln, Yvonna S. (eds.), *Handbook of Qualitative Research.* Thousand Oaks: Sage Publications.

Roberts, Bryan R. (1973), *Organizing Strangers: Poor Families in Guatemala City,* Austin and London: University of Texas Press.

Rootes, Chris (1992), 'Political Opportunity Structures, Political Competition, and the Development of Social Movements', Paper Presented at First European Conference on Social Movements, Berlin.

Rosenthal, Naomi and Schwartz, Michael (1989) 'Spontaneity and Democracy in Social Movements', *International Social Movement Research,* Vol.2, pp.33-59.

Rucht, Dieter (ed.) (1991), *Research on Social Movements: The State of the Art in Western Europe and the USA,* Boulder, Colorado: Westview Press.

Sabato, Larry J. (1981), *The Rise of Political Consultants,* New York: Basic Books.

Sallach, D.L., Babchuk, N. and Booth, A. (1972), 'Social Involvement and Political Activity: Another View', *Social Science Quarterly*, Vol.52, pp.879-892.

Saunders, Peter (1980), *Urban Politics: A Sociological Interpretation*, London: Hutchinson University & Co. (Publishers) Ltd.

Schuurman, Frans and van Naerssen, Ton (1989), *Urban Social Movements in the Third World*, London: Routledge.

Schwartz, Michael and Shuva, Paul (1992), 'Resource Mobilization Versus the Mobilization of People: Why Consensus Movements Cannot be Instruments of Social Change', in Morris, Aldon D. and Mueller, Carol McClurg (eds.), *Frontiers in Social Movement Theory*, New Haven and London: Yale University Press.

Schwartz, Michael; Naomi, Rosenthal and Schwartz, Laura (1981), 'Leader-Member Conflict in Protest Organizations: The Case of the Southern Farmers' Alliance', *Social Problems*, Vol.29, pp.22-36.

Scott, Allen (1990), *Ideology and New Social Movements*, London: Unwin Hyman.

Scott, I. (1989), *Political Change and the Crisis of Legitimacy in Hong Kong*, Hong Kong: Oxford University Press.

Selznick, Phillip (1970), 'Institutional Voulnerability in Mass Society', in Gusfield, Joseph R. (ed.), *Protest, Reform, and Revolt*, New York: John Wiley and Sons.

Shapiro, Thomas M. (1985), 'Structure and Process in Social Movement Strategy: The Movement Against Sterilization Abuse', *Research in Social Movements, Conflicts and Change*, Vol.8, pp.87-108.

Sharpe, E.B. (1978), 'Citizen Organization in Policing Issues and Crime Prevention: Incentives for Participation', *Journal of Voluntary Action Research*. Vol.7, pp.45-58.

Shils, E.A. and Janowitz, Morris (1948), 'Cohesion and Disintegration in the Wehrmacht in World War II', *Public Opinion Quarterly*, Vol.12, pp.23-26.

Sit, V.F.S. (1982), 'The Policy of Deliberate Urbanization: A Case Study of Hong Kong', in Sit, V.F.S. and Mera, K. (eds.), *Urbanization and National Development in Asia*, Hong Kong: Summerson Eastern Publishers.

Smart, Alan (1992), *Making Room: Squatter Clearance in Hong Kong*, Hong Kong: Centre of Asian Studies, Hong Kong University, Occasional Papers and Monographs, No.102.

Smelser, Neil (1962), *Theory of Collective Behaviour*, New York: Free Press.

Smith, David Horton and Pillemer, Karl (1983), 'Self-Help Groups as Social Movements Organizations: Social Structure and Social Change', *Research in Social Movement, Conflicts and Change*, Vol.5, pp.203-235.

Smith, Michael Peter (1989), 'Urbanism: Medium or Outcome of Human Agency', *Urban Affairs Quarterly*, Vol.24(3), pp.353-358.

Snow, David A. and Benford, Robert D. (1988), 'Ideology, Frame Resonance, and Participant Mobilization', *International Social Movement Research*, Vol.1, pp.197-217.

Snow, David A., Rochford, E. Burke Jr., Wordon, Steven K. and Benford, Robert D. (1986), 'Frame Alignment Processes, Micromobilization, and Movement Participation', *American Sociological Review*, Vol.51, pp.464-481.

Snow, David A. and Cynthia L. Phillips (1980), 'The Lofland-Stark Conversion Model: A Critical Assessment', *Social Problems*, Vol.27, pp.430-447.

Snow, David A., Zurcher, Louis A. Jr. and Ekland-Olson, Sheldon (1980), 'Social Networks and Social Movements: A Mirocstructural Approach to Differential Recruitment', *American Sociological Review*, Vol.80, pp.787-801.

Staggenborg, Suzanne (1986), 'Coalition Work in the Pro-Choice Movement: Organizational and Environmental Opportunities and Obstacles', *Social Problems*, Vol.33, pp.374-390.

Stoecker, Randy (1994), *Defending Community: The Struggle for Alternative Redevelopment in Cedar-Riverside*, Philadephia: Temple University Press.

Stokes, Susan C. (1991), 'Politics and Latin America's Urban Poor: Reflections from a Lima Shantytown', *Latin American Research Review*, Vol.26, pp.75-101.

Synder, David and Tilly, Charles (1972), 'Hardship and Collective Violence in France, 1830-1960', *American Sociological Review*, Vol.37, pp.520-532.

Tabb, W.K. and Sawers, L. (1978), *Marxism and the Metropolis*, New York: Oxford University Press.

Tannenbaum, Arnold S. and Kahn, Robert L. (1958), *Participation in Union Locals*, Evanston, Ill.: Row, Peterson and Co.

Tarrow, S. (1989), *Democracy and Disorder: Protest and Politics in Italy, 1965-1975*, Oxford: Clarendon Press.

Tarrow, S. (1988), 'Old Movements in New Cycles of Protest: The Career of An Italian Religious Community', *International Social Movement Research*, Vol.1, pp.281-304.

Tarrow, S. (1982), *Social Movements, Resource Mobilization and Reform During Cycles of Protest*, Western Study Programme Project, Social Protest and Policy Innovation, Working Paper, No.1, Ithaca, N.Y.: Cornell University.

Taylor, Verta and Whittier, Nancy E. (1992), 'Collective Identity in Social Movement Communities: Lesbian Feminist Mobilization', in Morris, Aldon D. and Mueller, Carol McClurg (eds.), *Frontiers in Social Movement Theory*. New Haven and London: Yale University Press.

Tillock, H. and Morrison, D.E. (1979), 'Group Size and Contributions to Collective Action: A Examination of Olson's Theory Using Data from Zero Population Growth, Inc', *Research in Social Movements, Conflicts and Change*, Vol.2, pp.131-158.

Tilly, C. (1978), *From Mobilization to Revolution,* New York: Random House.

Troyer, Ronald J. (1984), 'From Prohibition to Regulation: Comparing Two Anti-smoking Movements', *Research in Social Movements, Conflicts and Change,* Vol.7, pp.53-69.

Tsang, Wing-kwong (1993), 'Who Voted for the Democrats? An Analysis of the Electoral Choice of the 1991 Legislative Council Election', in Lau, Siu-kai and Louie Kin-sheun (eds.), *Hong Kong Tried Democracy: The 1991 Elections in Hong Kong,* Hong Kong: Hong Kong Institute of Asia-Pacific Studies, The Chinese University of Hong Kong.

Turner, Ralph, H. (1970), 'Determinants of Social Movement Strategies', Shibutani, Tamotshu (ed.), *Human Nature and Collective Behaviour.*

Turner, Ralph H. and Killian, Lewis M. (1987), *Collective Behaviour,* 3rd edition, London: Prentice-Hall, Inc.

Useem, Bert (1981), 'Models of the Boston Anti-Busing Movement: Polity/ Mobilization and Relative Deprivation', *Sociological Quarterly,* Vol:22, pp.263-274.

Useem, Bert (1980), 'Solidarity Model, Breakdown Model, and The Boston Anti-Busing Movement', *American Sociological Review,* Vol.45, pp.357-369.

Useem, Michael. (1975), *Protest Movements in America,* Indianapolis: Bobbs-Merrill.

Van Garderen, Ton. (1989), 'Collective Organization and Action in Squatter Settlements in Arequipa, Peru', Schuurman, Frans and Ton van Naerssen, (eds.), *Urban Social Movements in the Third World,* London: Routledge.

Verba, Sidney and Nie, N.H. (1972), *Participation in America: Political Democracy and Social Equality,* New York: Harper and Row.

Vidich, Arthur J. and Lyman, Stanford M. (1994), 'Qualitative Methods: Their History in Sociology and Anthropology', in Denzin, Norman K. and Lincoln, Yvonna S. (eds.), *Handbook of Qualitative Research,* Thousand Oaks: Sage Publications.

Walsh, E.J. (1981), 'Resource Mobilization and Citizen Protest in Communities Around Three Mile Island', *Social Problems,* Vol. 29, pp.1-21.

Walsh, E.J. and Cable. (1989), 'Realities, Images, and Management Dilemmas in Social Movement Organizations: The Three Miles Island experience', *International Social Movement Research,* Vol.2, pp.199-211.

Walsh, E.J. and Warland, Rex H. (1983), 'Social Movement Involvement in the Wake of a Nuclear Accident: Activists and Free Riders in the TMI Area', *American Sociological Review,* Vol.48, pp.764-780.

Walton, John. (1993), *Sociology and Critical Inquiry: The Work, Tradition and Purpose,* 3rd edition, Belmont, California: Wadsworth Publishing Company.

Walton, John. (1979), 'Urban Political Economy: A New Paradigm', *Comparative Urban Research,* Vol.7(1), pp.5-17.

Wang, L.H. and Yeh, A.G.O. (1987), 'Public Housing-Led New Town Development: Hong Kong and Singapore', *Third World Planning Review*, Vol.9(1), pp.41-63.
Weissman, Harold H. (ed.) (1969), *Community Development in the Mobilization for Youth Experience*, New York: Association Press.
West, Guida and Blumberg, Rhoda Lois (eds.) (1990), *Women and Social Protest*, New York and Oxford: Oxford University Press.
Wilson, James (1973), *Introduction to Social Movements*, New York: Basic Books, Inc.
Wilson, James Q. (1961). 'The Strategy of Protest: Problems of Negro Civic Action', *Journal of Conflict Resolution*, Vol.5, pp.291-303.
Wilson, K.L. and Orum, A.M. (1976), 'Mobilizing People for Collective Political Action', *Journal of Political Military Sociology*, Vol.4, pp.184-202.
Wolf, Eric (1966), 'Kinship, Friendship and Patron-client Relations', in Banton, Michael (ed.), *The Social Anthropology of Complex Societies*, New York: Tavistock Publications.
Wong, A. (1972), *The Kaifong Associations and the Society of Hong Kong*, Hong Kong: Orient Cultural Service.
Wong, C.K. (1988), *Social Movements and Hong Kong*, Hong Kong: Twilight Books. (In Chinese).
Wong, K.Y. (1982), 'New Towns - The Hong Kong Experience', in Cheng, J.Y.S. (ed.), *Hong Kong in the 1980's*, Hong Kong: Summerson Eastern.
Wong, R.Y.C. (1992), 'Privatize Public Housing', Paper Presented in the Conference on 'Residential Housing in Hong Kong', jointly organized by the Department of Business Studies, Hong Kong Polytechnic and the Department of Economics, The Chinese University of Hong Kong.
Wong, R.Y.C. and Staley, Samuel (1992), 'Housing and Land', in Cheng, Joseph Y.S. and Kwong, Paul C.K. (eds.), *The Other Hong Kong Report 1992*, Hong Kong: The Chinese University Hong Kong Press.
Yeh, A.G.O. (1986), 'New Towns in Hong Kong', in Choi, P.L.Y. et al. (eds.), *Planning and Development of Coastal Open Cities - Part Two: Hong Kong Section*, Hong Kong: HKU, Centre of Urban Studies and Urban Planning.
Yeh, A.G.O. (1985), 'Employment Location and New Town Development in Hong Kong', in Hills, P.R. (ed.), *State Policy, Urbanization and the Development Process: Proceedings of a Symposium on Social and Environmental Development, October, 1984*, Hong Kong: Centre of Urban Studies and Urban Planning, University of Hong Kong.
Yeung, Vincent, F.Y. (1987), *An Investigation into the Professional Ideology of the Neighbourhood Level Community Development Project Community Workers*, Unpublished M.S.W. Thesis, Hong Kong: Department of Social Work and Social Administration, University of Hong Kong.

Zald, M.N. (1991), 'The Continuing Vitality of Resource Mobilization Theory: Response to Herbert Kitschelt's Critique', in Dieter, Rucht (ed.), *Research on Social Movements: The State of the Art in Western Europe and the USA*, Boulder, Colorado: Westview Press.

Zald, M.N. (1969), 'The Structure of Society, and Social Service Integration', *Social Science Quarterly*, Vol.50, pp.557-567.

Zald, M.N. and Roberta Ash. (1966), 'Social Movement Organizations: Growth, Decay and Change', *Social Forces*, Vol.44, pp.327-341.

Zald, Mayer N. and McCarthy, John D. (eds.), (1987), *Social Movements in an Organizational Society: Collected Essays*, New Brunswick: Transaction Books.

Zald, M.N. and McCarthy, J. D. (1980), 'Social Movement Industries: Cooperation and Conflict Amongst Social Movement Organizations', in Kriesberg, Louis (ed.), *Research in Social Movements, Conflict and Change*. Vol.3, pp.1-20.

Zald, Mayer N. and McCarthy, John D. (eds.). (1979), *The Dynamics of Social Movements: Resource Mobilization, Social Control, and Tactics*, Cambridge, Massachusetts: Winthrop Publishers, Inc.

Zald, Mayer N. and Useem. (1987), 'Movement and Countermovement Interaction: Mobilization, Tactics, and State Involvement', in Zald, Mayer N. and McCarthy, John D. (eds.), *Social Movements in an Organizational Society*, New Brunswick and Oxford: Transaction Books.

Zimmer, Basil G. (1956), 'Farm Background and Urban Participation', *American Journal of Sociology*, Vol.61(5), pp.470-475.

Zukin, A. (1980), 'A Decade of the New Urban Sociology', *Theory and Society*, Vol.9, pp.575-601.

Government Publications

Hong Kong Government (1993), *Hong Kong 1991 Population Census: Main Report*, Hong Kong: Census and Statistics Department, Hong Kong Government.

Hong Kong Government (1990), *Hong Kong: Public Housing*. Hong Kong: Hong Kong Government Printer, May.

Hong Kong Government (1967), *Kowloon Disturbances, 1966: Report of Commission of Inquiry*, Hong Kong: Hong Kong Government Printer.

Hong Kong Government, (1984), *Green Paper: The Further Development of Representative Government in Hong Kong*, Hong Kong: Government Secretariat.

Hong Kong Government, Various Years. *Hong Kong Annual Report*. Hong Kong: Hong Kong Government.